A Historical Sociology of Childhood

What constitutes a 'normal' child? Throughout the nineteenth century, public health and paediatrics played leading roles in the image and perception of children. By the twentieth century, psychology had moved to the forefront, transforming our thinking and understanding. André Turmel investigates these transformations both from the perspective of the scientific observation of children (public hygiene, paediatrics, psychology and education) and from a public-policy standpoint (child welfare, health policy, education and compulsory schooling). Using detailed historical accounts from Britain, the USA and France, Turmel studies how historical sequential development and statistical reasoning have led to a concept of what constitutes a 'normal' child and resulted in a form of standardization by which we monitor children. He shows how Western society has become a child-centred culture and asks whether we continue to base parenting and teaching on a view of children that is no longer appropriate.

ANDRÉ TURMEL is a Professor in the Department of Sociology at Université Laval.

A Historical Sociology of Childhood

Developmental thinking, categorization and graphic visualization

ANDRÉ TURMEL
Département de Sociologie
Université Laval

CAMBRIDGE
UNIVERSITY PRESS

CAMBRIDGE UNIVERSITY PRESS
Cambridge, New York, Melbourne, Madrid, Cape Town, Singapore, São Paulo, Delhi

Cambridge University Press
The Edinburgh Building, Cambridge CB2 8RU, UK

Published in the United States of America by Cambridge University Press, New York

www.cambridge.org
Information on this title: www.cambridge.org/9780521705639

First published 2008

Printed in the United Kingdom at the University Press, Cambridge

A catalogue record for this publication is available from the British Library

Library of Congress Cataloguing in Publication data
Turmel, André, 1945–
  A historical sociology of childhood : developmental thinking, categorization,
  and graphic visualization / André Turmel.
    p.   cm.
  Includes bibliographical references and index.
  ISBN 978-0-521-87977-4 (hardback) – ISBN 978-0-521-70563-9 (pbk.)
  1. Children–History.   2. Child development–History.   I. Title.
  HQ767.9.T85   2008
  305.23109182'1–dc22
                                                              2008015651

ISBN 978-0-521-87977-4 hardback
ISBN 978-0-521-70563-9 paperback

This book is dedicated to my children, Antoine and Aude, and to my grandchildren, Naïmé, Emma, Clémentine and Éli

First we nursed our babies; then science told us not to.
Now it tells us we were right in the first place.
Or were we wrong then but would be right now?
                    Mary McCarthy, The Group, *1954: 228*

Contents

Illustrations

Figures

Forms

Charts

Tables

While every effort has been made, it has not always been possible to
identify the sources of all the material used, or to trace all copyright
holders. If any omissions are brought to our notice, we will be happy
to include the appropriate acknowledgements on reprinting.

Acknowledgements

I am grateful to many colleagues in the childhood studies field for their contributions to our debates and talks in several conferences over many years. In this respect, I thank the members of the Childhood Research Network of the European Sociological Association and the members of the groupe de recherché 'Sociologie de l'enfance' of the Association Internationale des Sociologues de Langue Française. I am obliged to all researchers involved in the exchange of views over earlier versions of Chapters 4 and 5 in the different meetings of the above-mentioned groups as well as some other research groups.

I am especially indebted to Nicole Ramognino, a wonderful sociologist at the Université de Provence, for our long-standing collaboration of more than thirty years.

I owe special thanks to Nigel Gearing in London; to Philippe Desaulniers, Étienne Girard, Emilie Lapierre, Mélina Bouffard, Jocelyne Martel and Étienne Rivard from the CIEQ in Québec City; and to Matthias Schwerdt and Monika Sommerer from the Max-Planck-Institut für Wissenschaftsgeschichte in Berlin.

Introduction

The areas covered by *A Historical Sociology of Childhood* are of relevance to sociologists, to historians and, more broadly, to social scientists. The title deserves some clarification. From an analytical standpoint, it alludes to two distinct sets of meaning. The first that comes to mind evokes, at least for readers familiar with social sciences, the emergence of modernity – and, afterwards, its design and patterning – in a sociological and theory-driven approach to history. It brings into play the work of historians to a sociological purpose, namely explanation in a comparative framework focusing on large-scale processes, which, it should be borne in mind, are the core of classical historical sociology: capitalism, bureaucracy or the state (Delanty and Isin 2003). However, the historical sociology of childhood put forward here is somehow different: it does not arise primarily from the aforementioned processes. It rather proceeds from compounded social operations such as the circulation, translation, standardization and stabilization of children, which were crucial in shaping modern childhood; these will be spelt out later on.

A second meaning pertains to a more unusual thrust with regard to these complex operations, for it was tucked away under layers of connotation, piled up one above the other for over two centuries. They were rendered feasible by what is known as statistical thinking and reasoning with its share of technologies. As the nineteenth century discovered statistical thinking and reasoning through large-scale empirical investigations – understood as population studies conducted by state authorities (Farr, Villermé, Quételet etc.), the statistical concepts of population, and of sub-population, came of age. Within the large movement aiming to delineate the national population in western countries, these statistical investigations brought to light the peculiarities, hitherto unknown, of different parts of the population, among them, children. Accordingly, the condition of children – health, work, education, social problems (abandonment, neglect, truancy, delinquency etc.) – was gradually uncovered; let alone the extensive history of child welfare or health policy and the sustained struggle against infant mortality. The net outcome was to frame children's situation in an entirely novel way as an autonomous category of thinking and acting thereupon in the national population: the historical rise of the category of childhood was set forth within this specific context. *A Historical Sociology of Childhood* outlines the statistical concept of the child population, henceforth the empirical discovery of their characteristics and idiosyncrasies.

The subtitle of the book, *Developmental thinking, categorization and graphic visualization*, also warrants some explanation. The starting point of the analysis, the acknowledgement of children's particular situation, came about in the wake of the rise of an autonomous category of 'childhood'. Although it is an astonishing social achievement, it is one that is estimated equivocally. What is a child, above the peculiarities brought to light by those large-scale inquiries? The question remained unanswered by the end of the nineteenth century. While it faced substantial uncertainties such as the appalling rates of infant mortality, the community – the childhood collective, as we shall find out later on – was nevertheless in search of a cogent answer to this issue. The discovery of 'childhood' launched an enormous research effort culminating in the systematic investigation of childhood. This effort took place in scientific domains such as public hygiene, paediatrics, psychology, education etc., and paved the way to social interventions leading to the onset of a specific form of childhood regulation.

This study covers a period of almost one century, from 1850 to 1945, which is considered as the apex of the developmental paradigm. The latter is understood in a broader sense than in developmental psychology as it applies to society as a whole: a model of history, which amounts to a model of progress, assuming that all societies follow the same course of transformation, with each going through identical stages of development, in brief from archaic or primitive to modern or advanced societies. This overarching model has been altering all social sciences from the outset, whether investigating global societies or changes in family life for instance; all societies are pegged at diverse stages along a uniform development continuum of stages and sequences (Thornton 2005). The influence of developmental thinking is broad: the decline in infant mortality and female fertility – known as the demographic transition – is an interesting case which will be looked at later. This paradigm is conveyed in numerous ways in the nascent science of childhood – notably although not exclusively via developmental psychology – integrating it into this substantial trend of the scientific community in the second half of the nineteenth century. I shall examine how developmental thinking impacted on the science of childhood and the consequences of this.

The answer to the question 'What is a child?' varied substantially according to its social inscription, whether it came primarily from the community at large – parents, social workers, teachers, welfare activists etc. – or from researchers in laboratories circulating scientific knowledge in a broader context. Beyond these variations, we are likely to find common ground providing a conceptual/empirical space within which to think about and act upon the child's body away from biological determinism. The nub of the issue is the manner in which social accounts or narratives of children's bodies, wherever they come from, tend to include and emphasize the likelihood that children's lives bear a material, as well as a discursive or representational, component (Barad 1998; Suchman *et al.* 2002: 101). Childhood as a social phenomenon is not basically the outcome of clear-cut ideas – the Hegelian pure idea[1] – produced by philosophers, for the child as an object is configured in social practices.[2] In contrast, the chapters of this book show the possibility of apprehending childhood differently, via the rise of a childhood collective – numerous social actors interacting together to frame children and regulate their behaviour – using diverse artefacts such as graphs and charts.

Whether these arguments are credible or not, the key point remains: it will map the way scientific investigation and public policy muster data and resources relevant to children, which then go on to influence their lives. It will explore, accordingly, the decisive historical trends leading to our current awareness of children. Population studies were

---

[1] Philosophy, in this respect, is not considered as a universal thought which transcends all particular situations from a unifying superior standpoint, but rather a singular and contingent thought produced in a specific society under particular conditions. This epistemological stance draws on the tradition, inaugurated by Marx, of a strong critique of philosophy. See his *The Poverty of Philosophy* (1847).

[2] Although Aries' hypothesis – the relatively recent solicitude regarding the child in western culture – was widely debated in the scientific community, it is generally acknowledged that concerns about the child took a new form and received a decisive impulse with the passage to modernity.

indispensable in this process: vital statistics, large-scale inquiries and data collection during systematic investigations by the Royal Statistical Bureau in the UK or its equivalents in France and the USA. These studies' categorization and classification rendered possible the emergence of an autonomous type, childhood, and the methodical comparison of children, thus ushering in the elaboration of norms of development.

For several complex reasons that this book will consider extensively, after a period in the nineteenth century during which public hygiene and paediatrics played a leading role in the social fabric of childhood, psychology progressively moved to the forefront in the twentieth century. It became the core of the nascent science of child research with the coming of age of the category of the normal child and, in the aftermath, the rise of the developmental paradigm. There were always tensions in the childhood collective: tensions between child experts and parents, between paediatricians and psychologists, between public authorities and welfare activists, and today between childhood research's new perspectives, with children's views provided either from a socialization standpoint or from developmental psychology. These tensions are a driving force in the process of child research understood as 'a culturally patterned and socially structured mode of already being in the world' (Alanen 1997a).

My goal in this book is to examine the inception of this key modern development in the social fabric of childhood. I am primarily concerned with explaining it sociologically, whereas others did so psychologically or philosophically, hence from various other scientific perspectives. My aim is, rather, to understand child research both as a historical achievement and a social production, and, accordingly, to show a science more in tune with the modern world and its major trends and characteristics.

A historical sociology of childhood

Though the subject matter of this book is original – so far no historical sociology of childhood has been written[3] – its general topic, childhood,

---

[3] It is essential to raise this core distinction in order to clarify a specific space in the scientific field, since historical sociology must be set apart from the more widely known history (British, American, French etc.) of children that is already partly

is not. Psychologists, historians and specialists in education or social work have written at length on the issue from their specific standpoints, all stamped in the developmental paradigm. Without undertaking an extensive review of this sound literature, I shall examine what a historical sociology of childhood is about, what it means and why it is needed. This venture takes place in the wake of N. Elias' disturbing concern: 'The Retreat of Sociologists into the Present', as the core statement of a general analysis of sociology's main trends over the past fifty years.[4]

The historical part of the question is broached at the outset: why and how is childhood a historical achievement? The sociology of childhood has, for the past twenty-five years, been very forceful, yet diligent, in putting forward a genuinely sociological standpoint on childhood. As the childhood field was overwhelmingly dominated since its inception by psychology – sociology being historically confined to the field of family studies[5] – the breakthrough of an insightful sociological stance still looks promising, be it only by putting forward a fresh view directly challenging the predominant psychological perspective. Unfortunately, some weaknesses can be detected in this. One of the most blatant flaws pertains to the ahistorical outlook implicit in most sociologists of childhood research, thus reiterating psychology's patent

---

written. Historical sociology, in the usual sense of the tradition, refers mainly to a specific type of analysis: 'macrohistory', long-term patterns of political, economic and social change (Collins 1999). It alludes largely to the rise of empires, world systems, global capitalism, modernization and so on. But the scope of the historical sociology perspective is now broadening towards new scientific objects and its scope is no longer restricted to macrosociology. A good example is Mackenzie's *Inventing Accuracy: A Historical Sociology of Nuclear Guidance Missile* (Mackenzie 1990).

[4] 'This retreat, their flight from the past, became the dominant trend in the development of sociology after the Second World War ... That it was a retreat is evident if one considers that many of the earlier sociologists sought to illuminate problems of human societies, including those of their own time, with the help of a wide knowledge of their own societies' past and of earlier phases of other societies. The approach of Marx and Weber to sociological problems can serve as an example ... The narrowing of the sociologists' focus of attention and interest to immediate present' (Elias 1987: 233 *et seq.*).

[5] Everything happened as if a form of scientific division of labour occurred by the end of the nineteenth century according to which psychology took hold of the field of childhood, whilst sociology became restricted to family studies, thus kept apart at the scientific level from the awakening and development of the childhood collective.

misconceptions as an ahistorical and acultural domain grounded in the assumption of a universal child.[6] The dangers of an ahistorical inscription of children must not, in any circumstances, be underestimated: a sound concept of childhood does emerge from society's real historical processes – past and ongoing – in which children are an integral part. 'Therefore, by placing concepts of childhood in the historical process in which childhood has emerged and developed, a more valid conceptualization of childhood can be approached' (Alanen 1992: 99).

This book reveals how wrong it is to assume that childhood is either a natural or universal entity, which amounts to an inconsiderate denial of its historical processes. Psychologists may be able to set up in a causal form their own experiments upon children in a quasi laboratory-type setting from the developmental paradigm. Sociologists have to wait for the passage of time: social changes gather together the phenomena and operations that draw their attention in the form of a historical process (Elias 1987).

The historical processes upon which the social fabric of childhood basically rests cannot be restricted to the most obvious aspects of its course. Childhood is neither an inevitable consequence of the historical accumulation of western societies' public policies, be it in the form of infant welfare, compulsory schooling or whatever, nor a simple outcome of experts' advice to parents and others. It is, rather, the product of a complex movement of cooperation, conflict and resistance between a broad range of social actors, including children themselves, in a historical process of moulding a form via diverse social actions: the child as a social form to be moulded throughout 'a sequence of biographic trajectory' (Bourdieu 1980, 1986).[7]

In such a process, the invention of childhood – to adopt Aries' wording – has fuelled, and been fuelled by, artefacts or social technologies:[8] graphs, charts, IQ, tabulation and so on, which regards

---

[6] Psychology's universal child is a direct product of developmental psychology's and, more broadly, developmental thinking's origins, which lasted until now in psychology's mainstream with a few remarkable exceptions (Woodhead 1990).

[7] Bourdieu defines the social trajectory as 'the series of positions successively occupied by an agent (or a group of agents) in a space itself in the becoming and subjected to unremitting transformations' (Bourdieu 1986: 62–63).

[8] The syntagm 'social technology' is used in contrast to the more conventional term of technology: soft technology as opposed to hard technology such as computers or the electricity network. The distinction is purely pragmatic and

graphic visualization as an essential patterning of children's condition. These were a shaping force and, thus, are considered as worthy ideas concerning child-rearing or abstract philosophical propositions pertaining to children in the overall historical process leading to our current understanding of childhood.

Understanding childhood as a historical social process creates particular consequences in need of being addressed. The Ariesian proposition relating to 'the invention of childhood' can be misleading to a certain extent. Childhood is not solely social to the point of invention and then self-sustaining thereafter. Its very conditions of possibility are always social from the onset and along the whole course of its trajectory leading to adulthood. Therefore this amounts to asserting that childhood cannot, in the first place, be restricted to an exclusive biological or psychological phenomenon, nor be considered a pure outcome of external conditions such as public policies. As a historical achievement, childhood pertains to broader processes gathered together under the aegis of social practices taking place in a collective within a fully pluralistic model of human societies as Elias suggests.

The latest explanations regarding social practices, which are tantamount to a clarification of the sociohistorical character of childhood, establish the three main reasons why the perspective of this research should be sociological as well as historical. Some are relatively patent, others less so. They allude respectively to the sociology of scientific knowledge, actor–network theory and the concept of collective cognitive dispositif to give an account of the now predominant developmental thinking framework.

Studying childhood amounts – it is an explicit objective – to throwing light on the historical processes of childhood social fabric more generally, and in particular those that have been kept in the dark for so long. The aforementioned processes were crucial in the rise of the concept of the normal child and developmental thinking at the turn of the twentieth century. It is acknowledged that the childhood collective was disturbed and rather chaotic and a subject of great anxiety for families, various reformers, public authorities, the state

does not pretend, in any case, to have theoretical foundations, the Foucaldian tradition being quite different in this respect. The distinction raises two serious questions: first, the relations between social actors and artefacts; second, what is technology from a sociological standpoint, which will be addressed later.

and the like. Children were threatened by appalling rates of infant mortality and unknown diseases; the questions of child work and compulsory education were still divisive; problems such as delinquency, truancy and cruelty to children needed to be addressed. Concerns about the normal child and its development were voiced publicly. Accordingly, the continuing uncertainties brought forth by the condition of children demanded to be resolved, and yet the collective required stabilization.

One must keep in mind that, although public concern about the plight of children was deep, very few devices were available for the appraisal of the child and its accurate measurement; no precise criteria or standards were widely recognized. The starting point is unquestionably the lack of scientific and technological instruments for the purpose of the knowledge of children. It is crucial to recall that issues such as infant mortality rates and compulsory education set up the context – namely, social environment and conditions – within which large-scale inquiries took place.[9] Children's bodies started to be observed, recorded, described, weighed, measured with diverse technologies, and physically as well as psychologically assessed at specific intervals in socio-medical encounters.

In tune with the line of argument brought forward, I shall emphasize that several social technologies relating to the condition of children contribute decisively to shaping childhood thoroughly; these technologies emerged as one of childhood's critical conditions of possibility. I do not intend to study these technologies technically but sociologically, via the sociology of scientific knowledge,[10] as they have materialized in the childhood collective nowadays to the point of being self-evident. At any rate, social technologies form a set of threads central to normality, hence to developmental thinking, for

---

[9] To a certain extent, social technologies, emerging in the wake of population studies and linked to developmental thinking, pertain to the implementation of a technical system in the social world. However, it must be asserted that these social technologies are very different from large technical systems such as transportation, electricity, water distribution and so on (Coutard 1999).

[10] The sociology of scientific knowledge has developed over the last thirty years as it moved beyond the classic Mertonian sociology of science. This new field purports to a set of empirical studies which examine social processes at the heart of the production and the assessment of knowledge by science. The most direct sustainable effect of this upon social technology arises because it also produces knowledge through categorization and classification.

every childhood collective has to confront the question of the child's transformations – growth, maturation etc. – in both its body and mind.

These threads inform the childhood social fabric by means of the basic activities of the observation and recording of children. They paved the way to a more formal knowledge-driven activity, namely, the categorization and classification of children leading gradually to developmental thinking's sequences/stages framework.[11] The height and weight chart appears in this respect as the typified form of the latter, the first step among several others leading to the sequential development of childhood. Charts were the very first technologies brought forth to appraise child development, once related contagion and diseases were mastered; in other words, once the threat of infant mortality was no longer insuperable. The childhood technologies not only set up extensive categories – normality/abnormality etc. – but more finely-tuned ones, as we shall see with feeble-mindedness and, above all, with Binet's intelligence tests (Bijker *et al.* 1987).

Technical devices such as graphs and charts provide knowledge to a given collective and yet, as artefacts, they realize this exclusive task in a performative interface with other actors by way of parameters in need of clarification. Asserting that technical devices provide knowledge in the form of graphic visualization amounts to saying that technology bears a particular status, radically different from the usual purely instrumental status (as a residue) which mainstream sociology abides by. These considerations bring the line of argument to the complex question of the intricate relationships between social actors and technologies in the construction of a stabilized common world; this is where actor–network theory (ANT) comes to the fore.

The essential feature of ANT, relational materiality, denotes the power of science and technology: it arises from the action of both human and non-human actors linked together (Prout 1996).

---

[11] The stages/sequences framework leads quintessential developmentalism as I shall argue in this book. The steady emergence of the concepts of stage and sequence is generally considered as an outcome of statistical reasoning applied to population studies and their large-scale inquiries. They played a vital role in the creation of a common world – namely, the wording of children's predicaments and the implementation of an efficient framework to cope with their maturation – and in the process to stabilize it. Moreover the concepts of stage and sequence were not restricted to the childhood collective as they percolated into other scientific fields (Desrosières 1993; Hacking 1990; Ménoret 2002).

Accordingly, its object constantly focuses on the deeds of mediation between the two distinct entities. I shall assert that ANT is particularly relevant to the circulation of graphs and charts in the childhood collective. Hence my hypothesis asserts that the assorted technical devices are mediators as well as translators, which operate as such in a network of relationships, namely a collective. A graph or a chart circulates – and interposes itself – between children, parents and the like by adding new resources to the collective which play a decisive role in the stabilization of a common world, thus raising the stakes.

Translation concerns the materials, which produce the practices ordering and patterning social life. It emphasizes the relational, constructed and process-oriented character of social life for it constitutes children as social beings emerging from the continuous interactions of humans among themselves throughout the inter-connectedness of a vast array of non-human objects with human actors. Mediation, on the other hand, is understood as an operation that furthers the circulation between human and non-humans. Non-human entities (technological devices such as graphs and charts) bear the status of an extension of human action, which then becomes more efficient and coordinated: the hammer is a prolongation of the hand that holds it just as the computer is a continuation of the fingers and the mind typing on the keyboard. Mediation transforms the collective's relationships in startling ways in the process of stabilizing it. To establish technical devices as mediators indicates that something happened, an event occurred. Charts and graphs make new connections while opening up new possibilities to the collective: novel forms of inscription and graphic visualization of children. They have the capacity to transform data and observations into visualized documents that interpose themselves between actors with a view to stabilizing the collective.

From a chaotic and disturbed situation in the last third of the nineteenth century to a more stabilized common world by the 1930s and 1940s, children's conditions were mediated and translated into diverse technical devices bringing forth developmental thinking. This passage – the trajectory leading to sequential development – is understood as the most acute attempt to stabilize the childhood collective. How was this massive achievement made possible? The answer to this question requires the concept of the collective cognitive dispositif, for it focuses on learning procedures, cognitive schema and institutionalized practices, all of which provide actors with resources to stabilize a common world, that is the childhood collective (De Munck 1999; De Munck and Verhoeven 1997).

The collective itself is a dispositif of inter-individual and inter-group coordination depending on rules and powers. Rules bear the status of heuristics and patterns – rather than binary prescriptions – for situated behaviour pertaining to childhood, and beyond. Collective cognitive dispositifs provide learning to social actors as they operate as mediators. They do so for the past as their rules condense anterior learning in a selective and operative manner; they allude, however, to ulterior learning for they are supports for actors' reflexivity. Finally, they maintain a global coherence within numerous situations. I shall argue that the developmental paradigm and thinking operates precisely as a collective cognitive dispositif, which provides coherence and stability to the childhood collective.

Beyond the social studies of childhood, this book draws on emerging ideas associated with the heterogeneity/hybridity of categories and phenomena related to childhood: children's interconnected and networked status as expressed in actor–network theory; Bourdieu's claim to the complexity of society; the theory of normality and the sociological ideas of De Munck and Ramognino pertaining to the cognitive collective dispositif. These topics pervade this book. Although I do not give a systematic account of these, I outline them selectively, when it is timely for the exposition of my argument.

The structure of the book

This book will draw out the implications of a historical sociology of childhood for our contemporary understanding of children, both across scientific investigation and public policies.

Chapter 1, 'Children in the collective', puts forward a cogent and legitimate historical sociology of childhood, disentangled from the plain drawbacks and limitations of sociology's sole concept of childhood: socialization. Beyond history's empirical descriptions, it will seek to describe the most decisive social processes leading to our current awareness of childhood. This broad movement takes place within a redefinition of the national population via its rationalization by public authorities, the rise of statistical thinking in the wake of manifold population studies, ushering in the systematic investigation of childhood; how the implementation of an autonomous category of childhood tallies with the rise of the concept of the normal child. Accordingly, the question of childhood regulation emerged both in the public sphere and in several scientific fields: public hygiene, paediatrics, psychology, education etc.

The appropriate research question concerns the specific translation of children's conditions yielded by the sciences of childhood: namely, how developmental theory – with the figure of the normal child – and its cognitive devices – graphs and charts – gradually became the usual way of thinking about and acting upon children that has abided ever since. By setting out an alternative conceptualization of the social sphere with regard to the child as an actor in its own right, by investigating how children's methodical measurement induces its classification and standardization, by considering how actor–network theory is relevant to a historical sociology of childhood, the chapter will present some empirical analytic propositions pertaining to the historical rise of the category of childhood with respect to the normal child and its historical seizure by developmental thinking.

Chapter 2, 'Graphs, charts and tabulation': the textual inscription of children, asserts that the very idea of childhood and a novel child figure were mainly sustained in science and in literature at the end of the nineteenth century. In this case, buoyant new fields of investigation, and technologies alike, spread throughout the second half of the century alongside less elaborate forms of child observation and recording, leading to a monographic form of children's inscription; the diary, either of a sophisticated or mundane type. Some scientists grasped these opportunities and pervaded the emergent domain of child study, which was hitherto under the authority of welfare groups or philanthropists; accordingly, they restructured the inscription of children into a visualized form and stabilized its network of relationships.

This chapter will emphasize the new resources introduced by the scientific investigation of children: technical devices, inventive knowledge, unusual expertise etc. From the outset, one cannot but be struck by the constant and steady presence of graphs, charts and tabulations in scientific journals or books related to the empirical study of children, which departed ceaselessly from the enormous advice literature offered by welfare groups. The complex of descriptions, vocabularies, reasoning and visual depictions evolved in such fields as anthropometry, hygiene, paediatrics and psychology that researched the child. These original ways of observing children are connected with the upsurge of empirical knowledge about childhood, which thoroughly transformed our apprehensiveness and our practices with respect to children.

Chapter 3, 'Social technologies: regulation and resistance', will stress how new methods of observation, and of recording, are put into place. They rest upon two prerequisites, social and technical alike: measurement and classification. One cannot conceive of recording, especially in its scientific rather than its monographic/diary form, without the practice of measurement according to explicit delineated parameters: the height–weight–age tables epitomize the exercise of children's measurement established during that period. Thus, a child becomes an object of scientific knowledge, with the investigation of the precise distinctiveness that identifies it as extensively different from other social actors.

Measurement categories inducing children's classification and enumeration are far from neutral within the collective. Classification bears consequences for the children classified, mainly in behavioural habits: this is regulation. And the other way around: this is resistance, by numerous actors opposed to standardization. Monitoring – and, therefore, regulating children's behaviour – through the social technologies is considered a task of a public as well as private apparatus. The technologies I shall be looking at are those established mainly by paediatrics and child psychology and implemented in the aftermath by public authorities: charts, record forms, well-child conferences, intelligence-testing and child-guidance clinics.

Chapter 4, The normal child: translation and circulation, asserts that a child is recognized as normal when classified or categorized as such, different in most features from anomalous children, in the wake of the implementation of developmental standards in the collective. Standards of development or normalcy? It remains to be seen if and how the two are equivalent, thus, substitutable one for the other, and this chapter will investigate the question. The enthusiasm for normalcy and standardization at the turn of the twentieth century percolated the childhood collective as it became a distinct entity in the national population; public authorities expressed concerns about the condition of all but few children. Developmental standards, which are produced at the same time through technologies of regulation, bring about three different forms of normalcy: the normal child as average, as healthy, and as acceptable.

Data collection, measurement and classification muster numerical facts, statistics, probabilities, means and correlations to bring up a new framework of thinking that seizes hold of the child. Statistical thinking introduces consistency in the investigation of the child: the institutional knowledge of children started to grasp its object in terms of statistical laws and probability. The normal child emerged as a cognitive being whom parents, physicians etc. taught about in their everyday practice, and as an administrative device to rationalize against. The processes of statistical assessments of children's posture pertain to some of the most cogent meanings of the child figure and the way it was shaped by the larger social trends in which it was embedded. The analytical perspective consists of apprehending the emergence of the normal child in its three predominant social forms.

Developmental thinking paved the way to the idea and the practice of the normal child as Chapter 5, 'Developmental thinking as a cognitive form', will investigate. While normality was a notion far from being indisputable, large-scale regularities played a huge part in outlining what a normal child should look like, both physically and mentally; different actors in the childhood collective began consequently to be on the look-out for new criteria suitable for adults in their daily relations with children. Moreover, parents, teachers and the like started gradually to behave along the main line of the cognitive device outlined by developmental standards as a particular way of thinking/acting to stabilize the collective.

I shall hypothesize that the introduction of cognitive devices induced a translation of children's 'predicaments' into a broad question of normality/development. Children's uncertainties in the collective are translated into novel standards and criteria of behaviour, for it provided a grounded and visual knowledge, via artefacts, to qualify specific situations such as children's illnesses and quandaries. One of the primary consequences of this translation consisted in a major redistribution of the network of relationships surrounding the child, the focus of the crucial distinction being displaced towards normal and abnormal children. Development brings stabilization to the collective by implementing a shared practice and knowledge-strengthening relationships among actors in regard to children's unsure situation: actors interact effectively for they do indeed share a common world, namely a mutual problematization of the situation. Stabilization conveys a shared framework, which raises actors to common-ness with regard to the situation of children as a prerequisite for action and focused intervention to put into place a stabilized collective.

The new direction designed for the study of childhood comes in the form of a historical sociology of developmental thinking. It is a call proposing that developmental thinking is the predominant framework of our current understanding and capacity for thinking and acting upon children. It should be borne in mind that this framework was, and still is, a credible alternative to western adults' endless capacity to sentimentalize, identify with or project onto children. The figure of the child, released from developmental thinking, helped shape feelings and concerns into structured thought. The visualized form of children's predicaments stabilized the movements of relationships in the collective between actors and objects for they are a means of cognition and ways of action that helped shape common-ness among actors: a means of bringing them together.

1 | *Children in the collective*

For the past twenty years, the various childhood studies produced have been less keen on providing a relevant analytic framework than on pointing out new ideas for forthcoming research in the area. Such an endeavour, however, bears a double-edged effect of which sociologists should be aware. On the one hand it helps a self-sustaining community of researchers, relatively isolated from mainstream sociology, to mark out its own field of activities by consolidating and unifying its object, by structuring the knowledge thus yielded around the issue of childhood. On the other hand it could lead otherwise well-intended empirical researchers, entirely absorbed in their daily work and fully devoted to the understanding of children, into a theoretical stalemate.[1] So many well-documented ideas have arisen from childhood studies that much energy has been concentrated on translating these into everyday knowledge; accordingly the capacity to theorize childhood has been set aside with unfortunate consequences (James *et al.* 1998).

These effects act as constraints on the development of sound knowledge of childhood. While this is not to suggest that contemporary sociology of childhood is in need of a theoretical overhaul, there remain urgent questions to address. The coming of age of a theoretically more productive approach can be seen as a sign of maturity; perhaps childhood is no longer either a residue of social theory or a peripheral phenomenon of adult society (Alanen 1992; Ambert 1986; Turmel 1998).

An ongoing debate must be sustained. We shall do so, first, by making a basic critique of socialization in regard to sociology's viewpoint. Second, by addressing the question 'what is a child?' from

---

[1] Such an assumption should be understood with respect to the important work done in the field of the sociology of childhood where a breakthrough happened both at the theoretical and empirical level. For the theory of childhood, cf. among others (Armstrong 1983; Bernard-Bécharies 1994; James *et al.* 1998; Lallemand 1993; Lee 1998; Quentel 1997; Qvortrup *et al.* 1994).

a sociological standpoint. Third, by setting out an unconventional conceptualization of the social. Fourth, by considering how such concepts as mediation, network, circulation and symmetry might be relevant for this process. Fifth, by setting out some analytic propositions.

1.1 Sociology's children

In both contemporary and classical sociological theory, one can find hardly any trace of that particular form of social agent, children, or of that special feature of social life, childhood. Whether in Durkheim's *Suicide*, or *The Rules of Methods*, Weber's *The Protestant Ethic* or *Economy and Society*, Marx's *Political Economy* or *Das Kapital*, whether in modern textbooks, Giddens' *Sociology* for instance, or in any of the diverse work of the major social theorists[2] of the twentieth century, childhood and children bear the weight of sociology's 'unthinkable object'. Such a situation is intriguing in some respects and it appears that to bypass this very phenomenon – childhood as sociology's 'unthinkable object' – constitutes a crucial weakness that needs to be addressed. This section will attempt to raise some of the issues related to the 'unthinkable object'.[3]

The objective here is not to propose a scholarly analysis of the intellectual, scientific and epistemological situation alike of such a domain as sociology in the second half of the nineteenth century. The prevailing situation – circumstances, state of affairs, specific juncture, critical theoretical conditions and the like – in the field of social sciences, of which sociology was an active part, is still only slowly becoming unveiled, and much still remains to be known in this

---

[2] With the notable exception, in my view, of Ulrich Beck, whose *Risk Society* and *The Normal Chaos of Love* put forward some stimulating and thought-provoking hypotheses with respect to children in the reflexive modernization – the second modernity – and in the individualization of society.

[3] French sociologist N. Ramognino proposed that language was sociology's 'unthinkable object' at the conceptual level. Although drawing on her work, my point is slightly different and less epistemological: childhood is an unthinkable object for mainstream sociology at the core body of its theoretical knowledge. The empirical phenomenon constitutes a black hole – a blind spot – for researchers. It is understood that sociology of childhood is still peripheral and has not yet strictly connected with mainstream theoretical sociology (James *et al.* 1998; Qvortrup *et al.* 1994).

respect. Hence a new contribution to knowledge of this particular question extends beyond the scope of this research.

I shall put forward the hypothesis according to which, toward the end of the nineteenth century, there was a scientific division of labour between psychology and sociology: the former embraced children and childhood, leaving the latter with family, which has since become a traditional topic of mainstream sociology. Sociology took this responsibility so seriously that it surrendered to this division of labour without questioning and started investigating the family issue by more or less excluding the child, thus leaving it to psychological enquiry. This hypothesis can be assessed institutionally:[4] in these specific areas of research, the scientific production of psychology is overwhelmingly child-oriented whilst sociology's outputs revolve massively around the family: all in all, a form of structural inversion.

Two unintended consequences of this division of labour have arisen progressively over the years. Sociology relied uncritically on developmental psychology to assess children until they become mature adults, thus having the capacity to participate fully in a given society as responsible, autonomous citizens (Prout and James 1990). As much for Durkheim as Parsons or Bourdieu, to name but a few, it is possible to suggest that their conceptualization of the human subject – of the child becoming an adult, an individual – relies substantially on a formal psychological reference. In Durkheim's case, the formal reference is that of Pierre Jamet (1859–1947), a student of both Ribot and Charcot, and his ideas concerning psychological automatism (Karsenti 1997: 53). Parsons' formal reference would be Freud – the universal patterns of the Freudian Oedipus complex – with the internalization of social value-orientations. Bourdieu on the other hand illustrates a conceptualization of the subject whose formal psychological reference is Piaget and Piagetian paradigms, whose theory is considered the epitomized form of developmental psychology (Lahire 1998).

Within the conceptual frameworks which command their respective empirical analyses, these sociologists, beyond their striking differences, share a fundamental common affinity: their conceptualization

---

[4] Institutionally along its classical parameters: journals, conferences, research programmes, laboratories, controversies, etc. It is also understood that, nowadays, psychology devotes a comparatively small amount of attention to family, and sociology likewise to childhood.

of the human subject – the child being nothing more than a human form maturing toward adulthood – rely formally on psychology in general and on developmental psychology more specifically. Sociology's inability to give a convincing and satisfactory account of childhood throughout its own history – children as a 'muted group' in social theory (Hardman 1973) – is not an isolated phenomenon: this enormous difficulty has always been experienced in proposing a coherent and global theory of the human subject.[5] The pre-eminence of a psychological construction of children at the heart of sociology is considered as the central feature of a major trend: the massive and disturbing silence surrounding children in sociological theory (Prout and James 1990: 8).

The second unintended consequence of the division of labour, related to the first, pertains to socialization as the sole concept that sociology has ever advanced in relation to children: how to bring them into mature adulthood with the necessary inculcation of appropriate rules, norms and behaviours. Since Durkheim is generally considered the first sociologist to propose a theory of socialization, the concept refers 'to social forces that make social life possible by drawing individuals together into a community' (Alanen 1992: 83). Society then must embody in the child the fundamental conditions of its own permanence: namely, to prepare the child for the requirements of social life (Prout and James 1990: 13). All types of sociologies, beyond their classic forms (functionalist, structuralist etc.), relate to childhood through different theories of socialization and their institutional sites – family, school, church and so on. Socialization constitutes a transformation of the child into a competent adult via methods and procedures such as constraint, inculcation, patterning and control (Jenks 1996: 35).

Prior to all refinements of different sociological traditions, the basic concept of socialization relates to the axiomatic idea of 'growing up' – children's immaturity and incompleteness are questions to be

---

[5] This theory should stand by itself; namely, it should not depend substantially upon the two main flaws of any sociological theory of the human subject – forms of psychological or economics e.g. rational choice theory. My hypothesis is that leaning on such theories for the conceptualization of the subject is equivalent to a theoretical abdication, even though one recognizes the inherent difficulties of a project of this extent. The corollary of this hypothesis is that a sociology of childhood offers a unique opportunity to fill that gap, providing that certain intricate questions, the nature of children's agency for instance, be addressed.

addressed later on (Hockey and James 1993); growing up as a transitional process between two distinct stages in the life-cycle. Socialization is thus considered as sociology's main attempt to explain this transitional process as a general and binding framework.[6] 'Socialisation research (makes up) the core of a sociology of childhood' (Fürstenau, quoted from Zinnecker 1997: 1) whose implicit counterpart is developmental psychology: the obverse and the reverse side of the same fragment of social reality. Among the various sociologists working within the socialization paradigm, Parsons is probably the most explicit in his attempt to link socialization with child development.[7] In his mind, socialization alludes firstly to the process of child development; it relates to the stablest and the most enduring elements in setting the child down onto the trajectory leading to adulthood (Parsons 1951: 207).

The outcome of this scientific division of labour was predictable. A massive psychological advance in the knowledge of childhood took the form of developmental psychology, thus enhancing a pervasive framework of explanation: childhood as a distinct stage of the life-cycle requiring specific child-rearing training and practices. Accordingly, the very limited knowledge of children in sociology pertains to the concept of socialization proceeding from a basic postulate:[8] children are adults-in-becoming, childhood as a lack which society has to fulfil during the socialization process: 'although the focus of the data collection ... may be childhood, the focus of theoretical interest is apt to be adulthood ... the issue of the concern is the functioning of the adult, not the life of the child' (Harkness and Super 1983: 222).

---

[6] This second unintended consequence of the scientific division of labour refers to sociology's own history and the 'doxa' as well: 'socialization has been foundational for sociological understandings ... Cultural common sense ... gives support to socialization as reality: children, who are born without language and knowledge of social organization, do become induced in the social worlds around them' (Alanen 1997a: 2).

[7] According to Jenks, Parsons has institutionalized social system's constraints upon the child into socialization theory through social norms understood as the ground rules of social life. 'As a concept it [socialization] incorporated the massive constellation of processes and accompanying paraphernalia that comprise "person building". In precise Parsonian terms socialization involves the lodging of the system's basic instrumental and repressive drives into the structure of individual personalities' (Jenks 1996: 18).

[8] The socialization perspective still prevails in mainstream sociology even though it has come under sharp criticism as will be indicated later on.

Childhood is only a short passage in a lifetime, 'a surface on which the completing process can be registered and observed' (Lee 1998: 463). So sociologists must focus on the different paths to adulthood and improve ways of yielding the best possible mature beings; children as receptacles of adult teaching and wisdom (Mayall 1994). Therefore sociological worlds ended up being populated by adults only (Alanen 1992: 1).

Socialization theory reckons on an explicit psychological model of child development that appears extraordinarily resistant to criticism, so strong is its position as a corner-stone of sociological theory. There it figures alongside family and childhood in a 'solid matrix of signi-fication' (Alanen 1992: 91) which is theoretically self-sufficient; this matrix is a digest of a general theory of social order which attempts to integrate children's difference into adults' standard social life.[9] The relevant question then becomes: how is such a process working upon the child,[10] how does it become an adult? The overall answer to this question revolves around the idea of internalization (of norms, rules and appropriate conduct), especially in the Parsonian tradition of internalization as a psychological process.[11] It emphasizes that socialization through internalization, whether in its psychological (Parsons) or structural (Bourdieu) model, appears a universal process in which the form of socialization[12] is overwhelmingly predominant over its content 'in each and every case' (James *et al.* 1998: 25).

[9] Ramognino proposes that every general theorization in sociology is either a theory of socialization or of communication. In this perspective, socialization is understood in a very broad sense, not in the rather restrictve common sense of family education and schooling. Thus it is possible to hold a topic like social regulation as an integral part of a theory of socialization: the extension of social regulation to the lives of children through medicine and hospitals, welfare and public health, charts, record forms and intelligence testing, conferences and clinics on child-rearing and child guidance, courts and prisons is deemed as a programmatic movement toward an attempt at a global socialization of children. This movement reinforces the family model, that is the use of human capacities in the family through technology for social ends: the moulding of the child's behaviour (Donzelot 1977).

[10] This point concerns Bourdieu's theory of symbolic violence, where socialization operates through inculcation and the concept of habitus.

[11] Internalization as a semiotic process: the logic of my argument will later connect the concept of childhood being unfolded here with semiotics via actor–network theory.

[12] Both Parsons' and Bourdieu's concept of socialization rests upon a certain conception of internalization – how the external world is poured into the internal world of the social actor. Reflecting on Piaget's specific developmental

An extensive critique of socialization theory has already been made. Beyond depreciatory qualifications of the concept as 'outmoded', 'dubious' or 'boring', it appears a necessary step in this argument to recall some key points of such an assessment. The main critiques can be summarized as follows:[13]

- Very schematically, the child is described as a passive recipient of adults' wisdom and society's culture, an outcome of global social processes that completely swathe it through the metaphor of the empty jar to be filled up (Corsaro 1998; Qvortrup 1995; Waksler 1991).
- The child is incompetent, irrational, irresponsible, because it is incomplete and immature, i.e. the imperfect *infans*, thus meaning that the child is acted upon, regulated, disciplined and determined, although in many different ways; this leads to the question of agency which will be looked at later (James and Prout 1995; Lee 1998).
- The concept is ahistorical and somehow acultural pertaining to the universality and naturalness of an abstract idea of the child heralded in the Piagetian form of developmental psychology (Elder *et al.* 1993; Prout and James 1990).
- Socialization theory is deterministic, characterized by individualistic naturalism, unreflexive adulthood, forward-looking, goal and output-oriented (Alanen 1997a; Jenks 1996; Thorne 1993).

To these classic assessments of socialization theory, the following two elements will be added so as to give as complete as possible a picture of its ongoing reappraisal.

- Socialization is identified by a unidirectional movement: out–in (that is, the outside world is poured into the child's body and mind); the human subject acquires personhood via a process of internalization which compels the community's lineaments into the child; Bourdieu's theory of reproduction through inculcation – habitus,

---

theory, Morss puts forward that 'for Piaget, ontogeny – like evolution – consists of the internalization of external conditions, a transmutation of the exogenous into the endogenous. In both cases, development is inherently and essentially progressive' (Morss 1990).

[13] This critique draws generally but not exclusively upon German sociologist Jürgen Zinnecker's presentation: 'Children as Agents. The Changing Process of (Re)producing Culture and Society between Generations' at a Conference on Childhood and Children's Culture in 1997, in Esbjerg, Denmark.

ethos etc. – represents its most implacable form (James *et al.* 1998; Ramognino 1987).[14]

- Socialization (that is, becoming social) is a transition from nature to culture, children becoming social only if they gradually ceased being natural;[15] this raised the issue of children as socially and biologically unfinished, thus of culture being burdened with the responsibility of finalizing the process; more generally, childhood appears as a transition phase between nature and culture (Prout 1999).

These critiques of socialization theory, some of them quite far-reaching, had various effects on sociology, but above all on the sociology of childhood. Zinnecker, while acknowledging the necessity of emancipating the research on children/childhood from socialization theory, argues nonetheless that sociologists should abide by the concept while they aim to shape inescapable changes to it (Zinnecker 1997: 10).[16] Alanen sees in socialization a limiting notion and calls for its suspension in researching children and childhood (Alanen 1997a: 3). A suspension does not mean, in Alanen's mind, the final relinquishment of the notion, for the paradigm may remain constructive within specified historical limits (Alanen 1997b: 253). Qvortrup, on the other hand, goes a step further by upholding the rejection of the concept as a condition for researching childhood nowadays; the concept can be convenient only at a meta-level of

[14] James *et al.* talk about the necessary inculcation of society's rules into its participants' consciousness. Although consciousness might not be the appropriate term to characterize suitably the transfer process, 'the direction of influence is apparent: the society shapes the individual' (James *et al.* 1998: 23). I would dispute their claim that Parsons constitutes the very symbol of the 'hard' form of socialization theory; Parsons being a functionalist, his version of structure is a rather 'soft' one. Bourdieu, on the contrary, coming from the Levi-Strauss school of structuralism, embodies the harshest form of the theory.

[15] In this respect, one can claim that socialization pertains to a theory of conformity, via its notions of interiorization and inculcation, which is a psychological theory (Moscovici 1988).

[16] In another paper, 'Sociology of Childhood, or Socialization of the Child?', Zinnecker asks the question: is the socialization frame simply outmoded and deserves to be exempted from the study of childhood? The wording of the title is a clear indication of the emerging opposition between a sociology of childhood and socialization theory (Alanen 1997b: 252). In other words, a sociology of childhood stands in its appraisal of children on as completely different a ground as one could possibly imagine.

analysis (Qvortrup 1995: 13). In brief, sociologists of childhood raise objections to children's marginalization by socializing them as 'becomings' (Lee 1998: 461).

For the most part, the assessment which advocates the forsaking of the concept came from a sociology of childhood which did not see any serious reason to hold to a theory that denies so systematically the possibility of researching children in their own right, for themselves and not as the carriers of the reproduction of the social order.[17] The focus of research veered to children in themselves and not as adults-in-becoming. James and Prout proposed that the 'black box' of the child remained resolutely shut within socialization theory – children being constrained by the environment – whilst the sociology of childhood has begun 'to pry open its lid' (James and Prout 1995: 90). Therefore, a tension – a euphemism for crisis – arose between the sociology of childhood and both socialization and child development theory; it had already begun destabilizing classical models of socialization and creating a fundamental shift in meaning.

It is now time to look at the sociology of childhood and try to understand how it began to pry open the lid of childhood. Opening the black box of the child was not sociology's sole task; other scientific fields such as history and anthropology were instrumental in this respect. These attempts are characterized by a number of common basic postulates to a post-socialization theory of the sociology of childhood:

- They downplay many presumed differences while emphasizing similarities between children and adults; there is no ontological difference between these two types of actors, the presumption of difference being a construction, situated and dated. This heightens the status of such a topic as the child's immaturity and incompleteness (Lee 1998).
- They recognize and emphasize children's agency: children as subjects in their own right and competent social actors in the realm of their own life: children actively construct their everyday lives just as they resist adult instruction. To affirm the child's

---

[17] Beck goes as far as saying that socialization is a 'zombie' category: a category that is dead but still alive, thus put to use in the mode of a 'ready-to-think' concept.

agency is a necessary but insufficient step;[18] to avoid the flaws of treating children's agency in an essentialist and humanist way, the question ought to be raised: agency for what? (Bernard-Bécharies 1994; Mayall 1994.)

- They emphasize that every concept of childhood is socially constructed: there is no universal child, childhood is a time–space construction that varies historically and from one culture to the other. Social construction is doomed as a rallying cry against any core truth, whether developmental psychology's linearity or biology's naturalness of any kind, although it dwelled too much on representational aspects of childhood whilst downgrading its material corporality (Prout 1999).

These basic postulates and the critiques of socialization theory alike amounted to a conceptualization of childhood in itself – both as an analytical category and an empirical object – as an integral part of a general sociology; the theories, the concepts and the methods historically legitimized in the field, rather than as a sub-field of the discipline such as social movement, stratification, family and the like. Among these, it is important to mention:

1. Childhood as a social category and a social status: childhood is both a social form revolving around a collective fabric and a culturally patterned as well as socially structured mode of being in the world, as opposed to a preparation stage for entering social life (Mayall 1994, 1996a); nor is it a fixed variable or another 'dependent variable' in the classic pattern of hypothesis–deductive methods. This view challenges both socialization, which enacts children individually, and the incompetent 'developing child' who is deemed to be a preparation stage for entering social life. Such a perspective leads to a focus of research 'on locations and situations in which children are among themselves, without the presence and interference of adults, within their own creation of "peer cultures"' (Alanen 1997c: 3). A child-centred approach pertains to ethnographic work.[19]

---

[18] The whole issue of the child's agency is a reiteration of the aforementioned theory of the human subject which sociology has been reluctant to address and has usually failed to address convincingly.

[19] Alanen's proposition of focusing research on children among themselves without the presence or interference of adults raises very difficult questions.

2. Childhood as an institution: the most serious attempt to pry childhood away from the stereotyped topics of family and schooling, to listen to children's own experiences and their resistances to the childhood planned for them by adults. Institutions are understood as a set of dispositions, socially and culturally constructed around an activity, that tend to survive in time and space (Näsman 1994; Turmel 1997). The institution of childhood refers to a patterned set of expected behaviours: stable designs for chronically repeated activity sequences; an active set of social relationships within which the early years of human life are constituted (DiMaggio and Powell 1991: 25).

3. Childhood from a structural and constructionist perspective in which children are conceptualized in relational terms: a particular generational ordering of social relations is materially constituted of structures of positionality, such as childhood, teenage years and adulthood 'which makes topical the linking of children's everyday worlds to the structural conditions for the childhoods we may observe' (Alanen 1997c: 2). This ordering connects children's modes of participation (resources as well as constraints) to social activities, particularly in relation to age (Qvortrup 1990). A semiotic configuration of symbols and meanings provides the construction through which the positionalities and their inter-relationships are yielded, and performed as culturally meaningful.

4. Childhood in which the child is taken hold of as 'being', in sum as a social actor in its own right, rather than 'becoming', the developing child.[20] This perspective supplies an analytical framework to the sociology of childhood, providing signposts for its progression. 'We offer an understanding of, first, the ways in which thinking about childhood necessarily reflects the nature of the social, and,

---

Studying childhood from the child's point of view heightens the question of how to achieve it. How are we to be sure that the perspective of the child presented is genuine rather than a recollection or reconstitution? It evokes Geertz's argument: 'Anthropologists do not have to turn native in order to argue from the native's point of view' (James *et al.* 1998: 183). The adult could be absent but still, however, present. Cf. the debate around the visible, the immanent, the metaphysics of presence etc. (Law 1999).

[20] The child in-becoming relates to the developing child, developmental psychology's way of conceiving of the child as a set of specific stages in a preordained sequence: the traditional model of the socially and cognitive developing child pertains to the growth metaphor (Morss 1990).

secondly, childhood's own contribution to furthering our understanding of that social world' (James *et al.* 1998: 200). An adequate
account of the social requires addressing childhood, which is a
fundamental statement in regard to social theory. The issues at
stake raise very serious difficulties: the relationship between child
and social order and core oppositional dichotomies such as nature/
culture, public/private, structure/agency, identity/difference, local/
global, continuity/change and adulthood/childhood, which is disput-
able from both a theoretical and an epistemological standpoint.

From socialization theory and developmental psychology to the
innovative sociology of childhood, a great distance has been covered.
The critique of the former is now well-established, firm and assured;
for sociologists at least, it is increasingly intricate, if not awkward, to
come to terms with childhood within the socialization framework.
This major breakthrough is considered an achievement. On the other
hand, the sociology of childhood has put forward some very critical
issues in the scientific account of the phenomenon of childhood.
Accordingly, these features have raised complex questions in regard
to the child that will now be addressed: what is a child from a
sociological point of view?

1.2 Unfolding the black box

The crucial question: 'what is a child from a sociological standpoint?',
has been variously addressed. Although the answers have proved to be
quite fruitful in many respects, thus paving the way for an original
sociological perspective on the child topic, they have nevertheless
raised serious problems in the very movement of their own answers.
To assert that children should be understood as 'beings' rather
than 'becomings' and, accordingly, be conceptualized in relational
terms, constitutes a necessary but insufficient step forward. Debates
surrounding these propositions are indicative in this respect.

This section will try to approach the obstacle from the side whilst
not trying to add another stone to it, so to speak. Thus taking a critical
look at social constructionism as a theoretical orientation, however
important its role in launching a sociology of childhood, does not
constitute the privileged way of coping with the basic question, perhaps because it tends to emphasize the dichotomy between material

and representational entities (Prout 1999). The paralysing effects of such dichotomies, along with others aforementioned, come within the scope of a long tradition of sociological dichotomies (Ramognino 1998a).[21] To overcome these drawbacks, a standpoint will be introduced which draws on Karsenti's reactualization of the work of Marcel Mauss, especially of his concept of totality (Karsenti 1997). In his book, *L'homme total* (*The Total Man*), he reasserts Mauss' outlook as elaborated in his seminal work, *The Gift*, around the concept of total social fact.

In the task of unfolding the black box of the child, the concept of totality is thought-provoking in a double specific sense. First, totality is a new way of integrating into a specific complexus of relationships scientific domains so crucial to understanding the child: biology, psychology and sociology as well as ethnology, history and linguistics in a general anthropology whose aim is to maintain the total unity of the human figure in all of its dimensions. The structuring tension among its components, especially between the physiological, psychological and sociological aspects, is an operative condition for the social to become the essential operator of the required synthesis. Social reality must then be viewed in the plurality of its dimensions, each playing a legitimized part in the composition of the whole. The major problem in this respect is the fraught relationship between psychology and sociology. When psychology attempts to dictate to the human sciences, it appears that the field is organized into a hierarchy around this schism: the individual and the collective whose institutional demarcation revolves around psychology and sociology (Karsenti 1997: 14).[22] These relationships are still at odds today and the concept of totality more relevant than ever in this respect.

---

[21] Bourdieu considered his concept of 'habitus' as a direct attempt at overcoming the gap between one of the most paralysing dichotomies of sociology, interior/ exterior: how to bring the exterior world into the subject and vice versa. Law castigates the paralysing effect of sociological dichotomies; his critique is implacable. 'In this scheme of things entities have no inherent qualities: essentialist divisions are thrown on the bonfire of dualisms. Truth and falsehood. Agency and structure. Human and nonhuman ... Sacred divisions and distinctions have been tossed into the flames. Fixed points have been pulled down and abandoned. Humanist and political attachments have been torn up' (Law 1999).

[22] Mauss wrote on this particular subject concerning the relations between sociology and psychology, outlining not so much a programme but rather a

The figure of the total man, in other words the totality of person-hood, is a complex three-dimensional structure in what Mauss calls a whole complexus. Mauss' man has three dimensions – psychology, biology and sociology – 'because he is not split up by the demarcation line between the individual and the social' (Karsenti 1997: 101). The three levels are distinct as well as interdependent; it is a unitary totality, indivisible and non-hierarchical.[23] It indicates a complete reformu-lation of the link between psychology, biology and sociology. Most notably, it ushers in a new sociological perspective on individual fact, whether psychological or corporeal; individual facts are not the sole property of either psychology or biology.

The 'total man' hypothesis amounts to the introduction of a legit-imized sociological aspect in the observation of the human subject considered as an individual. It takes into account the distinction drawn by Dumont between, on the one hand, the individual as being an empirical subject – the concrete subject of word, thought and will – and, on the other hand, the individual as value – the moral, inde-pendent, autonomous and essentially non-social subject which is a pure product of western ideology (Dumont 1986).

Beyond the possibility of a recomposition of the relationships between psychology, biology and sociology, the concept of totality provides a very stimulating breakthrough for integrating childhood into personhood, thus conceptualizing childhood as one of its basic, indispensable components. Accordingly, this small-scale movement – the categorization of childhood as a basic consituent of personhood – could very well go unnoticed, were it not for the enduring challenge to the homogeneous and unidimensional form of personhood that is still prevailing in sociology. If we are to accept the hypothesis of person-hood as a totality, then childhood becomes an essential part of its conceptualization as well as ageing, so depriving adulthood of its monopoly. The questioning of sociology's unrepentant adultism must

perspective, the totality, which aimed at unifying the knowledge of the human sciences. May I suggest that, presently, this analysis still appears relevant given the state of affairs as seen above.

[23] This is perhaps the main point of Mauss' argument. Regarding personhood, the three disciplines stand at the same level without any privileges granted to one or the other in any respect. Sociology does not invalidate psychology or biology, but combines itself with the others to propose its own perspective, which is to produce a specific articulation of the individual and the social (Karsenti 1997).

be firmly grounded in the soundest theoretical perspective:[24] the concept of totality provides the most promising opening and novelty for the sociology of childhood to establish its own theoretical framework upon the most reliable basis.

A proposition of such extent is scarcely new, however. Even before psychology made any statement about it at the turn of the twentieth century, various writers of both religious and secular persuasion agreed that the early years of childhood were highly consequential for the individual's character: early experience determined later behaviour, with regard to both emotional and intellectual development. In western societies, there exists a strong belief that previous training has a profound and lasting effect on a child's development; this belief rests on the premise that society is perfectible through the 'socialization' of its children (Richardson 1989), while establishing child behaviour as a legitimate subject for empirical scientific investigation (Lomax *et al.* 1978). Thus, infancy and childhood came to be progressively seen as a unique opportunity to mould final adjustment, that is adulthood.[25]

Moreover, in compliance with Bourdieu's hypothesis, modern societies do not fix a clear frontier line between different stages of life, mainly because the border is always being displaced, moving in one direction or the other according to historical tendencies (Bourdieu 1980). The boundary between stages or age categories is always both a matter of negotiation among various social groupings and a matter of conflict between them as well. The public debate in western societies about ageing, particularly about the age of retirement, is indicative

[24] This unrepentant adultism finds its most pre-eminent extension in the 'economics complex' of sociological realism after those sociologists who try to be taken as seriously as the economists' work in the neo-liberal society of the millennium. Their earnest concerns revolve around such topics as globalization, market, rational choice and power. In this respect, social reality is reduced to power, work, job market, technology, economy and the like. But could they compete with the economists on their own ground? Drawing on Caillé's incisive critique of Bourdieu: 'La sociologie des intérêts est-elle intéressante?' ('Is a Sociology of Interests Interesting?'), one can ask: is a sociology of power powerful?

[25] Consequently, childhood is never completely overcome in adulthood as the recurrent theme of the inner child illustrates: 'I should have learned from my experience with Sally that the simplest way of restoring a lost parent was to become one yourself; that to succour the abandoned child within, there was no better way than having children of your own to love' (McEwan 1993). See also Ivy 1995.

in this respect; the age of retirement is always a fiercely argued issue, its border being regularly displaced. Likewise debated are the demarcation lines between youth and adulthood, the question of the voting age being of consequence. Childhood also figures here, its confines being less and less firmly delineated. Above all, it is now widely recognized that childhood persists into adulthood in various forms,[26] so that one can conceive of childhood and personhood as irretrievably intertwined (Turmel 1997b; Turmel and Hamelin 1995). The concept of totality provides a unique opportunity to disentangle ourselves from a residual conception of childhood, characteristic of sociology's adultism, whilst putting forward the notion of personhood's integrality.

Karsenti sees the concept of totality as the main element of a general conceptual framework, and an original method, which he calls archaeological. Conceived as the methodological constituent of an underground research into a forgotten foundation – in Mauss' words, 'one of those human rocks upon which our societies are established' – but nevertheless essential to the comprehension of present time, it stands to prevent sociology from applying to society and, thus, to the social the schema of historical progress.[27] A sociologist has to keep himself from doing history, that is to say, from formulating historical hypotheses as a basis for an explanation of social phenomenon; history and ethnography alike are reservoirs of facts that serve to help understand present time. Historical sociology is never in this sense a research of origins; the archaeological method does not view the past as a relic of some sort, but as a plurality of forms whose effects, even systematically forgotten, are ascertainable in present time. Sociology's object is concentrated into an 'eternal present' and claims a double function: that of a synthesis of facts and that of an appraisal of the present signification; a sociologist assesses the scope of the data, their generality and their actual signification (Karsenti 1997: 310). In regard to this specific perspective, the social is conceived as a totality.

---

[26] The persistence of childhood into adulthood is not liable to a solely psychoanalytic reading. Although psychoanalysis pioneered the way in this respect, both topics of family and childhood memory are interesting modes of approaching the question.

[27] The schema of historical progress always continues to offer the possibility of an evolutionist conception of reality. The archaeological method is a bulwark against evolutionism.

If childhood is not a stage in life – neither a natural state nor a matter of age – but a basic component of personhood devised as a totality, then it is worth considering that childhood is a figure of life, a nomadic and mobile figure, continuously re-emergent, outlined and moulded in a given culture; that is to say that the figure varies in time and space accordingly. Thus such plain demographic facts as a decline in birth rate or in the child mortality rate can be regarded as a way of behaving toward oneself – the person as a totality – and its constant transformation in historical time, with layers of significations gathered over time, most of them being forgotten although still effectual in the 'eternal present'. This specific behaviour is a mediated form of conduct[28] which is not immediately and directly accessible to those involved; a detour is necessary to reach it (Molino 1978; Ramognino 1987). In modern societies, a form of conduct with regard to childhood is mediated through professional expert advice and scientific practice such as paediatrics, child psychology etc. (Jones 1983). Is it possible to conceive the experience of childhood, to recall that experience before it was captured by scientific discourse e.g. by the experience of measurement and its assumptions for how or what we now know about childhood, since a measurement presumes a representation of the object, a pre-theorized conception of what is being measured? What is the measurement of children all about as a practice of mediation?

The concept of totality – personhood as a totality – is established as the most promising foundation for reinstating childhood as a basic, unbypassable component of personhood; it thoroughly eschews the stage/age-division conceptions pertaining to childhood. Moreover, the totality standpoint conceals other conceptual potentialities, the most likely being the possibility of overcoming the body/representation dichotomy which embodies a tension bearing on the theorizing of childhood. The nub of the issue is that various forms of conceptual accounts of childhood tend to de-emphasize the possibility that the child has inextricably a material or corporeal as well as discursive or

---

[28] Mediation is not an intermediate between people, things and phenomena, but a detour that the human subject operates so as to act and to behave in the world; mediation adds something to the behaviour under consideration that was not there before. Molino introduces the distinction between a technical and a symbolic conduct, the latter being related to language as a mediator between oneself and the outside world (Molino 1978).

representational component (James *et al.* 1998).[29] The concept of totality provides the possibility of conceiving the child as both a material and representational entity, avoiding biological reductionism and semiotic mitigation alike (Prout 1999). Totality upholds an integrating perspective in which the child from its very inception is intertwined as a corporeal and discursive entity, neither of which carried an a priori entitlement to the core reality of the child, both of which are apprehended symmetrically at the analytic level.

The child as a material/corporeal entity, the body/child is indeed a crucial constituent of the sociology of childhood (James *et al.* 1998). Accordingly, and so as to overcome any biological account of children's bodies, we will examine the impediments underlying a theory yielding a sociological perspective on children's bodies. The questions at stake revolve around the immaturity and incompleteness of children. The child represents an acute figure of corporeal immaturity: he is 'constitutionally incomplete' (Lee 1998: 465). There already exist biological and psychological accounts of this immaturity: deterministic physiological growth and brain development. Child development can be looked at as a quasi-natural path to cognitive competence.[30] So far sociology's own account has been condensed in socialization theory: the child in a state of 'becoming', in its movement toward complete adulthood, thus duplicating the latter (Burman 1994; Morss 1996).

The obstacle for sociology consists of sketching an alternative set of attributions for the child, centred on the concept of agency, as immaturity has always been the soundest basis for depriving children of their agentic capacities. Understood in a non-essentialist form, a

---

[29] A strong reaction arose in the literature regarding the body against the linguistic turn in various social sciences which establish discourse at the foremost of scientific concern. 'In the social constructionist version, the body/child becomes dissolved as a material entity and is treated as a discursive object ... an effect of discourse ... social action is (generally speaking) embodied action, performed not only by texts but by real, living corporeal persons' (James *et al.* 1998: 146).

[30] Lee goes further by saying that classical psycho-physiological accounts of children inform a dominant set of attributions bearing upon children: 'It provides a default assessment of children as incompetent and irrational. This set of attributions precedes each child in their movement through the social to ensure that they are treated differently from adults, thus maintaining age-based hierarchy. It completes children as incomplete' (Lee 1998).

child's agency is not the property of a subject, but rather is derived from a distributed network of subjects, bodies, materials, texts and technologies; namely, childhood as heterogeneous and complex. The core of the question lies in the possibility of a sociological rationale of such phenomena as age, physiological change, language, cognition and, more broadly, the importance of embodiment in children's social life; this rationale is based on the assumption that the child is socially able, as opposed to the child's incompetence postulate adumbrated by decontextualized developmental theory. Embodiment appears the key point: children experience social life and expand their capacities and abilities, hence their competencies, mainly through embodiment.[31] The production and the experience of gender appear as a keystone in Prendergast's work on how British girls experience menarche (Prendergast 1992, 1995). A category such as menarche is not solely biological; nor can a phenomenology of the bodily experience with its symbolic referral deplete its meaning. Prendergast takes into account the material resources shaping the body practice with respect to this experience. This leads to the notions of heterogeneous materials and hybrids, central in actor–network theory, which enable us to under-stand the relationship between bodies and technologies. We shall look at these notions later.

The child as a discursive/representational entity consists of treating the child solely as a discursive object, as a pure effect of discourse in the way classical semiotics does. The discourse/child opens up radical questions in regard to the relevance of the child as a sociological object: how relevant are the representations bearing upon children for the construction of the child as a sociological object?[32] The approach put forward here questions and renders debatable the taken-for-granted outline given in the social practice: the child as an empirical object. The content of a symbolic form, a discursive/representational entity, should

---

[31] To speak of children's competence is not in any respect an implicit affirmation that their competences match in one way or another those of adults. There is a clear difference which needs to be asserted analytically, ethically and strategically (Lee and Stenner 1999: 110). Children have competences concerning the school: not about the curriculum obviously, but in regard to the school spatial organization, the spatial design of the yard for instance.

[32] The child as a sociological object refers initially to a specialized field of intervention so named and outlined; this design, already given in everyday social practice, appears to correspond to actors' social experience in a particular area of activity.

not be referred to the empirical child as one of its properties. If so, it then means that the social form would grant the child a status, features and sociological qualities which imply in the aftermath diverse determinations with regard to the description and the analysis of the object (Ramognino 1987). Therefore, such an impediment is all the more puzzling, since confusion emerges between symbolic entities and empirical elements of the social experience, thus attributing to the former sociological features of the latter; there is a continuity with the immediate social experience. Classical sociology does not distance itself in a convincing way from the factual outlines inherent in the pragmatic social practice; there is no direct connection between the empirical and the discursive child. The discursive/representational entity is a mediation, a translation; both the transparency of discourse or the immediacy of the child as an empirical object should be questioned (Turmel 1993; Turmel *et al.* 1991).

Opening the black box, a second concept will be looked at: rationalization, more specifically rationalization of the social in the context of modern societies,[33] drawing from Weber's seminal work. The cardinal topics of Weber's analysis are well-known: modern societies are driven by an irresistible process of rationalization which leads to an increasing bureaucratization of social life and to the theme of disenchantment with the world; the three forms – the typology – of rationalization are liable to a comprehensive sociology considering the individual actor and his intentions as the basic unit of analysis. There seems, however, to be a missing link between the individual as the foundation of the social and the inexorable necessity of rationalization at the societal level.[34] Rationalization is thus a social form which is constituted historically but which, sometimes, tends to be essentialized in certain types of analysis. This tendency must be avoided at all costs.

Specialized rational intervention in the field of childhood based upon science – constitutionally futuristic, thus allowing an extension of rational intervention – opens up a new social temporality, modernity,

---

[33] The context of the present study is the turn of the twentieth century. There was a particular form of rationalization process at that period of time (Beck *et al.* 1994).

[34] For a critique of this particular aspect of Weber's theory of rationalization, see Ramognino 1987.

which presupposes a rupture in the linear continuity of temporality; drawing up an opposition to traditional child-rearing and more broadly to the past. Rationalization of the social is an operation upon time, the future and history (Pomian 1984: 300). Modernity entails a rupture in the linear continuity of temporality, thus opposed to the past and to a tradition deemed outdated (Atlan 1979). Rational intervention reveals a new quality of time, that of modernity: through an intervention, a future is possible along the arrow of time. A conception of modernity as an opening of time–space for rational intervention is understandable only through this particular form of rationality born by science in its foreseeable, objectivist and positivist aspects (Ramognino 1998b).[35]

In regard to modern childhood, the rationalization process is directly related to science both as a unique method of apprehending the world and as a set of rules and norms for one's conduct in acting in the world. Once the causes of illnesses and pathogenic risks are recognized, rational intervention arises as an action coming within the scope of linear temporality: past/future. Sciences such as public hygiene, paediatrics and psychology have introduced a singular method, which is measurement: moreover accurate measurement of an uncommon object, the child, presupposes, as a corollary, a critical refinement of the object's observation toward more rigorous practices (Apple 1987; Armstrong 1983; Crisler 1984; Rodriguez Ocana 1998; Turmel 1997a). According to its own findings, science defines which features are desirable in the child and which ones are not; the power of definition that experts and scientists started acquiring from the last third of the eighteenth century received a new momentum with the great discoveries of the nineteenth century: Pasteur, Koch, Fleming etc. In the domain of childhood, purposively 'rational' action is gradually substituted for action guided by tradition: the 'natural' community between child and mother is given a new basis in the process (Cohen 1985; Cravens 1985b; Lomax *et al.* 1978).

State intervention and regulation of childhood took place within a broader process of the rationalization of the social. The three

---

[35] A complementary hypothesis is also conceivable. Rational intervention itself develops the science(s) it needs. For instance, it can be shown that mass schooling as a rationalization of socialization yields the development of a psychology of intelligence and child psychology alike (Ramognino 1998b).

basic lineaments of the rationalization process impinging upon childhood are:

- Rationalization of the national population; the various nation-states in western societies, each with its own specific traits,[36] went through a process of transformation of its national population and the groupings that comprised it: unyielding defined groupings, which individuals unavoidably belonged to. This new conception of the population as comprised of groupings, arranged in a hierarchy of superior and inferior ranks, was both thoroughly materialistic and naturalistic. Children constituted a distinct group within the national population, thus presuming that children were legitimate objects of scientific study. Child scientists shifted their focus to the normal child as part of a larger transformation of the notion of the national population and its taxonomy.

- Rationalization of the family through its structural transformation: the institution of the family owes its durability primarily to intrafamilial processes of rationalization, which consist of more egalitarian patterns of relationships, further individuated forms of interpersonal interactions, and alternative liberal child-rearing practices. The family, founded on affectivity and intimacy, saw itself as a bulwark against the constraints of the external world, which operated more in accordance with the schema of methodical and rational action. The regulation of the mother–child bond is guided by professional expert advice and the empirically grounded knowledge of paediatrics and psychology: the natural community for the satisfaction of needs existing between mother and child is given a new basis whilst the normative model of mother-love is still playing a central role. The individual development of women took place within families and the husband–wife relationship gradually enters a lasting period of transformation.[37]

- Rationalization of personhood: the formation of a personality structure capable of a methodical and disciplining conduct of life as

---

[36] British concerns converged upon the 'dangerous classes' and their possible degenerative effects on the future of the nation. While the French population crisis revolved around national anxieties concerning exhaustion and the decline of the country, the Americans focused on the quality and the ethnic composition of their population (Klaus 1993; Meckel 1990).

[37] These ideas are developed by both Habermas and Beck (Beck and Beck-Gersheim 1995; Habermas 1979, 1984).

a result of Calvinism's clear ascetic goal. The epitomized form of education consists of teaching children to be disciplined and to carry out their duty because it made its recipients capable of a methodical conduct of life which applies only to males. The childcare techniques, which emerged in the historical development of the handbooks of medical advice in regard to child-rearing, were to be used in dealing with the peculiarities of the infant's body, the control of the child's inner nature by means of scientific calculation. Age-based hierarchy – the division of life's process in age-defined divisions, which is a specific categorization of the nineteenth century – also introduced the notion of sequences of stages in child development as discrete stages of cognitive capacity.

Both concepts of totality and rationalization convened for the unfolding of the black box. Totality is introduced and operated not as an umbrella notion intending to link disparate notions, but as an integrating, unifying general perspective which allows us to think of childhood as a core element, rather than a residual one, of both sociological theory and the social. Rationalization, on the other hand, is a characteristic concept of modernization, which shaped and designed the diverse forms of the social at this specific period of time. The next section will look at the concept of the social so as to avoid the drawbacks of relying on an implicit theory of it.

1.3 The social: unity and heterogeneity

As a general category in sociology, the social is usually understood either as a particular domain of society – one of the four sub-systems of a general theory, amidst the cultural–symbolic, the politic, the economic – or as a very loose sphere including the vague meaning of 'being-together', the various ways in which actors behave and operate. Moreover, it can pertain to the area of social engineering (such as social work or social policy), that is to say the ways in which a specific community manages its social problems. In any case the category of the social is above all anything but accurate at the analytic level: the category is confined to something specific. Although a worthwhile category, sociologists use it accordingly: in an unrestrictive and indeterminate sense. They rely on an implicit theory of the social, which, because it is implicit, always yields inappropriate effects in the analytical process (Ramognino 1998a).

This is not to say that the social is a weak category. On the contrary, provided the concept be circumscribed and rendered explicit within a particular analytic framework whose premise requires that any account of the social – and of sociology – is deemed incomplete without childhood. The best possible way to approach this question is to start with the rise of social intervention and the cutting out of a specific sphere from the totality as well as its autonomization.[38] Social intervention cannot materialize without alliances, the most important being science: science can develop itself gaining access to a specific 'territory' and insofar as social actors are interested in its development in accordance with the territory's situation.

The processes of rationalization bore upon three main categories of activities: the economic, social and familial order insofar as socialization took place initially within the family and then was partly transferred to the social order. The rationalization of the social order by the political sphere at the time of the democratic shift took the form of a double movement: a rationalization of education and of health with new practices and institutional forms in both sectors. It should be borne in mind that the child as a sociological category refers initially to a specialized field of intervention so named and based on a Weberian type of rational foundation. This specialized intervention was based on a body of evidence, which is the 'continent' of empirical children.

This political rationalization of the social was historically carried out through the opening up of original space–times of social intervention. This overture arises only if the political rationalization can proceed with allies, both actors and objects. An intervention always occurs in a specific social field, which is the historic outcome of previous cutting-out within the framework of social interventions in a spatial projection. A social intervention is constituted insofar as it takes over an explicit space to rationalize. The social is therefore projected upon a surface, a territory, and a field of intervention. So as to take place, social intervention must outline a spatial form; that is, it must cut out from the totality the specific sphere of its intervention.

[38] I owe much to Ramognino's unpublished paper, 'L'Enfance handicapée' ('Disabled Childhood', May 1998), for the following line of argument concerning the social and its progressive autonomization.

Among the historical transformations yielded by the specialized intervention, the categorization effect occupies a significant place; the category of childhood carries on a homogenization attribute – to render homogeneous elements of the category while separating them from other categories (Ramognino 2000). Rationalization of the social was primarily observable in education as a space–time of intervention through compulsory mass education; it amounts to diverse forms of training of the child's body so that it can perform adequately in the new economic environment: education as embodiment.[39] As another space–time of interventions, health is the second area where rationalization of the social was observable: in this respect, health is conceived as work upon the body to enhance its capacities and abilities with specific consideration for the linking of the bodily and the cognitive (Mayall 1996).

Classical sociology puts forward a construction of the social in terms of structure. It could rightly be considered as a hierarchical conception of the social where the emphasis is laid on the unequal relationships between groupings, class and actors within a particular society; the metaphors of the pyramid and the ladder constitute the visual imagery of this usual construction of the social.[40] Although one will find some variation from one theory to the other – approximately from a firm structuralist perspective to a loose social structure point of view – the lowest common denominator remains the hierarchical devising of the structure and therefore the social.

Foucault provides a powerful analytic tool with the concept of dispositif and notions such as heterogeneity and network: it is somehow different from a structure albeit it seemingly refers to what sociologists call the social. He stated that a dispositif is the network that one can establish between the heterogeneous elements of the social. He is chiefly interested in the changing nature of the link between these heterogeneous elements; some might suggest the circulation amidst the entities.

---

[39] As already mentioned, the economic order was already rationalized and, thus, required specific types of skills and abilities from workers. Those were seemingly provided by the education system which was at that time undergoing a rationalization process.

[40] Such an understanding – the social designed as a structure, thus as a hierarchy of class, actors etc. – is so widely held an idea that young sociologists are initiated to the discipline by representing society as a structure or a hierarchy (Sewell 1992).

Foucault's dispositif invites a double reading. A pessimistic version dwells on regulation, control, prohibition and reduction; the huge apparatus of constraint and control that can explain the continuity of the narratives – the narratives of childhood for instance – over a period of more than a few hundred years (Armstrong 1983, 1986; Rose 1985, 1991).[41]

The optimistic analysis of Foucault puts the emphasis on the habilitation side of the dispositif, which is generative: it also reveals and multiplies.[42] The generative power of the dispositif depends upon its aptitude to create and make use of improved capacities in the actors who achieve through it. The socio-technological network makes possible the emergence of a subject as it enters a dispositif, thus launching or retooling a new kind of being by the multiplication of new abilities that it lets arise in the subject (Gomart and Hennion 1999). Dispositif abets the advent of a new kind of being. 'Those who created a science of children's psychological development were hardly aware that they were assisting at the birth of a new kind of being. The child is now "officially" a psychological being as well as a physical one' (Wong 1993: 128).

Taking into account these concepts, it is now possible to anticipate that the social is produced in and through patterned networks of heterogeneous entities. These entities find themselves not only to be heterogeneous, but also to be hybrids: people, bodies, minds, artefacts, objects and so on enter into a wide variety of shifting and negotiated associations and dissociations. 'The social becomes a construction not

---

[41] For a critique of Armstrong's and Rose's Foucaldian perspective, see Prout 1999 and Gurjeva 1998. Prout disputes the mainly discursive and narrative effects via an analysis of children's bodies. About the regulatory effect:

The relevance of Foucault for our purposes is that whereas conventional liberal histories have tended to emphasize progress in the fields of child social and legal welfare and public health, and other scholars have seen the whole process of reform in social welfare, health and education in either Marxist and/or patriarchal terms, Foucaldian accounts examine what is called the 'regulatory impact' of these practices. This means that through welfare, health, education and legal provisions, children are 'monitored', 'surveyed', 'calculated' – nearly always in relation to their families – and that their health and welfare is fused with the broader political health of the nation (Hendrick 1997).

[42] Foucault's concept of dispositif is seen as the harshest castigation of the notion of progress: the history of childhood as an unending progress toward the betterment of children's conditions.

only of and by humans (whether adults or children), not only of and by bodies (not to mention minds), but also of and by technologies' (Prout 1999: 14). Is it conceivable to explore the idea that the social possesses the unusual property of not being made primarily of structure, but rather of being a circulating body trying to picture a movement, a trajectory between the hybrid entities? (Latour 1999a).

The major effect of veering from a structural to a circulatory conception of the social revolves around the very nature of the social fabric: what is accordingly included and excluded in society? Traditionally, a society has been for sociologists the study of humans among themselves, thus excluding objects and artefacts considered as residuals.[43] If one starts to envisage things the other way around, it then becomes plausible to consider that non-human entities are part of the social fabric because, as semiotics tell us, they are an extension of humans in the production of social activities (Molino 1978).

Objects as extensions – and not as reflections – of the self acquire the status of variable-geometry entities, the common world designed of both elements of the social and the natural world:[44] 'an exchange of human and nonhuman properties inside a corporate body' (Latour 1999b: 193). Together they compose a collective where humans and non-humans cannot be disentangled one from the other and many properties are constantly being exchanged.[45] Techniques are mediators

---

[43] Regarding technical conduct which is the usual way to give an account of objects and artefacts, the conceptual repertoire of mainstream sociology does not seem to go any further than the conventional game of homologies and inversion – the metaphor of the mirror – with which we are familiar (Molino 1978; Ramognino 1987). Classical theory is unable to explain why artefacts enter the stream of our relations, except by abetting a conspiracy theory: society is hiding behind the fetish of techniques (Latour 1999a). The critical tradition is in an even worse position with respect to the analysis of technical conduct according to both Gergen (1994) and Gomart (Gomart and Hennion 1999: 226).

[44] It is of the utmost importance to avoid the expected critique from mainstream sociology not to extend subjectivity to artefacts, to treat humans like objects, to give machines the status of social actors. The question at stake seeks to capture the ways by which a collective extends its social fabric to other entities; no more than that.

[45] ANT's concept of collective consists in understanding the ensuing displacement of the relevant unit of sociological analysis: 'We now find ourselves confronting productions of nature-cultures that I am calling collectives – as different, it should be recalled, from the society construed by sociologists – men-among-themselves – as they are from the Nature imagined by epistemologists – things-in-themselves' (Latour 1994b: 107).

that bear upon the social fabric. Science and technology multiply the non-human entities enrolled in the fabric of the collective.

Those are the heterogeneous entities, the hybrids – objects as extension of the self – that recompose the social link, extend its scale and give new impetus to the social body. The relation between the collective and non-human entities is crucial for the latter mobilizes and circulates elements connected with a more finely woven social fabric. This supports a novel construction of the social centred on circulation rather than structure.

A second aspect of the standard conception of the social involves the problem of agency. Traditional sociological theory has denied the capacity of agency to certain types of agents children being the first among them: the theme of the child as dependent, in need of protection and so on. In reaction, sociology of childhood reconstitutes children as social actors by highlighting the ways in which they are also active participants shaping as well as being shaped by society (Mayall 1994; Prout and James 1990; Qvortrup *et al.* 1994). However there remains the danger of treating children's agency in an essentialist and humanist manner. To avoid both of those drawbacks, this decisive question will be discussed widely, first by stating certain basic postulates.

- Rather than the essentialist conception according to which agency properly belongs to individuals, it will be asserted that the sociological subject is a relation: actor as a relational concept (Law 1999; Lee 1998; Ramognino 1987).[46]
- Disentangling agency from the context-independent possession of a subject paves the way to its conception as social attribution: the relevant question regards the ascribing of agentic capacities to non-human entities as an extension of humans (Ashmore *et al.* 1994).
- Accordingly, agency is yielded as an effect of relations among actors and between them and heterogeneous entities (Callon 1991: 134).

---

[46] A relational conception of the actor entails correspondingly a congruent construction of the social and of society. 'In Bhasktar's transformational model of social action [the relational formation of the social world as its primary characteristic], society is the ensemble of positioned practices and interrelationships reproduced or transformed by activity. So whilst no one ever makes their relationships, because we all come into a world which is historically already made for us, people have the power either to reproduce or transform their society with the materials at hand' (Burkitt 1998).

- Such propositions are based on an indeterminacy of the actor: agency provides actors with their capacities to act, with their subjectivity, with their intentionality amidst a distributed network of relationships (Latour 1999a).

This set of arguments reconstitutes children's agency as an effect of the relations, the connections and the circulation made between a heterogeneous array of materials including bodies, representations, objects and technologies. Human entities achieve their form and acquire their attributes[47] – their abilities, capacities, competencies etc. – as an effect of the network of relations in which they are located with other entities (Law 1999). In this scheme, the relational theory of the formation of the human subject (Burkitt 1998; Gergen 1995), actors are performed in, by and through an active network of relations and entities, both human and non-human. Thus subjectivity, intentionality, agency and competence alike are no longer a property of human individuals; they are supplied to the actor in its circulating process. Circulation is what provides actors with their features as a subject (Latour 1999a). A person is seen as an intersection in a network of relationships upon which it broadly depends. So, at birth, one can observe a total dyad in the first months between the mother and the infant; gradually this closed relation expands into more differentiated relations as an infant relates to siblings and other relatives, makes friends at kindergarten, enters school and so on. Much as the child depends on others in the early years, yet as a person grows up the network of relationships is overturned as others come to depend on him or her; in other words, the balance of dependencies shifts as the individual becomes less reliant and more entailed. In old age the network lessens again and dependence expands once more (Swann 1990: 11 and 22). Lee puts forward a similar idea: growing up is a matter of proceeding from one social order to another, extending and differentiating it; that is accelerating the pace of network relationships

---

[47] The question of agency is dissociated, here, from a sociological theory of the subject. As important as the latter ought to be, its scope largely exceeds the issue of agency albeit there could not be any construction of agency without an underlying conception of the subject. Among the various topics related to a theory of the subject should be mentioned the problem of subjectivity in relation to interiority, the processes of subjectivation, individuality as a figure of subjectivity, the difference between the empirical individual and the individual as an abstract value.

building and slowing it down (Lee 2001: 137). The different stages of the expanding, the condensing and the contracting of the network's relations through which an actor circulates gives a general overview of the relational theory.

From a purely sociological standpoint taking its distance from a structural perspective, agency tallies neither with subjectivity nor with interiority of the actor: 'Individuals construct themselves as subjects through language, but individual subjects – rather than being the source of their own self-generated and self-expressive meaning – adopt positions available within the language at a given moment' (Naussbaum 1988: 149). Taking on the relational concept of actor, agency would rather rely on the notions of network, intersection, connection, circulation and so on; agency emerges then as an effect of the actor's distribution and circulation in a specific network (Callon 1999: 182). People are always negotiating their relationships with others (Strathern 1999: 158): an intermediary regarded as having the capacity to put other intermediaries into circulation (Callon 1992: 80).

Trajectory, movement, connection and displacement are the key elements that lead from a construction of the social as a structure to a surface where entities circulate. In this substitution, we encountered classical sociology's proclivity for structure and its vision of society as a hierarchy. The rationalization of the social, with its setting up of dispositifs in the education and health area, was revealed to be a key point for introducing the notions of network and heterogeneity. Furthermore, agency was also networked, thus departing from an individualistic conception of it. The next section will look more closely at a number of concepts already put forward in the previous elaboration.

1.4 Translation, mediation and circulation

An adequate answer to the questions raised requires a detour via the paradigm of actor–network theory. The essential feature of ANT is that the power of science arises from the action of both human and non-human actors linked together. Accordingly, its object constantly undermines a sharp distinction between culture and nature by focusing on the deed of mediation between them.

ANT as a relational materiality is a non-dualistic theory of the space or fluids – a network – circulating in a given situation (Law

1999: 3). It says that by following circulations one can achieve more in terms of analysis than by defining entities, essence or actors and so on. It makes possible the description of an effect by referring not to actors but to circulation among them. Network means a series of transformations – translations, mediations etc. – that could not be grasped by any of the traditional notions of sociology – 'structure', 'power' and so on (Latour 1999a: 20).

In this respect, my hypothesis would be that ANT is particularly relevant for a study of the circulation of graphs, charts, tabulations and the like in the field of childhood at the turn of the twentieth century. The five cardinal principles of ANT are established as follows:

A. Agnosticism: impartiality between actors engaged in controversy such as rationality and irrationality: the two are considered analytically equal and no privilege is given to either side of the dichotomy, which becomes an outcome of analysis rather than its starting point.

B. Symmetry: commitments to explaining conflicting viewpoints in the same terms: none of the opposing positions enjoys privilege with respect to the explanation of a given phenomenon; the relations between human and non-human entities are symmetrical, thus sharing the reliability for action (Latour 1999a: 179).

C. Human action: the extension of the symmetry principle levels the very traditional distinction between humans and non-humans, or society and technology; and by logical progression between adults and children. Society is not generated solely through human action, but via patterned networks of heterogeneous materials and shifting associations between human and non-human entities (Prout 2005).

D. Free association: abandonment of all a priori distinction between the natural and the social or nature/culture; what is natural and what is social becomes blurred; it is neither social nor natural whilst at the same time it is both and at once thoroughly materialist.

E. Technical mediation or technical translation: which means 'displacement, drift, invention, mediation, the creation of a link with and through circulation that did not exist before and that, to some degree, modifies the original two entities already in relation' (Latour 1999b: 179). 'The mediation, the technical translation, that I am trying to understand resides in the blind spot in which society and matter exchange properties' (Latour 1999b: 190).

I shall concentrate my attention on some of those principles, mainly technical mediation and symmetry, while, however, modifying them somewhat. The hypothesis put forward henceforth is that the various devices looked at in this study – graphs, charts and tabulations – are technical mediators/translators which operate as such in a network of relationships that inherently consist of both human and non-human entities, treated symmetrically at the analytic level. A graph or a chart circulate and interpose themselves between children, parents, peers, paediatricians, nurses, teachers, experts, school apparatus, neighbours, clinics, offices, laboratories, institutions, welfare associations etc. which amounts to patterned networks (Figure 1). They add new forces and new resources to the network because they show, indeed visualize, bodily elements.

These are general features and the need for some more accurate specifications concerning the sociological intelligence of technology will lead to certain of its features to frame a coherent and informed analytical perspective: delegation, socialization of non-humans, complex transactions and mediation.

- First, I shall define technical action as the form of delegation that allows us to mobilize in interaction movements, which have been executed earlier, at some distance, and by other actants, as though they are still present and available to us now.
- Second ... the traditional definition of techniques as the imposition of a form ... should be replaced by a much more accurate, definition as the socialization of non-humans.
- Third, the most important consequence ... is that when we exchange properties with non-humans through technical delegation, we enter into a complex transaction.
- Fourth ... techniques are not means but mediators, that is, means and ends at the same time, and this is precisely why they are brought to bear on the social fabric.

(Latour 1994a: 792)

With the purpose of understanding the crucial transformations in the specific field of childhood at a particular point in history, the turn of the twentieth century, two basic ANT guidelines must be clearly asserted. First, the social bond – the network of relationships – does hold, mobilize and stabilize itself with and through the non-human

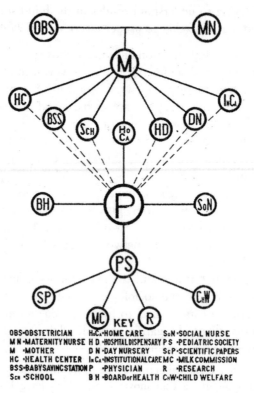

The above chart is a suggestive representation of the inter-relationship which exists between the physician, his Pediatric Socety, and the child in the various environments in which it is found.

Figure 1: Paediatrist in the community
Source: Bradley 1915

objects (graphs etc.) which mainstream sociology considers as a residue. Second, the status of these non-human objects, far from being residual, is closely interwoven with humans in the social fabric by adding something new, something supplementary, to the circulation, mobilization and stabilization of the network of relationships.[48] The

---

[48] The paediatrician's core tasks included, for instance, the circulation of rules and norms, in regard to age-appropriate behaviour in children as well as parenting; but the circulation was also directed at schools and teachers, as well as other settings and institutions.

relations between human and non-human entities are reshuffled on an entirely new basis; the social and technological will no longer be considered as two separate and opposite entities but as doggedly intertwined (Latour 1994a; Law 1999).

The emerging question then becomes: what does this circulation/ mobilization introduce or interpose into the social fabric? What does a chart or graph bring up and muster in a network of relationships? Proceeding any further requires us to give a few more indications concerning the concept of translation:[49] how and in what ways is technical mediation a translation process and how does this process relate to childhood: what do we learn from mediation/translation that we could not learn otherwise? The sociology of translation is concerned with the materials from which social life is produced and the practices by which these are ordered and patterned. It emphasizes the relational, constructed and process-oriented character of social life in a generalized way whilst it tells us nothing at all about how it is that links are made; and it restates a form of sociology in a way which places materiality in relation to the other social entities (Prout 1999). One of the most crucial matters that arises has to do with the account of complexity; the complexities stemming from social life might be lost in the process of cutting up and labelling, but ought to be taught: pattern, ordering, heterogeneity, distribution, hierarchy and so on.

The process of translation constitutes children as social entities emerging both from the continuous interactions of humans – parents, kinship, peers, teachers and medical experts for example – and through the mutually unending interconnectedness of a vast array of non-human objects and resources (Place 1999). The sociology of translation alludes to basic formal units of substance which enter into networking relationships by way of encounters (Brown and Capdevilla 1999: 34).

---

[49] The two different aspects of the process of translation are not mutually contradictory, but rather complementary:

> On the one hand, translation is the process of making two things that are not equivalent, the means through which different forms of matter are articulated (Brown and Capdevilla 1999; Latour 1987). On the other hand, translation as a semiotic operation – a 'socio-logic' in Callon's terms – creates 'convergences and homologies by relating things that were previously different' (Callon 1980: 211). Thus the ordering and organizing of signification, interests and concerns.

The analysis focuses on the translations – the network of mediation[50] – between these different entities, both human and non-
humans. Mediation must be understood as an entity, which furthers
and accelerates the circulation between them; non-human entities
such as a technological device bear the status of being an extension of
oneself, not an intermediary amidst human entities (Strathern 1999).
'mediators – that is, actors endowed with the capacity to translate
what they transport, to redefine it, redeploy it, and also to betray it'
(Latour 1994b: 81). Technical mediators are the extension of human
action, allowing certain human capacities to migrate to objects.[51]
These in turn become efficient, intelligent, coordinated or 'purposeful'. Extension is the pivotal notion, along with circulation, in this
respect: the hammer is a prolongation of the hand, which holds it just
as the computer is a continuation of the fingers and the mind typing on
the keyboard. It does not consist in extending subjectivity to things or
to pretend that machines are operating like social actors. The nub of
the question is avoid using the subject–object distinction at all in order
to talk about the encounter of humans and non-humans: how any
given collective extends its social fabric to other non-human entities
(Latour 1999b: 194 and 198).

The network is an opening: inscription into objects render these as
prolongations of activities already initiated elsewhere; the circulation

---

[50] 'To shuttle back and forth, we rely on the notion of translation or network.
More supple than the notion of system, more historical than the notion of
structure, more empirical than the notion of complexity, the idea of network is
the Ariane's thread of these interwoven stories' (Latour 1994b: 3).

[51] Latour's Pandora's Hope distinguishes five types of operations in technical
mediation:

1 translation: the means by which we articulate different sorts of matters;
2 crossover: which consists of the exchange of properties among humans and
   non-humans; we exchange properties with NH through technical delegation
   in a complex transaction;
3 enrolment: by which a non-human is seduced, manipulated, or induced into
   the collective;
4 mobilization: of the non-humans inside the collective, which adds fresh,
   unexpected resources, resulting in strange new hybrids;
5 displacement: the direction the collective takes once its shape, extent and
   composition have been altered by the enrolment and mobilization of new
   actants.

(Latour 1999b: 194)

is like a 'translation drift' where charts and graphs move progressively further away from their natal sites in the process of network-building (Brown and Capdevila 1999: 29). Translation is concerned with tracing the processes by which these heterogeneous entities – sometimes called hybrids – mutually enrol, constitute and order each other, processes which always involve something being upheld, something being aggregated and something being taken away. 'Of quasi-objects, quasi-subjects, we shall simply say that they trace networks. They are real, quite real, and we humans have not made them. But they are collective because they attach us to one another, because they circulate in our hands and define our social bonds by their very circulation. They are discursive, however; they are narrated, historical' (Latour 1994b: 89).

The object-mediators transform the world in startling ways.[52] Talking of children: what is being upheld, aggregated, taken away by such objects as charts, graphs and tabulations in the process of circulation, mobilization and stabilization? The charts and graphs make new connections between the heterogeneous entities while accelerating the circulation among them. The socio-technological devices[53] of measurement bear witness to the family and to the medical clinic (paediatricians, nurses and so on) also as an isolated unit, but to the whole connection/circulation between families, peers, schools, clinics, hospitals and the state. For instance, charts stressed parental demand for developmental standards, enforced their obligation to conduct oneself in accordance with the standards; parents wanted to measure their children against the prescriptions of the charts, with the active cooperation of relatives, neighbours and teachers.

---

[52] To see objects as mediators amounts to indicating that something happens without inevitably falling back on action and actors. An event occurred and it has a positivity of its own, limited neither to its origins nor to its effects. The focus shifts from the agency question – who acts? – toward the 'what occurs' issue: it is a turn toward events, toward what emerges, what is shaped and composed, what cannot be reduced to an interaction of causal objects and intentional actors, rather than what is performed (Gomart and Hennion 1999). According to the principle: something occurs with the arrival of immutable mobiles such as graphs, the focus of analysis is redirected.

[53] Technical mediation amounts to the summing up of interactions through various kinds of devices, inscriptions, procedures and formulae; specific forms, social relations and circulation took place through these devices, inscriptions and formulae.

Accordingly, new questions arose: how can a given collective modify its fabric by articulating through technical mediation different associations and circulation among its components? What were the ongoing operations that were put forward and thus adumbrated in a new form of social relations?

1. A new form of child observation: the transformation of child examination from the diary form of laypersons to the systematic protocols of a scientific laboratory.

   In this particular site, in the paediatrician's clinic the child is connected to sets of technological artefacts, which enable detailed examination of various segments of its body. The processes surrounding children's observation and their intensive combination with medical and psychological technologies generate artefacts which amount to a set of symbols: traces, numbers, graphs, charts and so on.

2. A new form of inscription of observations: the translation of heterogeneous elements of observation into a text in the form of charts, graphs, formulae, diagrams etc. – is considered as the main strategy of inscription.

   A natural object, the child's body is visualized in the form of an inscription produced as an observation chart: inscription devices are artefacts by which naturally occurring phenomena are transformed into visualized devices. Paediatricians and nurses take the visualized device of the body – the observation as inscribed in graphs and charts – as having an unproblematic relationship to the child's body. Numbers generated by inscription devices reveal the corporeality, whether in the form of a body or a mind in the case of intelligence.

3. A new form of graphic visualization of the observation/inscription: the translation of aspects of the physical body into an abstract figure enables the generation of tabulated data organized in a graph/chart form which visualize the child's body.

An over- or under-weighted body becomes a critical body as it is sorted out into a numerical, scientific, form. Once ordered, it is also visible in its tabulation form. Throughout the process of monitoring the child, there rests an underlying working assumption according to which the visualized tabulation simply throws light on a concealed reality: there is a consonance between what the chart shows and how the child is or behaves. The network of both human and non-human entities within a collective is designed so that it can be accurately seen. Once the visualization is available, other actors can be convinced it is the child's body or intelligence.

If such technologies are conceived of as inscription devices, they have the capacity to transform data and observations into visualized documents. By way of translation, mobilization and enrolment, technical mediation transforms matter from one state to another, in this case from a private, affectionate child–parent bond to a scientific relationship – observed, measured, tabulated etc. A network can be stabilized and at the same time allowed to be moved and recombined with other such entities (Place 1999: 154).[54]

The second relevant ANT principle is the principle of symmetry proposed in the field of sociology of science (SSK) by Bloor to explain scientific controversy in the same terms (Bloor 1991). This principle was later extended as generalized symmetry in ANT with the explicit purpose of blurring the rigid dichotomy between human and non-human – that is, between society and technology (Latour 1994b). It was a question of establishing equality among the various entities involved by setting the scale at zero. The analysis consisted of registering the differences: asymmetries were considered as the outcome, not as the starting point.

With respect to childhood, the principle of symmetry will be displaced from a commitment to explaining the conflicting viewpoints in the same terms to a commitment to explaining two different sets of actors, the child and the standard adult, in the same terms; that is, in the same perspective and within the same conceptual framework. This will of course raise certain questions: traditionally the child's immaturity concurs with the pre-social period of life, while an adult's maturity and rationality amount to full human status. The symmetry principle disputes these distinctions and questions – what Qvortrup

---

[54] Accordingly, in the process of connection to the artefacts, the child is ordered and patterned and its boundary extended. What exactly constitutes a child's body and mind is open to negotiation, as these are constituted by, and contested through, their extension in technological entities. The child becomes circumscribed by both corporeal (human) and technological entities (Prout 1999).

calls 'the structural inconsiderateness towards children' (Qvortrup 1993: 12).[55] What else does it mean, in analytical terms?

1. Certain signs do not mislead: with the reappearance of mendacity, unemployment, soup kitchens, vagrants in towns and suburbia, returned the social figure of a child-worker whose iconography is portrayed in Dickens, Hugo and Zola; this figure used to be typical of the nineteenth century, then it progressively disappeared after the economic crisis of the 1930s. The recent predicament brought back this image: the United Nations estimates that around 250 million children are working, among them some as young as five years of age.[56] Most of them work in the poor countries of the South – in agriculture, the informal economy, domestic work, the carpet mafia, prostitution networks and so on[57] – but some of them are also working in the countries of the North which blurs the North/South divide to some extent, at least from the perspective of children's work. This goes as far as suggesting that, at least in the North, child work is not exclusively related to poverty since children from relatively affluent families also work (Morrow 1994).

   How can sociologists describe the empirical phenomena and give an account of it?[58] In the mainstream sociology of work, children

---

[55] We have seen above how certain of these ideas – immaturity, incompleteness, socialization etc. – are so strongly and deeply rooted in mainstream sociology in its classical adultist perspective. Perhaps should we refer to it as the social production of indifference.

[56] In the European Community alone, it is estimated that up to two million children are working, especially in countries characterized by liberal reforms such as Great Britain, or in countries generally considered as socially progressive such as Denmark and the Netherlands. Ignacio Ramonet, 'Enfances fracassées', *Le Monde Diplomatique*, 526, January 1998, p. 1.

[57] The classification of child work can vary significantly,

   'recognizing its wide variety and complex character; domestic work such as cleaning the house, preparing food and taking care of other siblings; subsistence work in fields or workshops which provides goods that can be exchanged on the market; work as apprentices living and working in other households while learning a trade or craft; as slaves or bonded labour, sold to others and put to work for their benefit; as beggars working the streets on their own behalf or as part of a collectivity, be it family, clan or gang; as labourers earning a wage in the fields, workshops or factories' (James *et al.* 1998: 103).

[58] 'Whatever the place of children is thought to be in industrialized societies, it is not usually regarded as "at work". What children are supposed to do is play and learn – but that is not generally recognized as work. If they are seen to be

are surprisingly but effectively inconspicuous, albeit this invisibility might be an effect of a specific conception of the child as dependent and non-productive (Morrow 1995: 226). If childhood were to be part of a general sociology, if there were not any scientific account of the social without addressing the child question, then children's work should symmetrically and consequently be considered within the same parameters and in the same terms as adult work, especially as a very large part of this child work is similar to adult's work and could be performed by adults. There should not be any ontological or theoretical difference between the two forms of work. Children should not be treated differently from adults with respect to work. Drawing on different fieldwork, some researchers argue strongly for this. 'In the fishing community children bait fishing lines alongside, adults and each baiter is expected to complete the task irrespective, considered within the same parameters and in the same terms as adult work especially as a very large part of this child work is similar to adult's work and could be performed by adults. There should not be any ontological or theoretical difference between the two forms of work, of their status. Child labour . . . is in this account presented as a normal dimension of these children's lives. Children are capable members of the baiting team' (James *et al.* 1998: 186). In this particular case, both forms of work belong to the same theoretical frame and conceptual network.

Arguably, the same assertion and the same reasoning can be made for child prostitution (Kincaid 1992: 76; Steedman 1995: 106) as well for the child-soldier whose pathetic figure was broadcast on television screens in relation to the different civil wars in Africa and elsewhere.[59] 'Children under 18 participated in 45

---

working ... the reflex is towards constituting this as an aberration or an outrage' (James *et al.* 1998: 101).

[59] The French magazine *Le Nouvel Observateur* published in May 2000 a special issue on the child-soldier. The magazine estimates at 300,000 the number of children, aged between ten and eighteen (and often younger), who are enrolled generally by force in various armies, guerrilla units and militias in Kosovo, Chechnia, Sierra Leone, Afghanistan, Burma, Palestine, Rwanda, Congo etc. According to Olana Otunnu, then United Nations' deputy secretary general in charge of this particular area, children are forced, in some specific conflicts, to perform the most horrendous acts imaginable. See also the online database available at www.rb.se/childwardatabase/ (Halsan Hølskar 2001: 360).

conflicts around the world between 1994 and 1998, and many as 35 of those disputes made use of minors under the age of 15. Their current estimate is 300,000 underage soldiers worldwide' (Halsan Hølskar 2001: 340).

2. The second point concerns a 'fait divers' which happened in Liverpool, UK, in 1993. It is the culmination of a step-by-step discovery that the very symbol of children's innocence – so strong is the association in western culture of those two semiotic categories 'innocent' and 'child' (Higonnet 1998) – is being rudely questioned by empirical phenomena discreetly concealed under the classification of 'child offender'. The first phase is the recognition that children are subject to physical exploitation and that their ascribed innocence is shattered by adults: child abuse come to light. The second phase is the discovery that child abuse is usually performed by adults who had themselves been sexually exploited in their childhood. The third phase was the disclosure that those who rape, abuse, torture and occasionally kill children are children themselves. Let us remember for instance the case of young James Bulger, aged two, who was abducted from a shopping mall in Bootle, near Liverpool by two ten-year-old boys from a deprived area, Jon Venables and Robert Thompson.[60] They led him onto a railway embankment, stripped him, battered him to death with bricks and an iron bar, and possibly abused him sexually. Killer children: when children kill other children, even though this is a topic which 'society' would prefer not to think about, uniting rather in moral panic,[61] what do sociologists suggest by way of explanation?

The trial of the two young offenders that followed offers a good idea of what is still the dominant frame of reasoning and explanation: the boys were not animals or evil as the popular press depicted them; they turned out to be all too human and weak despite their obvious cruelty. From demons, the two boys became victims, the demonization being transferred to their family situations. Both had disturbed backgrounds; one grew up in a broken family where violence was endemic, while the other displayed a desperate ferocity at school. Both lied extensively about James' death. The question at

[60] Morrison 1997.
[61] The other well-known and well-documented case is that of Mary Bell (Sereny 1999).

stake in the Bulger case is precisely the one raised by Jenks: what is 'the child'?

That children are capable of violence . . . and even murder, is an idea that clearly falls outside traditional formulation of childhood . . . newspaper headlines echoed confusion . . . It is supposed to be the age of innocence so how could these 10 year olds turn into killers? (*The Sunday Times*, 28 November 1993)

This problem raises a question of classification: can children who commit such violent acts still belong to the category of 'child'? What about the differentiation, the boundary between the categories of 'child' and 'adult', so firmly established in the modern period? Are they not becoming blurred or weakened? (Jenks 1996: 127). Therefore the very notion of childish innocence is being questioned, indeed undermined. Questions arise: if children are capable of terrible deeds, whose responsibility is it? The common sense response revolves around bad parenting, the availability of violent pornography, the new poverty of exclusion and so on. This might be trustworthy, but these forms of explanation, disturbed backgrounds or bad parenting, raise enormous difficulties, mainly because it is almost impossible to define firm boundaries between good and bad parenting, between disturbed and 'normal' backgrounds, these boundaries being always disputed and, from time to time, displaced.[62]

May I propose that the symmetry principle arises as the main basis at our disposition for a sound explanation of such phenomena as the Bulger case (and others such as child work/prostitution) without falling into the drawbacks of bad parenting or disturbed backgrounds? The question at stake does not relate at all to relativism; that is, to argue that adults and children are equivalents and interchangeable in social reality. 'In the case of childhood and representation, it is neither analytically, ethically nor strategically satisfactory simply to declare that they have the same competences as adults' (Lee and Stenner 1999: 110). It is patent that they do not have

---

[62] This last example heightens the question of child agency. From the Bulger case, can we say the two abductors behaved with full knowledge of what they were doing? Can they be held responsible for the consequences of their behaviour? To what extent can a child be granted agency, and what kind of agency?

the same competences; on the other hand the principle of symmetry does not chiefly apply to child and adult competences as such.[63] The standpoint proposed is analytical and methodological. It requires us to consider adults and children on a strictly symmetrical relational term at the point of departure by giving the same credit to the activities and behaviour of each from an analytical point of view. If the two aforementioned propositions – that childhood is an integral part of a general sociology; that there cannot be any account of the social without childhood – were to be investigated to their full extent, then the symmetry principle would be considered as a major element in any venture which attempts to give as total an account as one can: 'the principle of symmetry aims not only at establishing equality but at registering differences – that is, in final analysis, asymmetries – and at understanding the practical means that allow some collectives to dominate others' (Latour 1994b: 107).

Symmetry is a general principle of equality that has totally modified the sociology of science in the last twenty years. The hypothesis that it can produce the same effect in the field of childhood should be seriously examined: it is the only way to demarginalize children and to take the opposite view of developmental theory which deems children as irresponsible, unproductive and in need of protection. Technical mediation, on the other hand, should be a central feature of a sociology of childhood as a process involving the crafting of resemblance between the child's corporeal body and its visualized form in the technology in which it is, literally and figuratively, embedded. The next section will investigate how these theoretical reflections can be turned into analytical propositions.

1.5 Childhood, measurement and standardization

The theoretical framework for a historical sociology of childhood being in place, the task of carrying out an analytic scheme must be completed promptly. First, we shall take a critical overview of the direction that social constructionism took in a field such as the sociology of childhood with the intention of firmly grounding and sharpening it. Then the role of science in the emerging field of

---

[63] ANT is not chiefly about structure, agency, competence or hability, but about circulation: the transformation of the social from a surface into a circulation.

childhood will be closely looked at; special attention will be given to the technologies that emerged from the systematic investigation of children. Finally, drawing on the propositions recently put forward by well-known sociologists, some ideas pertaining to the normal child and developmental theory will be introduced.

For once the metaphor of social construction bore the promise of a conceptual and analytic innovation. This new idiom with its under-lying original theoretical propositions attracted scholarly interest, particularly in the field of the sociology of childhood where it became a token of exchange for a legitimized approach to the question of childhood. Social construction brought legitimation as it stood as the most pre-eminent theoretical stance to oppose biological reductionism and developmental theory's expansionism by helping to create a conceptual space within which to think about the non-biological and the non-psychological (Prout and Christensen 1994). Nowadays, social construction tends to prove either too narrowly or too loosely defined: it is becoming tired. Rightly, it tends to overemphasize the representational and discursive aspects of childhood, thus leaving the whole question of embodiment and materiality aside.

The critical difficulty however pertains to the definition of the concept itself which is hardly accurate by any criteria. Most sociolo-gists of childhood have taken the concept for granted, rather than challenge orthodoxy, as if constructionism was unproblematic. Why such a hazy process? If it entails the battle cry against any form of reductionism, social construction also offers the possibility of exam-ining childhood as a phenomenon inscribed in historical and spatial variability, and thus of enacting it as a social rather than natural issue, so sharpening the traditional distinction between nature and culture. In brief, it meant historicity and spatiality alike; moreover, an insist-ence on a social or cultural account of childhood beyond the flawed argumentation surrounding the concept.

The sociology of childhood's stance on social construction is understandable if one agrees with Lynch in seeing it as a useful term to collect together studies with eclectic surface affinities (Lynch 1998). The exact signification of the concept remains an open question and a clear and undisputed formulation of its constitutive elements remains to be established.

Hacking's castigation of social construction cannot be ignored under any circumstances by a sociology of childhood (Hacking 1998).

Hacking's purpose is to limit but also to sharpen the project of social construction by framing six theses.

1. Most items said to be socially constructed could be only constructed socially, if they are constructed at all.
2. There is a wider range of construction ideas than is commonly acknowledged.
3. The metaphor of construction should retain one element of its literal meaning: building or assembling from parts.
4. Many construction analyses aim at unmasking an idea or practice, in contrast to refuting that idea or showing that the practice does not serve its purposes well.
5. Analyses that chiefly aim at unmasking are to be distinguished from those that primarily aim at refuting.
6. Construction analyses have been applied primarily (a) to ideas and socio-political aims and (b) to knowledge of inanimate nature or metaphysical aims.

(Hacking 1998: 49)

In order to establish more firmly the construction of a historical sociology of childhood, Hacking's theses 1, 3 and 4 will be looked at more closely.[64] In 1, Hacking stresses the idea that almost all of the sociological objects said to be socially constructed could only be so because they were objects grounded in either cultural or social practices. If one accepts the hypothesis that sex is the biological category and gender the social one, how therefore can gender be constructed other than socially? A sociology of childhood will thus be considered socially constructed primarily if it impedes us from viewing childhood predominantly as a natural (biological) or psychological phenomenon.

With 3, Hacking goes back to the root metaphor of construction and steers the attention to its core meaning of building or assembling from parts, i.e. putting together. 'Anything worth calling a construction has a history. But not just any history. It has to be a history of building' (Hacking 1998: 56). It also has to do with space, to be consistent with the argument put forward above.

---

[64] In the discussion of these theses, I shall rely decisively on Hacking's arguments, since he raises very crucial questions for a sociology of childhood in the constructivist perspective (Hacking 1998).

Hacking's thesis 4 introduces the distinction between unmasking an idea or a practice and refuting it. Unmasking has to do with denunciation on one hand and deconstruction on the other; refuting refers to showing a discourse or doctrine to be false.

In this framework, a historical sociology of childhood takes into account Hacking's critique of the construction of childhood as being unavoidably social without being anything other than socially constructed. It will concentrate on thesis 3, by analysing the emergence and institutionalization alike of a concept (normality), a practice (observation and measurement), a body of knowledge (paediatrics and child psychology) and a new form of child (the normal child). Accordingly, this study is chiefly concerned with the advent of a new kind of being, the normal child, and the way specific sciences moulded its very existence: science yielded a new knowledge pertaining to childhood via new methods, techniques and protocols.

The malleability of the normal child must be put back in the broader context of the concept of normality, in the nineteenth century. It all started with the implementation and the use of specific techniques of medical or psychological investigation, later translated into the public domain, the definition of the normal child being gradually extended to diverse realms of childhood. Each phase in the extension of the notion of the normal child relies on the establishment of a previous construction: from the refinement of observational techniques to the different charts or graphs (the height–weight chart etc.) the expansion of the notion encompasses more and more behaviour, skills and abilities. The contingent character of the historical as well as spatial circumstances under which this expansion occurred must be stressed.[65]

The moulding of the category of the normal child owes much to both new techniques of observation and the rapid increase of research and knowledge in such fields as hygiene, paediatrics and psychology (Graff 1995; Rollet 1990). Much as this research will be aware of exposing the pre-established rhetorical tracks of such scientific

---

[65] To clarify the primary focus of this research, it should be borne in mind that, contrary to the main trends in classical sociology, the analysis will not overemphasize either the context or the circumstances of the phenomenon under study, but rather study the phenomenon in itself. Priority is given to internal analysis (Canto-Klein and Ramognino 1974; Gardin 1974; Molino 1974).

knowledge, it will focus rather on the triad of method–technique–procedure with which a specific – relevant, accurate – scientific knowledge of childhood was established in paediatrics and other fields (Lomax *et al.* 1978; N. Rose 1991). To this extent little attention will be paid to the rise of a group of professional experts alongside the transformation of the category and the field of childhood (Chauvenet 1988; Halpern 1988).[66]

As a core element of the rationalization of the social, science has to do with the regulation of childhood; it also had something to say about the role of the child's experience, and yet how it can say this must be specified in one way or another. The displacement of the child's status from a topic for discussion among well-educated people to an object of scientific observation in a laboratory – or through mass investigation of schoolchildren, for instance – had important effects. As a somehow unusual if not revolutionary scientific object, the child presents serious obstacles to researchers. There was little established knowledge available and very few methods, techniques or procedures to produce the required intelligence to monitor children as requested by state authorities and various reformers.[67] Thus children began to be observed, described and measured on an extensive scale. What are the chief concerns of this research, and what are their consequences? [68]

The line of argument of the following chapters will cover the path from the first experiments in scientific observation of children and their measurement to the creation of the original graphs and charts to the production of the behavioural benchmarks of the normal child. The question of parents' compliance – notably of middle-class mothers of young children – with experts' prescriptions, hence the diffusion of scientific findings, advice and guidelines, proved to be fundamental. Much as most studies have addressed the problem in a

---

[66] Reference is made here to the theme, so well analysed by Halpern (1988), of professional experts in search of a market or trying to expand their own share of an existing market.

[67] So as to achieve this goal, researchers and paediatricians needed new techniques on the one hand, and a refinement of measurement and observation procedures too (Rosenkrantz 1978). Their first goal, however, remained the fight against the high rate of infant mortality.

[68] This particular concern – focus – is substantially different from other studies' concerns such as scientific management of children or scientific childcare (Gurjeva 1998), scientific motherhood (Apple 1995), scientific paediatrics (Rodriguez Ocana 1998) or scientific psychology (Hornstein 1988; Rose 1985).

classic diffusionist approach – applications of science as a sign of its influence and maturity – it is nonetheless possible to conceive of it rather in a different way: as a rationalization process operating within an ANT modus operandi of translation and network-building.[69] The authority of science, accepted as a premise, is questioned by paying as much attention to parents' resistance as to focusing on science's empirical operations. For the moment, the continuity/discontinuity between scientific regulation of childhood and routine domestic practices remains open; in this matter parents do not inevitably lag behind experts. It is the commodification of childcare that yielded the standardization of care procedures (Gurjeva 1998: 105). Measurement, quantification and graphic visualization paved the way to child hygiene and child development as guiding principle of care both domestic and institutional.

For the purposes of this study, considering science as a core element of the rationalization of childhood, special attention is given to the following features which fundamentally reshaped the whole field:

- observation, recording, measurement, quantification and precision, and the technology which supported it;
- standardization of protocols and the transformation of scientific indicators into standards, criteria, and finally social norms through a schematic visualization of the child's body;
- the schema of regularity/firmness/rigidity, an outcome of the technology of measurement, as a decisive component of the normal child; schedule of the child as a watchword;
- childhood as a sequence of discrete stages of development, each with its own behavioural expectations and benchmarks, with special regard to physical and intellectual growth and character-formation alike;
- the relation between science and the abstract notion of universal childhood as a natural state – i.e. culture-free and timeless – and their embeddedness in the normal child.

These features must somehow be completed for they do not exhaust as complex a subject as childhood (James and Prout 1990a; James *et al.* 1998; Javeau 1994; Quentel 1997; Qvortrup 1993).

[69] Most ANT key figures see their theory as a viable alternative to the classic diffusionist system (Latour 1994b).

- Childhood is primarily neither a social category, a form of social structure nor a minority group, but a never-ending process, which has no arbitrary or peremptory beginning and is never fully completed.
- Childhood is an integral component of the totality that is human-hood; accordingly, no general account of either the social or the actor is relevant without a theory of childhood; the concept of a total person provides a unifying perspective capable of going beyond sociological dichotomies.
- Developmental theory's descriptions of the various stages of a child's development constitute the core of the category of the normal child and are related to specific cultural strata, thus to the Western middle class.
- Developmental theory as a pre-ordained and articulated sequence of discrete stages, in the usual Piagetian sense, is deeply embedded as a cognitive form in Western culture.
- Childhood is a situated space–time form, thus varying accordingly; notions of age as well as age group are deemed to be a decisive feature of childhood, but above all of the normal child.[70]
- This study is constructionist in the original sense of the metaphor: building from parts which are both historical and spatial, then contrived into larger structures within a broad cultural framework.

The seeds of a legitimate historical sociology of childhood, disentangled from the plain drawbacks of sociology's conception of children which prevented it from blooming, are now sown. This chapter started with a critical review of mainstream sociology's sole notion of childhood – socialization and its inherent limitations – and later continued with the task of unfolding the black box: what is a child from a sociological standpoint? This work ushers in the concepts of totality – providing a unifying scene to overcome childhood's theoretical ghetto – and rationalization as a central feature of modern societies, both of them leading to a specific theoretical perspective for a historical sociology of childhood. An important clarification of the concept of the social actualized these two basic concepts: its conception as a complex set of heterogeneous entities in a network of

---

[70] This proposition must be understood as being different, situated at another level of analysis, from James and Prout's examination of the timeless culture or the institution of childhood (James and Prout 1990b: 228).

relationships led to a reshuffling of the classic structure–agency device; a primary form of rationalization of the social was reached via the implementation of a specific space–time for social intervention, thus for childhood regulation.

The clarification of the concept of the social was a first step, soon to be followed by others in the direction of ANT as a theoretical stance offering much to fulfil it. To be consistent with both the purpose of this study and the notion of heterogeneity, we reconceptualized the relations between human and non-human entities, the latter deemed as a prolongation of the former and being inextricably natural, social and discursive. The notions of translation, mediation and circulation achieve a theoretical framework which allows to view the outcomes of the systematic investigation of childhood as something other than a mere residue: graphs, charts and tabulations are considered vital players in their own enabling as well as demarcating new forces to be introduced in the field.

The conceptual framework being designed, it was necessary to complete the process by bringing together analytic propositions. Instead of being proposed as a vague general umbrella, social construction had to become more specific about what is meant by the analytic operation understood as construction. The role of science was clarified with respect to a historical sociology of childhood: neither a demiurge nor a mere instrument, it decisively transformed the pattern of relationships in this field, so that developmental theory became a usual way of thinking and acting upon children. The next chapter will look at where it all started: the new observational device and the textual inscription of the child.

2 | *Graphs, charts and tabulations*

The textual inscription of children

British historian C. Steedman points out that, during the nineteenth century, the child figure and the very idea of childhood were sustained in literature and in science above all (Steedman 1995). In this latter case, buoyant new fields and new technologies of investigation spread throughout the century and some scientists grasped these opportunities, particularly in the emergent domain of childhood research. From the outset, one is struck by the constant, steady and hence huge presence of graphs, charts, tabulations and the like in scientific journals and books related in one way or another to the empirical study of children. These original ways of observing the child from within a scientific discourse are connected with the increase of knowledge, notably technical knowledge, about childhood. The complex of descriptions, vocabularies and visual depictions evolved in such fields as anthropometry, hygiene, paediatrics and psychology that researched the child.

First, I shall propose that a growing body of scientific texts became available, initially in specialized circles and afterwards to a larger public, alongside the enormous advice literature provided by the welfare groups. This specific discourse involved a textual inscription[1] of children whose form is relatively different from the previous ones. The second purpose of this chapter is to consider the radical novelty introduced by this specific textual inscription of children in the form of graphs and charts etc. Third, this chapter offers a detailed account of both the first forms as well as the more elaborate forms of child observation and recording as a background to twentieth-century scientific textual practices. Fourth, this argument will consider some

---

[1] Inscriptions are operations which allow the production of plain facts. This means everything which functions as traces, points, diagrams, numbers, histograms and figures. It concerns the transformation of matter into writing, into visual writing most of the time (Latour 1986).

of the main graphs and charts of the turn of the twentieth century, their specific constituents and effects.

2.1 Inscription and embodiment

For a long time, both in academic circles and by educated members of the public, history was considered as both a representation and a discourse that a culture tells to itself: the main scene of a society's memory. More recently, however, theoreticians have started to argue through new epistemological approaches that history is objectivized in many ways via institutions and the body.[2] Both institutions and bodies are accumulated, incorporated and objectivized throughout history. Above all, the body is liable to those social institutions that 'we live through' (Bellah 1991: 3). The process of becoming a social actor is initiated and achieved by embodiment and the framing of the actor by the institutions. The line of argument developed here will probe further how embodiment is carried on and how inscription articulates it in some specific ways.

The entry of the body into sociological theory goes back to the early forms of organic theory in the nineteenth century, when sociologists drew comparisons between biological and social systems' equilibrium through the organization metaphor, as an important component of social theory in the second half of the century. The idea that the body functions as a classificatory system is not new to anthropology but sociologists have generally ignored it, with the exception of Durkheim and Mauss whose work, *Primitive Classi-fication* (1963), was an important first step in this direction. From then on, the body was disregarded as a preoccupation of the average sociologist and as a topic for social theory.

From a historical perspective, the body was not a corner-stone for social theory to build upon. At the end of the twentieth century, however, the configuration of sociology was transformed, the body being considered as an object worthy of scientific investigation. Today, new approaches in social theory recognize the importance of the body, of embodiment more specifically, in the processes through

---

[2] Institutions are understood as a set of dispositions socially and culturally constructed: 'stable designs for chronically repeated activity sequences' (DiMaggio and Powell 1991: 25).

which human beings become social actors and are thus enabled to participate in social life. 'It is widely agreed that an adequate social theory must account for the body and the part it plays in social relations' (James *et al.* 1998: 147).

Society is not only a matter of social structure and economic processes, political organization or ideology. A major proposition in this respect would then be that a social actor learns both his society and culture through embodiment and inscription (language, codes etc.). We learn by and through our body. This fundamental proposition, unusual amongst sociologists, needs to be explained further. The actor's relationship to his own body is a decisive factor in a social structure; that is to say, social structure is about the production and reproduction of embodiment as one of its main functions. This relationship is, in a certain sense, beyond awareness and consciousness. To understand with one's body means 'that social action is (generally speaking) embodied action, performed not only by texts but by real, living corporeal persons' (James *et al.* 1998: 147).

The instruction of the body observable in the family with child-raising as well as in other settings cannot be reduced to Foucault's disciplined body and the repressive hypothesis. Institutions such as churches, schools and armies emphasize corporeal training: activities like exercises, prayers, gymnastics, sports and rituals of different kinds are all directed to train the body in one way or another.[3] The sociological construction of embodiment is broader than Foucault's discipline while also incorporating it. A sociologist would not question that the army practices corporeal discipline: the training of a good soldier occurs through the embodiment of a discipline into the social actor. My perspective is different: it tries to identify the ways society and culture inhabit a social actor and how these ways come by embodiment.

Practical behaviour is neither the sole outcome of a constraining norm nor a voluntary adherence to official dogmas, but rather a state of the body that is established and materialized in predispositions[4]

---

[3] Corporate loyalty, team spirit or bodily disciplines exist in most organizations – the Church, the army, political parties, industrial concerns and so on – 'this is to a great extent because obedience is belief and belief is what the body grants even when the mind says no' (Bourdieu 1990: 167).

[4] Or a habitus in Bourdieu's terms: lasting, regulated and transposable dispositions functioning as a matrix of perceptions, appreciations and actions. Bourdieu's insistence on the embodiment aspect of the concept of habitus must

which entitle an actor in a given field. The corporeal form is the pragmatic realization of a permanent disposition that is a durable manner of behaving, of walking, of talking, of feeling things or persons. Such injunctions as: 'don't hold your knife with your left hand' or 'stand up straight', and all other trivial things such as posture, ordinary behaviour or corporeal manners are embodied as a practical operator into an operating sketch. Being a sketch, and therefore a constitutive part of someone's dispositions, moves these corporeal manners out of the area of conscience and explication.

Relationship to the body, because it is an integral part of one's dispositions, cannot be reduced to either the body image or the body concept. What is learned through the body is not something that one has but rather what one is. Elias' account of the way social actors acquire specific table manners is a convincing example of the theory of embodiment (Elias 1978: 84). Children are socialized to those table manners through work upon their body: 'Do not hold your knife this way'.

One becomes a social actor by incorporating dispositions into one's own body that are always class-defined. In this sense, the corporeal form is a sketch that outlines the legitimate definition and usage of the body in a given culture according to specific class dispositions. The body is linked to class dispositions, each class developing its own matrix of perceptions and actions in that respect. To live in one's own body with ease and grace or to experience it with discomfort, ill-being and timidity: that is the difference between being able to recognize a code – inscription – and being able to embody it.[5] This arises from the gap between the socially legitimate use of the body and the body that one has and is 'an account of how practices of a non-inscribed kind are transmitted in, and as, traditions' (Connerton 1989: x). The passage from an oral tradition to a literate culture generates the transition from incorporating to inscribing practices. This transition, he adds, does not mean that incorporation and embodiment are not relevant or salient any more. In a literate culture they take other forms.

---

be emphasized. The dispositions are bodily learned, appropriated and inculcated into the social actor through the institutions that frame him.

[5] The French maxim: 'Il faut y être né' ('one has to be born to it') refers to class dispositions, especially those of the bourgeoisie. One does not enter into that magical circle by a spontaneous decision of the will, but either by birth or by a slow process of initiation that is the equivalent of a second birth.

These last remarks introduce the question of the actor's inscription. The sociological construction and differentiation between the concepts of incorporation and inscription is fundamental and may represent one of the most original contributions to social theory. What is the nature of the relationship between social structure and corporeal dispositions? Social structure establishes itself both through institutions and social organization, but also through corporeal dispositions.

In the latter case, the line of argument developed earlier strongly maintained that a social structure must grasp social actors and achieve their embodiment to be suitable and effective, as seen above. In the former case, social structure comes to the actor through the process of inscription: learning a language and, generally speaking, the linguistic and speech codes; learning the codes of behaviour and social conduct; learning the stories and the narratives of one's own family and culture that enables one to situate oneself within a history and a trajectory that began long before one's own birth; learning, and becoming familiar with, the specific social memory of one's own culture[6] and so on. This does not mean that social structure is mostly a matter of language and of discourse, but rather that inscription cannot be bypassed in conceptualizing social structure and is the very beginning of it. Social structure is implemented not only in the mind (cognition, culture, representation and the like), but also in the actor's body; both implementations are a condition of efficiency in maintaining social structure, as Figure 2 illustrates.

For a number of complex historical reasons, not least because sociologists are scientists who emphasize theoretical explanation, sociology often relied heavily on inscriptive processes to give an account of society and social change.[7] Is it necessary to put forward for those who are not mainly statistical sociologists and whose data are primarily linguistic that sociology is caught out by the hermeneutic

---

[6] Connerton constructs memory as embodied practices that are transmitted through both commemorative ceremonies and bodily practices. By bodily practices, he means techniques like gesture and postural behaviour, rituals and ceremonies, all of which have a function in the transmission of memory. He argues 'that images of the past and recollected knowledge of the past are conveyed and sustained by ritual performances and that performative memory is bodily' (Connerton 1989: x).

[7] To avoid excessive generalization, in large segments of sociology, notably in economic and political sociology as well as in structural sociology, to mention a few, inscription did not prevail as the core of the explanation.

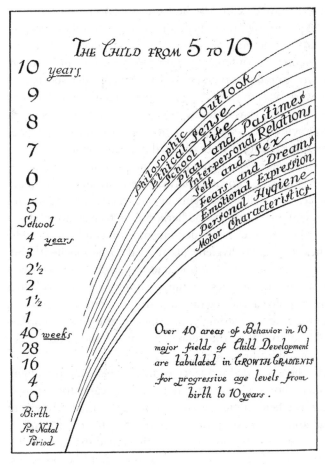

Figure 2: The child from five to ten
Source: Gesell 1946b

paradigm that entitles above all inscription of the actor and, accordingly, leaves incorporative processes in the shade?[8]

---

[8] This is noticeable in the strong trend summarized under the semiotic metaphor of society as a text able to be read: dense description of Geertz, Foucaldian archaeology, Derridean deconstruction etc. are among the main thrusts of the semiotic metaphor of society: language and text become the primary unit of empirical knowledge of society. Everything becomes a discursive object, the

The semiotic metaphor can best be summarized in the Derridean proposition: 'There is nothing outside the text.' This radical proposition had certain effects among social scientists, since it challenges deep-rooted assumptions, inferences and postulates. The most noticeable of these was to induce some sociologists to consider social phenomena they were working on as textual phenomena, thus focusing exclusively on specific forms of inscription processes at the expense of all others. Following the lasting effect of Ariès' *Centuries of Childhood*, major research efforts were directed at such thematic areas as the image, the representation of the child at different historical periods in different societies; the enormous advice literature for the primary caretakers of children, chiefly parents and teachers;[9] the politics of childhood from infancy through 'toddlerhood' to 'teenagehood', from schooling to welfare, and from delinquency to child labour; the question of health, mental hygiene (as it used to be labelled), children's emotional life and child abuse; and so on. It is not an overstatement to say that these types of study, within the framework that was theirs, menopolized the energy and the working capacities of researchers in the field. Accordingly, inscription came to be identified with and reduced to either the representation of the child or the various forms of advice literature.

Reactions to the expanded influence of the hermeneutic paradigm, the semiotic metaphor and Derridean reductionism came forth slowly and steadily; in the field of childhood, it took the form of a return to the body/child and the question of embodiment as the main markers of the child's materiality. In this respect, some argued that the child is not merely an effect of representation: 'the body/child becomes dissolved as a material entity and is treated as a discursive object – the product not of an interaction between "nature" and "culture" but purely an effect of discourse' (James *et al.* 1998: 146). Hence the return to the embodiment problematic initiated some time ago.

What conclusions can one draw from this rather severe critique of the inscription processes coming from researchers amenable to

---

child among others, upon the basis that nothing, no fragment of reality, ontologically exists and is grasped outside discourse, outside the way actors talk about it.

[9] It is worth paraphrasing the well-known warning to historians by Mechling: 'Advice to Historians on Advice to Mothers' (Mechling 1975: 44–63) and questioning sociologists on the same ground and from the same perspective.

investigating children's embodiment? It might be a unique opportunity to focus on the construction – that is, translation and mediation – or the apprehending of inscription as separate from the semiotic metaphor and any other form of Derridean reductionism; a unique opportunity also to try to appreciate inscription outside any notion of the child's image, or representation. That is to say that the task ahead is enormous, mostly because the path, unfamiliar and unusual, is quite narrow. I shall, however, emphasize the two elements that offer the best possibility of a way out of the representation quandary.

The first inscription scheme is narrative, a family narrative for instance, provided one acknowledges the hypothesis according to the intelligible figure of narrative separately from any form of representation or semiotic discourse. Narratives are essential to both personal and cultural identity. The transformation, or the progressive mutation of a biological entity – a newborn infant – into a thoroughly established social actor, legitimately enabled to perform in the polity upon the actualization of its capacities and abilities, requires more than biological and sexual maturation. It demands the transmission of a cultural heritage.

Transmission of a cultural heritage is established in a long-term project, assigned to various institutions: family, school, church and media. Throughout a narrative over a period of years, a child is steeped into an institutionalized family form of which it has neither an immediate experience nor a direct memory. This narrative is a circulating discourse that is not set forth by any specific, identifiable narrator. 'It is through hearing stories ... that children learn or mislearn both what a child and what a parent is, what the cast of characters may be in the drama into which they have been born and what the ways of the world are. Deprive children of stories and you leave them unscripted' (Macintyre 1984: 216).

The second inscription scheme came into sight in the second half of the nineteenth century in a very specific and limited domain of human activity: in hygiene, in paediatrics, and later in psychology. The systematic scientific investigation of childhood which began at that time had some major effects, the most important of them being the changing translation of the normal child and thus the normal family, the varying social practices surrounding child-rearing, monitoring etc. that ensued (Morel 1989; Rollet 1990). Science was instrumental in this new mediation (Crisler 1984; Richardson 1989) and was effective in a number of ways; one of them was its innovative instrumentation, namely measurement and statistics (Hacking 1983: 234).[10]

While it appears to be inappropriate at this stage of the argument to examine why such scientific specializations as hygiene and paediatrics started to probe children, it seems relevant to bring to light the specific methods – techniques and procedures – used to investigate childhood systematically. Whatever the reason was for physicians to intervene in childhood research,[11] they had to frame a specific type of intervention and, above all, to bring together the various requirements of their intervention; chiefly, and equally, the cognitive conditions and the technical instrumentation supporting it. The physicians' intervention turned out to be in line with the general trends characterizing the scientific field and different methods already used in other areas of medicine (Halpern 1988).

With his usual explicitness, Kuhn asserted that the fairly novel passion for measurement was entirely in place by the end of the nineteenth century. Since the world was now conceived of in a rather more quantitative way, and conceptualized in hard science by numerical magnitudes, science comes to be buried beneath an avalanche of numbers. The mathematization of physics after Newton in the course of the nineteenth century built clarified criteria for problem-solving and for experimental protocols. The outcome of these experiments was their accuracy and the new technology of measurement that they fabricated. 'Our conception of numbers and measuring is clear and unquestioned at the end of the nineteenth century' (Hacking 1983: 234).

---

[10] The observation of objects or events is usually done with instruments. In this respect, Hacking raises the following questions:

- Do we fully understand the point of the most precise, delicate, and admired measurement in history?
- Is measurement an inherent part of the scientific mind?
- Do measurements measure anything real in nature, or are they chiefly an artefact of the way in which we theorize? (Hacking 1983)

[11] Whether to secure a new professional field of intervention, or as a result of the pressures from public authorities in the face of such scourges as infant mortality, delinquency and child labour, the physicians mastered the task of intervention in two ways: as professional advisers to parents, but also as producers of the necessary knowledge required for intervention.

The knowledge of the child consists of a specific form – 'the long history of child-watching' (Steedman 1995: 138) – of recording children's lives and bodies on a very large scale, unknown before the second half of the nineteenth century.[12] In different settings such as the doctor's surgery, the school, the family home through visiting nurses and so on, children were observed, measured, weighed and physically assessed – and later on psychologically assessed – in brief, described and classified. Following domestic child observation, the professionalized mass observation of children in the late nineteenth century became more 'scientific' in its methods, techniques and procedures. Everything is then observed and systematically recorded: from 'the daily watching of children's heads, tongues, cries, gestures and faeces' (Steedman 1995: 70) and the patient scrutiny of 'another level of observation, of the circulatory, respiratory and digestive functions' (Steedman 1995: 71) to the methodical registration of weighing and measuring children. Robert's appeal to *Lancet* readers for help in achieving a cycle of observations to measure the height, weight and chest girth of English children was made within an international framework: 'Roberts already had 15,000 observations on boys' (Steedman 1995: 76). Galton's large-scale anthropometric measurement of children around the 1880s as well as the US Children's Bureau's gigantic campaign for recording children's heights and weights – 5,000,000 cards distributed – after the Second World War are seen as strong indicators of this trend.

Knowledge of the child involved large-scale recording, and yet the practice of recording and the tables produced thereafter remained nonetheless problematic, in sharp contrast with today where they are taken for granted both as a way of thinking and as material objects. If tables bear the status of anchoring and materializing general ideas of human development – in sequences of episodes embodied as markers of development – it is understood that tabulation requires specific skills which, then, were far from obvious, outside the laboratory setting. Tables were in fact 'a complex technical and social accomplishment' (Gurjeva 1998: 165). The fabrication of graphs and charts rested upon the tabulation of an impressive amount of data collected from parents, teachers, nurses, reformers, child study activists and the

---

[12] Kincaid (1992) is relevant on the personal forms of child observation and recording: the habit of domestic observation.

like; their cooperation was essential to the project. This topic raises a very intricate problem: how do these actors acquire the necessary tabulation skills so as to collect the relevant data?[13]

The other question at stake with respect to tables and graphs concerns their status as material objects. Tables, graphs and charts are pivotal in the standardization and normalization of child development. As objects, they play a crucial role in the emerging network of relationships of both human and non-human entities, being at once a mediator and a translator. As mediators, they circulate between children, parents, teachers, paediatricians etc.; they mean displacement while creating a link. The thrust of the argument introduced below assumes that tables ensure a new form of cooperation between these heterogeneous groups by translating their conflicting viewpoints, agendas and practices into a stable visualized design of child development. The emergence of material objects such as tables reshuffled the relationships among actors by successfully recognizing the likelihood of collective action across divergent social groupings; thus yielding a relative stability in the field of childhood (Fujimura 1992). In this sense, they are considered as inscription devices.

This large-scale measurement and recording by the medical establishment informs a totally new textual inscription of children. These bodily assessments are mapped into charts, graphs, numerical regularities, tabulations and the like. This institutes a textual inscription of children, quite different from the traditional representation and inscription. Such a form of textual inscription ushers in distinct ways of thought, which amount to a new form of thinking: the relationship between children and visualized entities – graphs and so on – becomes at once a form of cognition (Moran-Ellis 1998; Quentel 1997; N. Rose 1991).

Moreover, this in-depth description of children in almost every conceivable aspect of their lives and bodies involves therefore their classification according to specific parameters and benchmarks in relation to pre-defined developmental and behavioural norms (Rosenkrantz 1978). From description to classification lies the passage of inscription to embodiment as the child's body is objectified through

---

[13] The question of the acquisition of tabulation skills is outside the scope of this study, albeit fundamental and deserving of mention. Gurjeva devotes an entire chapter to this question in her work (Gurjeva 1998). I am indebted to Gurjeva for this development.

the technological apparatus of statistics (Crisler 1984; Luc 1997). The child's body observed through statistics and visually transformed in charts and graphs is afterwards reconfigured via 'the medical gaze' (Armstrong 1983; Richardson 1989). Hence the implementation of a medical reference within the classification processes acknowledged and paved the way for the comparison, the standardization and the normalization of children's developmental behaviour. The standardized norms were accordingly embodied in the child as both parents and children were expected by medical and welfare experts to conform to the charts.[14]

Such processes of measurement and description are examined as a textual inscription of children with their fundamental results in the aftermath of the child's embodiment. Children's lives became permeated by the extensive textual inscription of their being and childhood. The next section will look at the relationship between this technological device and the cultural context in which its theory emerged.

2.2 The statement

By the end of the nineteenth century, the new category of the 'normal child' emerged. Physicians and hygienists began to classify children in distinct ways, the most prevalent of these categories being the normal child.[15] The latter became an institutionalized category to classify and inscribe children in public hygiene and in paediatrics. Thus appeared an original manner of being acquainted with children, of producing knowledge about them and, above all, of behaving toward them: social classification and categorization constitute a specific form of knowledge embedded in the cultural context of a given society.

---

[14] The two processes, inscription and embodiment far from being totally autonomous, incompatible or opposed one to the other, constitute rather a pair of Siamese twins, so to speak: the obverse and the reverse side of a sheet of paper. No inscription without embodiment and vice versa.

[15] This reconfiguration is a direct consequence of the scientific investigation of childhood of the nineteenth and twentieth centuries. It is the main hypothesis of this research. Note that the question of the normal child emerged at the same time, in the same context and in the same semantic field as the question of delinquency, raising the problem of the construction of a new citizenship (Sutton 1988).

The cultural, social and scientific context that witnessed the rise of the normal child is rather complex;[16] it requires us to look at the transformations of scientific practice to understand its effects on childhood investigation with such devices as charts, tabulations and the like. The methodical medical examination of the child is not an isolated practice within the larger scientific domain, but an integral part of it, as it is constituted when the fundamental transformations of scientific practice are already implemented. Therefore the major trends of both scientific theories of that period become basic elements in the process of institutionalization of the normal child.

A sudden trend dominated the scientific context of the turn of the twentieth century: the erosion of deterministic thought and the rise of probabilistic theory. Hacking does not hesitate to characterize this major cultural transformation: 'the most decisive conceptual event of twentieth century physics has been the discovery that the world is not deterministic' (Hacking 1990: 1). Perhaps for the first time in the history of human society, it seems plausible that the past does not strictly determine the future, that what happened in history is not indicative of what will occur next. This original cultural perspective opened an unusual space for uncertainty and doubt, but also for projects bearing societal orientations. The structures of society were no longer taken for granted (Touraine 1992), but the product of human activity and social relationships. Social scientists turned to considering structures, practices and organizations as a product of society and humankind that could come up with knowledge on the basis of empirical research and the new technologies of statistics and probability.[17]

As a result of this cultural shift, the Enlightenment's cardinal idea of human nature, predominant for a long time, underwent a major transformation as the deterministic perspective eroded and faded

---

[16] Emphasis is put on the scientific context in the logic of this text. Strong social demands found their way to the public authorities concerning new ways of raising children, health and hygienic preoccupations, school performance, improvement of social behaviour and so on (Elder *et al.* 1993; Klaus 1993). The hygienist, as a specialist of public health, stands in between the physician and the expert in urban planning, mid-way between scientific and technical knowledge.

[17] The shift from a deterministic to non-deterministic perspective in the account both of the natural and the social world, paved the way to a new knowledge and to a political transformation of the society.

away.[18] This concept is gradually substituted in the scientific sphere by a model of normal people statistically constituted with laws of dispersion that emerged within the cultural framework of indeterminacy. The model soon percolated in the larger circles of the wider public: 'to see that the world might be regular and yet not subject to universal laws of nature. A space was cleared for chance ... society became statistical' (Hacking 1990: 1).

The practice of measurement became generalized around the mid-nineteenth century, revolving on the measurement of the nineteenth-century's newly discovered object of scientific investigation: population. The extension of this practice beyond its traditional scope bore major effects in the social sciences as well as in public hygiene and in paediatrics: it opened up wide new fields of enquiry, almost totally intact until then. The systematic examination of children took place within the newly emerging vast domain of population studies. It was carried on, paradoxically, not in the social sciences, but in the medical field, at least in the beginning. The methodical and formal collecting of data and the gathering of these data into identifiable patterns provided an original form of 'objective knowledge', different from any other forms that were available at that period of time. Knowledge of the child as an important outcome of a long historical trend became a core expertise excluding lay persons (Halpern 1988).

'Take so seemingly unproblematic a topic as population' (Hacking 1990: 6). It seems altogether familiar, at least for social scientists: regular census data render familiar images such as the number of people in a city or country, the number of suicides, births, deaths etc. These figures make sense because institutions established what the category of population means.[19] This was not the case in the nineteenth century. The concept of population, in its statistical meaning, was still unknown. A representative sample of a given population had yet to come into being. 'This has required techniques of thinking

---

[18] The idea of human nature survived the erosion of the deterministic perspective and still appears to be pervasive in the twentieth century. The concepts of normalcy and normal people carried on the mutation of the idea of human nature.

[19] Concerning the question of categorization and classification by institutions, see Douglas 1986 and Turmel 1997. Douglas' book, *How Institutions Think*, is a course of study in itself as well as a strong metaphor. It supports the point that institutions have a life of their own and indeed produce social objects such as classification.

together with technologies of data collection. An entire style of scientific reasoning has had to evolve' (Hacking 1990: 7).

Hacking puts forward, after Crombie's work regarding various ways of thinking, the notion of 'a style of reasoning' concerning statistical analysis of regularities of population, that is new forms of reasoning and argumentation. Although the great burst of statistical thinking arose in the nineteenth century, it illustrates that a style of reasoning is not solely a matter of knowing or thinking, but of action. It has to do with 'the idea of making up people. I claim that enumeration requires categorization, and that defining new classes of people for the purpose of statistics has consequences for the ways in which we conceive of others' (Hacking 1990: 6). And for the ways in which we inscribe and embody others in various social settings.

This question has to be conceptualized. The notion of regularity in the social world was then deeply distinct from the regularity observed in nature, and thus from the universal laws of nature explaining it. The enormous flood of numbers gathered by the states' apparatus for collection of statistics paved the way for the notion of statistical laws of society. An intrinsic belief with respect to laws about people was nonetheless agreed upon; this was a pre-condition for probability being read into those numbers. Numerical regularities relating to disease were widespread by the 1840s. The idea of statistical laws of the human body was making its way. The first half of the nineteenth century witnessed a society shaped by numbers and measured in every aspect of its configuration. The measurement of society occurred in every branch of human activity, not only in health or population studies. Accordingly, a new type of law[20] concerning societies came into being, as the exact opposite of the causal laws of nature: these laws, expressed in terms of probability, pertained to people, their relationships and the way they behave, for probabilities are attributes

---

[20] Today it is more accurate to talk about rules than 'laws' used by nineteenth-century social scientists in a context where positivism and measurement were in close association with each other as positivism usually means numerical data and regularities. The distinction between nature and culture, the proper methods to give account of both objects and the German debate between explanation and comprehension had not made yet its way to empirical research. On the other hand, statistics and probability were brought together for probability was instrumental in determining mortality rates of a particular population.

of groups rather than single individuals (Rothstein 2003). Before proceeding, however, a basic question must be addressed: what does a statistical law of the human body devise in the social world?

These two transformations, the erosion of determinism and the rise of probability, appear to be connected; the former and the latter linked in the same process, as being the two faces of the same problem. In the new emerging cultural configuration, public authorities deemed certain human behaviours such as vagrancy, prostitution and delinquency to be the main social problems of the period (Cravens 1985b; Pinchbeck and Hewitt 1973; Sutherland 1976; Sutton 1988). Published tabulations of numerical facts relating to such behaviour appeared to researchers surprisingly regular from year to year. By the 1830s myriad regularities about vagrancy, delinquency and the like with their relative frequency – by month, sex, region etc. – became visible with the publication of printed graphs, tables and charts.

The gathering of data on suicide is first initiated with the collection of huge numbers and the publication of printed tables; its model is set in the 1820s by the *Recherches statistiques sur la ville de Paris et le département de la Seine*.[21] When the statistical technologies were generalized and later became the usual way of thinking in a matter such as suicide, data took the form of average and dispersions around the mean; they became statistical with the legitimized seal of probability. So were the data in regard to other social problems. One thinks for instance of Durkheim's classic study, *Suicide*, although the probability form of thinking was already implemented at the end of the century when Durkheim published his research. These figures, derived from probability, were the numerical and visual expression – graphs and charts etc. – of the social phenomena under consideration. They specifically carried with them and emphasized graphically the notion of normalcy, thus the connotation of normal people. People positioned near the average are considered the norm, meaning that other people, those at both ends of the bell curve, deviated from the norm. Well-armed with such data and figures, reformers at the end of the nineteenth century launched a new kind of social engineering,

[21] *Recherches statistiques sur la ville de Paris et le département de la Seine*, Paris, 1821–1829, four volumes.

namely the medical regime,[22] for the purpose of controlling the underclass and their undesirable behaviour (Swann 1990).

Two important elements need to be fully understood at this point. First, the non-deterministic cultural configuration contributed to the emergence of probability theory, paving the way for the notion of normal people against the Enlightenment idea of human nature. Normalcy meant average people living within the socially acceptable norm and people deviating from it.[23] The notion of 'average' influenced heavily what was considered to be normal for social actors. One must not underestimate the feedback effect of these laws and of the analysis based on those technologies; human behaviour came under scrutiny and social actors were summed up to behave according to these figures; that is, to what the charts and the graphs brought out: clear, indeed obvious, tendencies.

Second, on the more empirical ground of self-consolidation, the nation-states needed theories and technologies to frame their own population while facing the harsh realities of the Industrial Revolution; specifically to regulate deviant fractions of the underclass. These needs became imperative as soon as it appeared to public authorities and to the ruling class that the deviant behaviour was a direct threat to

---

[22] The institutionalization of the medical regime is complex and revolves around the instrumentation that renders it possible.

A medical regime has established itself over the population of modern societies. In everyday it exists in an extensive but not very intensive version: it operates through mass screenings, routine tests, physicals for insurance and job appointments, and school and company health check-ups ... Entire categories of apparently healthy persons are declared, a priori, medical subjects: pregnant women, infants, senior citizens ... This is a consequence of technological and organizational innovations in medicine: the technical progress concerns the improvement and refinement of diagnostic machinery. The organizational innovations concern the mass examinations of complete populations in preventive campaigns (Swann 1990: 60).

This leaves open the problem of the articulation of the medical regime with the medical gaze, thus with inscription through medical categories.

[23] The question of why and how a norm becomes socially acceptable is a stimulating though difficult question. The argument will come up with this question concerning the normal child. 'People are normal if they conform to the central tendency of such laws, while those at the extremes are pathological. Few of us fancy being pathological, so "most of us" try to make ourselves normal, which in turn affects what is normal. Atoms have no such inclinations. The human sciences display a feedback effect not to be found in physics' (Hacking 1990).

public order (Cohen 1985; Graff 1995). This was particularly compelling.

The state needed the means to collect data and to draw up statistics; an apparatus, the statistical office,[24] had the power to publish official statistics on a wide range of subjects. The initial investigations referred mainly to deviant social actors whose conduct public authorities tried to regulate within certain acceptable boundaries (Hopkins 1994). Within the office of the Registrar-General for England and Wales where he was a health statistician and a hygienist, William Farr institutionalized British vital statistics in the 1840s and 1850s; he was highly preoccupied by the high urban death rate, especially among infants, which in his view reflected a society's moral standing. The British were already convinced, after the medical arithmetic pattern, that there were laws of sickness whose regularity was akin to that of mortality. The office's system for recording and analysis became a model for the rest of the world (Farr 1875). Social scientists gathered huge amounts of data expressed customarily in terms of probability. Statistics became the most relevant instrumentation not only for observation and description of a particular type of population, but also for understanding and explaining the course of behaviour and events, therefore extending medical quantification to public health. There lies the widely held belief that it is possible to improve the behaviour of the underclass with worthwhile public policies based on data gathered by sound enumeration, taxonomy and classification (Donnelly 2005).

The nation-states launched the campaign to count, classify and categorize their citizens, specifically for the two traditional purposes of government: taxation and army recruitment. The need to classify very soon exceeded those purposes. The laboriousness attending the creation and the enforcement of new categories should not be underestimated.[25] Categories were designed to be convenient both to an

---

[24] Namely the Italian cities and their elaborate statistical enquiries; the Swedish pastors and their accumulation of data on births and deaths; the French Napoleonic bureaucracy committed to imaginative statistical investigations; Britain's Registrar-General, Board of Trade and Board of Agriculture; the Prussian statistical bureau; the Royal Statistical Bureau in Berlin; the United States Census and the like.

[25] The gigantic task of collecting and tabulating data presupposes a classification of disease and social problems that were completely renewed. Classification and categorization are empirically and conceptually inseparable problems (Eco 1988; Molino 1989).

accurate description of the various populations and to the needs of the state. The official reports set up categories which classified actors according to the social problem under investigation. Therefore people inscribed under official categories happened to see themselves consistently in terms of these classifications. Moreover they began behaving generally as such; that is to act in conformity with the socially acceptable norms. It became an implicit prescription.

The scientific, basically statistical and probabilistic, investigation of populations ensued in a systematic collection of data regarding social actors, their conduct and their habits, that utterly transformed society's self-conceptions and inscriptions in the long-term. It affected not only the ways in which state bureaucracies observe and describe various social classes, but also the trends of people's agency, actions and achievements, the different categories in which they inscribe themselves, the aims they pursue and the social forms in which they embody other people's selves. Defining new categories for social actors both for the purposes of the state and for the relentless reform action of progressive groups bore consequences: potentialities and possibilities of agency were framed in a somehow different way as well as people's inscription in various social settings.

As the next section suggests, the social forms of child observation and child recording have a long history culminating in the statistical and probability technologies. What are then the main differences in the perspective of the child's inscription?

2.3 Observing and recording

One way or another, there is nothing we do so much of with children as watching them (Kincaid 1992: 364).

The practice of child observation was an Enlightenment imperative (Steedman 1995: 68). The zeitgeist of the Enlightenment had buoyant effects on childhood, with its changing conceptions, its ebullient concerns and its keen watchfulness of the child. Parents as well as pedagogues, physicians and experts were assigned to their duties of watching the child; through this observation, the knowledge of childhood became more accurate, reliable and trustworthy. It is nonetheless legitimate to throw light on the social forms of observation[26] that came into being as part of the Enlightenment imperative; these forms took place within a long-term process that put childhood at the forefront of public authorities' concerns, thus putting an end to the long public silence relating to children.

The practice of the observation of children became well-established throughout the nineteenth century, the scientific and lay forms intermingling with one another to a certain extent. This section will look at the two forms of child observation, highlighting both their specific and shared traits, observation being: 'a process that defines structures of proper development and constructs social forms of caregiving' (Varga 1991: 71). This investigation will start with families', chiefly mothers', pragmatic watching of the child before moving on to a more systematic form of observation carried out in the second half of the century by such figures as Darwin, Preyer and Binet, whose scientific aura did not prevent them from empirical domestic observation.

The rise of child observation took place in the context of high infant-mortality rates and growing public awareness: physicians were tireless in their efforts to overcome it while being prolific in their advice to families. The infant's physical wellbeing was the centre piece of these efforts: maternal duties could not tolerate any compromise. Hygienists and physicians, as well as moralists, thought the education of the mother was essential to the young child.[27] Essential, but not always sufficient, some would estimate. A genuine mother should always be present for her infant, for the education of a toddler requires meticulous observation, respectful of scientific recommendations. Accordingly, parents of the educated classes are told with a certain insistence to keep records 'made on the progress of their children in a book kept for that purpose' (Steedman 1995: 68).[28] Although this method was already advocated by such thinkers as Fénélon, Locke, Buffon, Condillac and,

---

[26] Talking of the generalization of child observation far beyond the scope of this practice, Kincaid says that, in the twentieth century, 'parenthood has become largely an extended series of "watchings"' (Kincaid 1992). Piano, ballet, tennis, swimming and computer programming lessons are turned into displays of skills, with parents watching either with admiration or critical eyes the child's demonstration.

[27] The explicit proposition underlying these expectations is twofold: do not entrust your infant to an incompetent nurse; do not listen to incompetent advices from friends, neighbours, family or kin.

[28] Christian Augustus Struve, *A Familiar View of the Domestic Education of Children* (Steedman 1995: 68).

above all, Rousseau, the observation and book-keeping method were gradually set up at the beginning of the nineteenth century by writers, moralists, pedagogues and several child supporters.

Various lay persons as well as pedagogues and physicians asserted action in the same direction. Buffon, for one, had a friend, the Comte de Montbeillard, who took measurements of his son's height at various ages; although it is unclear why Montbeillard carried on these measurements, Buffon published the findings without any commentary (Tanner 1981: 102). The observations by the German Dietrich Tiedemann of his son's birth up to two-and-a-half years of age were published in 1787;[29] it is to some extent considered to be the first scientific study of children's conduct through the observation of their sensory and mental capacities. He did not pretend to any generalization, but wished that others would make known their results so comparison might become possible. Profoundly influenced by Rousseau, Johann Heinrich Pestalozzi, a pedagogue of the end of the eighteenth century, made interesting experiments in teaching young children from a principle stipulating that education should be moulded to natural growth; he suggested that education should follow the natural growth of a child's capacities (Chudacoff 1989: 31). He is nonetheless most remembered for the diary he wrote in 1774 based on his observations of his three-and-a-half year old son, teaching him drawing and languages (Latin and German).

An unstinting advocate of child observation and recording, Mrs Adrienne Necker de Saussure, a Swiss pedagogue whose prominent book, *L'éducation progressive ou étude du cours de la vie*,[30] contains abundant indications of the methodical investigation of childhood she upheld, is considered the leading figure in the area. She urges mothers to record systematically, in a manual outlining a substantial framework of observation, what they notice in their child's daily life.[31] 'I keenly exhort young mothers to keep an exact record of

---

[29] They were not translated (first into French, then English) until the mid-nineteenth century. The English version is available as 'Tiedemann's Observations on the Development of the Mental Faculties of Children' (trans. C. Murchison and S. Langer), *Journal of Genetic Psychology*, 34, 1927: 205–230.

[30] The first volume was published by Garnier in Paris in 1828, and the second in 1838.

[31] The following three quotations are in my translation.

their children's development in a specific book ... in chronological order, the magnitude of a child ... Ideas, knowledge, emotions, language, everything that is an acquisition and develops in the aftermath' (Necker de Saussure 1828: 86–87).

Mrs Necker de Saussure was herself a fine and acute observer of children's lives. She was already sixty-three years of age when she wrote her first volume, published in 1828; drawing on her own memories, she also relied on a network of much younger friends whose information and observations constituted a primary source for her own writing.[32] Duchess Albertine de Broglie, herself the mother of two girls of seven and six years of age and a boy of three years of age, wrote in November 1824, to her friend, Baroness Sophie Anisson-Duperron, a young mother of two children, a boy of eight and a girl of two years of age, asking her 'to gather together all the observations in relation to your children, to write about their small progress and everything you notice. Write a diary' (De Staël 1896: 123–125).[33]

She goes on concerning Mrs de Necker's project to write on children's education and her need to access information from mothers with young children; both women will become precious assistants to Mrs de Necker. What was Mrs de Necker's particular mode of observation beyond the watchword and the general frame that she suggested? She first introduces different periods in the child's life:

- the first two years;
- the period from three to five years of age;
- the period from five to seven years of age.

Within this taxonomy, she goes on to habits at two years of age, to the activities and the imagination at three years of age, and to consciousness at four years of age. The turning point between the second and the third year witnesses a remarkable development: the child becomes more decisive, its imagination becomes much more salient,

---

[32] This development of private child observation owes much to the work of Jean-Noël Luc. It draws also upon Carolyn Steedman's as well as Egle Becchi's books. The translation of the quotations is mine.

[33] Albertine de Staël, Duchess of Broglie, *Lettres*, published by her son the Duke of Broglie, Paris, Calman-Lévy, 1896, p. 338. These two ladies belong to the nobility of the Ancien Régime; this observation is congruent with Aries argument that the 'sentiment de l'enfance' first appeared among the higher classes before circulating among the popular classes.

its intelligence develops in relation with the progress of its language: 'to witness the child's intelligence slowly come out ... it ... expands every time it discovers a new phenomenon ... the need to enter the world of words ... that will soon supply instruments to his thought' (Necker de Saussure 1828: 137).

Mrs de Necker's book was translated in 1835.[34] Elizabeth Gaskell was much influenced by this book after her first child, Marianne, was born. Concerned with Marianne's moral, intellectual and religious progress, she devoted a great part of her diary to observing her child's behaviour in accordance with Mrs de Necker's guidelines and Combe's *Principles of Physiology* (1834) alike. She acknowledged that, at nine months of age, Marianne's change of temper was related in one way or another to a corresponding change in her body. This allowed her to look at Marianne's progress in terms of faculties in development: her capacities of intelligence, will and memory expanded in time which means that they blossomed alongside the body's growth.

The practice of child observation was slowly becoming established in its monographic form; the reading of signs in children seems to develop with time, being taught to physicians in training and to parents. Physical health was then the primary target and mothers were urged to train their skills in decoding the child's gestures in both health and sickness in the strict sense of the word:[35] every change of manner, gesture, mood, temper and smile is noted and considered as a sign to be unravelled. Physicians by then emphasized 'the necessity of observation and attention to the smallest and most trivial symptom' (Popham, quoted in Steedman 1995: 69).

The second half of the nineteenth century saw an important diversification in child observation as it became more systematically organized, especially in Great Britain, through distinct societies meant for children's observation in London, Cheltenham, Manchester, Derby, Newcastle and Edinburgh. The prime mover of these societies, Miss Louch, influenced by American psychologist Stanley Hall,

---

[34] Necker de Saussure, *Progressive Education; or, Considerations on the Course of Life*, London, Longmans, 1835.

[35] Two references: the 1831 anonymous *Letters to a Mother on the Watchful Care of Her Infant*, London, Seely and Burnside, 1831; J.-B. Fonssagrives, *Livret maternel pour prendre des notes sur la santé des enfants*, Paris, Hachette, 1869.

published the societies' journal, *The Paidologist*, whose aims were clearly stated: helping parents with observations of the periods and aspects of childhood and providing teachers with some guiding principles in relations to the perplexing variety of activities confronting them (Caws 1949).

These concerns rapidly found their way in childcare manuals. In Britain, prior to the 1870s the quasi totality of childcare's manuals for mothers were written by physicians; but from the 1870s on matrons started to write more systematically about childcare, albeit in a different genre, that of domestic advice literature, which has to be distinguished from medical studies. The matrons drew on their own experience as well as on scientific or medical findings. Gurjeva identifies two distinguishing features among the two genres: first, for matrons science is an external source of authority and, second, they integrated scientific discoveries into the narratives of their own experience (Gurjeva 1998: 49). As a specific genre in itself, childcare literature did not stress particularly any form of observational work in the family for the parents (or mothers) although they tended to conform to medical prescriptions in that matter.

Quite different from the previous domestic child observation by mothers or other lay persons, another form of investigation is identified, set up between the latter and a more systematic form of scientific investigation. Almost all authors classified hereafter are either physicians or scientists, but they perform their observation alongside their official careers and sometimes in a rather unsystematic manner. An untiring curiosity and the zeitgeist of the scientific community appear to be the main spurs behind their recording.

Locke and Rousseau[36] are usually considered the precursors of this form of child observation, neither a professional nor a scientific form in a strict sense. Rousseau, whose influence spread throughout the western world, outlined an innovative image of the child pertaining to a specific nature endowed with an autonomous intellectual activity, even though aloof from reasoning abilities, and subjected to a well-balanced developmental process. He insists on an education first centred on the corporeal instruments of intelligence, thus setting the

---

[36] Jean-Jacques Rousseau, *Emile ou De l'éducation*, in *Œuvres complètes*, edited by G. Gagnebin and M. Raymond, t.IV, Paris, Gallimard, 1969; John Locke, *Some Thoughts Concerning Education*, 1st edn, London, Churchill, 1693.

child in situations favourable to the gradual awakening of its capacities and virtualities (Py 1997: 266–301).

At the turn of the eighteenth century, a most valuable experience took place in southern France: a wild child was first sighted and later captured in the forests of the Aveyron area. The child, later called Victor,[37] was assumed to be around eleven or twelve years of age. Psychiatrists examined him and issued a diagnosis and later on Victor was entrusted to the care of Jean Marc Itard, a physician at the Deaf and Dumb Institute sponsored by the Society of the Observers of Man, who tried in the following years to acculturate him whilst recording his experience. At the time of his capture, he behaved as an animal, showing only physical deprivations (food) but neither intellectual nor affective deficiencies; he was a primitive being, a child of nature whose humanity has been shaped by the sole circumstances of his physical existence. Convinced from the outset that he was not an imbecile,[38] but a child with anti-social habits, a blunted sensibility, a persistent inattention and inflexible organs, Itard began the moral education of Victor. It proved to be a genuine novelty as he was not only a human, wild of nature and untouched by human socialization, but also a child. Itard introduced him to the world of mankind and culture; he tried to make human a wild child completely ignorant of language and cultural traditions as well as of intellectual performances and affective behaviour.

Itard concluded that the education of the child was possible, although not entirely conclusive; he was endowed with the free exercise of all human senses, giving continual evidence of attention, of recollection and memory; he attested his abilities to compare, distinguish, judge, and finally to apply his understanding to goals relative to his training. The scientific community was stunned and a debate arose thereafter on the educability of manhood. Through this experience, a new picture of childhood comes of age: the transition from nature to

---

[37] Victor is one of a long list of abandoned children reared by animals, a most prevalent figure and legend in the popular imagination of our societies. Julia identifies the wild child as one of the three emblematic figures of childhood at the end of the eighteenth century, the two others being the child prodigy with Mozart as its epitome and the child hero that arises during the French Revolution (Julia 1998: 85).

[38] Or an autistic child as some physicians thought he was at that period of time. Cf. Lane, op. cit.

culture, from wild to social life, from 'pathology' to 'normality', as Itard used to say. These progressions above all happened and were observed in a child in the course of its life: his entrance into the world of culture and into society.[39]

To talk about the child becomes again a difficult task. If one refused to take up the approach of eighteenth-century philosophers, the only way left was that of meticulous observation and description.

Within the long history of child observation and recording, many people kept diaries and reported on their own children's development; we have already noticed the domestic practice of child-watching mostly by concerned women and pedagogues. We now turn to people who perform this duty at the same time as their career, looking with curiosity at their children in the nineteenth-century context of evolutionary theory. Philosopher Hippolyte Taine, who was already working on intelligence, observed, between 1873 and 1875, two infants, of which one was his own infant daughter, between twenty-one months and three years of age (Luc 1997). Chiefly concerned with the acquisition of language, a major concern at the time, he consigned his observations to a brief text that was published both in French and English.[40]

The most famous of these child-watching diarists was Charles Darwin himself: he conferred scientific respectability on child observation. First in his own autobiography and, above all, in a short text, *A Biographical Sketch of an Infant*, he gave an account of the observation of his son, William Erasmus, born in 1839.[41] It

---

[39] On the wild child of Aveyron, cf Lucien Malson, *Les enfants sauvages*, Paris, Union Générale d'Editions, 1964; T. Gineste, *Victor de l'Aveyron: Dernier enfant sauvage, premier enfant fou*, Paris, Le Sycomore, 1981; Harlan Lane, *The Wild Boy of Aveyron*, Cambridge, MA, Harvard University Press, 1976; Roger Shattuck, *The Forbidden Experience. The Story of the Wild Boy of Aveyron*, London, Secker and Warburg, 1980; François Truffaut's film, *L'enfant sauvage* (1969), in which he plays Itard, raised much interest in the phenomenon.

[40] Taine's paper, 'Notes sur l'acquisition du langage', was first published in *Revue Philosophique*, 1876, pp. 6–20; then translated shortly after and published as, 'M. Taine on the Acquisition of Language by Children', *Mind*, 2, April 1877: 252–259.

[41] *The Autobiography of Charles Darwin*, London, Collins, 1958; Charles Darwin 'A Biographical Sketch of an Infant', *Mind*, 2:7, July 1877 : 285–294. Darwin's observations of Doddy were published thirty-seven years afterward. Both Taine's and Darwin's papers were published in the same journal, Darwin's text being considered a response to Taine's assumptions and in support of his evolutionary ideas, thus launching a debate (Bradley 1989).

constitutes a phenomenological chronicle which the father begins at the birth of the child and which goes on for almost three years; it might have been the embryo of the natural history of newborn infants that Darwin was planning to write, but never did. This short text relates the first months of a child as observed by his affectionate father; an emotional expression but according to classic parameters: fear, anger, pleasure, timidity, affectivity, idea association, reasoning, the unconscious, moral sense and communication etc. (Becchi 1998).

Darwin brought out the most detailed diary of all: 'My first child was born on December 27th, 1839, and I at once commenced to make notes on the first dawn of the various experiences which he exhibited, for I felt convinced, even at this early period, that the most complex and fine shades of expression must have had a gradual and natural origin' (Darwin 1877: 285). He wrote within both a cultural context, briefly described above, and a family tradition that goes back to his grandfather, Erasmus Darwin. Looking at Doddy, he explores a variety of explanations for early kinds of behaviour and their form of expression (Bradley 1989).[42] Fear, for instance:

When nine weeks and three days old – whilst lying on his back cooing and kicking very happily – I happened to sneeze – which made it start, frown, look frightened and cry rather badly – for an hour afterwards every noise made him start – he was nervous (Bradley 1989: 20).

The first sign of Doddy's ability to reason is recorded as such:

April 20th – aged 114 days – Took my finger to his mouth and as usual could not get it in, on account of his own hand being in the way; then slipped his own back and so got my finger in – this was not chance and therefore a kind of reasoning (Bradley 1989: 20).

The child's reactions to the mirror brought Darwin's attention to the capacity for deduction:

When four and a half months old, he repeatedly smiled at my image and his own in a mirror, and no doubt mistook them for real objects, but he shows sense in being evidently surprised at my voice coming from behind him. Like

---

[42] In his critical introduction to child psychology, Bradley goes back to Darwin, whose labelling as the forefather of this sub-specialty of psychology he questions. Morss develops a similar perspective with respect to Darwin (Morss 1990).

all infants he much enjoyed thus looking at himself, and in less then two months perfectly understood that it was an image; for if I made quite silently an odd grimace, he would suddenly turn round and look at me. The higher apes which I tried with a small looking glass behaved differently (Bradley 1989: 20).

This last assumption indicates Darwin's main interest: his involvement with natural history and evolutionary theory. The basis of the theory of natural selection was already in place by the time of his child's birth in 1839: Doddy played no part in *On the Origins of Species*. But later in his career, Darwin worked to marshal evidence for human evolution that would corroborate his main evolutionary hypothesis. Only then did the observation of his son's development intervene in the fabric of his thinking.[43]

The original ideas concerning childhood burgeoned in the specific context of the nineteenth century, characterized by the progress of science; new theoretical hypotheses on the nature of the world; the generalization of universal education and, in some cases, compulsory schools; the new attention to the infant and the gradual decline of infant mortality (Wong 1993). Everything converged toward the child and its new position: the place of the human being observed, defined and constructed (Becchi and Julia 1998: 153). This happened within the great Weltanschauung of evolutionism: the child becomes the hub of scientific conceptions that take it as an object of investigation. 'The child thus stands at the threshold of the boundaries between different fields of knowledge' (Bourne-Taylor 1998: 91–92); namely as a collection of heterogeneous orderings.

The second half of the nineteenth century saw many scientists intrigued with explicit parallels between child and animal, child and primitive human beings such as aboriginal people, or the beginning of human history and child development within evolutionary theory. A child's development was believed to divulge the secluded arcana of the species (Clarke-Steward *et al.* 1985). Evolutionists of the nineteenth century came to see the child as the missing link between

---

[43] 'Darwin's deliberations about babies draw on two theories of mental dynamics. The first is epitomized by the idea that infants are born with innate mental faculties or 'instincts'. The second assumes that mental characteristics are habits built upon association between events and reactions which have occurred together in the past' (Bradley 1989). The difference between Darwin's work and, for instance, Mme de Necker's preoccupations is vast.

nature and culture;[44] the development of the child leading to the path of the evolution of the human species became commonplace in logic and reasoning. The logic worked in both directions: just as child development proved to be a keystone to constructing a genetic argument for human evolution, so evolution operated to illustrate and decode child development.

Young children's development was an example of the gradual evolution of human faculties in Darwin's theory (Morss 1990). Darwin was a biologist whose interest in child observation illustrates persuasively the idea that human beings are products of evolution. In trying to bridge the gap between human species and animals in relation to intellectual abilities such as speech, intelligence and reason, Darwin focused on infants because their behaviour is seemingly uncluttered by culture and learning. In this respect, there was no absolute gap between humans and animals: the infant's development provided a link. 'Darwin ... made connections between evolutionary progress and the development of the faculties in young children' (Steedman 1995: 83). It is nonetheless crucial to understand that Darwinian evolution opened the way to such a concept as development and the relevance of this concept to the knowledge of the transition from infancy to adulthood (Stainton Rogers 1998: 193). 'The Darwinian legacy to childhood studies was to root them in biology' (Prout 2005: 57). Prout adds that much of developmental psychology is rooted in this approach.

By the beginning of the 1880s, the emergent child psychology is already upheld as one of the most promising branches of psychology. In 1882 a text was published that turned into a benchmark in the history of the nascent scientific child development: W. Preyer's *The Mind of the Child*: 'I proposed to myself a number of years ago the task of studying the child' (Elder *et al.* 1993: 192). Scientific alertness to children's mental development was on the rise. Preyer's material and data come from observing his own child three times a day in all his behaviour, describing systematically month after month the state of his intellectual dispositions from birth to three years of age. These fatherly observations are complemented by the

---

[44] Marivaux's play *La Dispute* can be considered, in literature, as an anticipation of this argument. I owe this point to a remark made by Nigel Gearing.

examination of other children so as to be in line with the multiple-case rule prevalent in the new scientific domain.

From the first days after his birth, Preyer studied his son's sensory development, his will, his intelligence and his language. He tried to identify and seize the various stages of intellectual and emotional maturation. 'I witnessed some examples of attention, memory and intelligence during the third year, where one would not suspect these to exist' (Luc 1997: 94).[45] From all accounts, Preyer's approach to child development germinated under the intellectual authority of evolutionary theory, provided the latter is accepted as a non-monolithic paradigm underscored with conflicting tensions. Although Preyer is still in the realm of domestic child observation, the specific requirements of scientific psychology were such that he had to widen his observations to other children so as to legitimize his work in the eyes of the scientific community.

Like so many scientist of the turn of the twentieth century, French psychologist Alfred Binet, whose name is automatically associated with intelligence testing, observed his own children, Marguerite and Armande, and reported his experiments in *L'étude expérimentale de l'intelligence* (Binet 1903). He first studied his two daughters at the early stages of motor development (Wolf 1973: 118–135). At the ages of eleven and ten-and-a-half, they were tested rather systematically to contrast their cognitive development in a series of tests, some of which were already available for schools.

1. Writing 20 words, unobtrusively timed.
2. Verbal explanation of the associations, images, etc. involved.
3. Writing 20 sentences, also timed.
4. Completing sentences, also timed.
5. Developing a theme, also timed.
6. Writing lists of 10 memories freely chosen, also timed.
7. Describing a presented object: a cigarette or a picture.
8. Describing an event, e.g. a train journey during which Binet was in a position to note selectivity in response.
9. Crossing out letters, also timed.
10. Immediate memory for digits.
11. Copying words and lines.

---

[45] Quoted from the French edition of 1887: my translation. The English translation of the German book came out in 1890.

12. Copying designs shown for a short interval.
13. Reaction time.
14. Memory for verses.
15. Memory for words.
16. Memory for objects.
17. Memory for a read prose passage.
18. Memory for designs.
19. Reproduction of lines of specified lengths with eyes closed.
20. Perception of intervals of time.

                                                        (Reeves 1965: 233)

Later on, Binet put forward the data for broad analysis and discussion. Although Binet's observations of his two daughters was strictly speaking domestic, he can be considered as a symbolic example of someone who bestrides domestic and scientific observations, the former providing insights and the latter data.

Domestic child observation and recording, which prevailed throughout the nineteenth century, did not end with the emergence of scientific child psychology. One has only to recall Piaget's observation of Jacqueline, his own daughter in the 1920s, to note that this form of experience was carried on well into the twentieth century. As a method of child investigation, domestic observation has never completely fallen out of favour. Nonetheless, the emergence of scientific child psychology considerably modified the rules and the practice of observation; the diary records were discarded as an inadequate form of data collection. Preyer is considered as a reference-point in this respect, for he was the first psychologist, labelled as scientific, whose work was at least partially based on domestic child-watching. From this perspective, Preyer is appraised as a denial of Anderson's remark: 'The few persons who kept records of children were scientists who used their own children as subjects. Usually they were satisfied with the production of a baby biography' (Anderson 1956: 182).

From the philosophers of the eighteenth century – Rousseau etc. – to Itard's experience with the wild child of Aveyron, to Mrs de Necker and the different pedagogues' observations, to Darwin, Preyer and finally Binet, we have surveyed the various forms of domestic child scrutiny and some aspects of their intermingling with scientific and theoretical debates of that period. Domestic observation became more and more systematic towards the end; the statistical and probability technologies were remote. The next section will look at scientific forms of child observation and recording in an attempt to specify the main differences from the previous domestic forms.

2.4 The scientific forms of child observation

At the turn of the twentieth century, the practice of child observation reached a turning point as the investigation of childhood became systematic and generalized. It stamped the experience of child-watching and, above all, of child recording in a specific form which we shall take up again with the question of graphs and charts. This major transformation took place within a specific social and scientific context whose main features revolved around a growing public concern in relation to childhood: on the one hand, the progressive control of child labour, compulsory schooling, the various aspects of delinquency, the child's health and welfare concerns etc.; on the other hand, while the knowledge of childhood undoubtedly grew, questions remained with regard to the reliability and the trustworthiness of this – a theoretical controversy raised by evolutionary theory as well as empirical uncertainty concerning both recording methods and samples of the observation practice.

Historically, domestic observation is the informal form of the empirical study of children.[46] Those who devoted themselves to it worked without strict guidelines; they were simply mindful of the various manifestations of the child's growth and development. They studied children in their daily life in a family setting, or while travelling, even in their own childhood memories. Starting with Preyer, the investigation turned more systematic in its methods and its processes, while being institutionalized with the notable development of hospital registers. Scientists leaned towards a more sophisticated type of instrumentation to measure children's development; among many others, we shall look at the work of Sully, Hall, then Gesell; thereafter Holt and paediatrics. 'They (children) also found themselves being examined under the influence of "science", whose main institutional forum was the Child-Study movement' (Hendrick 1990: 47).

---

[46] 'The textual codification of a medicine of childhood (paediatrics), at least for English-speaking writers, is usually traced back to Thomas Phaire's *The Boke of Chyldren* (1554; quoted from Tomalin 1981)' (Stainton Rogers and Stainton Rogers 1992). On the other hand, Morel lists a series of influential eighteenth-century medical textbooks pertaining to childhood (Morel 1989).

The more prominently the young child stands as an important object of scientific investigation, the more he appears to be the bearer of the elementary forms of social and psychological life. In other words, the child is located in the same position as the savage and the insane; from a scientific point of view, he therefore carries out the basic forms of social life that needed, as a preliminary step, to be understood so as to explain the more elaborate and contemporary forms.[47] 'The modern psychologist, sharing in the spirit of positive science, feels he must begin at the beginning, study mind in its simplest forms before attempting to explain its more complex and intricate manifestations.' (Sully 1881: 544).

'Mental science', which later gave birth to well-defined forms of developmental theories, was a newly established discipline in the nineteenth century both as an additional field of theoretical knowledge and as a meaningful offshoot of medicine. It examined some central questions such as cognition, memory, will and self-knowledge from a materialist perspective based on empirical research in physiology, instead of the abstract scope of metaphysics. At the end of the century, it manifested itself socially in the child-study movement on both sides of the Atlantic: the Childhood Society, the Child Study Association, the Child Study Society etc. G. Stanley Hall initiated the child-study movement (1880s–1914) out of a burgeoning interest in the population of children; it was designed to provide as complete a description as possible of the child from birth to adolescence, thus inspiring numerous studies of child development. Child study happened at a meeting place of science and society, at the crossroad of two major trends: the condition and the quality of the child as a whole (health, welfare etc.) and the individual child with an interest in the details of its development (Wooldridge 1995: 11). Sully introduced these questions from the vantage point of the forms of child observation.

Professor of Philosophy and Psychology at London University – the Grote Chair of Mind and Logic – as well as being the most influential figure of the British Child Study Association, James Sully was instrumental in establishing developmental child psychology,

---

[47] This is the pattern of knowledge, common at that period, followed by Durkheim in his classic, *The Elementary Forms of Religious Life*: the elementary forms were the simplest, leading to more complex forms. Within and outside evolutionary theory, this pattern of knowledge was general.

particularly because he was critical of psychology's tendency to place human and animal development on a direct continuum: from his perspective, animal growth was not relevant in researching infant development. He nonetheless advocated that psychology must proceed by dividing the complex phenomena into simple factors, e.g. from the complex mind of the adult to the simple mind of the child, and therefore of the 'savage', which is a standard evolutionary position Darwin himself (who was interested in the natural history of babies) could have held (Morss 1990: 22). 'The emphasis in nearly all of the works cited here is on the Darwinian question of human development rather than on statistical analyses' (Wong 1993: 106). Sully turned out to be a highly visible advocate of mental evolution in the UK: understanding the human mind amounts to mapping its functioning at lower stages (the child and the savage alike) as well as fathoming its development.

Both of Sully's books – *Babies and Science* (1881) and *Studies of Childhood* (1895) – are characterized by recapitulationary logic. He puts forward the idea that childhood is at the same time the origin and the point of culmination of the adult self: the child retrieves the possibility of revealing the adult's past within the framework of developmental theory.[48] It is properly known that in developmental psychology and in psychoanalysis the path to the adult's past is a crucial issue. Sully advocated a uniform order of development of faculties, developmental change being labelled by progress i.e. from simple to complex, from vague to distinct knowledge (Morss 1990: 22). Within the child-study movement, a group of parents and teachers interested in child development, he advocated the systematic study of child development while emphasizing the scientific basis for child-rearing and education (Valentine 1999a).

Sully's method departs from previous ones although he did make some domestic observations of his own children, Edith and Clifford; his was ethnographic in exploring the child's symbolic world, drawing inspiration from cultural anthropology. 'Sully was primarily interested in genetic psychology (i.e. developmental psychology in a broad sense);

---

[48] Freud's unconscious was not very far from Sully's position. 'Cited by Freud and standing, in a sense, on the threshold of psychoanalysis, Sully's work highlights the connections and tensions between mid-nineteenth-century theories of the unconscious and the concept of childhood and evolution' (Bourne-Taylor 1998).

his preferred methodology was the holistic study of individual children, based on naturalistic observation in every situation' (Valentine 1999b: 11). It is therefore a composite site: a mixture of parents' and teachers' diaries, literary and autobiographical recollections of childhood (George Sand, Goethe, Stevenson etc.), children's drawings, question-naires, extensive personal observation etc. Sully was well aware of the need for mass evidence both because evolutionary biology relied on a large number of cases and because statistical technologies required huge standardized observations to avoid the discrepancies of indi-vidualities and to identify the stages of normal development. Taking an active part in the child-study movement, he made contact with potential observers of children who would then forward their data to his laboratory (Gurjeva 1998: 211). The teachers helped him gain a better access to children since parents' cooperation was needed for observations in domestic settings.[49] He promoted the idea of having 'mothers and aunts busily engaged in noting and recording the movements of children's minds' (Wooldridge 1995: 39).

Sully can be regarded as a go-between for child-study activists and scientific psychologists. He was in a position to exert considerable influence over the course of developmental theory in both research and domestic contexts. Though he held a professorship in psychology, Sully remained very critical of Baldwin or Münsterberg's methods of observation and experimental psychology because they attempted to simulate laboratory conditions with all the drawbacks one can imagine; thus he remained marginal to scientific psychology (Bourne-Taylor 1998: 101). Sully's method is a mid-way point between domestic and extensive scientific observation. 'James Sully symbolises the link between amateur Child Study and professional psychology' (Wooldridge 1995: 47).

G. Stanley Hall is usually considered the first major scholar to address childhood as a genuine object of academic research rather

---

[49] Parents' and teachers' cooperation was deemed essential for any reliable observations of children. Sully published an appeal in *Mind*, 1893: 'Professor Sully will be greatly obliged if parents or teachers of young children can supply him with facts bearing on the characteristics of the childish mind. What he especially desires is first-hand observations carried out on children' (Valentine 1999b: 4). 'Karl Pearson appealed to teachers and parents through the *Educational Times* in January 1901 for "aid in the measurement of children"' (Gurjeva 1998).

than domestic observation. He was by far the most active and prominent element, the bellwether of the movement who wanted to bring observation, reflectivity and rationality to bear upon childcare and child-rearing; he nurtured the scientific study of children. He emphasized the importance of gathering scientific data about large numbers of children: primary schools and institutions in charge of toddlers provided the critical mass of children to scrutinize for extensive research.[50] Child study was the great leap forward to the topic of childhood investigation in the legitimation of a scientific perspective which bolstered the medical and psychological model. Hall's lasting research involvement rested upon his two basic convictions: that manhood should be investigated scientifically, and that education should be based on the needs of the child.

Hall's construction of children was in part a refinement of the conceptualization of Rousseau's noble savage completed with Darwin's notion of the survival of the fittest and an organismic concept of growth (Richardson 1989). Hall worked within the framework of diverse stages[51] in the normal development of childhood and adolescence, as a reflection of natural processes in the recapitulation theory of the history of the human species.[52] He asserted that children underwent distinct

[50] One can think of British infant schools, France's *salles d'asile*, Aporti's toddler schools in Italy and Froebel's kindergartens in Germany. 'One development, above all others, turned children into attractive research-subjects, namely the opportunities afforded to investigators by mass schooling' (Hendrick 1990).

[51] Already acknowledged, at least in scientific circles and amongst the educated public, the very framework at the base of developmental theory is that childhood can be segmented and distributed in different categories that are as many as stages of development. This idea goes back as far as Rousseau's view of childhood as a series of discrete mental and physical stages culminating in adolescence and is linked to recapitulation theory that made the notion of stages more persuasive and less speculative (Lomax *et al.* 1978).

[52] From the evolutionary model to the post-Darwinian theories, the grander scheme of thought was the recapitulation theory, which stated 'that a higher organism, such as a child, passed through developmental stages that were apparently identical with those of lower forms – such as fish, reptiles, and primates – from which human beings had evolved' (Lomax *et al.* 1978). 'The theory drew on two intellectual sources ... The sociological theory insisted on the parallel between the psychology of the child and the psychology of primitive man ... The biological theory maintained that ontogeny recapitulates phylogeny – that the embryological development of the members of any species repeats the evolution of the genus to which the species belongs, with the human embryo passing through all the stages from fertilised egg to primate' (Wooldridge 1995).

stages of mental and emotional development. Broadly speaking the question at stake concerns the relationship between an individual and social institutions. 'Hall made essentially a sociobiological theory of child development out of this idea. Biological maturation brings about successive "nascent stages" of children's thoughts, feelings, and will. With each stage, the form of governance that the child can accept and participate in changes' (Elder *et al.* 1993: 215).

In *The Contents of Children's Minds*,[53] his first child study paper, Hall researched 200 schoolchildren from Boston, two-thirds of whom were aged between two and four. Nothing was to be excluded from the study: thought, emotions and behaviour were to be charted and listed by drafting. This seems to reflect his concern with the emotional basis of good schooling in the 1880s. The pedagogical seminary (1891–1894) reflected Hall's concern with scientific pedagogy. He dealt mostly with child development and education during the kindergarten and elementary school years. Even though child study was seen as research by and for teachers, he was uncertain about the exact way in which child-study research might have a utility for educational practice by providing guiding principles. He also offered advice to parents; 'train early', 'touch the child', 'the mother must stay calm and tranquil' etc.

He was the first American psychologist to study explicitly the development of the child scientifically based on psychological, socio-logical and anthropometric methods:[54] mass questionnaires – 194 different surveys between 1894 and 1915 – and personal observation, albeit from a very elementary methodological basis – data gathering from teachers 'providing memories of their own childhoods, and their observations of children in their classrooms' (Varga 1997: 40). He carried on what was considered extensive research at that period of time, gathering an enormous amount of empirical data on American children: 'on their sense of humour, their appetites, their collections, their reactions to light and darkness, their fears, dreams, feelings of anger, envy and jealousy, their dolls and toys, and their moral and religious experiences' (Wooldridge 1995: 28).

---

[53] Published in 1883 in the *Princeton Review*.
[54] For further details concerning Hall and the child-study movement, see: (Ross 1972; White 1990: 131–150); for a list of the surveys, see: (Lomax *et al.* 1978: 221–236).

Critics were prompt to react to the methodological expedients. In their view, Hall's work fails to be convincing because the sum of its technical elements does not lend persuasiveness to its request for the generalization concerning child development. Questions were raised concerning the representativeness of the sample, for instance. Baldwin's critique was devastating: 'They lack the first requisites of exact method'.[55] As normative data results from the questionnaire method appeared of little value, by the 1900s the method had come into disrepute: the samples were unknown, the conditions of data collections were not standardized. Hall had trouble deciding on an exact scientific method for child study: 'His unwillingness to set rigid criteria and firm definitions for the behaviour that he wanted his unpaid assistants to code led the surveys to degenerate into accumulations of ambiguous, anecdotal information that was essentially uninterpretable' (Lomax *et al.* 1978: 33).[56]

Was Hall unable to achieve his purpose of designing a genetic schedule of development because of the nature of its method, its qualitative orientation, its inability to deal with a large amount of collected data, its unsystematic observation and recording procedures; in short, because its data could not be quantified? The rise of modern psychology was based on scientific experimentation and the idea of service to community: families and parents. Once the physician no longer held the infant's survival in his hands due to sharp decrease in infant mortality rate, parents started reacting against the rigours of aseptic medical rationalism: the doors were thus open to developmental psychology. The demand for scientific knowledge was growing rapidly, despite the fact that very few tools were available for measurement. Scientists saw in the child-study movement a legitimate domain for the search for rationality, measurement and lawfulness in human behaviour: to count and measure; to find pattern and law in

[55] J. M. Baldwin, 'Child Study', *Psychological Review*, Vol. 5, 1888: 218–220. Positivist criticism was harsh: 'Most of the so-called child psychology is partly history, partly economics and ethics, partly physiology, partly nothing at all, but decidedly not psychology' (Hugo Münsterberg, 'Psychology and Education', *Educational Review*, 16, 1898, 114).

[56] Is it paradoxical that the present-day appraisal of Hall's work is much less critical than his own colleagues in the scientific community at the turn of the twentieth century? 'Hall's framework is an interesting and plausible basis for thinking about children's social development. The recapitulationism to which Hall subscribed is incidental – consistent with his framework' (Elder *et al.* 1993).

HOME WEIGHING RECORD

	19	19	19	19	19	19
January	lbs.	lbs	lbs.	lbs.	lbs.	lbs.
April	lbs.	lbs.	lbs	lbs.	lbs.	lbs.
July	lbs.	lbs.	lbs.	lbs.	lbs.	lbs.
October	lbs.	lbs.	lbs.	. lbs.	lbs.	lbs.

NOTES

Form 1: Home weighing record
Source: Veeder 1926

nature as well as in society. In this context, Hall's work was rapidly dismissed as unscientific under the devastating impact of his peers' criticisms. In the long history of child observation, he nevertheless occupies the unique place of being the first scholar to initiate extensive research into childhood.

The potential for measurement, quantitativeness and lawfulness was carried on by some of Hall's former students: Barnes, Thorndike, Cattell, Terman, Goddard, but above all, by Arnold Gesell who held degrees in both child psychology and medicine, enabling him to support his view with both clinical and experimental documentation.[57] The first US-employed school psychologist, he later set up, in 1911, the Yale-Psycho clinic – later to become the Yale Clinic of Child Development – funded by the Laura Spelman Rockefeller Foundation with a general mandate to investigate the child's mental development and to circulate such findings through parent-education activities (Richardson 1989).

The broader context – namely, a growing demand for objective (quantitative) procedures of systematic observation and recording of children's behaviour (Form 1) – sheds light on Gesell's unique contribution to child observation: 'he raised the observational study of children to a degree of sophistication undreamed of at the turn of the twentieth century' (Lomax *et al.* 1978: 37). Gesell pioneered innovative observation methods and recording procedures as well; at

[57] Gesell is a graduate in psychology (1906) from Clark University where Hall taught and he held a medical degree from Yale (1915); he wanted to become a physician because he wished to make a 'thoroughgoing study of the developmental stages of childhood' but 'lacked a realistic familiarity with the physical basis and the physiological processes of life and growth' (Gesell 1952: 128). The section on Gesell's methods owes much to the work of Donna Varga.

the Yale clinic, his extensive child-watching with formal procedures put him in the forefront of the field of childhood in the 1920s, when he issued the first timetables of normative chronological schedules of development for children from birth to age five (Ames 1989). The sequential phases of development rested, from his perspective, on the child's genetic apparatus: biological maturation, rather than experience, was the determining factor.

His conception of normal child development is made up of a movement from one stage to another within a stipulated period of time.

- He characterized children's development as a series of distinctive but accumulative stages;
- Normal development calls for the completion of an explicit stage before the next stage can occur;
- A prevalent stage of development is the sign of the effective completion and retention of past stages.

(Varga 1997: 41)

Although Gesell's main contribution to childhood research was not only in developmental theory – it should be bore in mind that the idea of sequential development as a framework for understanding children's path to adulthood and maturity goes back to the eighteenth century and Rousseau (Lomax *et al.* 1978) – the proposition of a schedule of development, far from being discredited or abandoned in the aftermath, was always taken up again by each succeeding generation of child observers and given a new impetus towards what can be considered not its definitive form, but one of its most refined and accurate ones: Gesell's timetables of normative chronological development in children's emotional, physical, mental and social capacities. These schedules were based on the premise 'that behavior develops in a patterned, more or less predictable manner' (Ames 1989: 152).

Furthermore, the clinic proposed that, beside physical and mental developmental schedules, children should mature socially through observable 'normal patterns' (Low 1998: 19); accordingly, the schedules always had a social behaviour component, alongside motor, language and adaptive components.[58] Gesell's tireless efforts also

---

[58] Developmental theory always had a specific, although marginal and varying, feature concerning social behaviour. It goes back to the common belief that, if science prevented disease, it could accordingly prevent psychological as well as social disorder.

brought him from the schedules for observing children to the implementation of a developmental diagnosis and supervision method: a
method of care to optimize development; he also brought into focus the
developmental quotient – relation between chronological age and the
child's general development, physical and mental – and launched
the Developmental Record Form.

What were Gesell's innovative approaches in child observation and
recording? In what sense did he depart from Hall and became more
scientific in a positivistic rationalist perspective?[59]

- First, Gesell worked within laboratory conditions, thus departing
  from the usual direct child study in everyday settings or household;
  it provided the psychologist with a better control of the whole
  observational process. This is the language of experimental science:
  the Yale clinic was intended to be a laboratory setting.
- Second, the observations of children were systematized and the
  recording protocols standardized. As long as laboratory conditions
  were used optimally, they provided the best suitable arrangements
  for objective observation: a similarity of environments for consecutive observations, the cautious management of the various influences
  impinging upon the child's behaviour etc.
- Third, the fact that the child was unaware of being observed was
  considered a necessary aspect of a scientific methodology, so as to
  preserve the naturalness of its behaviour. Otherwise, the child's
  awareness of an observer's work was reputed to have two weak
  outcomes: inhibiting the child's reactions and stimulating undesirable behaviour.

At the Yale clinic, the observation laboratory consisted in its
elementary form of rooms filled with play equipment for the children's
use; more elaborate settings would include provision of specialized
non-play devices. A variety of observational laboratories were set up;
a guidance nursery, the examination or clinical crib, the observation

---

[59] Gesell once said in a National Film Board of Canada documentary: 'The mind
manifests itself in patterns of behavior, which take on characteristic shapes
throughout infancy and childhood. We have identified the behavior patterns
which may be used as standards of reference in the clinical diagnosis of child
development. When you observe the work of this clinic, you will see how these
diagnostic standards are applied' (Low 1998: 19).

compartment whose purpose – naturalistic observation – consists in freer body adaptation of a child unaffected by a conventional test situation; the observer would note body (hands, eyes etc.) adaptations (Gesell 1929: 47).

The inevitable condition for having as objective as possible an observation was that the observer's presence be almost invisible. The observation alcove was a space sub-divided from the child's area and set up so that the child, while being in complete and continuous sight of the observer, could not behold the latter: the use of a viewing room equipped with a one-way window. From their position on the other side of the one-way window large enough to provide an unobstructed view, the psychologists were thoroughly able to watch the child in all the areas of the laboratory while preserving the child's unawareness of being observed: a unidirectional way to proceed. The technology and their recording were adapted to the maturational pattern in which growth is a process that cannot be observed at once. 'To some extent, then, the methodology of the observation of growth depends upon adjusting the durational interspaces between cross-sectional surveys of behavior levels in such a way as to yield a picture of the course of development' (Gesell 1929: 25).

Standardized complex record-keeping forms were used by Gesell's team, quite different indeed from the narrative diaries. The main difference is surely that the diary is a daily consecutive narrative, while the record-keeping forms segregate the various kinds of behaviour one from the other: a particular behaviour observed at one point can be dissociated from the following one and combined with another noticed later or earlier for the purpose of manipulating and comparing children's behaviour. The second crucial difference is that the textual inscription of the child's behaviour renders development visible: it could then literally be seen.[60] Accordingly, the child's different kinds of behaviour are analysed as independent units, then combined and pooled together to constitute generalized norms for developmental schedules. A mobilization of actors connected and supported the trajectory from record-keeping to sequential

[60] Both observation and record-keeping could then be considered as a technology designed to monitor child development. Record-keeping in particular was set up in a standardized format with characteristics to be observed and a space for recording (Varga 1991).

development. Gesell's abridged developmental schedules are indicative in this respect.

The first five years in the cycle of development are the most fundamental and the most formative:

- In the *first quarter* of the *first year*, the infant, having weathered the hazards of the neonatal period, gains control of his twelve oculomotor muscles.
- In the *fourth quarter* (40–52 weeks) he extends command to his legs and feet; to his forefingers and thumbs. He pokes and plucks.
- By the end of the *second year* he walks and runs; articulates words and phrases; acquires bowel and bladder control; attains a rudimentary sense of personal identity and of personal possession.
- At *four years* he asks innumerable questions, perceives analogies, displays an active tendency to conceptualize and generalize. He is nearly self-dependent in routines of home life.
- At *five* he is well matured in motor control. He hops and skips. He talks without infantile articulation. He can narrate a long tale. He prefers associative play. He feels socialized pride in clothes and accomplishment. He is a self-assured, conforming citizen in his small world.

(Gesell and Ilg 1949: 62)

Gesell was innovative in utilizing photographs and the motion-picture camera as an additional means of recording children's behaviour. In 1919, he initiated a systematic longitudinal study of several hundred healthy and normal children from birth to age six. This series of experiments resulted in the publication in 1925 of his first major book on child development: *The Mental Growth of the Pre-School Child*, which featured the first schedules of sequential development (Beekman 1977: 154; Halpern 1988: 89). He went on in 1927 with a new and more detailed study, using the motion picture camera as an innovative mean of recording behaviour (Lomax *et al.* 1978: 37). He considered the camera superior to direct observation: 'The "objectivity" of the camera, and the record's unchanging nature over time made them superior to the human eye and memory' (Varga 1991: 78).

In his account of developmental progress, *An Atlas of Infant Behavior* (1934), Gesell published more than 3,000 photographs, arranged in sequences, of children engaged in various activities – feeding, mastering mobility, postures, social interactions etc. – that were asserted to depict the visualization of genetic developmental

patterns. 'One excerpt from it will give an example of its character ...
A triumphant moment, the first steps, beautifully, simply and
dramatically recorded' (Beekman 1977: 158).

Photographs provided still pictures; successive still, different angles
of the same behaviour. Motion pictures provided the possibility of
dissecting a behaviour over and over again in increasing detail:
behaviour can be segmented in minuscule duration and the motion
picture can be stopped, reversed, slowed down, moved forward at
various speeds etc. The photographic images are then coded onto data
sheets that are later analysed. This proved to be extraordinarily productive as the individual child can be measured, compared etc. on a
very small and accurate scale in its developmental progress. Gesell's
entire work consisted of delineating specific behaviour patterns
expected for children in sequential stages of development by as exact
and systematic a method as one can conceive for that period of time.
'The normal child could now be seen in full view' (Wong 1993: 127).

While developmental psychology was still fighting for its institutional recognition as a scientific domain, such was not the case in
paediatrics where the problem of scientificity of this particular specialty
was never really at stake as it was in psychology; paediatrics emerged in
a very well-established and legitimized scientific field. The question
under consideration here is less the professionalization of a medical
speciality than, in order to keep in line with the argument put forward,
the particular way that paediatrics put into place specific modes of child
observation;[61] the work of Holt appears a fine piece in this respect.

At the end of the nineteenth century, paediatrics emerged as a
specialty in a medical context characterized by major scientific
discoveries that greatly affected the way medicine and paediatrics
intervened in questions of health. The extension of human knowledge
concerning the bacterial origin of many forms of disease through the
work of Pasteur is justifiably considered as the greatest achievement in
the medical progress of the nineteenth century; it marks an epoch in

---

[61] In his chairman address to the American Medical Association Section of
Paediatrics in 1923, Borden Veeder stated that a paediatrician 'is not a
specialist of childhood diseases, but of the knowledge of the child'. 'Child
hygiene is at present the most important motif in our work, as it will continue
to be in the future, and in child hygiene work it has been the child that has been
the topic of consideration – not disease or medicine' (Halpern 1988: 96). What
then was this particular knowledge of the child?

scientific progress generally speaking. Thought and enquiry were propelled in new directions, and preventive medicine was raised from its speculative depths and claims into consideration on a scientific basis. Anatomy and experimental physiology had exploded but the application to medical practice was only moderate until Pasteur's discoveries in the 1870s created the new science of bacteriology, thus providing a rational basis for basic therapeutics in the treatment of disease and public-health techniques for its prevention, the most important of these being the pasteurization of milk. The contribution of biology and bacteriology to paediatrics was the discovery that children did not merely develop according to hereditary determinism or in response to environmental incentives, but were subjected to the devastating effects of germs and other micro-organisms, causing diseases and infection as the fundamental findings of bacteriology indicated.

There is a long French tradition in medical infant care that goes as far back as the seventeenth and eighteenth centuries (Morel 1987, 1989). This tradition is rich, diversified and mainly twofold; it has a research component and a welfare as well as a state intervention component (Klaus 1993; Rollet 1990). The research aspect culminated with Pasteur, bacteriology and the discovery of germ theory in the second half of the nineteenth century. The welfare constituent, on the other hand, has always been remarkable in its capacity to set up innovative programmes and agencies for childcare (Fonssagrives 1882). One can think of the setting up of *gouttes de lait* (milk depots), or the maternal education programme established by Budin at the Hôpital de la Charité in Paris, or the *consultation des nourissons* (infant-health consultation) a follow-up instruction programme for infants and their parents set up to prevent infant sickness and death at home in the first year.[62] The paediatrician was chiefly concerned with children's physical growth, and not only in the French tradition; mental development will come in due course hereafter.

---

[62] Let us mention the foundation, in 1902, of the Ligue Française contre la Mortalité Infantile; in 1905 the first international conference on infant welfare while France hosted the initial meeting of the Congrès International des Gouttes de Lait; in 1907, under a new name, in Brussels this time, the Congrès pour la Protection de l'Enfance du Premier Age. More or less equivalent initiatives were undertaken in Great Britain (the National Conference on Infant Mortality in 1906), Germany and the United States for example with the International Union for the Protection of Infants (Meckel 1990).

Since the beginning, paediatric texts gave much attention to the physical needs of infants, much more than the other needs considered negligible. These physical needs, as well as their counterpart physical growth, were seen as relatively precise and measurable in contrast to the other needs which were deemed elusive and unmeasurable: 'It was not so much that the diseases of early life are peculiar, as the patients themselves are peculiar' (Meckel 1990: 47). Paediatricians' concerns with the diseases of children and their consequences shifted to more effective ways to bring up a healthy and normal child; the physical concerns of paediatrics extended beyond pathological conditions towards a more holistic orientation. In a certain way, its chief concern veered from the anomalies and diseases, which are encountered in the infant and child only to the scientific study of healthy children whose benchmark was the implementation and generalization of a medical examination for the healthy child.[63] The presidential address of Abraham Jacobi, founder of the AMA Paediatrics Section, is indicative of this concern for the child's physical growth and wellbeing: raising the standard of physical health to possible perfection according to the principles of sound and scientific physical hygiene.[64]

From the mid-nineteenth century, there was a growing interest in the sheer external size of children of different ages, sexes, nationalities, including prenatal size. Physical growth became a central focus of paediatrics' developmental study as the child's physical wellbeing involves:

- first of all, system and order in the routine care;
- regularity in the hours of sleep, of bathing, of feeding and exercise with a suitable room for the child's sleeping hours as regards ventilation, sunshine and quiet;
- a proper judgement in the preparation of suitable food including the adjustment of the child's food to its individual capacities to avoid the evil effects of overfeeding, or to meet its lowered capacities while sick;
- a thoughtfulness providing proper clothing and bed covering to suit the temperature and weather.

(Coit 1910: 728)

---

[63] This should not be underestimated as a cultural phenomenon. The medical examination of a healthy child was a major cultural transformation as the usual visit to the physician up to the turn of the twentieth century occurred only when a child was sick.

[64] A. Jacobi, Presidential address to the APS, 1889, *Archives of Pediatrics*, VI/11, Nov. 1889, p. 760 et seq.

The practice of paediatrics lay in establishing objective criteria for the major determinants and stages of maturation. Specialists sought criteria that were scientifically grounded. Instrumentation played a key role in establishing these criteria; for instance, so far as skeletal structure was concerned, Roetgen's discovery of X-ray photography in 1895 represented a major instrumental breakthrough for the study of growth. The standards established by both researchers and clinicians were applicable to all normal children. What was then, one can inquire, the translation of standards in the emerging domain of childhood? Gesell provides a strong argument in support of standards in the appraisal of the child's health and growth.[65]

> The scientific and the practical function of the standard in child health work is measurement, not compression into a mould. The standard is a formula which represents a bit of information which may be used as a landmark of reference. We use the height and weight chart not to standardize physical growth, but to interpret it. Standards are lenses through which we observe the child's growth to determine whether it is pursuing a favorable course ... The hygienic supervision of physical growth, therefore, depends upon standards (Gesell 1926: 46).

The weight–height–age chart turned out to be the most widely used technology by paediatricians in this respect: a standard to assess and interpret children's physical growth based on the scientific study of physical growth. Whilst acknowledging that physical standards were still imperfect, Gesell advocated that the situation could only be corrected by more standardization, not less: available standards had to become more adequate for an accurate clinical appraisal of the child (Gesell 1926). Sleep, exercise, feeding and nutrition were beginning to be better understood. Everything possible was regulated, including: the time, numbers of feeding and the quantity of food given; the amount of sleep required; the precise time of bathing and the order in which the baby's face, body and limbs were to be washed.

---

[65] By the 1920s and 1930s, concerns and critiques were raised as regards the question of normality – there is no such thing as a normal child; all children differ, no two are alike – and with standardization – children are not factory automobiles; we should avoid standardization of children. One of the strongest voices in this period was Grace Adams, for numerous years head of the US Children's Bureau, in her book *Your Child Is Normal*: 'The American craze for standardization has given us, among thousands of other standardized objects, the standardized child' (Adams 1934).

Paediatricians thoroughly endorsed the proposition according to which public health, school apparatus and social work seek discriminating standards for children so that they can carry on with the core of their task, which is assessing and classifying children.

Holt's book, *The Care and Feeding of Children* (1894), is generally considered a good example of a systematic approach to infant care characterized by regularity and firmness: strict schedules for both feeding and sleeping. The fact that it enjoyed 28 editions and 75 printings (Apple 1987: 104) is indicative of a wide circulation and a substantial consideration. In his book, Holt gives detailed coverage to the question of feeding and physical growth: 'Nutrition in its broadest sense is the most important branch of paediatrics ... the largest part of the immense mortality in the first year is traceable directly to disorders of nutrition. The importance of correct ideas regarding the subject can hardly be overestimated ... which shall tend to healthy growth and development' (Holt 1914: 122). He believed that perfecting and monitoring infant feeding was the most important activity of a paediatrician. He was also a staunch proponent of mother's milk (Apple 1987: 110). Holt's manual gives what amounts to a very elaborate dietary chart of feeding practice for the child.[66] The child's life, especially in the early infant stages, is divided into specific cycles – early months, middle months, etc. – each one of these being subdivided into various periods; every period has a series of formulas appropriate for the child.

Apart from feeding practice, Holt's manual advised mothers on several other subjects such as pain, temper – never give a child what he cries for, let him cry himself out – illness, habit and play – 'Babies under six months old should never be played with, and the less of it at any time the better. They are made nervous and irritable, sleep badly' (Beekman 1977: 117). The important point to notice here is that, by the turn of the twentieth century, paediatrics was already established in its methods and its intervention. The practice of child observation and intervention were totally under the scope of classical positivist rationality and methods. There was then no other legitimized way of looking at and observing a child. 'Observation, measurement, recording, analysis, the serious work of studying real children as

---

[66] 'In the 140 pages of the 1904 edition, 20 have to do with "care" (bathing, airing, etc.), 30 deal with miscellaneous problems, from playing with children to "bad habits" and 90 pages have to do with feeding' (Beekman 1977).

they grow and learn, had by 1930 been under way for more than a quarter-century ... It was in these dry bones of fact that the course of modern child raising was set' (Beekman 1977: 154).

This chapter has followed, over a period of almost two centuries, the profound transformation of the practice of child observation from a speculative activity of philosophers in the eighteenth century, to the domestic child-watching of the first half of the nineteenth century, to the scientific form of child observation and recording of the turn of the twentieth century. This progressive modification happened within the context of the collection, classification and enumeration of the population that the technologies of statistics made possible. The child was modified from an issue for discussion and speculation to an object of scientific observation; children began to be observed, measured, weighed and described. The most visible outcome of this observation took the form of tables, graphs and charts. The twentieth century began in this respect by charting and graphing children; its two most pre-eminent disciplines generated an impressive sum of technical knowledge, which culminated in positioning the child in a peculiar and specific form of textual inscription: specialized language, tables, protocols, visual depictions and the like. This textual inscription had a particular enduring effect upon children: it implemented in them abstract variables and developmental benchmarks whose consequences one can still speculate about.

Paediatrics is, in this respect, on the threshold, or to put it otherwise, at the interface of child observation and child monitoring. The main concern of paediatricians is no longer to put into place or to implement a sound and scientific methodology for observing the child, but to monitor it so as to protect against some of the worst social harms. In accordance with the perspective elaborated in this chapter, paediatrics (with Holt at the forefront) is no longer in the realm of observation, but henceforth in the practice of supervising, thus regulating child-rearing. Not only were paediatricians and psychologists writing manuals such as Holt's and Gesell's – or many others such as Galton and Burt in England; Budin, Binet and Simon in France – but they were by that time, as the next chapter will indicate, in the position of creating and implementing social devices and technologies to frame the behaviour of children as well as that of their parents.

3 | *Social technologies: regulation and resistance*

A child becomes an object of knowledge when it is identified as such, different from other social actors, and as methods of observation and then of recording, are discovered or implemented. These methods rest on two prerequisites: measurement and classification. One cannot conceive of recording, especially in its scientific rather than its diary form, without the practice of measurement in compliance with specific predefined parameters: the height–weight–age tables symbolize the exercise of measurement put into place. Accordingly, measurement of children in conformity with discrete parameters takes place within a system of categories: the activity of classifying children is fundamental in this respect.

The classification, enumeration and collection of data concerning children are activities by no means without consequences. On the contrary, classification directly affects the children being classified: this is regulation. And vice versa: this is resistance. 'In medicine, the authorities who know, the doctors, tend to dominate the known about, the patients. The known about come to behave in the ways that the knower expect them to. But not always. Sometimes the known take matters into their own hands' (Hacking 1995: 38). In between the two stands an apparatus in charge of monitoring children's behaviour. Children are monitored through specific forms, the social technologies,[1] considered a

---

[1] The general context within which these social technologies were set up revolved around the contemporary belief that scientific knowledge and professional expertise could indeed solve social problems. Between 1890 and 1940, two distinct phases are identified. During the first phase (1890–1915), the dominant theme was reform: the transformation of the circumstances of children's lives through public policy. The second phase (1915–1940) saw the use of human sciences and technologies as the necessary precondition of further public action (Cravens 1985b). It is during these two periods (1890–1940) that children started to constitute a distinct group within the national population with their own status, institutions etc.

by-product of scientific investigation, both of the recording methods and of the activity of classification.

This chapter examines the social forms – the technologies – which contributed to social change throughout the process of delineation of a national population in a given society. It concerns some of the most cogent social technologies set up to supervise, that is, to regulate children's behaviour;[2] and their reactions, as well as their parents', to this supervision, that is, their resistance. The perspective is twofold: regulation/resistance, and furthermore, it takes into account the fact that these forms vary in time and space. In this respect, I shall focus my attention upon the technologies that paediatrics and child psychology have established from the turn of the twentieth century to the interwar period; and those public authorities and reformers of different kinds – the apparatus – implemented in the aftermath. The technologies that will be looked at consist of the following:

a. the charts;
b. the record forms;
c. the well-child conference;
d. intelligence testing;
e. the child-guidance clinic.

3.1 Technology and visualization

The devising of the various charts rests upon the achievement of anthropometric measurements of children and their tabulation as their most distinguishing outcome. Measurement stands in this respect as a mediation between scientific observation in the laboratory and children's daily lives in their households; the link between scientists' concerns or purposes and parents' willingness, indeed readiness to apprehend a child's development. 'The Victorians were the first to become enraptured with numbers (it was seen as bookkeeping applied to society), and through their gradually accumulating statistics a

---

[2] The question of regulation was on the agenda of public authorities. In this respect, the nineteenth century can be seen as the beginning of the regulation. Different social problems became visible and very worrying, such as delinquency, runaways and vagrants. Measures were taken to control the most threatening of these manifestations: such as the juvenile court system (Sutton 1983, 1988). Other institutions – the Boy Scouts, the YMCA – were introduced for the purpose of regulating the behaviour of youth (Cohen 1985).

picture of society emerges' (Beekman 1977: 97). The tables appear to be a crucial material element in this mediation. A table takes the form of a material object manipulated in settings such as houses, infant clinics and schools and liable to standard protocols (Gurjeva 1998).

Physicians and psychologists requested parents to supply data by filling in the tables handed to them. Parents' collaboration – as well as that of older children, at school for instance – was deemed essential for the relationship to be workable and productive. Physicians could not in any way pursue their goals, whether scientific or more policy-oriented toward monitoring, without the active partnership, which they explicitly sought of the other party, either the parents or the children. There is a long tradition of physicians and paediatricians advising parents, particularly mothers, on note-taking about their children, on how to handle the table effectively. For instance, in 1869, Professor Fonssagrives published in Paris a maternal booklet for note-taking on children's health made up of important remarks to this effect (Fonssagrives 1869; Luc 1997: 106). Its English counterpart of the 1880s, *The Mother's Record*, was configured with issues on observation and notes on record-keeping (Cavanaugh 1985: 196). In this very distinct social relationship, which, it must be emphasized, operates more on an exchange basis, parents and children have the opportunity to resist the requirements of both paediatricians and the apparatus. The latter, however, had powerful means in their hands to convince the former.

What is meant by social technology? From the outset, it is important to distinguish between technology and the general advice literature so widely studied (Ehrenreich 1978; Hardyment 1983; Mechling 2001). The main difference appears to be that the advice literature takes almost exclusively a narrative form, while technology has the form of a material object such as a chart or graph possibly sustained by a discourse.[3] It is a device of some type, which has the

---

[3] A pamphlet issued by the Boston Board of Health in 1876, *Rules for the Management of Infants and Children*, is considered as a good example of advice literature.

1. The child should be kept clean, bathed daily in warm water and changed as often as he becomes dirty.
2. The child needs fresh air.
3. Children's clothing should not be too tight [a final warning against swaddling?]

capacity of being a mediator between categories of social actors. Following Callon's proposition, 'agency cannot be dissociated from the relationship between actors' (Callon 1991: 134), we shall consider technologies as entities within a complex network of relationships in a particular social setting, but entities less gifted with the capacity of agency or subjectivity, rather than viewed as an extension or prolongation of humans. 'If humans and nonhumans are to be regarded as equivalent objects in sociological analysis, then agency is no longer the sole preserve of humans. Liberated from its containment in human entities, it dispersed through the networks' (Ashmore *et al.* 1994: 735). Accordingly, the social technologies of childhood will become entities of their own in a network of relationships with social actors.

The technologies of childhood are considered as inscription devices.[4] The crucial point revolves around the possibility of an effective collective action across divergent social groupings (Figure 3) in the field of childhood, thus yielding in it a relative stability (Fujimura 1992). Some of the problems under examination in this respect have been encountered although, alas, not yet adumbrated: how to muster different groupings with conflicting viewpoints in a specific field? How is the mobilization of new resources achieved in this collective action? We shall look at the way someone convinces someone else to accept and assume a proposition, to circulate it, to find new allies, to muster support and cooperation (Latour 1990). As the line of arguments put forward does not rely on such explanations as 'interests', 'capitalism', 'culture' and 'modernity', the textual inscription of children through graphs, charts and tables becomes the focus of analysis.

4. Children need as much sleep as they want.
5. The basic diet of a child is milk, which should be given every two hours when he is small and gradually lengthened to every four hours. 'All prepared varieties of so-called infant's food are to be avoided.'
6. Children are to be weaned by the ninth month.
7. Children are to be vaccinated; children are not to be given cordials (opium); the doctor should be sent for when the child is ill.
8. After a child reaches two years, 'regularity of hours of sleeping and eating should be insisted on'.

(Beekman 1977: 103)

[4] For an overview of the notion of inscription device, see Latour (Latour 1987).

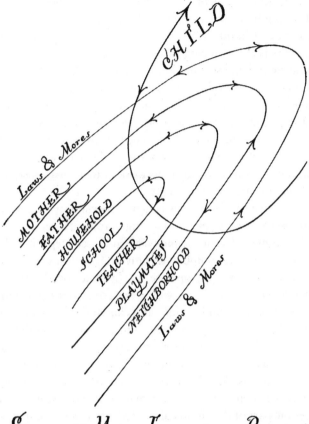

Schematic Map of Interpersonal Relations

Figure 3: Child relation map
Source: Gesell 1946b

Artefacts such as charts and graphs are socialized non-humans and operate as mediators/translators in a network of relationships that inherently consist of both human and non-human entities, treated symmetrically at the analytical level. Objects and artefacts are analytically examined: how can they succeed in making social actors behave in a certain manner, and vice versa.[5] It has to do with the

___

[5] The status of objects and artefacts has a primary aspect which will be developed below. 'And this can best be done by studying artefacts and

practice of making an instrument work effectively up to the extent of considering the sociologically inconceivable question: 'how objects construct the subject' (Latour 1994b: 82). The outbreak of AIDS in the past thirty years is a convincing case: a virus, that is, an object of scientific knowledge, relentlessly modifies human conduct. The question then becomes how a device such as a chart intervenes in human conduct. In other words and to put it bluntly, how technologies such as charts and tables contribute to the production of another subject.[6] From this standpoint, the unit of analysis is neither the paediatricians, nor the children (or their parents) nor solely the technologies in themselves, but the socio-technological network of their relationships, with the latter being central to this chapter.

The question of technology remains cogent, especially in regard to the mobilization issue. Aiming to avoid a long ontological regression, which is familiar to mainstream sociology when the concept of technology is examined, my questioning in this investigation can be reformulated as: how does technology operate in a specific social setting? One of the possible answers lies in the way groups of actors argue with one another using diagrams, tables, signs and charts; they result in the transformation of an object, say children, into an inscription device which could then, along with other inscriptions, be combined, rephrased, superimposed, and above all circulated. The crucial point in the inscription device is that children are rendered visible: they can now be seen, whereas before they were a matter of discussion. They accordingly become part of the visual culture (Alpers 1983), the spatial location and perspective – the interchanges and bonds between painting techniques and scientific discoveries in Renaissance Europe (Edgarton 1975) – deemed so important in the rediscovery of the scientific object (Fabian 1983, 1984; Turmel 1986).[7]

---

quasi-objects which are a combination of all the different dimensions of human life, incorporating the human and non-human, the social, semiotic and material. Artefacts are created within relations of communication and relations that transform the real' (Burkitt 1998: 129).

[6] The principle of generalized symmetry amounts to the simultaneous production of humans and non-humans. The social scientist puts himself in a median position where he can observe the ascription of both human and non-human properties in a given social process – how humans and non-humans exchange properties (Callon 1986).

[7] Both Edgarton and Alpers wrote about the history of art. Rightly so, they point to science's visual language. Pauwels edited a book regarding visual

If one supports the proposition that science is not solely about describing or replicating reality then this endorsement opens up a space for rendering the world more legible and intelligible; this likely brings up the complex issue of graphic visualization and depictions in a historical perspective among other things. Pauwels' visual culture is understood in a fairly material sense: how a society literally sees the world and makes it visible, which leads to a form of objectification in the broader context of observation, measurement, tabulation, graphs, analysis and so on. Therefore a visual culture in the scientific world – in the emergent science of childhood and its concomitant collective for instance – relates foremost to the practices enabled to make things – problems and phenomena – visible and accountable. Visualization and legibility: it remains to establish how the former entails the latter. I shall therefore examine how research objects – whether IMR, IQ or developmental standards – were transformed over time and cautiously moulded into graphic data that were afterwards measured, investigated, printed and circulated. The graphic visualization amounts to the transformation of raw data into legible ones, which are then circulated in the collective. Lynch rightly puts forward the idea that these data are graphically embedded (Lynch 2005). He goes on to say that it has to do with the clarification and the tuning of scientific reality: what object is studied under which circumstances? In an emergent scientific field, diagrams, figures and tables and so on, in bringing about a schematic plan, give a unique advantage in a debating situation: one can show some sort of synoptic evidence (Curtis 2002). The science of childhood comes forth from such a trend towards visualization.

Nowadays it is usually recognized that no scientific discipline can come into legitimized being 'without first inventing a visual and written language which allows it to break with its confusing past' (Latour 1990: 36). The same basic rule applies to a 'science of childhood': diagrams and graphs can be more easily suitable, fathomable and intelligible. Among the advantages of visual inscription devices, Latour mentions that: they are mobile, immutable and reproducible – they can circulate without alteration; the scale of the

representation in the production of scientific reality, namely making it more accessible and understandable in various ways: not only representing reality, but somehow revealing it.

inscriptions can be modified although the internal proportions are maintained; inscriptions can be reshuffled, recombined and made part of a written text. From now on, we shall concentrate both on the visualization of children and on the operations yielded by the devices in the networks of relationships.

The further one gets inside a medical clinic, revealed here as a threshold space in which the critically weighted/heighted body is constituted, the more the clinical gaze of paediatrics moves away from the child's body towards those devices which visualize its corporeality. The same is true for the psychological clinic in some respects. Such a process constructs the reality of the child's body or intelligence independently of the means by which it is scrutinized and known; namely, the body exists prior to its visualization. Accordingly, if a child's body is observed then that observation must be directed at those locations – graphs, charts, tables etc. – where that body is made visible, thus intelligible. The relative success or failure of technologies of visualization can be regarded as a product of a stable network of heterogeneous elements.

The introduction of the above-mentioned technologies was already carrying parents and children into a different cultural and material world: the world of mediation and that of the socio-technological network of relationships. The establishment of social technology in child-rearing, and more broadly speaking in general childhood matters, introduced a new entity in a set of relationships while also changing the very nature of these relationships: the technological device has its own autonomy within the network. It operates and recomposes the social link by extending its scale. It gives new impetus to the social configuration under consideration: subjects and objects alike enter into a new set of relations.

So as to assess both the usefulness and the relevance of such technologies, one has to keep in mind that, although public concern about high infant-mortality rates was deep, very few tools and technologies were available for measurement and appraisal of the child.[8] 'It was the

---

[8] The quest for measurement and quantitativeness must not be underestimated. 'The broader political culture . . . lent enormous weight to quantitative method as a means of bridging the chasm between scientific research and practical application . . . with the institution of a national census, numbers eventually became the lingua franca of American progressivism . . . all lent power to numerical treatments of social issues' (Brown 1992). This trend was part of a

schools which had provided the information for the analysis. The paraphernalia of statistics and graphs which accompanied it...' (Cunningham 1991: 193). It is crucial to remember that such features as infant-mortality rates set up the context, that is the social environment and conditions, within which the socio-technological network of relationships takes place.

The Pasteurian revolution, which introduced a fundamental and gigantic step forward in medicine and public hygiene was already on its way to altering, through the germ theory and its application, infant-mortality rates and to mastering its most obvious causes (Dwork 1987).[9] The western world was transforming its condition of existence in the wake of the breakthrough in medicine (Meckel 1990).[10] So what we shall now be examining is the other side of the sheet of paper, so to speak: as it pertains to childhood, once the basic necessities of securing the survival of the infant were met, the issue at stake turned to prevention and then to development. How to ensure the best possible chances for the child and how to assess its development with the best conceivable technologies to ensure these purposes?

3.2 The charts

The charts arose as the most visible and enduring of all the social technologies that were implemented. Their lasting effect can still be

---

broader zeitgeist that aimed to find sound principles and scientific methods for child-rearing. 'The child-care book... reiterated time and again that maternal instinct was not sufficient for healthful rearing of children... established science as the informing agent in child-rearing and health matters' (Apple 1987).

[9] This topic of the Pasteurian revolution is a difficult and complex one that directly affected infants' survival. 'The domains of medicine which pertain to pregnant women and new-born infants may be those that most quickly took advantage of Pasteur's discoveries' (Rollet 1990: 155). The topic is mentioned here not only because it forms the background of the issue that I am looking at, but because it is considered as a precondition of its emergence (Apple 1987; Meckel 1990).

[10] Meckel identifies three general social developments that played a catalytic role in the infant welfare domain. First was the concern over national deterioration with France playing the leading role with its declining birth rate and the necessity of saving infant lives. Second was the huge increase in public concern with different aspects of child welfare. Third was the awareness that the infant death rate was not declining at the same pace as the overall death rate (Meckel 1990).

noticed, if not ascertained, in the modus operandi of public health bodies of the twenty-first century, albeit in a very different framework; descendants of the height–weight–age charts are still in use in obstetrics wards, in paediatricians' surgeries and school offices, which is indicative both of their ubiquitousness and of the enormous weight they carry in the inscription-embodiment of children. The other technologies did not last that long, in their initial form at least, with perhaps the noticeable exception of the IQ tests (Hacking 1995: 97). This section starts by looking at the prerequisite of the charts, the tables and the tabulation; it will then examine the epitomized form of the chart, the height–weight–age chart; thereafter it will review other influential charts such as the feeding, sleeping and posture charts.

The tabulation of parental observations of children, note-taking and recording started in the scientists' laboratories and first took the form of charts and graphs (Gurjeva 1998). Charts are a peculiar form in a socio-technological network set up to mediate, that is, to interpose, but not solely on a purely technical basis, rather in the sense of incubating children's development amidst a cluster of heterogeneous social relationships at once material, technological, discursive and cultural, involving human and non-human resources.[11] The actors involved are researchers, laboratories, physicians, paediatricians, clinics, parents, children, social reformers, welfare workers, their organizations, and the charts. At the heart of this heterogeneous network lies the mother and her child on the one hand and the medical professionals (physicians and paediatricians) on the other.[12] The French triad of Roussel, Budin and Strauss paved the way for highly progressive social welfare measures around the endowment of the

---

[11] Some institutions were already monitoring childhood from a medical standpoint. In prenatal clinics, such a supervision had a decisive effect upon reducing the high infant mortality rate of the newborn during the first few weeks of life. Infant welfare clinics, known as *la consultation des nourrissons*, were supervising the baby from birth up to two years old. For the preschool children (from two to six years old), British infant schools, France's *salles d'asile*, Aporti's toddler schools in Italy and Froebel's kindergartens in Germany as well as the Boston clinics were considering a new set of specific problems which differ from the former: school hygiene, supervision of school buildings by public authorities and systematic physical examination of children by physicians etc.

[12] Most historians do agree that the mother, regularly deemed as ignorant by the medical experts, was at the centre of any plan of action to overcome such problems as infant mortality (Meckel 1990).

Ligue contre la Mortalité Infantile; the British threesome of News-holme, Newman and Pritchard stressed indigence and ignorance as a continuum rather than two discrete categories; and the American trio of Jacobi, Rotch and Holt were perfecting and monitoring infant feeding from the perspective of preventive medicine in early life.

Charts were among the very first technologies brought forth to appraise child development from a perspective of prevention once infection and diseases related to it were conquered; in other words, once the threat of infant mortality was no longer insuperable.[13] This threat over the infant's survival in its first year being surmounted, physicians looked for different types of instruments, measurements and technologies that would support them to frame the child's growth and progress from infancy to adolescence. Thus the experts' attention came to be directed to normal growth in childhood in the 1850s and 1860s (Steedman 1995: 75). How did the charts intervene as a mediator of child development in this peculiar network of relationships?

The starting point is unquestionably the lack of scientific instruments for the purpose of paediatric research: 'very few tools available for measurements and little established knowledge on developmental stages' (Lomax *et al.* 1978: 8). The concern in regard to normal growth in childhood found one of its most earnest manifestations in the work of anthropometry, which is the measurement of the human body within the wider frame of reckoning populations.

In England particularly, the 1833 Commission on the Employment of Children in Factories instructed its administrators to measure the height and weight of children to evaluate the difference between factory children and other children; they measured 1,933 children between nine and eighteen years of age in the Manchester area and

---

[13] Infant mortality was one aspect of a vast campaign concerning the protection of children, labelled as a war measure.

This aim – the public protection of mothers and young children – is only part of the program of the campaign, which is fivefold. The other four aims are; to maintain the standard of home care and the income on which proper care of children depends; to see the restrictions on child labor and the requirements of school attendance laws are not broken down under war time pressure; to insure to every child opportunities for the outdoor life and recreation which are essential to health, and to provide for children in need of special care – the dependent, the neglected, the delinquent, the subnormal – the care that they require. (Meigs 1918: 50).

found the factory child to be shorter and lighter than the non-factory child.[14] Factory work was detrimental to children, hindering their growth (Tanner 1981: 147). Physicians appointed under the Poor Law or under local agreement to schools began the large-scale anthropometric studies as early as the 1860s and up to the 1880s; in 1888, the British Medical Association established an Anthropometric Committee to carry on the task of measuring children (Cunningham 1991: 197). The school provided a specific area for the observation of growth and physical development of children.[15]

Their American counterparts (Bowditch and Porter) gathered important data with respect to children's heights and weights (Young 1979: 225). These were raw statistical data that could not be considered to provide useful and, above all, imaginative knowledge; they lacked the categorization and tabulation to do so. 'This had now become possible by means of statistical analysis; all that was needed was careful classification, tabulation and calculation' (Wong 1993: 87).

Thus the first technologies that were designed and established are characterized by the fact that they were elementary. It became so. 'This had more complex and more sophisticated as it proved helpful to researchers, physicians or parents; and useful for monitoring children, and for regulating certain types of behaviour. Some charts persisted over the years and some of their descendants are still used today in a more advanced form while others did not last very long or were limited to that very period of the turn of the twentieth century and whose usefulness as a social technology did not persist. The former will be examined first.

Among the various kinds of charts, the most widely known technology for assessing physical growth and children's general development was the weight–height–age charts.[16] 'The weight is one of the

---

[14] In 1837, another administrator, Leonard Horner, coordinated a large study of children's heights and weights in the Manchester–Leeds area, where 8,469 boys and 7,932 girls were measured (Tanner 1981).

[15] As an example, Steedman relates to C. Roberts' series of observations on the height, weight and chest girth of 15,000 English children; according to Roberts himself, these series were incomplete. On the other hand, in 1875, Henry Bowditch from the Harvard Medical School weighed and measured 24,000 Boston schoolchildren.

[16] The main characteristic of this type of chart as compared to the following ones (feeding and sleeping charts) is the length of time that it remained

primary data that it is necessary to obtain' (Anonymous 1912: 32). 'Nevertheless, the most generally useful and concrete index of health is the child's weight' (Wood and Lerrigo 1925: 551). 'A normal gain in weight is one of the essential attributes of growth in childhood and is the best single comparative, objective measure of normal physical development...expressed in figures...the height and weight charts' (Brennemann 1933: 14). The weight–height–age chart became the most extensively used technology in this respect. Paediatricians, researchers and public-health practitioners produced these tables. Holt's manual recorded two weight charts: one for the first year of the infant's life, the other for ages one to fourteen.[17] *Archives of Pediatrics* published one of the first scientific charts in 1910 (Rotch 1910a: 568).

What were those charts? How were they collected? 'I may explain the weighing and measuring test briefly as a test in which as many as possible of the children under 6 of a community are weighed and measured, and these measurements compared with a table of average heights and weights at different ages' (Meigs 1918: 52). The tabulation of these individual tests was done by researchers on the basis of very large samples; the 1918 American campaign by the Children's Bureau aimed at tabulating 300,000 individual tests. It is clear from the outset that parents' collaboration was essential to the project: without it, it would have been much more difficult to gather the relevant information allowing the final tabulation of the data. Charts were regularly printed afterward in scientific journals as well as booklets for the general public and diffused on a large scale. Both the American Medical Association and the American Child Health Association (ACHA) distributed the chart throughout their various affiliated organizations. By the end of the First World War, the device was openly recognized as one of the most useful that physicians and parents had to assess children's development.

The validity and the reliability of the charts was raised in scientific circles: the measurement was questioned rather than the status of the

---

salient: modern forms of those weight charts, although more complex, are still used today by paediatricians to assess children's development, albeit in a more cautious and careful way.

[17] In his book, *The Diseases of Infancy and Childhood* (1897), Holt incorporated a complete chapter on child growth. The height and weight charts were already in use for adults at the end of the nineteenth century as Young has documented (Young 1979).

technology itself.[18] 'Information as to the weight and measurement of children is only beginning to be reliable. Much that is erroneous has been published concerning the weights during the first year and very little data has been published as to the gain in weight and height of children under the good conditions' (Freeman 1914: 203). The doubts did not last long because the practice of measurement became progressively more sophisticated, the tables being able to discriminate more effectively.

Different forms of weight charts were circulating at that period. The descriptive aspects of the charts conveyed factual information that experts and possibly parents could find useful:

It is interesting to note that in the first 6 months the rate of growth is in direct ratio to the birth weight, while in the third 3 months the rate is about the same for all babies, and in the fourth 3 months the rate of gain is in inverse ratio to the birth weight. This may be construed as meaning that heavy infants bring into the world a relatively strong growth impulse which gradually diminishes toward the end of the year, while small infants have at first a weak growth impulse which gradually grows stronger during the year (Faber 1920: 249).

The text goes on with reflections in regard to seasonal variations in growth in infants, seasonal variation in birth weight, and the considerable variation in birth weight between boys and girls.

Basically two types of charts were distributed. Some were more research-oriented and produced by laboratories tabulating data empirically collected and plotting graphs to indicate visually the curve of the normal child's weight according to height and age (Chart 1). Researchers worked on a large scale, in university laboratories or research centres, tabulating raw data conveyed by those who, in schools, clinics and offices, were in charge of their gathering. Borden Vedeer's *Preventive Pediatrics* is a good example of a research graph.

Some of the charts were more normative in their orientation and designed to be a tool for paediatricians and parents in their daily

---

[18] Rotch took a publicly critical stance toward this particular type of chart. 'There is a manifest need for some developmental index by which physicians ... shall be able to determine the fitness ... The means formerly used for this purpose are inadequate, whether they may be height, weight, teeth ... Height and weight have long been known to be very inadequate for determining' (Rotch 1910b: 26).

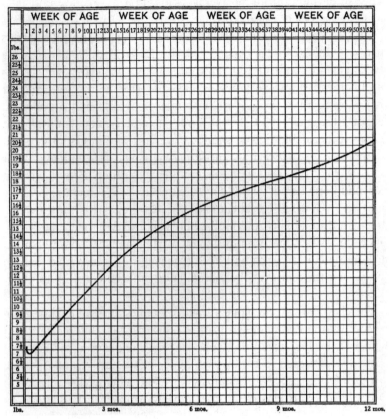

Chart 1: Weight for baby's first year
Source: American Child Health Association (Veeder 1926)

handling of the child. The physician assessed a child's growth by comparing its weight to the appropriate average of same age (and same sex) children already tabulated by researchers; it was usually understood that a deviation of more than 10 per cent below or 20 per cent above the mean was, in this respect, expressive of abnormality (Baldwin 1924; Palmer 1925: 5). Percentages might vary though: 'It is quite generally accepted that there is something wrong with a child who is persistently more than 5 or 7 per cent below the standard weight for his age and height' (Wood and Lerrigo 1925: 551). It is interesting to

notice here that abnormality is relative to the average – it is a certain
range of deviation from the average – and that the average implicitly
denoted the idea of normalcy.[19]

On the other hand, 'children that are under good control so far as
diet, rest and exercise are concerned, show a great advantage over the
data at hand concerning other children both in weight and height
during the first twelve years of life; and that at the twelfth year
they surpass the average by 20 pounds in weight and 6 inches in
height' (Freeman 1914: 208). 'Children under good control' is a
euphemism establishing a specific form of social relationship, an
asymmetric link between the medical experts and the children or their
parents. This logic also applies to children as a group in itself, a group
not undifferentiated, but highly organized into a hierarchy: those
who are well-cared for and those who are not. 'This shows a surprising advantage of the well-cared for children over the other'
(Freeman 1914: 208). Can this hierarchy be a replication of the usual
dichotomy between rich and poor that was so pervasive not only in
the nineteenth century,[20] but throughout the whole history of childhood?

The chart was a technology grounded in the statistical methodology
of comparison and designed for the assessment of children's growth
which is the best measure of physical development: a child is positioned with regard to the average of the other children of the same
age group in a process of comparison. 'With the height–weight–age
tables children are classified as per cent over or under the average, or
standard, weight, of a group' (Palmer 1930: 50). The methodology of
comparative research bore the very idea of normality and, thus,
abnormality: to compare consisted not only of classifying children,
but also in sorting out the categories which circumscribed the average

---

[19] This topic of normality/abnormality in relation to the average and a deviation
from the mean was addressed in Chapter 2 (section 2.2) and will be debated in
Chapter 4.

[20] A direct social class interpretation of childhood, especially for children of the
'dangerous classes' is, however, quite typical in a certain progressive literature,
particularly among historians (Cunningham, Steedman, Hendrick etc.): 'This
had particular relevance to the urban slums, where informed opinion held that
the poor – a race apart – needed to be civilised. Indeed, there can be no proper
understanding of ... the social legislation affecting children without an
appreciation of ... the significance of social class' (Hendrick 1994).

in child growth and development.[21] This involved specific consequences in the construction of childhood.

Therefore there are social relations in the classic sociological sense:
relations between social actors, leaving everything else aside, and
saying for instance that the paediatrician is in charge of the process, the
parents provide the basic information, the physician issues a diagnosis,
a welfare clinic does the follow-up. The social scene does neither appear
to be solely indebted to social actors in the restrictive sense, nor bring
the paediatrician face-to-face with the child[22] or the parent, or the
nurse/clinic with the child: in this relation, there are no one-to-one
confrontations, no duels. Another agent is present, acting, exchanging,
enforcing limits and aims, redefining the social bond from a distinct
perspective: that of the chart. Although their cooperation is essential in
the whole process, both children and parents are tagging along behind
the medical experts and the clinic whose knowledge and authority are
deemed indisputable. What about the chart then? How is the paediatrician's knowledge and authority brought to bear upon the chart?
What does the chart introduce between the conventional social actors?

In the 1890s, France, through the *consultation des nourissons*
and the *gouttes de lait* (milk station),[23] stated clearly that one of its
aims was to weigh infants in its global struggle against infant
mortality.[24] A trilogy of essential constituents formed the ritual of the

---

[21] The ideas of average, mean, normal distribution, bell curve and so on
embedded the concept of normality. The mere operation of comparing children
would lead to the crude fact that some would be in the recommended
pattern and others would not.

[22] The encounter of the trio (paediatrician–child–parent) always takes place in an
institutional setting such as office, clinic or hospital. Later, the school will
become the main location for the connection between these actors.

[23] A few notes on the history of France's child welfare will prove helpful. 'The first
Consultation des Nourissons was opened by Professor Pierre Budin at the
Charité Hospital, Paris, in 1892, for the children born in the hospital. In 1893,
Dr Gaston Variot, a leading French paediatrician, opened a consultation at the
Belleville Dispensary, Paris, and in 1894 the first consultation organized as a
separate institution was opened at Fécamp by Dr Léon Dufour, who called it
Gouttes de Lait. The name became popular.' (McCleary 1935).

[24] France had a long tradition of wet nurses. The practice of sending infants to wet
nurses was a particularly important social problem in regard to the infant
mortality rate. This is why specific measures such as visiting physicians,
medical inspections and state control of wet nurses were taken (Rollet 1993;
Sussman 1982).

Consultation: a weighing scale, some milk and the physician. The material support of this ritual rested upon a register, a card, a scale and so on. The combination of these elements laid the basis of the network of relationships: the scale, the card and the register were positioned as unascertainable players in this particular setting. Budin, the founder of the Consultation, was fairly explicit in regard to the network represented by the setting. Although women leave the maternity hospital already trained to breastfeed, yet upon their return to the Consultation they present a card consisting of the date and the delivery registration, the infant's weight at birth and at its exit from the hospital. The infant is examined and weighed, the appropriate information being written down on a new card. These data are transferred onto a register, so that the staff can easily establish the weekly curve, which is done for every one of the infants (Rollet 1990: 356).

Other countries, not outdone, launched other intiatives. In 1918, the US Children's Bureau for one, with the aid of the Women's Committee and Child Welfare Department, orchestrated a 'children's year' campaign whose aim was to save the lives of 100,000 children under five years old. It could do so by setting up organizations to provide for children in need of special care, the young infant and the pregnant mother being the main target. The campaign focused on a weighing and measuring test as a standard procedure to improve children's health or growth. It was designed to impress on the public the need for preventive healthcare. The Bureau proceeded to distribute five million cards for recording and reporting height and weight. The campaign was a massive effort to enhance children's health and frame their growth. 'The demand for cards for the test has gone far beyond our expectations: 5,000,000 cards have been printed and distributed. A campaign in which 5,000,000 families and many thousands of communities have taken part is one which is talked of and thought about' (Meigs 1918: 51).

The campaign – almost a crusade for welfare activists – turned out to be massive: thus, recording height and weight, and their tabulation by statistics through sound classification and categorization, confirmed public concerns with child development. This tremendous effort came some time after the apex of the hygienist movement, which had already transformed the British, and other countries', system of health, although the two overlapped at some point.[25] If the weighing charts proved from the beginning to be a useful technology in the hands of the paediatrician as well as the parent, how did the chart affect the social actor's behaviour?

The circulated charts produced a number of effects in the network of relationships. Most historians and sociologists consider that the management of the healthy child, as opposed to the child of the hygienic and the high infant mortality rates (IMR) period, positioned the paediatrician in a new relationship to the family for it was a radical cultural innovation (Apple 1987; Lomax *et al.* 1978; Steedman 1992). The paediatrician's core tasks now included the circulation and diffusion of rules, if not norms, in regard to age-appropriate development and behaviour in children and parenting (Halpern 1988: 108). The trend in western societies was obviously toward enforcing standards of physical development put into effect by expert advice connected to the technology of charts. Historians and sociologists speak of the normative regulation of childhood by experts. My concern in this respect is somewhat different: it is to look at the technology upon which this management was based, and moreover to try to find out how the new player acted in the network, thus, in so doing, how social actors behave differently.

Charts stressed parental demand for developmental standards and their obligation, in terms of regulation, to behave in accordance with the standards usually accepted, implemented and enforced by institutions in addition to legitimized authorities. Developmental reasoning gradually instilled the principle by which children started to be taught. Parents, especially upper- and middle-class mothers, wanted to align their children with the prescriptions of the charts because the data reported above yielded the idea that mankind's development in every aspect of its maturation pertained to specific laws visually expressed by the charts and discursively emphasized by the experts. Accordingly, the charts became the best possible way to help parents gauge their child's development:[26] 'sub-normal' attainment was a sign of great concern, if not apprehension, for children and parents.

---

[25] The threat of infant mortality was still present in everyone's mind and the fight against it was not yet won in a hygienist temporality. With child development, we are henceforth in another temporality.

[26] From the 1910s on, public opinion led by medical experts and medical associations alike came to see the charts as the most reliable technology to configure child's development. 'The weight of the child, considered in relation

The natural effect on the mother when confronted by a standard was to proceed to standardize her child, to make him weigh what he should for his height according to the tables...the child rebelled against a system that allowed him no choice as to time, place, kind, amount or manner of taking his bottle and his later foods, and which did not consider whether he was hungry or thirsty or indisposed at the time (Brennemann 1933: 14).

It produced, among other things, eating disorders in children too strictly monitored by their parents so they might perform in conformity with the charts; these appeared as the objective standard against which the child's development would be ascertained (Wong 1993: 92). Brennemann warned that the next step would be the creation of other behavioural and developmental benchmarks. 'The child who will not eat is, ipso facto, a behaviour problem...In one situation the mother tried to standardise her child physically, with such results as we have seen; she is now being confronted by the far more delicate and intangible problem of standardizing him behaviorally' (Brennemann 1933: 16).

Resistance took various forms from the refusal of working-class parents and children to attend compulsory schooling to the refusal of regular weighing or to abide by the charts and its provisions put forward by the experts (Bliss 1991; Comacchio 1993; Turmel 1997a).[27] The resistance also took the form of puzzlement, quandary and confusion. 'The weight–height–age table in the hands of the uncritical examiner may be grossly abused. The abuses of the tables are due to...' (O'Shea 1924: 23). Children's relationship, and likewise that of parents, to the medical apparatus was mediated by the technology of the chart, which stood as the standard to appraise child development; the chart constrained the actors who, on the other hand, would not always handle the demands suitably. 'G. Stanley Hall has told us how difficult it was to measure the height and weight of school children because parents objected to the invasion of the children's right'

---

to height and age, is the best single, practical, concrete...Moreover, the one most helpful and practical index is the orderly and normal increase in weight' (Wood 1924).

[27] The charts were endorsed willingly by middle-class parents in various societies; working-class parents in the USA seemed to be just as impressed, but offered more resistance in other societies. Can we presume that this pattern prevailed elsewhere and generalize from the American model? Nothing is certain.

(Anderson 1956: 182). Gesell, for one, devoted a considerable amount of space in his later books to the defence of the individual against the statistical average, reacting against a normative view of his behavioural benchmarks by parents, teachers and the like. He advocated a more flexible reading of the benchmarks in response to both parents' resistance or those following along. 'He felt that his works were being misused by parents who constantly compared their children to his behavioral tables, just as earlier parents had weighted their infants against the curve in Holt' (Beekman 1977: 158).

From the outset, researchers were aware of the limits of such a device, especially if it was used in a one-dimensional way: the average child at each stage of its development upheld the impersonal standard for gauging each child's growth. The earlier forms of charts were too rudimentary in design to become a sophisticated technology for they did not indicate any deviation from the average. That is the statistical critique. 'That it is unscientific and unfair to set 'average weight' as a goal for all children or for an individual child' (Whitney 1930: 41).

The relationship between weight, height and age had to be more cautiously articulated in that respect, according to paediatricians and general practitioners alike. 'What the child should weigh is determined by his individual physical build largely, and not by an average of a number of the other children's weights who are of his age and height' (Whitney 1930: 42). This is more of a medical critique as experts were trying to select features of nutritional status. Retan stated two basic propositions in a study on measure and development of nutrition:

- first, there is a great variation in weight for any given age;
- second, the relation of age to weight does not separate the normally nourished children from the undernourished children (Retan 1920: 33).

The consequences of these findings were significant.[28] Specialists discovered that the relation of height to age was much more complex than they first thought: it could not be a standard of nutrition because the relationship of height to age – as physicians of the 1920s taught – would measure the rate of development in stature and had nothing to

---

[28] Physicians and researchers acknowledged the complexity of the chart: what a child should weigh was determined largely not by the average of other children's weight but by individual physical build so as to give an appropriate account of the child's development.

do with nutrition. Moreover, the charts were based on average weights; but as this measure included a rate of 20 per cent of undernourished children and 3 to 4 per cent of overnourished, it could hardly represent the average of normally nourished children.

Two important outcomes would eventually follow: first, normal weight is a variable that should be represented by a zone instead of a concrete number in the charts; second, the links between the average and the normal became looser, and therefore more intricate. So researchers worked at the creation of a more complex standardized chart which would include measurements of hip width, chest width and depth, girth of arms and calves so as to give an account of the nutritional status of a child.[29] They searched for developmental indices by no means limited to physical growth while coping with the idea of complexity in children's development. This paved the way to a much more complex idea of physical development and growth.

In 1905, *Archives of Pediatrics* published a text from Dr Jennings in regard to the medical supervision of schools. Physicians and paediatricians alike manifested a sustained interest in schools' affairs: their conferences and meetings would feature seminars and lectures on topics ranging from school architecture and playgrounds to the curriculum. One question at stake related to the connection between sleep and intellectual work prescribed for children, with over-fatigue and over-stimulation being the principal concern; physicians usually found the amount of work sought by teachers too demanding for young children.[30] 'Knowledge of the physiology of childhood emphatically reveals how seriously inadequate is the provision for brain rest in the whole scheme of school education. No attempt is

[29] These charts could not be used reliably as an indication of nutritional status, which is the physical condition responsive to food, sleep and exercise; weight was not a satisfactory measure of this status because it was insufficiently discriminating. The charts progressively appeared as an index of skeletal framework, the skeleton being the principal factor in determining weight and being influenced by genetics (Palmer 1930).

[30] An unpublished manuscript of Steven Schlossman, 'A Sin Against Childhood: The Crusade Against Homework, 1897–1941', sets the tone on the question of sleep and homework. 'Sleep concerns . . . substantial crusade against homework during the early decades of the 20th century. Several major cities abolished homework in all or most of the elementary grades, and the anti-homework crusade gained ground thereafter, even for middle-school students . . . on the grounds that it overstimulated the brain and prevented decent sleep' (Stearns *et al.* 1996: 361–366).

THE HOURS OF WORK AND SLEEP ADAPTED TO THE VARIOUS AGES
OF CHILDREN.

Ages of Pupils.	Hours of Work per Day.	Hours of Sleep per Night.
From 5 to 6 years............	1	13½
" 6 " 7 "	1½	13
" 7 " 8 "	2	12½
" 8 " 9 "	2½	12
" 9 " 10 "	3	11½
" 10 " 12 "	4	11
" 12 " 14 "	5	10½
" 14 " 16 "	6	10
" 16 " 18 "	7	9½
" 18 " 19 "	8	9

Chart 2: Hours of work and sleep
Source: Jennings 1905

made to adjust work and sleep to the physiological demands of the young, growing child' (Jennings 1905: 490). Jennings published a chart tabulating the hours of work and sleep required for children in elementary and secondary schools (see Chart 2).

The US Children's Bureau[31] soon became involved in the question of children's sleep. It published a brochure on the subject: 'Why Sleep? Sleep Helps Children Grow' (Anonymous 1929). This brochure was widely distributed across the country through the various organizations and associations associated with the Bureau, while the former *Archives of Pediatrics* chart (Jennings) was accessible mainly to physicians. The Bureau was trying to connect sleep and growth: 'A child grows most when he is asleep...If the child gets too little sleep his growth is hindered...The faster the child is growing, the more sleep he needs' (Jennings 1905: 3). The Bureau's position was double-sided as it proposed the necessity of establishing good sleeping habits in infancy. It recommended its own sleep chart that was more or less the same as the paediatrician's. But it also required parents to keep track of their child's sleep, noting each day on a diagram the

---

[31] The US Children's Bureau was established in 1912 as an outcome of the first White House Conference on children and youth held in 1909 (Halpern 1988).

time the child goes to bed and the amount of sleep he gets every night.[32]

The important point to notice here is the connecting of sleep and growth, the latter being the great issue in the medical field and in broader society alike. The preoccupation with sleep came at the same time as the interest in growth. 'Sleep issues did not loom very large during the middle decades of the nineteenth century. Manuals for parents... simply did not deal with children's sleep – in marked contrast to their counterparts by the 1920s' (Stearns *et al.* 1996: 345). Sleeping charts were intended to monitor children's lives the same way that the height and weight charts did; the desirability of regularity with the increase of the amount of sleep being the main features sought after. Children had to stick to the prescribed schedule with regularity. Again, sleeping charts came into being as a mediator between children and parents and between children and experts as well. In this set of social relationships, they outlined the social bond by introducing new forces in the network: schedule, regularity, specific amount of sleep, study, exercise etc. (see Table 1) were already translating the parent–child heterogeneous relationships into a new mode, into a new time–space.

Another chart put forward in these days was the posture chart (see Figure 4) aimed at maximizing body mechanics. One of these posture charts appeared in Veeder's *Preventive Pediatrics*, a manual intended to help paediatricians in their everyday practice.[33] Notice that the

---

[32] The White House Conference (WHC) on Child Health and Protection of 1930 looked into the question of children's sleep, through its committee on the infant and preschool child, which surveyed 3,000 American families. The data presented in the report stated that: the young child in the home, is thus the result of empirical research while the data from the Children's Bureau and from Jennings were normative: the fact that this survey indicates the mean, the median, the standard deviation and the number investigated is important in that respect.

[33] This survey was developed by a sub-committee of the White House Conference, who published a report of its own. But the Conference published its own work: *Growth and Development of the Child* (New York, NY, D. Appleton-Century Co., 1932), whose first volume, *General Considerations*, approached this problem of children's sleep from an empirical perspective. They reported different studies and tests made to ascertain how the soundness of sleep varies under certain conditions. They explicitly referred to studies such as the ones by the Institute of Child Welfare, University of Minnesota, Fleming, Hughes and Terman, and studies made in England, Germany and Japan. The last ones showed considerable variations from the American figures.

Table 1. *Weekly schedules*

TABLE 1.—Weekly Schedule in Hours for Schoolboys, Aged 6 Years

| | | School Days | | Week Ends | Weekly Total | |
		School	Home			
Activity	Study	14	0	0	14	40½
	Exercise	7	7½	12	26½	
Inactivity	Relaxation	10½	21	12	43½	127½
	Sleep	0	60	24	84	
Total.		31½	88½	48	168	168

TABLE 2.—Weekly Schedule in Hours for Schoolboys, Aged 8 Years

| | | School Days | | Week Ends | Weekly Total | |
		School	Home			
Activity	Study	17	0	0	17	48½
	Exercise	8½	9	14	31½	
Inactivity	Relaxation	9½	18½	11	39	119½
	Sleep	0	57½	23	80½	
Total.		35	85	48	168	168

TABLE 3.—Weekly Schedule in Hours for Schoolboys, Aged 10 Years

| | | School Days | | Week Ends | Weekly Total | |
		School	Home			
Activity	Study	21	0	0	21	55
	Exercise	10	9	15	34	
Inactivity	Relaxation	9	16	11	36	113
	Sleep	0	55	22	77	
Total.		40	80	48	168	168

TABLE 4.—Weekly Schedule in Hours for Schoolboys, Aged 12 Years

| | | School Days | | Week Ends | Weekly Total | |
		School	Home			
Activity	Study	22½	0	0	22½	62½
	Exercise	12	12	16	40	
Inactivity	Relaxation	5½	15½	11	32	105½
	Sleep	0	52½	21	73½	
Total.		40	80	48	168	168

Source: Smith 1920

34   GROWTH, PHYSICAL DEVELOPMENT, POSTURE

POSTURE STANDARDS
Intermediate-Type Girls

Excellent Good   Poor Bad

EXCELLENT POSTURE	GOOD POSTURE	POOR POSTURE	BAD POSTURE
1. Head up—chin in (Head balanced above shoulders, hips, and ankles)	1. Head slightly forward.	1. Head forward.	1. Head markedly forward.
2. Chest up (Breast bone the part of body farthest forward)	2. Chest slightly lowered.	2. Chest flat.	2. Chest depressed (Sunken)
3. Lower abdomen in, and flat.	3. Lower abdomen in (but not flat)	3. Abdomen relaxed (Part of body farthest forward)	3. Abdomen completely relaxed and protuberant.
4. Back curves within normal limits.	4. Back curves slightly increased.	4. Back curves exaggerated.	4. Back curves extremely exaggerated.

Children's Bureau, United States Department of Labor, Washington, D.C., 1926.

FIG. 5.—STANDARDS OF POSTURE FOR INTERMEDIATE TYPE GIRLS.
Wall charts similar to the above may be obtained through the Children's Bureau.

Figure 4: Posture standards
Source: Veeder 1926

posture chart is a normative chart; empirical research was, however, carried on so as to understand how schoolchildren would perform according to the chart's norms. In a survey on body mechanics managed by the WHC's sub-committee, the examination of 1,708 children revealed that 1 per cent had excellent posture, A; 7 per cent good posture, B; 61 per cent poor posture, C and 31 per cent bad posture, D, with very little gender difference: 92 per cent of the these children had a posture ranging from poor to bad at the time of the survey (WHC 1931: 84).

Thereupon, the schools initiated a rigorous training programme with a control group – an outcome of the generalization of statistical technology – so as to measure the effectiveness of the programme. The distribution of the posture grade at the first examination was much the same among the two groups. However, the distribution at the second examination indicates that the trained children's posture was significantly different (50 per cent in the A and B categories) from the control group (less than 10 per cent).[34] The posture chart illustrates well the following proposition: society moves forward through the use of the charts, for the charts reorganize childhood in a new way with body mechanics, a training programme, adequate posture and the like.

Let us mention another form of chart in this category: the feeding chart put out in the context of high infant mortality which public policy had tried so hard to diminish (Dwork 1987; Rollet 1993, 1994). The complexity of the situation was increased by the fact that mothers had already started artificially feeding their infants. Bottle-feeding for the newborn child proved to be a hazardous path, since cow's milk and the conditions under which it was produced were not safe enough to prevent those specific infant diseases such as diarrhoea and gastro-intestinal complaints; indeed it soon became the main cause of infant mortality (Apple 1987; Meckel 1990).

Knowledge about the physiology of infant feeding, particularly artificial feeding, was in its early stages. The discovery of a new device for artificial feeding based on the infant's weight instead of age was an important step forward in monitoring the passage from breast- to bottle-feeding; the regulation of the quantity of food was from now on based on weight rather than age (Anonymous 1890: 470). The feeding charts were an attempt to monitor the passage to artificial feeding and,

---

[34] The results of this survey may be briefly summarized as follows: 'Nine times as many children improved in body mechanics under special training as those without training. The groups given training in body mechanics decreased in rate of absence due to illness during the year' (WHC 1931: 194).

in so doing, lower mortality rates due to such diseases as diarrhoea (Douglas 1905: 748). The important point is not the control that paediatricians exerted on mothers, which is too conventional a type of sociology to yield a convincing explanation, but the fact that the chart acted upon the network of relationships.

The various charts were among the first social technologies of the regulation of childhood. Some of them did not remain very long while others lasted for a long span of time even though they were modified substantially along the way; such was the case of the weight–height–age chart whose various forms became more differentially settled over the years. The conventional height and weight chart is a formal inscription which contains facts about the child's body under scrutiny, visualizing bodily capacities. However, the processes of this translation are deleted. This is a body made visible by inscription and not merely a set of lines and numbers. It is a hybrid socio-technical network of interconnecting elements, an actor-network, which enables the statement 'this is what is happening in this body'.

Charts and graphs appear to be an essential, indeed unavoidable, actor redefining the whole set of childhood relationships. The standards of weight were received by mothers as a norm: a constraining behaviour to be implemented. From now on, the child's relations with parents and with experts alike were mediated with such technologies. As we shall see in the next section, the technologies did not always take the form of a statistical device.

3.3 Record forms

Record forms are social technologies designed to monitor a child's development as well; but where the charts have generally to do with schoolchildren up to adolescence, the record form is a technology that relates to children from the outset, from birth. At a point in time where the main concern was to combat the social problem of IMR (Hendrick 1994: 94) – appeals in this sense can be documented in journals such as *The Lancet*, the *British Medical Journal*, the *New England Journal of Medicine*, the *Bulletin de l'Académie de Médecine* and the *Annales d'hygiène publique et de médecine légale* – the way different countries confronted the problem varied considerably: physicians and paediatricians required specific technologies that would allow them to put this goal into effect and to tackle the various diseases causing such harm.[35]

There were substantial differences in the manifold national experiences with respect to the IM question (Anonymous 1914) – and these variances have been reliably analysed (Dwork 1987; Klaus 1993; Rollet 1993). 'The French population crisis stimulated an interest in infant mortality and a consensus in favor of maternal and child welfare programs which was not duplicated in the United States. American reformers were more concerned about the quality and the composition of the population than with the rate of population growth' (Klaus 1993: 6).[36] The British experience, somewhat different, was not distinct in this respect (Newman 1906). Starting with the Poor Law action,[37] there was a deliberately designed move to make children central to the national interest: 'a concern for the future of the nation and of the race ... Gorst's declaration ... "to bring home to the people of Great Britain a sense of the danger of neglecting the physical condition of the nation's children" ' (Cunningham 1991: 191). Above these

---

[35] Catherine Rollet's scholarly synthesis proposes four periods relevant to the struggle against IM:

   a) around 1860, a new awareness of IM as a social or national question;
   b) toward 1880–1890, the battle of milk;
   c) at the turn of the twentieth century, a new focus on the mother;
   d) after the First World War, the beginning of a family social welfare policy.

   (Rollet 1993)

[36] The French population crisis is attested in a book, *Dépopulation et puériculture*, published in 1901 by Senator Paul Strauss, considered a leading figure in the movement for infant and childhood welfare (Klaus 1993: 195–250; Rollet 1990: 128). French politics revolving around national anxieties concerning exhaustion and decline is described in Nye (Nye 1984). The Americans on the other hand 'focused on the ethnic composition of the population and the perfection of its physical, mental, and moral health' (Klaus 1993; Meckel 1990).

[37] The concern about the quality of the population was also a major preoccupation in Britain. The improvement of the quality of the race and the question of the 'dangerous classes' were central to this. No less pivotal was the relation of children to poverty, thus to the 'dangerous classes', 'a whole rethinking of the problem of poverty, a project to break up the poor into separate categories ... This process of categorization and labelling meant that "the poor" as a single entity no longer existed; there were different types of poor, different levels of poverty ... Children ... constituted a significant proportion within many of these categories' (Cunningham 1991).

concerns, up to the mid-nineteenth century, were those related to the reliability of the IMR, considered the most crucial problem: parish registers were not trustworthy mainly a significant number of births and infant deaths were not registered. The state had not yet made these mandatory; the latter is critical a condition to yield well-founded data on IMR. Medical arithmetic – not statistics – prevailed in the eighteenth century: a few officials such as Graunt and Black in England or Moheau and Montyon in France found that one in four infants died before the age of one (Rusnock 2005). Thereafter hospital registers were meant to establish more rigorous mortality estimates so that the problem could be fully assessed.

Despite these differences in the national experiences with regard to the IM issue, there is some scepticism: 'it remains extremely difficult to measure the efficiency of human and technical means ... So difficult that most historians and demographers do not want to venture in this direction' (Rollet 1998: 1). Technology, I suggest, is the common feature that runs through these different national experiences and allows us to look beyond their disparities: the unifying factor above the dissimilarities of the struggle against IM. It is unifying because the technology is encoded in specific protocols onto standardized inscriptions for the medical investigation of the child; it allows both parents and paediatricians to behave toward the child on account of a mediated gaze that reorganized relationships in the childhood collective. Thus the technology is not simply a mean or a passive device; it might even be the active constituent that links all the points together (Rusnock 2005).

Different types of technologies are put forward in the struggle against IM. The Pasteurian discoveries and some of their consequences in bacteriology – such as sterilization of milk – are considered technical means that played a decisive role in improving infant survival. Although the technology of the record form was not specifically designed for the sole purpose of monitoring the infant in relation to the IM question, it appears feasible to sort out common features in the diversity of the device and in its various forms used at distinct stages of childhood. I shall examine the technology of the record forms in its different patterns, from the health booklet to the developmental record form; this analysis does not seek to delimit the efficiency of this particular technology, or any other, but to establish how such a technology supports both classification and categorization through standardized inscriptions for monitoring children: how as elementary a technology as the health booklet intervened in the child's life as well as a more complex device such as the developmental record form.

The general context in western societies revolved around the high IMR which public policy and institutions were trying to lower.

1. In England in about 1900, an estimated 10,000 infant deaths went unrecorded annually, mostly in large cities; the issue of collecting and compiling records were acute.
2. 12,657 babies under one year of age died in New York City in 1918. 35 per cent of these died as the result of conditions arising before birth or accidents at birth, mostly preventable.
3. 5,818 babies under one month of age died in New York City in 1918. 75 per cent of these died as the result of conditions arising before birth or at birth, largely preventable.
4. The number of still-births reported in New York City in 1918 was 6,793. Only a small proportion are reported and the total loss of life including miscarriages and interrupted pregnancies is very much larger. Hundreds of these losses are preventable.

(ACHA 1920: 53)[38]

To reach this goal, it was acknowledged that the conditions of pregnancy, delivery and birth had to improve accordingly. 'The basic method used has been early examination and supervision throughout the whole period of pregnancy combined with aseptic delivery and adequate after-care... It is estimated that at least 75,000 pregnant mothers in New York City are entirely without medical or nursing oversight' (ACHA 1920: 53).

For medical experts, the two major problems inducing high IMR were prematurity and diarrhoea (Turmel and Hamelin 1995). 'Premature birth was a significant cause of infant mortality, being responsible for... Diarrhoea, known as the "recurring tragedy", usually became something of an epidemic in the summer months'

---

[38] ACHA (American Child Hygiene Association, formerly the American Association for the Study and Prevention of Infant Mortality) would, in 1923, merge with the Child Health Organization into the American Child Health Association; all these associations were dedicated to the promotion of child health. They usually met once a year and published the transactions of their meetings (Halpern 1988).

(Hendrick 1994: 94). The causes of high IMR were generally classified into three categories:[39]

a) developmental conditions (prematurity, debility, congenital defects);
b) diarrhoeal diseases;
c) bronchitis and pneumonia.

The fact that more mothers began to give birth in institutions such as hospitals and private maternity wards had a positive effect in reducing IM. This allowed physicians to monitor both the pregnancy and the child's birth, to intercede more effectively in such phenomena as prematurity with the emerging technology of the incubator, and thus to place newborn infants under strict medical supervision and stewardship. It is important to appreciate the depth of the change in the behaviour of the family described here.

The first step consisted of persuading the mother to deliver in hospital so that the conditions of birth could be monitored, enhancing the chances of the newborn traversing safely such a crucial period of its life. The second step amounted to physicians taking charge of the pregnancy; it was not a usual behaviour for a mother to seek advice from a physician, especially if her pregnancy was considered without significant difficulties. The third step involved setting up a framework and implementing a device with which it was possible to monitor newborn infants after birth and upon leaving the hospital, the first month of life being the most crucial of all.[40] This required a technology that would allow an efficient follow-up of the child's health and its evolution, once it left the institution and direct medical supervision. This technology is the record form in its various guises.

These first two steps, which mainly concerned the mother, were achievable at the time of the First World War, as an illustration of 'the

---

[39] This classification is the usual one at the turn of the twentieth century. There were variations from one country to the next in regard to the main cause of IM. The main cause of IM in France for instance was not the same as in Britain or the USA at certain periods of time (Rollet 1990).

[40] The discovery of the crucial character of the first month of life happened progressively in epidemiological studies (Bresci and Livi-Basci 1994).
According to Sykes, the baby was at greater risk during the first three months of life; moreover he showed that the first month of life was more dangerous than the second and third (Hendrick 1994). For the USA, see Apple 1987; Cohen 1985; Meckel 1990.

turn to the mother' that some historians have identified in the struggle against IM. 'First, concentrate on the mother. What the mother is the children are. The stream is no purer than the source. Let us glorify, dignify and purify motherhood by every means in our power' (Dwork 1987: 114). This turn to the mother would eventually take the form of 'scientific motherhood' in the USA (Apple 1995), 'mothercraft' in Britain (Hendrick 1994), and *maternage* in France (Klaus 1993). The record forms were instrumental in gathering data about prenatal care and the conditions of the pregnant mother: any particular diseases or any specific circumstances under which the pregnancy developed that deserved to be put on file.

The American Child Hygiene Association (ACHA) reported at its annual meeting of 1919 a double record form[41] which consisted of a maternity centre record form and a physician's record. The first one included such items as:

- personal and social history which collected data about nationality, language, occupation, work, insurance, housing, inmates, income, evidence of disease and alcoholism (information about past and present behaviour);
- history of pregnancies (excluding the present) that carried information about: miscarriage, premature stillbirth, at-term, spontaneous, instrumental, multiple, living, dead;
- items about the current pregnancy: general condition of patient at first visit and observation of patient during present pregnancy.

The physician's record on the other hand listed items such as:

- physical examination findings which consisted of the usual examination provided by physicians for pregnant women;

---

[41] Let me mention here the problem of the multiplicity, thus that of the unification, of the record forms. Hundreds of different forms were devised by physicians and institutions along the years. In the United States for instance, each hospital, city, region, state and professional association produced its own forms. These forms were not entirely different from each other, but they were not identical. Substantial differences from one form to the other in data collection made comparison almost impossible and, furthermore, would make a child's transfer from one institution to another difficult. Paediatricians complained about it. Professional societies such as the American Pediatric Society and the American Medical Association worked to formalize data collection and to produce a standard record form (Halpern 1988). For France, see Rollet (1990).

- record of baby and post-natal care: temperature, weight, umbilical cord, eyes, skin, feeding etc.;
- record of delivery, record of post-partum care, return visit record and post-partum examination.

This brief listing gives a good idea of what was a record form with respect to the pregnant woman: gathering data, keeping track of the pregnancy and its evolution up to delivery and the following days as far as the mother's health was concerned.

Once the process of pregnancy and delivery was under medical supervision, the remaining problem was the follow-up of the aftermath of the delivery and the first few weeks after both the mother and the child left the hospital; this is the third step mentioned above. First, new habits had to be devised and unfamiliar behaviour initiated so that the mother and her child would stay in touch with the medical apparatus in order to reinforce the supervision of both of them, even if their health was considered normal. Thus, secondly physicians needed a technology to implement these habits as a follow-up to the young infant's health.

Various patterns of record forms were introduced by physicians and by institutions (hospitals etc.). The general goal was to somehow keep track of the progress of the health of the newborn infant and his mother from the moment the two of them left the hospital, the focus being however the infant from that moment on, even though the mother's health remained a constant concern. It must be stressed that this was uncommon behaviour in the family; furthermore it had to be implemented to the point of becoming habit. The matter of records – that is, keeping systematic track of the infant's health especially in its first months – is considered of crucial importance in the plan to monitor children's lives in the grand struggle against IM.

As early as 1910, at its first annual meeting, the American Association for the Study and Prevention of Infant Mortality (AASPIM) published one of those record forms: History Blank, in use at the Babies' Hospital of Newark, New Jersey. It was a weight chart and nurses' record which featured general information such as management and care, environment, nourishment, medical history and diagnosis; it included a weight chart in the primary form, a record of monthly visits or weekly inspections, finally a monthly score card and a viability chart. However, there is no indication that this chart was widely used or endorsed officially by the former association. It was a case of what institutions were meant to do to implement a follow-up of the young infant (AASPIM 1910: 261; Coit 1910). In France, after the Roussel Law regarding the protection of children, the regulation of wet-nursing etc, and the 'Consultation des nourissons' as well as the *gouttes de lait*, a new legislative proposition comes into effect: the health booklet[42] became compulsory for each child, detailing information about vaccinations, height and weight, visits to the paediatrician, mode of feeding and so on. It was considered an extension of the medical certificate and of various booklets or notebooks in circulation at that period of time (Rollet 2003, 2004).

In 1914, the American Medical Association (Punch) issued a record form for postnatal work called: Standard Score Card for Babies (Form 2); as an official document of the AMA, it was diffused through its membership – which does not mean that it was immediately adopted, since there is always a form of passive resistance to the widespread implementation of a new technology.

What was this standard score card all about, beyond the fact that it aimed to be a synthesis of the pre-existing forms? A record form is mainly a method of book-keeping, whilst the periodic examination is a sort of annual statement of the child's health. In addition to the open history and record of the child containing data of attendance, changes in diet, a record of illnesses and medication, which the paediatrician kept as a matter of routine, the standard score card displays a chart of the infant's development that proved very useful; a graph in duplicate for both parents and paediatrician gives a clear-cut record of the child's growth and development which tends to maintain the interest of the parents for child's progress in this respect. Along with demographic features and general information, the standard card requested data in five sections:

I Mental Development (Form 3);
II Oral and Dental Examination;
III Eye, Ear, Nose and Throat;
IV Physical Examination;
V Measurements.

---

[42] Different steps were necessary before reaching what is known today as the health booklet: rearing booklet (*carnet d'élevage*), growth booklet, finally the health booklet. This is another aspect of the multiplicity of the record form (Rollet 2003, 2004).

STANDARD SCORE CARD FOR BABIES
ISSUED BY
THE AMERICAN MEDICAL ASSOCIATION
Copyrighted 1914 by American Medical Association.

Total score ....

Entry No. ....

Name .... Address ....

Male .... } Class { Rural.................... Age in months ....

Female .... } { City .... Age division ....

Weight at birth...................Lbs. ....Oz. | Father's name ....

Condition at birth: Strong............. Feeble............. | Address .... Age.............

| Nationality ....

No. of child of mother: 1, 2, 3, 4, 5, 6, 7, 8, 9, 10th child...... | Occupation ....

Breast fed............. How many months................. | Mother's maiden name ....

Bottle and breast fed......... How many months......... | Nationality .... Age.............

| Has birth been registered ....

Bottle fed............. How many months................. | Where ....

What foods .... | If not, why ....

Kinds of food at present.................................. | Baby sleeps alone ....

No. of feedings in 24 hours............................... | If not, with whom ....

Ounces of food at each feeding...................... | Sleeps in open air......... Day.......... Night..........

Examination held at......................... By........ | .... Date...........

I—MENTAL DEVELOPMENT   PERFECT SCORE FOR ALL AGES, 20

		Units	Tenths
	Attention, facial expression, irritability and disposition should be considered during the examination and included in the total marking according to the judgment of the examiner.		
SIX MONTHS	Child sits unsupported for a few minutes (3.).... Balances head (3.).... Eye follows a bright object (5.).... Looks in direction of an unexpected sound (5.).... Child seizes an object and holds it (4.).... - - -		
TWELVE MONTHS	Stands and walks with support (4.).... Makes a few sounds, such as mam-mam, da-da, co-oo (4.).... Plays with toys (4.).... Attempts to use paper and pencil (3.).... Shows interest in pictures (4.).... Clings to mother (1.).... - -		
EIGHTEEN MONTHS	Child walks and runs alone (5.).... Says a few words, such as Mama, Papa, Baby (5.).... Points to common objects in pictures (5.).... Imitates a few simple movements, such as placing hands on head or clapping hands (5.).... -		
TWO YEARS	Runs (4.).... Repeats two or three words (5.).... Knows features (4.).... Obeys simple commands, such as "Throw me the ball" (4.).... Imitates movements (3.).... - - - - - - - -		
TWO AND ONE-HALF YEARS	Talks in short sentences (5.).... Knows names of members of the family (3.).... Roughly copies a circle (4.).... Recognizes self in mirror (4.).... Imitates more complex movements (4.).... - - - - - - -		
THREE YEARS	Talks distinctly (4.).... Repeats sentences of six simple words (6.).... Repeats up to two numerals—meaning repeats first one numeral and then two numerals (5.).... Enumerates objects in a complex picture and attempts to describe it (5.).... -		
FOUR YEARS	Knows its sex (4.).... Names familiar objects, such as key, knife, etc. (5.).... Repeats three numerals (4.).... Compares two sticks (can select the longer) (4.).... Distinguishes the longer of two lines (4.).... - - - - - -		
FIVE YEARS	Compares weights and lengths (5.).... Copies a square (5.).... Counts four pennies (5.).... Describes a picture (5.).... - - - - -		

Examiner...

Mental score......

Score brought forward from reverse page..........

Total score......

Form 2: Standard card for babies
Source: American Medical Association, 1914

The crucial topic in this standard card is encompassed in the first section: mental development. For the first time, a record form incorporates such a specific topic and gathers data concerning mental development, thus providing a more complete picture of the child's

I—MENTAL DEVELOPMENT ᴘᴇʀꜰᴇᴄᴛ ꜱᴄᴏʀᴇ ꜰᴏʀ ᴀʟʟ ᴀɢᴇꜱ, 20

	Attention, facial expression, irritability and disposition should be considered the examination and included in the total marking according to the judgment examiner.
Sɪx Mᴏɴᴛʜꜱ	Child sits unsupported for a few minutes (3.).... Balances head (3.).... lows a bright object (5.).... Looks in direction of an unexpected sound Child seizes an object and holds it (4.).... - - - - - -
Tᴡᴇʟᴠᴇ Mᴏɴᴛʜꜱ	Stands and walks with support (4.).... Makes a few sounds, such as mam-mam co-oo (4.).... Plays with toys (4.).... Attempts to use paper and pencil Shows interest in pictures (4.).... Clings to mother (1.).... - -
Eɪɢʜᴛᴇᴇɴ Mᴏɴᴛʜꜱ	Child walks and runs alone (5.).... Says a few words, such as Mama Baby (5.).... Points to common objects in pictures (5.).... Imitates simple movements, such as placing hands on head or clapping hands (5.)....
Tᴡᴏ Yᴇᴀʀꜱ	Runs (4.).... Repeats two or three words (5.).... Knows features Obeys simple commands, such as "Throw me the ball" (4.).... Imitates ments (3.).... - - - - - - - - -
Tᴡᴏ ᴀɴᴅ Oɴᴇ-Hᴀʟꜰ Yᴇᴀʀꜱ	Talks in short sentences (5.).... Knows names of members of the family Roughly copies a circle (4.).... Recognizes self in mirror (4.).... } more complex movements (4.).... - - - - - - - -
Tʜʀᴇᴇ Yᴇᴀʀꜱ	Talks distinctly (4.).... Repeats sentences of six simple words (6.).... up to two numerals—meaning repeats first one numeral and then two numerals (Enumerates objects in a complex picture and attempts to describe it (5.)....
Fᴏᴜʀ Yᴇᴀʀꜱ	Knows its sex (4.).... Names familiar objects, such as key, knife, etc. (Repeats three numerals (4.).... Compares two sticks (can select the longer) (Distinguishes the longer of two lines (4.).... - - - - - ⁻⁻ ⁻⁻
Fɪᴠᴇ Yᴇᴀʀꜱ	Compares weights and lengths (5.).... Copies a square (5.).... Coun pennies (5.).... Describes a picture (5.).... - - - - - -
	Examiner................................... ....

Form 3: Mental development
Source: American Medical Association, 1914

maturation which was now set beyond physical growth while also integrating it. It would nonetheless be possible to discuss endlessly the items subsumed under the category of mental development.[43] My own argument seeks to establish both the idea of mediation and the proposition that such a device can have actors behave in some regards rather than others. A technological device, understood as a network of associations, is an active agent in a web of relationships operating to shape a new configuration of social interactions. The purpose of the standardization of the record form for post-natal care was rather explicit in the eyes of the committee responsible for it.[44]

[43] For instance, items such as 'child sits unsupported for a few minutes', 'rocks head', 'stands and walks with support or alone', 'clings to mother', 'knows its sex' and so on could be challenged as elements specifically related to mental development. But this is not the point of the line of argument extended here.

[44] In fact the committee on procedure and standard record forms worked on the standardization of three record forms: the first form dealt with prenatal care, the second with obstetrical care and the third with post-natal work (ACHA 1918).

1. To promote intelligent motherhood, including prenatal care and to foster maternal nursing
2. To keep well babies well
3. To prevent sickness and death in early infancy
4. To place babies under the supervision of infant welfare agencies as early as possible
5. To prevent the ailments of infancy and early childhood, particularly those which handicap or lead to defects and disabilities in later life.
                                                              (ACHA 1918: 259)

In 1926, the American Child Health Association distributed the Developmental Record Form[45] intended to aid physicians in assessing the progress of the child (Form 4). The form included a listing of behavioural benchmarks considered normal for children in specified age categories. If a medical health examination is an assessment of constitutional status, then a developmental health examination is considered as an assessment of specific progress in physical growth in mental maturation, in emotional stability, and in various other aspects of normal healthy childhood.[46] Developmental indices went well above physical growth as they incorporated psychosocial norms (Halpern 1988: 89).

The association between paediatrics and psychology meant: 'the close interrelation between physical growth and mental growth and the interdependence of the two' (Veeder 1926: 65). Psychology purports to a knowledge of the mind: how it works, how it develops, how it reacts, and the condition influencing its working; the paediatricians were not even thinking about child psychology. Gesell, especially through his influential book: *Mental Growth of the Preschool Child*, was instrumental in the introduction of the mental development chart (Ames 1989). He stated that the normal child was not the average child of the statistical method because, under proper expert supervision, the normal child could develop to the utmost of his

---

[45] American paediatricians, B. Veeder and G. T. Palmer, designed a Developmental Record Card, for the child of preschool age, one to six years of age. This chart was distributed through the Child Health Association and AMA; it provided a form for a yearly recording of the essential features of the child's growth and development (Veeder 1926).

[46] These other aspects of a healthy childhood included estimates of muscular power and coordination, of personal social reactions, of reasoning and the handling of factual material, of mechanical intelligence and ability, of self-reliance and emotional stability (Veeder 1926).

DEVELOPMENT RECORD

(1 to 6 Years)

| | | Number | Name |

Name_____Address_____

Date of Birth_____Is Birth Registered_____Nationality_____

Position of child in family____1____2____3____4____5____6____

Important Family Data_____

_____

_____

_____

Full term_____Delivery, Normal_____

Premature_____Forceps_____

Birth weight_____Asphyxia_____

_____Complication_____

	Birth	3 mo.	6 mo.	9 mo.	1 Yr.
Breast fed_____months					
Breast and comple._____ Weight lbs._____					
Bottle fed_____months Illness in infancy_____					
Type of food_____					
Supplement to breast or bottle_____					

	Year	Age			Year
Measles_____			Vaccination_____		
Scarlet Fever_____			Schick Test_____		
Chicken Pox_____			T. A. T._____		
Diphtheria_____			Dick Test_____		
Mumps_____			S. F. Toxin_____		
Pertussis_____			T. P. T._____		

Form 4: Development record
Source: Veeder 1926

physical, mental and moral abilities.[47] Almost all children, apart from the afflicted, could become normal, namely, reaching their fullest development and maturation under the supervision of professional child experts (Varga 1991).

---

[47] The debate between instincts and habits, namely between nature and culture could be stated as follows. All the instincts play an important role in the development of the child's mind and personality. From a purely medical standpoint, fear is one of the most important of the instincts and emotions; anger is a frequent source of behavioural problems in childhood, jealousy and temper tantrums likewise. Habits dominate our lives: they are acquired while instincts are inherited.

One of the most important achievements of modern psychology is the establishment of norms or levels of intelligence for age periods.[48] Psychometric measurements, or mental measurements as they were known in Britain through the work of Burt and Issacs (Wooldridge 1995: 112), are of importance not only in determining whether or not a child is mentally backward, but as a method of recording the child's normal development in the same way that the curve of growth is used for recording physical maturation. Properly used and interpreted, these tests, it was believed, have a place in paediatrics in that they supply a standard of mental development. 'The psychometrists... insisted... and, for them, the most important and interesting of these qualities was "intelligence" ' (Wooldridge 1995: 201). The physician should use them the same way he uses the X-ray, as an aid in forming a complete picture of the problem in the individual child.

The various record forms were designed to monitor the child's development from the very beginning of his life, and even before, if we include pregnancy. Some of these record forms, the health booklet for instance, are still in use today although in a quite different form, whilst others vanished over time. The record forms, charts and graphs, are essentially agents whose deeds are deemed unavoidable in a complex network of relationships establishing the configuration of childhood. Not only did it confirm that expert advice is needed, but it secured the centrality of the device itself as an unsurpassed mediator in this network. As the next section will indicate, the mediation did not always pertain to a device, graph or form.

3.4 Well-child conference and periodic MD exams for healthy children

Infant or child welfare is an inexhaustible object of research amongst social scientists. The diverse forms of child welfare clinics throughout Britain, France and United States performed mixed functions that varied in both time and space: from dispensing milk to centres for advice and educational works – instructing mothers on the care of infant

---

[48] The Developmental Record Form can be considered an American experience: the union of paediatrics and psychology. Both the French and the British experiences were rather oriented, as far as mental measurements and development is concerned, toward IQ tests with Binet and Burt.

feeding, hygiene etc. – to medical surveillance for infants and toddlers (Wile 1910). The emergence and consolidation of these child welfare clinics came about within the larger framework of the child movement whose focus shifted, from issues such as IM and child labour to the broader topic of child development (Halpern 1988: 84; Hendrick 1994; Norvez 1990).[49]

Child welfare has been extensively researched over the last twenty years. This section will not be a re-enactment of these studies. Nor is it a matter of either under- or overestimating the expansion of public health activity (Gagan 1988; Rodriguez Ocana 1998). Nor will it be a rerun of the endless debate between those who think that 'rising living standards and associated nutritional improvements have been the predominant source of mortality decline' (Szreter 1988: 34) and those who deem that welfare was the main cause; between those who advocate that mother's ignorance was inexorable and those who see poverty and socio-economic conditions as appalling (Preston and Haines 1991). The perspective upheld here is, however, different: neither the state's apparatus nor the public-health policy in themselves are the focus of analysis. The concern with social technology is constant; constant to the point of disputing Halpern's labelling of the well-child conference as a 'professional service', turning this construction upside down and looking at it as technology.

Despite substantial national differences in regard to child welfare in Britain, France and the United States, similarities and concordance alike are found in these different national experiences. In her comparative analysis of the origins of infant health policy in both France and the United States, Klaus comes to the conclusion that 'French *gouttes de lait* and American clean milk stations, French *consultation des nourissons* and American infant welfare centers had goals in common: the elimination of maternal ignorance, the dissemination of modern hygiene, and the distribution of pure milk' (Klaus 1993: 44). The Americans drew heavily on the French models when they sought methodical measures to prevent IM: weighing infants, encouraging breastfeeding, distributing sterilized/pasteurized

---

[49] 'With the development of this systematic plan of oversight and protection from conception to the age of employment, there exists one gap which merits attention. Insufficient provision exists for the health care of children during the pre-school age' (Wile 1920).

milk, supplying medical supervision of infants and advising mothers on modern hygiene (Chenery 1919; Hendrick 1994: 96).

The British situation also showed similarities. An advocate of mothercraft, Dr Pritchard set up the first Infant Welfare Clinic in England (St Marylebone) to monitor infant feeding, which he connected to the weight rather than the age of an infant. He drew both inspiration and information from Budin's *gouttes de lait* although Marylebone was not affiliated to the French organization (Lewis 1980). The Infant Welfare Clinic was somehow different. 'In general they provided clean milk to infants of varying ages but undertook little, if any, medical supervision' (Dwork 1987: 104). At St Helens, Liverpool and Battersea, the milk depots could neither make provision for medical supervision nor for infant weighing.[50] In the same period, the focus shifted to the education of mothers and to 'mothercraft': the instruction of the mother as a major medical task, thus moving toward the view of *The Lancet*. This shift found its empirical materialization in the health-visiting and infant-welfare system with the 'health visitors' and the 'ladies inspectors'. A similar trend can be noticed when McCleary observed that IM was less a problem of sanitation and rather a question of personal hygiene (McCleary 1935).

What is common to these diverse national experiences? Beyond their noticeable differences, is it possible to find a shared ground upon which these experiences could intersect and connect in some respect? Some authors kept doubts about this mutual ground alive. Rollet distinguishes between the French model and the Anglo-Saxon model; in the first, the methods of the medical protection of childhood, namely the home health visit and the *consultation des nourissons* and mother's education in the institution of the *gouttes de lait,* were united under medical supervision; whilst in Britain and the United States, the medical supervision and the education function were rarely associated in the same institution (Rollet 1993: 11) – an interpretation strongly denied by some researchers. Halpern states that infant-welfare clinics supplanted US milk stations and were constituted as centres for the medical supervision of infants and diffusion

---

[50] Although innovative, the impact of Pritchard's work was limited during his lifetime, because childcare authorities ignored his approaches concerning infant feeding (Gurjeva 1998). The reasons why milk depots did not last are described and looked at in length by Dwork (Dwork 1987: Chapter IV). See Hendrick 1994: Chapter 3.

of childcare advice (Halpern 1988: 84). Dwork concludes that despite the failure of the milk depot system in Britain it provided a stimulus and opened up new avenues for public health: the health visitor paving the way for the medical supervision of children (Dwork 1987: 122).[51]

I wish to propose that, beyond the dissimilarities, all national experiences tended to establish the habit of medical supervision for healthy infants and toddlers as well as to instruct mothers in the principles of hygiene.[52] This supervision was implemented through the technology of periodic medical examination for healthy children considered as a radical social innovation for it transformed to a large extent the behaviour of the actors involved. It is understood that it was unusual to visit a clinic when one was healthy, and that includes the child: only the sick child came to the paediatrician. This was a radical innovation because it reorganized the whole set of relationships in this hybrid socio-technical network: parents received advice from experts – and not only from the family and neighbourhood compound – as well as establishing an indispensable link with their paediatricians in this network (DeVilbiss 1915: 256). 'But, more important, they visit the homes where much needed aid is administered to the often ignorant and helpless mother. They form the indispensable link…they are the ones who give the pediatrist a working picture' (Jones and Hand 1935: 259).

Whether in the form of infant-welfare centre, health visitor or consultation des nourissons, the medical supervision of healthy children is achieved as a technology to regulate child's development from the moment it left the maternity hospital; the main problem being, as Budin had already noticed, that children left hospital in good health, but often sickened afterward and died at home. As for France's

---

[51] The British tendency, hitherto characterized as health visitor and education of the mother (mothercraft), gradually progressed towards the medical supervision of the child with such experiences as the Marylebone Health Society/Infant Welfare Centre (1905) and the St Pancras School for Mothers (1907). These dispositions are indicative of 'the growing official and medical surveillance of, and intervention in, infant care' (Hendrick 1994).

[52] It must be stressed that this technology of regular medical supervision was not intended solely for infants, but for all preschool children, even though these provisions, whether in Britain, France or the USA, were enforced in the context of the struggle against IM.

'consultations' they were conducted on similar lines and had three main objectives:

1) the systematic medical supervision of infant rearing;
2) the encouragement of breast-feeding;
3) the provision of sterilized milk for infants who could not be wholly breast-fed.

(McCleary 1935: 9)

The American example is thought-provoking in this respect. The well-child conference is a setting, fostered by the Council on Public Health and Instruction of the American Medical Association (DeVilbiss 1915: 256), where physicians or nurses weighed, examined babies and instructed mothers on the care of infants. It focused on the routine care of the healthy child giving advice on nutrition, habit training and mental hygiene. 'Habit training, modes of punishment and methods of education are as intrinsic a concern of the well baby clinic as are the regulation of diet and hours of sleep' (Fries *et al.* 1935: 28).

The difficulty of standardizing a protocol in a systematic way must not be underestimated.[53] The first visit occurred about three weeks after the child's birth; nurses weighed and measured the baby then took down a history from the mother, including information on feeding and daily routine; a physician examined the child afterward and inter-viewed the mother. Medical visits occurred at regular intervals: weekly during the early months, monthly until one year, every three months thereafter. The infant clinics set about persuading communities at large and mothers of the value of periodic medical supervision for healthy children. The whole training given at these conferences made mothers more observant of their child's health and more ready to seek the advice of their physicians for minor illnesses (Stuart 1928: 91). To a certain extent, however, there was a trace of cultural resistance to those regular visits; it took a long time to persuade parents to behave in this respect.[54] 'The mothers are much more difficult to manage after the

---

[53] Descriptions of a standard well-child conference are to be found in Bradley and Sherbon 1917; Stuart 1928: 96–97; Veeder 1926: 177–179; Yerington 1928: 71.

[54] It is very difficult to document this resistance because there are very few written reports concerning it. Resistance took diverse forms. Sometimes parents did not want to get too dependent upon the physician for childcare. I am much more cautious than Halpern: 'By the 1920s, American parents had a perceived need for expert child-rearing advice' (Halpern 1988). Stearns *et al.*, for instance, on

babies are two or three years of age, and it is often quite difficult to get them in for an examination, in contrast to the first year when they feel rather inadequate to the situation' (Jones and Hand 1935: 260).

As a technology of regulation, the well-child conference had a common framework: standard equipment, standard staff, standard procedure, a standard record sheet (Form 5).[55] Standardizing this technology (by national paediatrics societies, child-health organizations, and the Children's Bureau) as well as the practices related to it required agreed-upon criteria of what constituted normal development; this raised an enormous task for paediatricians and experts who devised such standards.

The standards had to be scientifically grounded. To do so paediatricians and experts looked to the up-and-coming domain of child development for guidance: 'the development of the baby's mind...the way in which his habits were being formed' (Wasburn and Putnam 1933: 518). How then is the category of habit constructed, what does it include, and why were habits considered so meaningful? (Camic 1986).

An examination is not complete unless the child's habits are studied. Many little children have bad habits of eating, sleeping, thumb sucking, nail biting, bed wetting, temper tantrums, disobedience. Does yours? The healthy child has good habits. He does not fuss about his food ... He eats three regular meals a day...He goes to bed early and sleeps 12 hours. He learns to obey...Parents must work together to help their children form good habits (Anonymous 1926: 132).

This leads to psychology, or mental development. As already noted in the Developmental Record Form, Gesell tried to sort out standards of mental health that would be as legitimate and feasible as standards of physical status. Child-health specialists and paediatricians alike quickly

children's sleep; 'Parents were perfectly capable of ignoring some experts arguments – they undoubtedly modified the most severe elements in Watson's anti-coddling approach' (Stearns *et al.* 1996).

[55] 'The equipment for the conference was simple – white washable furniture, small chairs for the children, comfortable wicker chairs for parents, a large examination table for the physician, smaller tables holding a scientifically designed measuring board for babies and a baby scale, a floor scale...Parents entered the pavilion...where the nurse received them and filled in the record sheet with a full family and personal history, including a habit history. The mother then went with the child to the dressing room, took off his clothes' (Anonymous 1926).

A. Feeding:
> Hours, foods (actual amounts).
> Time consumed at each feeding.
> Behavior (distractibility, speed, methods of rejecting, etc.).
> Variability of appetite.

B. Sleeping:
> Hours.
> Regularity.
> Quality of sleep (nights disturbed by internal stimuli, etc.).
> Effect on sleep of external disturbances (noise, being moved, etc.).
>
> Behavior when "put down" (special measures to induce sleep).
> > 1. At accustomed time and place.
> > 2. Under changed conditions.
> Behavior on waking.
> Effect of unusual day on sleep (upset schedule, unusual social stimulation).

C. Dressing:
> Bathing behavior.
> Changing.
> > Number of times daily,
> > Pre- and postchanging behavior,
> > Training measures employed.
> Undressing at night, rubbing, etc.

D. Play (alone or with others):
> Number of persons playing with the child. Type of relationship.
> Objects used in play.

E. Expressive behavior and personality traits:
> Crying
> > Explained,
> > Unexplained,
> > Time of day.
> > How is baby quieted?
> Laughing
> > Incidence,
> > Stimuli.
> Moods (sensitiveness to mother's moods; duration; changeableness).
> Demonstrativeness of or responsiveness of baby.
> Vocalization.
> Fears.
> Anger.
> Reaction to "discipline."
> Habits (thumb, pacifier, rocking, handling of contact type).

F. Behavior observations during time at clinic.

G. Suggestions made to the mother in the course of the interview.

Form 5: Procedures – well-baby conference
Source: Wasburn 1933

integrated Gesell's norms to the technology of medical supervision (well-child conference). Psychology attained a pivotal status in the domain of child development. Its contribution was not limited to childhood mental development. As the next section will indicate, psychology's main input to child development and to the network of relationships it constituted was doubtless the vast and unavoidable technology of IQ testing which blossomed at the beginning of the century.

3.5 Intelligence testing

Childhood investigation's encounter with psychology has a long history, beginning almost at the outset of the systematic investigation of children. The first formal laboratory of experimental psychology (1883) was set up by Wundt at the University of Leipzig with the general purpose of measuring the mind (Sokal 1987b; Wooldridge 1995). The child rapidly became a privileged locus of observation in this respect. In the aftermath of the first steps of experimental psychology, intelligence testing formally emerged as a technology of categorization and classification (Danziger 1990).

Whether in Britain with Burt (educational psychology and the evaluation of individual differences) in France with Binet and Simon (the creation of a scale for measuring intelligence) or in the USA with Terman (the development of tests and prescriptions for their use) intelligence testing was implemented and well established (Cavanaugh 1985; Cravens 1985a; Hearnshaw 1964). The history of IQ testing is a vast subject, and so is the controversy surrounding it. In this analysis we will focus on it solely as a technology: how does such a device of classification reorganize and stabilize relationships among actors? (Cohen and Pestre 1998: 725).

Historically speaking, however, concerns with regard to mental development as well as the search for standards and norms of behaviour came into the limelight in the 1920s, mostly via Gesell and Veeder's work. The question of child mental development was previously introduced while examining both the Developmental Record Form and the technology of medical supervision. These forms, it should be borne in mind, were designed to assess children's progress in their physical and mental course. The notions of mental growth and mental health became part of the usual language of paediatricians trying to disclose a global – holistic – image of the child's development (Cravens 1988; N. Rose 1991).[56]

---

[56] This movement is best understood as an outgrowth of the personality theory (an ongoing action system integrating self-esteem and life course) which

Mental development is considered part of the institutionalization of psychology in the form of IQ testing, the other major psychology technology of regulation under study here. IQ testing is a technology for classifying children in different settings, schools in particular, according to their ability and the age group average. 'Intelligence testing and other forms of measurement provided the technology for classifying children' (Chapman 1988: 11). This classification of children into ability groups, the channelling of children, it must be emphasized, is conducted with respect to a certain range of legitimized social norms (Rose 1985). The context of compulsory and universal education, its implementation and enforcement, had the effect of creating an institutional demand for the assessment and the classification of children (Brown 1992: 51, 60, 74).

In the context of compulsory education, school administrators and teachers had to deal with children presenting behavioural problems, some of them mild, others more serious: 'ill-suited to the rigours and disciplines of the school, and unable to fill the role of subject in the pedagogic technology of the normal classroom' (Rose 1985: 126). One need to be handled related to the 'feeble-minded': how to determine and to allocate the few spaces available in schools to those who were more likely to benefit from such an environment. A second need concerned the classification among normal children between those whose failure was a problem of retardation and those who could be considered delinquent. Adaptation was the master word of the period: adaptation of children to social norms and required standards of conduct.[57] The school's whole apparatus was looking for a technique that could accurately measure this adaptation and sort the children accordingly. The solution to these educational problems was related to the objective evaluation of the child's mental ability: it was then classified in relation to others and assigned to the appropriate school setting.

> replaced character study in the early twentieth century (Camic 1986; Youniss 1990). It is part of the child-development movement of the beginning of the century which, in itself, more or less succeeded the child-study movement (Sears 1975). It is also linked to the mental-hygiene movement, as psychiatry's involvement in promoting the general wellbeing of society (Brown 1992; Richardson 1989).
>
> [57] One can possibly understand how the dichotomy of adaptation–regulation was brought about as both feasible and relevant through such specific technologies as IQ testing and the like (Rose 1985).

In the first empirical studies, conducted by Preyer, Baldwin and Hall, children began to be weighed, observed, measured and described, so that the data would facilitate the understanding of their growth. Hall for instance excluded nothing: thought, emotions and behaviour were charted; Hall's concern with scientific pedagogy led him to study the emotional basis of good schooling.[58] Pragmatic investigation focused on children's educational progress. In 1890, McKeen Cattell, who studied with Wundt, first coined the term and defined mental tests in the perspective of quantitativeness and law-fulness.

Psychology cannot attain the certainty and exactness of the physical sciences, unless it rests on a foundation of experiment and measurement...by applying a series of mental tests and measurements to a large number of individuals. The results would be of considerable scientific value in discovering the consistency of mental processes, their interdependence, and their variation under differing conditions (McKeen Cattell 1890: 424).

Testing became a focus of strong interest among psychologists who saw formal, quantitative child research as an empirical applied science: numbers, measures, formal protocols for testing and for data analysis were fulfilled in the scientific appraisal of the child. 'Testing was equivalent to experimenting, for psychologists' (Wong 1993: 123). The requirements of education and scientific pedagogy focused the concerns on techniques by which individual differences in ability are measured so that schools can sort out children and channel them.[59] Intelligence tests were designed to meet this concern of school administrators and educators.

Britain had already a long-established tradition in measuring individual differences which started with Galton, gained impetus from the Anthropometric Committee of the Anthropology Section of the British

---

[58] At the same point in time, the possibility of a relation between physical size and mental development appeared in specialist discourse. Physician Porter declared that precocious children tended to be heavier and dull children lighter than the average child; he concluded that there was a physical basis for precocity and dullness. Anthropologist Franz Boas disagreed and there was a controversy.

[59] On the other hand, the standardized achievement tests appeared as another technology for those preoccupied by school standards: the effectiveness of different methods of teaching could be evaluated by the pupil's accomplishment.

Association for the Advancement of Science, was calibrated by
Pearson and applied to psychology by Spearman (Szreter 1986;
Tanner 1981). Galton launched a highly significant anthropometric
survey to study the fear of national deterioration, in which he refined
the research of individual differences and its methodology (normal
distribution, deviation etc.), thus paving the way to the rise of
psychometry.[60] Later on, extending the work of both Pearson and
Spearman, Burt completed this cycle of studies with the school
population while adapting intelligence tests to English children. His
appointment as official psychologist to the London County Council,
where the problem of mentally defective children was pressing,
allowed him to look at intelligence testing as a technology of child-
centred education; his work lay with three groups of children: the
backward, the gifted and the delinquent. The psychology of individual
differences rapidly turned itself into a mental-testing movement,
debating the nature of intelligence, arguing that children's substantial
differences in their intellectual abilities were induced by inheritance[61]
rather than by environment (Sutherland 1984).

An intelligence test device introduced in France, by Alfred Binet,
conducting research at the Sorbonne and working under the aegis of
the *Société libre pour l'étude psychologique de l'enfant* (Society for
the Psychological Study of the Child), developed in 1905 a diagnostic
method for measuring intelligence. French educational authorities[62]
were preoccupied with maladapted and backward children; they
looked for an objective method to assess children's levels, namely to
classify them into ability groups for school purposes (Richardson and
Johanningmeir 1998: 700). With Simon, he established a scale of
measurement, which had eluded Galton. For the first time, psychologists moved away from their usual tests of elementary reactions
to colours and so on and asserted it was possible to measure mental

---

[60] The 'ubiquitous Francis Galton', as Szreter refers to him, is a prominent figure
of British science, particularly statistics, of the nineteenth century.

[61] Burt argued 'that the correlation of scores on intelligence tests support the
notion of a general "g" factor, which was inheritable' (Richardson and
Johanningmeir 1998). The "g" factor would later become the intelligence
quotient, IQ. Before this step, Binet had to bring forth his own device. For the
reception of Binet in Britain, cf. Sutherland (Sutherland 1984: Chapter 4).

[62] The French Ministry of Public Instruction set up a committee in 1904, of which
Binet was a member, to consider the problem of distinguishing 'normal' from
'subnormal' in schools.

functions in a more accurate way by making correlations between chronological and mental age. This discovery represented a major step forward from the usual psychologist's practice concentrated on diagnosing problems of disturbed or mentally deficient children.

Binet's concept of intelligence came directly from Taine, whose notion meant 'thinking, but explained in terms of patterning and re-patterning of images derived from sensory experience' (Reeves 1965: 242). It was in the process of devising their methods to assess normal and maladjusted children that Binet and Simon began to differentiate intelligence and thought by reducing step by step the definition of intelligence and emphasizing a developmental approach in contrast to the dominant views; in this respect, the development of intelligence is never dependent on innate ability but on social and other kinds of fulfilments. Binet published an intelligence test designed after the concept of mental age: 'by the early twentieth century, another concept, that of mental age, was beginning to enter educational schemes and the culture at large' (Chudacoff 1989: 78).

Binet's test was a tremendous step forward because he departed from the abstract problem of conceiving a device to measure intelligence on the grounds of mental faculties; instead he proposed a means of ranking and classifying children according to their abilities and behaviour, which were considered relevant to their educational progress. Binet introduced the concept of intellectual level, designed to measure the child's mental ability. It was represented not by an absolute-zero point on psychological scales but in relation to the distribution of other children's responses.[63] By ascribing an age level to a range of intellectual operations, by establishing the age at which the average child could bring the task to an end, by rating children against their peers and against a normal developmental curve, he submitted the distinction between mental age and chronological age, therefore concentrating on the development of intellectual capacity (Wooldridge 1995: 89).

---

[63] It is a standard definition of the intelligence quotient: the ratio of mental age to chronological age, expressed as a percentage. To formulate Binet's breakthrough in another way: 'a scale of intelligence that matched item difficulty on each test to age expectations; that is, test problems were graded according to difficulty and to the age norms of different mental levels' (Chudacoff 1989).

This was the crucial transformation introduced by the Binet–Simon scale: the classification of children in terms of a single measure — mental age (development) – depending on their chronological age and from the point of view of abilities to perform certain tasks. Their test was reputed for its capacity to differentiate the normal child from the feeble-minded: intelligence became what was measured.[64] In *Les enfants anormaux*, they recognized their test as an administrative device: a means of classifying children into categories to provide for individual differences, to channel them into different paths – vocational, comprehensive schools etc. – thus to assign children to an education suitable to their aptitudes (Binet and Simon 1907).[65]

In 1908, Goddard translated and revised the Binet scale of intelligence, adapting it to American children (Zenderland 1987). Goddard claimed that the tests were capable of establishing discrete stages among normal mental levels of children up to the age of twelve. Goddard wanted to use the test to sort mentally deficient children in different mental levels (Wallin 1914).[66] Terman's revision of the Binet–Simon test (1915), known as the Stanford–Binet (Freeman 1917; Kohs 1917), 'had come into wide use' (O'Shea 1924: 266). It focused on the group's norms and averages. He used the notion of intelligence quotient (IQ), defined by the ratio of mental age to chronological age, to represent a child's mental ability by a single score. Terman's major thesis on human conduct, the fixed IQ, was, with Gesell's maturation theory, the major offshoot of child development from the 1920s to the 1950s.[67]

---

[64] Edwin G. Boring, 'Intelligence as the Tests Test It,' *The New Republic*, 35 (6 June 1923).

[65] Educational ability was, at this time, reputed to be distributed evenly in the school population: a few at the top and at the bottom with the majority in the middle. The difference between the middle/normal and the bottom/subnormal was a matter of degree on a continuum (Hornstein 1988).

[66] This social technology served Goddard to establish a hierarchy of mental defects by mental level; this was ultimately possible only at the cost of defining an unbridgeable and sharp line separating normal and subnormal types of children. But Goddard's translation did not work well; apart from the fact that it could be used by incompetent educators, it was criticized for classifying too many children as feeble-minded (Brown 1992).

[67] The breakthrough in mental tests came when researchers started to separate theoretical issues from methodological practice: despite the ongoing debate concerning the ontology of intelligence, they worked empirically. 'It was the genius of Binet to standardize mental age. Binet understood that intelligence,

In the 1908–1910 period, the testing movement took the form of a vast enterprise developed in a practical way and was fully implemented in public schools within the following decade. School administrators found in the IQ tests a device that met their language of efficiency since mental functions were constructed as a natural resource and education as a technical means of its use (Brown 1992: 46). The tests were designed to be superior to traditional assessments and were more accurate than teacher opinion and therefore supplemented it. By 1917–1919, psychologists had used intelligence tests on a sufficiently large population to be able to validate the results;[68] the normal distribution of intellectual ability in the general population was roughly established and IQ was seen as a useful predictor of school achievement; research would yield the norm for the rational guidance of educational practice. By 1925, the entire public educational system had been reorganized around the principles of mental measurement (Hornstein 1988).[69]

Intelligence tests have proven themselves a useful means of correcting and supplementing the more subjective methods of estimating human abilities... it is important to take account of... how reliably it measures what it purports to measure. It is especially important not to be misled by the apparent definiteness suggested by the numerical scores of tests (Stuart 1933: 32).

In the perspective developed hitherto, the focus was kept constant: a specific social technology, the regulation it provided and the

whatever it is, increases during childhood, and that it is more fruitful for a psychology of individual differences to concentrate on relative levels of intelligence than to try to measure such a nebulous concept on absolute terms' (Snyderman and Rothman 1988: 15).

[68] The First World War was a turning point: there was a universal draft and 1.7 million US Army recruits underwent tests of mental ability, achievement and physical examinations as well. Yerkes, Terman, Thorndike and Scott created the Committee on the Classification of Personnel in the Army. The military sought new techniques of training officers and recruits that would surpass the traditional methods of selection and instruction. In two respects, they were, in the majority, found sadly wanting; neither their teeth nor their literacy were adequate for military service: soldiers ought to be able to read and understand orders (Chapman 1988; Sokal 1987b).

[69] The advent of intelligence testing enlarged the purposes of school from their traditional goals of imparting facts and skills to one of acknowledging individual differences and channelling children in different paths.

resistance it stirred up. To a large extent, the debate in regard to the status of intelligence testing[70] is secondary to the argument taking place here: the effects of this technology of testing in the hybrid socio-technical network of relationship. 'Intellectual performance ... could be ... used "with precision" ' (Richardson and Johanningmeir 1998: 699). It appears that intelligence testing encapsulated at this time the state of the art of classification and categorization for children. The demand for classification came mainly from the school apparatus: 'useful in arriving at a correct estimate of cases referred for metal defect' (Anonymous 1912: 195). Much as school authorities were concerned with the feeble-minded, they were also looking for an objective means of classifying children in the school setting (Chapman 1988). Tests provided the classification and the comparison of children in such categories as subnormal, average and advanced as Figure 5 illustrates strictly or, as in Figure 6, in a more elaborate way.

However the category 'inferior' proved to be too large and general for effective social intervention. The problem of feeble-mindedness – 'an arrest in the normal development of the brain' (Anonymous 1912: 191) – turned out to be an extraordinarily complex question for school authorities: how to ascertain with sound standards and criteria children whose behaviour in the school setting happened to be problematic for teachers and school apparatus. Thus categorization and classification were refined:

made it possible to classify on the basis of mental age, but doubtless led to other differentiations, adopted tentatively ... :
Feeble-minded: Moron Mental age, 8 to 12.
Imbecile Mental age, 3 to 7
Idiot Mental age, 0 to 2
The whole question of the 'moral imbecile', 'defective delinquent', and other special and emotive types, was set aside for further consideration ... The morons are the higher group of intellectual defectives that can earn their own living under proper conditions; imbeciles, the intermediate group that cannot earn their own living, but can protect themselves from common physical dangers; idiots, the lowest group, that cannot protect themselves from common physical dangers (Rogers 1913: 302).

[70] Weinland gives a quick account of this debate (Weinland 1989: 224–227).

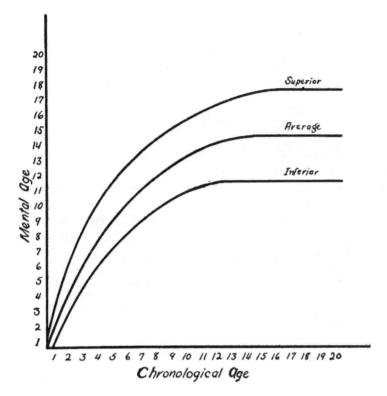

Figure 5: The average mental age
Source: O'Shea 1924

Binet is considered as the initiator of such a refined categorization for feeble-minded children. Working within the French school system, he elaborated a series of criteria based upon the logic/rationality of pedagogy, where language occupies a crucial position in the organization of criteria. An idiot is defined by its incapacity to speak; an imbecile, as someone who will never be able to write; a moron, as someone who cannot rise to abstract thinking (Quentel 1997: 288). The classification of children in such a typology of categories bore explicit repercussions, notably for the school:

there appear to be three duties falling to the school doctor. First, there is the necessity of determining the number of school children in each area who are mentally abnormal. Secondly, there is the work of diagnosis, differentiation

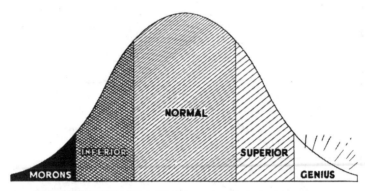

DISTRIBUTION OF MENTAL ABILITY IN CHILDREN

Children may be classified on the basis of mental ability into at least five groups—genius, superior, normal, inferior, moron. The percentage of children belonging to each category is about that represented in the space accorded above to each group; that is, the children of normal ability constitute half of the population, superior and inferior each constitute about one-fifth of the population, while genius balances the true moron group in one-twentieth each of the population. This curve of distribution of mental ability in a large population is calculated according to the theory of probability.

Figure 6: Distribution of mental ability in children
Source: Kugelmass 1935

and classification of such children. Thirdly, there is the duty of advising and supervising the character of their education. The primary question is, of course, that of detection and classification (Anonymous 1912: 191).

The entire question of classification cannot be reduced to that of the feeble-minded, although the latter were deemed highly important at that period. Psychologists produced other categories for children not included in the previous ones through the seventy-five tests of general mental ability that they then released (Brown 1992: 4). 'Normal, retarded, borderline, morons and imbeciles' (Porter *et al.* 1915: 77). 'Bright children, normal children, handicapped children, retarded children, deafened children, blind children; all types and kinds of children everywhere were measured and studied' (Anderson 1956: 183). Provisions were accordingly reckoned in both private institutions and public schools: homogeneous or ability grouping, tracking, classes for sub- or supernormal children, etc. Ultimately, children could not escape a binding classification in some form or another, being relentlessly ordered into categories which tied and bound them; for the practical purposes of school management, the age-level scale served as a helpful, ad hoc selection technology. Intelligence came to be seen as an adjustment to normatively measured levels according to socially relevant criteria.

The most confining of those categories proved in the long-term to be the dichotomy of normal/abnormal. One question comes to mind in this respect: when a child and its parents learned that it was classified as borderline or retarded, how could they possibly react, how was their network of relationships transformed? The technical mediation of a device such as intelligence testing bore within it all the characteristics of reorganizing the whole set of relationships in this childhood realm via the school administrative concerns in regard to classification and channelling of children. However, this reorganization goes a step further than the previous ones: it is binding inasmuch as once the apparatus has classified a child in one category, not only could not he escape it, but the child was stigmatized in a Goffmanian sense. A feeble-minded and a gifted child alike were no longer considered a normal child: they required special provisions, care, treatments and so on. Their whole life as well as their parents' revolved henceforth around this classification and its impediments.

The technical device eluded, to a certain extent, a political or social explanation. It introduces new agency into the topic, thus impinging on the state of relationships among actors; and, accordingly, involving new associations between those actors. This is not a question of ideas or theories, but of ways and means. 'The intelligence test also completely altered the terrain of child development...Now psychological characteristics could be studied just like physical ones...Enough of these tests would set the frame that would allow the normal child to appear' (Wong 1993: 125).

The entire history of intelligence testing is sparked with controversy and fierce disputes; these concern various aspects of the technology such as the eugenic argument pertaining to the relation between physical and/or social attributes and mental attributes;[71] the

---

[71] Such an argument goes back as far as Galton, hence finds its way to Terman's work – with its fascination with genius and upper-class children – and resurfaces again in the recent controversial book of R. J. Herrnstein and C. Murray, *The Bell Curve: Intelligence and the Class Structure in the United States*.

methodological argument regarding the validity of intelligence testing and the way it was used. One ought to remember the stormy contentions ignited by such leading figures as John Dewey and Walter Lippman in the USA or Richard Hoggart and Raymond Williams in Britain. Today almost all books related to intelligence testing devote a chapter to these controversies.[72]

Therefore, it should be borne in mind that controversies are only one form of resistance, albeit an important one; moreover, controversies are generated by people who have the capacity to debate with the intelligence-testing experts. The debate over testing came from three standpoints – the testing community itself, the media and school administrators (Chapman 1988: 129). But controversies triggered by experts and resistance initiated by lay persons are not to be amalgamated; they seldom even overlapped. The opposition of people in communities to intelligence testing is much more intricate to document than the controversies; it nevertheless truly happened. Some commissioner of education observed 'a perceptible fear' from both teachers and parents at the prospect of a low score in intelligence tests which would entail unfavourable comparison and provoke a disgrace 'that must be shunned at all costs' (Stenquist, quoted in Chapman 1988: 142). Children were often apprehensive of the tests, parents afraid of having their children tested, and teachers sceptical about the use of testing. At least, however, some of them resisted.

Although criticized, intelligence testing was regarded by psychologists themselves as a valuable improvement. 'The general mental test stands today as the most important single contribution of psychology to the practical guidance of human affairs' (Sokal 1987a: 113). Not only were psychological features described and measured, they were considered as genuine, substantial and tangible as children's weight and height. Such a technology was indeed immensely influential in schools, classifying and sorting children. But it was not limited to this area.

A device such as intelligence testing bore within it the characteristics of reorganizing children's relationships through schools' concerns for classification and channelling of children. However, this reorganization goes a step further: it is binding inasmuch as once the apparatus has classified (inscription) a child in one of these categories, not only

---

[72] The main books in relation to the controversies are: (Block 1976; Gould 1981; Kamin 1974; Modgil 1987; Snyderman and Rothman 1988).

could he not escape, but the child was consequently stigmatized. Classification of children, however, was not limited to the school setting; it was also used as a selective agency for child guidance. The next section will look at another form of marginalized child: the maladjusted child for whom a specific form of technology is established: the child-guidance clinic.

3.6 Child-guidance clinic

The mental development movement found its way first in Gesell's Developmental Record Form and afterwards in intelligence testing. The progressive refinements of mental measurements – the diverse forms of intelligence testing from Binet to Terman – have always been integrated into a developmental approach; the psychology of individual differences resorted to classification of children with its emphasis on the normal child (Sutherland 1984). Accordingly the channelling of children in different paths within the school system brought to light the obverse of the latter, the subnormal child.

Around the time of the First World War, the notion of maladjustment came into being as a counterbalance to the nineteenth-century category of delinquency, for example, runaways, truants, vagrants and orphans, and more broadly, problem children who lacked sufficient parental backing.[73] In the USA in particular, the shift from delinquency to child guidance was clearly grounded in a preventive approach; the juvenile delinquent was rapidly vanishing from the language of child-guidance workers. 'The change was justified on the grounds that "if juvenile delinquency was to be prevented, early intervention was required; once the juvenile court was involved, it was too late"' (Thom 1992: 206). This sets the general social context of the rise of child guidance, whose sources were threefold: the child-study movement, American psychological medicine (Gesell etc.), and the new psychology in Britain (Hendrick 1994: 162).

---

[73] The question of delinquency is a tremendously complex problem in itself. It literally haunted the public authorities, the reformers, the child experts, the child-saving professionals. It should be borne in mind that one of the first measures taken to face delinquency was to set up an autonomous juvenile delinquency court. By the 1920s, the public authorities had realized that once in court, it was already too late. Child guidance and maladjustment came as an alternative (Cohen 1985; Graff 1995; Sutton 1988).

The forms of problems encountered with delinquents – and their subsequent displacement towards prevention – established a new basis upon which these children's predicaments came to be regarded as developmental and, therefore, containing the possibility of early intervention. Maladjustment will hereafter refer to 'children whose academic achievements or social behaviour did not match up to their innate abilities' (Wooldridge 1995: 146). The maladjusted child was a social problem because it was presumed that maladjustment came from the environment, namely from the larger society; it meant preventing social deviance and enforcing behavioural norms (Cravens 1985b). The discrepancies between ability, achievement and behaviour opened up a space for social intervention with regard to the child's problems and eventual readjustment.[74]

From the training of the mind which intelligence testing was pledged to, child guidance was committed to the care of children's behavioural problems (Table 2) through the moulding of their emotional life.[75] Childhood was recognized as the critical time to intervene, a precious period in which to shape the final adjustment with respect to the regulation of character or behaviour disorders, if serious adult problems were to be avoided. This is considered as a constant trend among child experts and a cultivated public alike. The clinic offers an understanding of the difficulties the child is facing and their relation to his psychological state and to the experiences which he is exposed to. It provided the clinic's orientation by linking together the psychical, the familial and the social.

At the outset, before the Great War, a clinic such as Dr Healy's Chicago Juvenile Psychopathic Institute was primarily delinquency-oriented providing psychiatric examinations of adolescents brought before the courts. That did not last very long and, in the 1920s, both British and American practice turned to child guidance. It had a complex

[74] One of the questions at stake is the criteria for identifying maladjustment: 'Suffice it to say here that discrepancies between high scores in mental tests and poor school performance and/or disruptive behaviour came to be seen as one of the more obvious indications of maladjustment' (Sutherland 1984).

[75] The relationship between the child-guidance clinic and the mental-hygiene movement was steady and constant. Mental hygiene was at the forefront of child guidance both as a purveyor of ideas and at the organizational level. 'The primary function of a child guidance clinic is to present to parents and teachers the fundamental laws of mental hygiene ... The laws of mental hygiene are just as definite and clear-cut as the laws of physical hygiene' (Blanton 1925).

Table 2. *Child guidance problems*

CHILD GUIDANCE INSTITUTE 117

TABLE F. PROBLEMS AS REFERRED

FORTY MOST COMMON COMPLAINTS OF THOSE REFERRING PATIENTS

Problem Referred	Number of Cases
Disobedience, uncontrollable, etc.	42
Stealing	32
Temper	29
"Nervousness"	28
Lying	24
Disturbing behavior in school	20
Truancy, school	20
Truancy, home	20
Retarded in school	17
School failure	15
Enuresis	15
Masturbation	15
Quarrelsome	14
Destructive	9
Fighting with other children	9
Reading defect	9
Shy	9
Sleep disturbances	9
Stays out late	9
Fears	8
Does not get along with children	8
Restless	8
Sensitiveness	8
Undesirable companions	7
Excess phantasy	7
Impudent	7
Mother protective	7
Overdependent	7
Physical defects	7
Sex activity	7
Stubborn	7
Unhappy	7
Defective concentration	6
Cries easily	6
No friends	6
Irritable	6
Irresponsible	6
Obscene language	6
Annoys other children	6
Speech defect	6

Source: W.H.C. 1931

agenda revolving around, at one pole, the health and welfare of the child and, at the other end, boundless concerns clustered around mental hygiene. In the early 1920s, the Boston habit clinic dedicated itself to the mental life of children of preschool age in four distinct parts:

1. study of the environmental conditions and the personalities with which the child comes into contact;
2. study of the mental equipment of the child – his mental age in relation to his chronological age, his opportunities for development, and the intellectual equipment of the parents;
3. study of the personality of the child;
4. treatment:
   a. medical and psychological;
   b. social.

(Thom 1925: 30)

Such a major reorientation is observed in the new four-part protocol. The British experience though, under the auspices of the Child Guidance Council and the London Child Guidance Training Centre Clinic, took a similar approach both at the Tavistock Clinic and at the East London Child Guidance Clinic opened by the Jewish Health Organization in 1927 in Whitechapel and others in cities such as Manchester and Birmingham. By the 1930s, child guidance aimed at treating children with moderate behaviour problems, which meant a narrowing of institutional scope toward the child of normal intelligence who exhibited a range of behavioural and psychological problems known as maladjustment (Blanton 1925: 689). In insisting that 'There are no bad children' (an American child-guidance watchword) but only children with behavioural problems, the clinic's interventions dealing mainly with mild emotional difficulties were grounded in the belief that problems lay in the adjustment between the child and the environment rather than within the child itself (Table 3).

These interventions were also related to the idea of the vulnerability of the normal child. Psychiatry was instrumental in delineating a classification of those behavioural problems and mild emotional difficulties. The third edition of Henderson and Gillespie's leading *Textbook of Psychiatry* (1932) not only provided the rationale for psychiatrists' intervention in child guidance, but also yielded a classification of children's problems (Urwin and Sharland 1992: 190). The textbook bestowed on childhood 'its own particular repertoire of disorders' (Rose 1985).

Table 3. *Relation of sex to specific problems*

TABLE III

RELATION OF SEX TO SPECIFIC PROBLEMS

CONDUCT			PERSONALITY		
	GIRLS : BOYS			GIRLS : BOYS	
Negativism	5.0 : 1		Jealousy	3.5 : 1	
Laziness	2.9 : 1		Imaginary ills	3.2 : 1	
"Bossiness"	2.0 : 1		Apprehensiveness	1.9 : 1	
Nail biting	1.8 : 1		Fearfulness	1.4 : 1	
Stammering	0.7 : 1		Sensitivity	1.3 : 1	
Stubbornness	0.7 : 1		Timidity	1.2 : 1	
Thumb-sucking	0.5 : 1		Inability to get on with		
Destructiveness	0.4 : 1		other children	0.7 : 1	
Disobedience	0.3 : 1		Tics	0.7 : 1	
Truancy	0.3 : 1		Irritability	0.6 : 1	
Unruliness	0.1 : 1		Nervousness	0.5 : 1	
			Restlessness	0.5 : 1	
			"Spoiled"	0.4 : 1	

Source: Preston 1935

a disorders of personality: timidity, obstinacy, irritability, sensitiveness, shyness, day-dreaming, lack of sociability, and emotional disturbances;
b behaviour disorders: truancy, wandering, temper tantrums, lying, stealing, begging, sex misdemeanours, food fads, and refusal of food;
c habit disorders: nail-biting, thumb-sucking, incontinence, constipation, vomiting and stammering;
d glycopenic disorders (migraine, crises of collapse, insomnia, night terrors, cyclical vomiting);
e psychoneuroses (anxiety, hysteria, phobias, obsession and compulsions);
f epilepsy and mental deficiency.

(Hendrick 1994: 167)

Was the child-guidance clinic a technology set to visualize features of the children whom it was taking care of? Can any of the clinic's standardized procedures be considered as an inscription device? Its claim to rely on techniques was clear: 'Child guidance is one of a group of closely related and overlapping techniques and sciences dealing with human adjustment...received its impetus from several techniques' (Stevenson 1930: 252). The clinical protocol always included a three-phase sequence of study, diagnosis and treatment:

a. Study: examination of the case from the social, physical, psychological and psychiatric point of view:
  • an extensive social history of the child's early period: the social worker considered all aspects of the child's environment as well as relationship with family, friends and so on;

- psychological testing remained a constant feature over the different periods of the child-guidance clinic;
- extensive psychiatric evaluation;
- physical examinations were eventually dropped in favour of the reports of the family paediatrician.

b. Diagnosis: the results of the different parts of the study were pooled at a case conference meeting in order to be able to formulate an adequate diagnosis.

c. Once the staff agreed on a diagnosis and outlined a plan, the treatment phase began; it involved a continued contact with the child during which he was treated.[76]

The monitoring of children's behaviour is carried out through certain specific relationships, thus a constant form of circulation:

a. cooperation between clinics and public schools was insured through the work of visiting teachers, an intermediary between school, children and family who assisted in identification of maladjusted children at school;
b. interactions between clinics and local welfare agencies were established through a shared handling of agency-referred cases called the cooperative case method;
c. contacts were established with juvenile court judges and probation officers concerning certain specific cases referred to the child guidance clinic.

(Horn 1989)

An ineluctable lack of uniformity in child-guidance practice is part of the pioneering nature of the technology. In the 1920s, the leading trend was behaviourism with its hallmark insistence on habit formation, training, discipline and so on.[77] On the other hand, in the 1930s, behavioural models and intervention techniques were replaced by psychodynamic approaches which put emphasis upon emotional factors within the child; this shift is linked to professional behaviour rather than more effective therapeutic techniques (Horn 1989; Thom

---

[76] For a slightly different procedure in a child-guidance clinic, see Preston: (Preston 1935).

[77] In the 1920s, leading child psychologists agreed that:

- the child's character was fixed in early life;
- the early influence of parents was determinant of the child's later adjustment;
- the personality was shaped through habit training.

(Brown 1992; Horn 1989; Sears 1975)

1992).[78] The focus also shifted from advice to parents toward suggestions to the child: one must not underestimate the influence of psychoanalysis with its emphasis on the role of the unconscious and the importance of transference (Thom 1925: 30).

Thus a typical child-guidance clinic record would include the following entities from both preventive medicine and social health: the referral data; the social history; the physical, psychological, psychiatric examinations; the presentation of diagnostic interpretation; the treatment plans; the formulation of next steps in treatment; the successive steps which mark strategic points in the treatment itself (Sayles 1932). Was that sufficient to be considered as an inscription device contributing to translation and then to an accelerated circulation in the network? Rose raises the question of control and regulation in regard to the practices of child guidance: 'Abnormal behavior, antisocial conduct, eccentricities ... all these departures from the norm could be linked together as maladjustments, and as predicators of troubles to come' (Rose 1985: 165). One can, indeed, see the hand of the state – or of capitalism – behind these measures. But is control by the apparatus the nub of the question here?

The analytical stance being flouted here, the question at stake, concerns the mobilization of the various social groupings involved, that is, the possibility of an effective collective action across divergent social groupings. The mustering of these groupings around a common goal rests on the circulation of a convincing proposition. Can child guidance be considered an artefact such as a chart or graph, that circulates in the hybrid socio-technical network of relationships without being altered? Is child guidance a technology; if so, what and how does it visualize childhood?

I must stress that the adequate operation of the clinic needed from the outset the active collaboration of parents: 'the cooperation of the home is essential. Parents, as well as teachers, should be able to detect these suspicious signs' (Wood and Lerrigo 1925: 551). Parents were ready to use the clinic to solve household problems such as enuresis, night terrors and bad habits (Thom 1992: 209). Needless to say, mothers especially sought the clinic to supervise mild behavioural household problems; it had to do with both mobilization and

---

[78] For a view of the specificity of the British case and the particular role played by Burt and his methodology, see Thom 1992.

translation. The scope of mobilization in child guidance was rather narrow; from 3,000 to 4,000 a year were seen at the clinics in the mid-1930s in Britain while 25,000 to 30,000 were examined in the USA which is, all things considered, not very substantial.[79]

Above all, the translation that occurred in child guidance is deemed weak for it did not yield a device which could illustrate the maladjusted child. There were contradictory forces going through child guidance – different patterns of intervention and undefined boundaries which cases should be referred to: practitioners were unable to propose an undisputable device which would visualize the maladjusted child. Children with behavioural problems were translated into an inscription device which could be combined, rephrased and thus circulated. Their bodies, either badly adapted or never finally harmonized, were not visualized in the same way as their height and weight. Although an inscription device has the property to render its object intelligible, child guidance on this account could not give an accurate answer to the questions: which child is a problem child? What behaviour is abnormal? (Thom 1992: 216).

Chapter 2 followed the huge transformation of child observation from a speculative activity of lay persons to the scientific form of the laboratory, whose recording amounts to a textual inscription of children with its specialized devices. This chapter looked at these languages and devices as a way of embodying children who, in this respect, are not only textually inscribed, but also codified through technical devices which are accordingly patterned in specific normative ways. The status of the technical device was established from a sociological standpoint. The clarification of this concept was an important step forward. Starting with a proposition – technical objects are a prolongation of human entities – then their task is to activate the collective action of various, conflicting social groupings through their mobilization; thus enabling as well as limiting new forces introduced in the field.

The epitomized form of a technical device is the height and weight chart. Their lasting effect is still perceptible nowadays. They were produced to appraise child development as the most useful index of health once preventive medicine was on its way to mastering

---

[79] These are estimates, not accurate and rigorous figures. They give a general idea of the phenomenon of child guidance and the extent of its mobilization.

contagion and diseases. Considering the scale and the extent of children's height and weight measurements, it is said that mobilization was maximal; and enrolment likewise. Charts became immutable mobiles. Record forms – from the health booklet to the Developmental Record Form – were technologies put forward to monitor children's development and supported a standardized classification and categorization of children in systematically keeping track of the infant's health, both physical and mental, in the aftermath of Pasteurian discoveries. The medical supervision of healthy children was in itself a huge cultural transformation, for it was very unusual to seek medical consultation for a healthy child. Intelligence testing is considered as the technology which crystallized to a certain extent the notion of the normal child, whilst child guidance remained unable to give a satisfactory answer to the questions of the maladjusted child and abnormal behaviour.

The diverse technologies were meant to rally social groupings around the topic of child development. By introducing new forces in the field – inscription devices and immutable mobiles such as schedule, regularity, sleeping charts etc. – they sought to rearrange the social: they were already translating the parent–child relationship into a new mode, into a new time–space. The effect on the mother when confronted by a standard was to proceed to standardize her child, that is to make him weigh what he should for his height according to the tables: the child sometimes rebelled against a system that allowed him no choice as to time, place, kind, amount or manner of taking his food. By succeeding in standardizing the practices of child-rearing, the technologies raised the question of the normal child, which will be looked at in the next chapter.

4 | The normal child

Translation and circulation

A child is recognized as normal when it is classified as such, different in most features from anomalous children, and as standards of development are identified, implemented and generalized in the collective. Standards of development or normalcy – it remains to be seen if and how the two are equivalent, thus, substitutable one for the other; this chapter will investigate the question. The turn of the twentieth century's enthusiasm for normalcy – and for standardization (Adams 1934) – could not bypass the childhood collective for it was in the process of becoming a distinct entity within the national population; public authorities expressed concerns about all but few children's general condition. Developmental standards, which are produced at once and the same time by the activity of and by the technologies of regulation, bring about three different forms of normalcy.

Collection of data, measurement and classification: a new way of thinking, characterized by numerical facts, statistics, probability, mean, dispersion and correlation, seized hold of population studies. These new forces turned up in the childhood collective. Statistical reason, both in its cognitive and administrative lineaments, introduces consistency and regularity in the investigation of the child. This way of reading reality pertained to childhood as well: the institutional knowledge of children started to grasp its object in terms of statistical laws and probability. In this context, the normal met probability, mean etc. and overlapped with these notions. The normal child emerged as a cognitive being whom parents, teachers, physicians etc. taught about and as an administrative device to be rationalized.

This chapter examines the three social forms that materialized the normal child: normal as average, as healthy, and as acceptable. This analysis takes place within the larger context of the rise of statistical thinking (Hacking 1990) and the processes of its contribution to the definition of a national population with respect to children in particular. It pertains to some of the most cogent meanings of the figure of the child and the way it was shaped by larger social trends in which it was embedded. The analytical perspective consists of apprehending the emergence of a singular form in the collective while looking into the transformations of the network of relationships so implied.

4.1 The social forms of normalcy

The rise of statistical technologies, along with the fading away of determinism, led to the rediscovery of normalcy. Statistical thinking was also a condition of possibility for the ascent of a public space in which questions pertaining to the polity were debated; a necessary condition of democracy and of an enlightened debate (Desrosières 1992). These particular movements were embedded in the greater topics of the French Revolution and the Industrial Revolution. The latter spurred a burgeoning appeal for measurement in the economic sphere – trade, manufacture, steam-boats, railways and so on – which subsequently found its way into the social sphere, thus enhancing the public debate. The great quest for measuring children, which emerges in the second half of the nineteenth century, happened to be one of its most extensive manifestations.

The process of normalization is formalized in various domains and later yielded the concept of the normal child. Thus the argument subsequently developed must be more specific about the concept of normal. Historically speaking, the concept was rather equivocal and bore three different set of meanings: normal as healthy, as average, and as acceptable. The first step, however, to the examination of the concept of normal requires an appraisal of the ways in which statistical technologies transformed Western thinking about normality.[1] Then we shall probe how these three different set of meanings emerged both intermingled and successfully at the same time. Finally, the institutional consequences of both the emergence of normality and its various forms in regard to the child will be looked at considering the dynamics of the field of childhood.

---

[1] Although this argument concerns statistical thinking in a general way, there nevertheless exists a national tradition quite different from one country to the other, especially in the nineteenth century. These distinctions will not be emphasized here (Schweber 1996).

Statistical reason is related to the institutional enforcement of the modern nation-state, and this aspect ought to be emphasized, to the progressive disclosure of new social objects, among them the child. A key element in the erosion of determinism – thus in the rise of probability – had to do with social life and with the fact of gaining a new type of knowledge about social processes. Statistics bore the assurance of the consistency and the permanence, both cognitive and political, of the child as an object of investigation: thus bolstering the consolidation of new social objects (Schweber 1996: 119). Social actors living together in different communities, integrated in one society, were subjected to social laws whose nature was statistical and probabilistic.[2] Two consequences ought to be emphasized with respect to those statistical laws.

First, the state needed the means to collect numerical data and to perform statistical operations with them. Within the state, the statistical office had the power to publish official statistics on a wide range of subjects. The Italian cities, which some consider as the architects of the modern conception of the state – one thinks of the Medicis' Florence – made extensive statistical investigations and reports before everyone else. Sweden, it is understood, had the best organizational system, through its pastors, for collecting data on births and deaths. We have also mentioned that the office of the Registrar-General for England and Wales with William Farr institutionalized British vital statistics in the 1840s and 1850s (Eyler 1979; Farr 1875). France, too, had an established tradition since the eighteenth century in regard to statistics collection both with Condorcet, whose *Esquisse d'un tableau historique des progrès de l'esprit humain* set up the basis for social mathematics, Duvillard who was a civil servant specializing in data collection and Villermé.[3]

Above all, Prussia constitutes the finest historical example of the public use of statistics for Prussian intellectuals – and Leibniz is a

---

[2] John Venn's *The Logic of Chance*, first published in 1866, stated the fundamental conception of probability: a series which 'combines individual irregularity with aggregate regularity' (Hacking 1990: 126). Desrosières also considers aggregation as one of the fundamental operations of statistics (Desrosières 1992).

[3] *Recherches statistiques sur la ville de Paris et le département de la Seine*, which gathered data about suicides, is generally considered a model for the 1820s.

refined example of an intellectual interested in statistical questions[4] – stood up for 'the idea that the nation-state is essentially characterized by its statistics, and therefore demands a statistical office in order to define itself and its power' (Hacking 1990: 18). Prussia instituted a statistical bureau, which was to become a key resource for the offices of government. Thus was launched the Royal Statistical Bureau in Berlin, soon to be followed by equivalent offices in London, Paris and Washington. As one of the first involved in statistical data collection, Prussia designed the technology used in population studies, thus giving the state one of its main instruments of governance and control.

In the wake of this movement, society became numerical and statistical with the avalanche of printed numbers in nineteenth century. Thereupon Desrosières introduces an important distinction in statistical reason between two different types of device: the political–administrative and the cognitive (Desrosières 1992: 133). A system of registration, coding, tabulation and publication of statistics concerning the social world put progressively in place by the state's apparatus. The published tabulations gave an instant picture of the rough facts and vital statistics of a society both in written text and in visual presentations. By the 1830s, these tables showed myriad regularities from year to year: tabulations about natural events such as births and deaths, voluntary acts like marriage – distribution of age at marriage – seemingly illogical events such as suicide, crime, or even sickness (Porter 1986: 5). It thus paved the way for indexes related to public health (Danziger 1990: 75).

On the other hand statistics introduced, cognitively speaking, a new way of thinking: numerically, statistically, probabilistically, a scientific schema emerging from the numerical facts about social actors. This new way of thinking was not limited to population and health studies; it expanded to all areas of human activity. The British for instance came to believe that there were laws of sickness cognate to those for mortality; regularities about disease, unknown in 1820, were

---

[4] In a 1700 memorandum, Leibniz 'proposed a 56-category evaluation of a state, which would include the number of people by sex, social status, the number of able-bodied men who might bear weapons, the number of marriageable women, the population density and age distribution, child mortality, life expectancy, distribution diseases and causes of death' (Hacking 1990).

customary by 1840.[5] It was known as the law of large numbers: 'the term "law of large numbers" became entrenched, and it was taken to denote a profound fact about the world... When there are enough events, they display regularities. This law passed beyond a mere fact of experience' (Hacking 1990: 104). The institutions which launched population studies and data collection transformed our knowledge in two ways: by introducing the notion of statistical laws of society, akin to Newtonian laws of nature, and by putting forward the idea of probabilistic laws.

This leads to the second consequence. Grounded in a space of common representations carried out by a conventional language (Desrosières 1992), numerical regularities paved the way for the question of normalcy. While normality is a concept that has a long history which probably goes back to Aristotle – normal was then understood as typical (Hacking 1990: 162) – it secured its usual present connotation around the 1820s. It later became a parameter of culture, a way of thinking and reading reality, percolating almost every sphere of social activities, thus pertaining to childhood as well.

Normality may have seemed hitherto to be a rather homogeneous concept referring to a clearly delineated form of reality and bearing a specific meaning, were it not for the plurality of its historical roots: thereupon the emergence of the notion was much more complex. We shall instead dwell on three different forms of normality – which do not exhaust other forms as such – and examine how each of them is relevant to childhood: normal and average, normal and pathological, normal and acceptable.

A first form of normality as average[6] emerged in a specific cultural configuration. The bell curve[7] became the normative way to behave, everyone being required to stand by the norm imposed by both public authorities and common sense. 'It was he [Quételet] who introduced into practical work the Normal curve, discovered in another context

---

[5] William Farr introduced a new classification of diseases and a new method of analysis of the incidence of birth, life and death which became a model for countries involved in statistical investigations (Hacking 1990).

[6] 'First form' does not mean a priority of any sort. It must be understood as a convenient way of classifying the varied forms of normalcy.

[7] The bell curve is characterized by two quantities: the mean and a measure of dispersion around the mean. Concerning social problems, it is possible to imagine how the deviation from the mean could be interpreted.

by Laplace and Gauss' (Tanner 1981: 122). By the mid-nineteenth century, the idea that statistics could generate laws concerning diverse social phenomena was somewhat novel. Quételet introduced the notion that both natural and social phenomena were managed by laws; they pertained to the 'law of errors that astronomers advanced for standardising their measurements. He conceived human characteristics, physical, social and mental, as being normally distributed according to the statistical law of errors; social problems as well as natural phenomena should then be normally distributed' (Desrosières 1992: 138).

To do so, Quételet had to transform the astronomers' law of error and invert it.[8] Thus a series of measurements would give an accurate account of the people observed: the average height and weight of children at age X was a factual measure of that feature in the group investigated: Quételet measured children's heights and weights in Belgium and he discovered that an infant's weight temporarily drops shortly after birth (Young 1979: 219).[9] 'He provided us with one of the first examples of growth tables for children from birth to age 19 ... Quételet characteristically used these tables to derive an equation for the growth curve for height' (Wong 1993: 93). The notion of the average man came of age: 'The *homme moyen* was, of course, that fictive individual who had the average value' (Tanner 1981: 128).

The generalization of the notion of the average man introduced new objective measurements in statistics applied to society. Quételet's concerns with height and growth are well-known, indeed essential in the fine-tuning of new statistical measurements. His curiosity was endless: in 1846 Quételet seized the opportunity to measure a dozen

---

[8] From astronomy to social phenomena (and one must bear in mind that Quételet was the Astronomer-Royal of Belgium for a period of time) he introduced a major transformation: 'Quételet changed the game ... he transformed the mean into a real quantity' (Hacking 1990). He meant that the average (of a population of schoolchildren of seven years of age) became a real characteristic of this population. His work, both conceptually and instrumentally, allowed to pass from the height of schoolchildren to the measuring of an objective property of that population. The mean that objectively describes a population is a property of a collective entity, not of a single person.

[9] Quételet was interested in children whom he extensively studied in the 1830s at the Foundling Hospital in Brussels (Tanner 1981).

Objiway Indians (Cassedy 1984: 157). The notion of average man had some stimulating conceptual consequences.[10] As abstract a notion as the average man was, it nevertheless embodied the most standard features of children; from an abstraction, average height became a real feature of a population of children. How? 'He transformed the theory of measuring unknown physical quantities, with a definite probable error, into the theory of measuring ideal or abstract properties of a population. Because these could be subjected to the same formal techniques they became real quantities' (Hacking 1990: 108). Hacking considers this transformation as a crucial step: from being descriptive of large-scale regularities, statistical laws turned out to reveal intrinsic accounts and factualities concerning social life (Porter 1986: 57–70).

The cancellation of extreme variations in the balance allowed Quételet to uphold that the attributes condensed in the average man could be regarded as the type of perfection, the normal state, for children at a particular period: it would become the common standard by which other children could be compared. Those who depart from the dominant trends would be categorized as subnormal (Wong 1993: 80). The attributes of the average man – statistically speaking– translate the normal state for actors in a given population. 'Instead of referring to it as the "average child" they have tended more and more to speak of it as the "normal child" ' (Adams 1934: 17).

Normality is, in a second phase, connected with the potentialities offered by probability theory. Since normal is the mean of a normal distribution, the possibility of a deviation from the mean can be statistically attested. The proposition of a continuous deviation from the mean, e.g. the normal, comes from pathology.[11] In this respect, Comte, who coined the term sociology, is considered a figure of transition between the first – normality as average – and the second – normalcy as

---

[10] Quételet, who wrote in French, used the notion of 'homme type' usually translated as 'average man'. The literal translation of 'homme type' ought to be 'typical man'. The problem seems semantic, but could it also be conceptual? Desrosières makes a striking parallel between Quételet's *homme moyen* and Durkheim's concept of society as being *sui generis* realities, different from individuals, and calling for specific analytical methods (Desrosières 1993).

[11] The concepts of norms and standards introduce an essential distinction because it is impossible to have a deviation from either a standard or a norm. You meet the standard or you do not. There is no continuity away from the standard while the continuous deviation is possible from the mean, or from the normal.

healthy – form of the concept of normalcy as he introduced a vital tension in the concept of normal: normal as the prevailing average and the normal as an ideal of perfection that a society tries to achieve (Hacking 1990: 168).

Galton represents the outcome of this process: the construction of normalcy from a probabilistic perspective. While Durkheim saw the deviation from the norm as pathology, Galton called the deviation from the normal distribution excellence at one end and mediocrity at the other. Much as Durkheim identified the normal with the moral, Galton saw in the normal the mediocre. Excellence appeared to him as the aim which society should strive for: the ideal of perfection. He was accordingly very critical of Quételet's average man. The normal was, from his perspective, rather mundane, ordinary and mainstream, with excellence being a deviation from the normal; in the normal curve, one of the extremes was neither abnormal nor pathological but exceptional (Mackenzie 1981). The idea of intelligence testing is not only the best illustration of Galton's construction – one can think of Terman's fascination with gifted children – but also of what happened in the aftermath of probability: the endless fabrication of standards of normal behaviour for children and for other social actors alike.

This perspective was not universally accepted, even less shared. French experimental physiologist C. Bernard, working in the tradition of Bichat, still advocated a deterministic and necessary chain of causation for diseases; the physician's duty was to determine what causes disease, and what restores it.[12] A commentator such as Sir John Herschel was highly sceptical with respect to some conclusions concerning the average man (Tanner 1981: 128). Quételet's average man nevertheless provided a rational argument for the old maxim that social and political society was supported by judicious knowledge. Such knowledge was now upheld by statistical analysis of social phenomena, provided that norms with respect to actors are set up from the diverse features of those actors in a given group (Wong 1993: 81).

[12] 'I do not know why one gives the name law to results obtained by statistics. According to me, a scientific law can only be founded on certainty and on an absolute determinism – not on a probability' (Hacking 1990: 153). Hacking adds that Bernard's immensely successful *Introduction à l'étude de la médecine experimentale* 'is a running discussion of what he calls "determinism"'' (Hacking 1990: 152). He states the French word *déterminisme* should rather be translated as 'mechanism'.

The statistical view of normalcy as average paved the way for a notion of type based on the mean and sub-groups deviating from the mean. It also concealed the idea of progress grounded in a continuous distribution of attributes, thus embodying the idea that enhancement is possible (Rollet 1993; Szreter 1988).

A second form of normalcy, the normal/pathological one, emerged, historically speaking, noticeably apart from a statistical conception of the normal. For a rather short period, normalcy's domain was mainly medical and physiological: hence physiologists used to speak of a normal individual and the deviation from the norm that indicated bad health. Medicine, public hygiene and biology shaped the concept in its modern sense, although a figure like Comte played a crucial role in the generalization of the concept (Canguilhem 1966). The question at stake was the nature of the relation between the normal and the pathological: illness as the qualitative opposite of health and as the quantitative derivation of the normal state. When illness is conceived as evil, then therapeutics amounts to a re-evaluation; when it is apprehended either as a defect or as a surplus, therapeutics consists of a compensation, argues Canguilhem. How do these propositions impinge upon the normal child?

The conception of normal and pathological growth in childhood was transformed with the introduction of statistical thinking and technologies. Quételet's influence on physiological growth studies in nineteenth-century Britain and France is huge and recognized (Steedman 1995: 49). Quételet thought the concept of average man was crucial to medicine. His notion of normal, of being the average value of a specific attribute, entails a double connotation. It relates to actors in a given population, but it also has to do with value: the average means healthy and the reverse, a deviation from the average, refers to unhealthy (Hacking 1990; Tanner 1981). Social actors should endeavour to reach the normal state, understood as the healthy state, for to categorize a group of children as normal amounts to bestowing on them a status: namely, a capacity of translation/mediation which will accelerate the mobilization and enrolment of others in the transformation of its domain of activity (Steedman 1995: 75).

In France, the main medical authorities were the physiologists Bichat and Broussais. The latter took a key part in the coming of age of this form of normalcy. Before him, the pathological state referred to a completely different set of rules from those prevailing in the normal state; thus no continuity from one to the other. Broussais established a new link, by arguing that health and disease are fundamentally in continuity one with the other, differing only in intensity. Accordingly, the concept was usually not a self-sufficient entity, but paired with its opposite, pathology: the pathological became a deviation from the normal (Canguilhem 1966). As a deviation from the normal, all alterations were characterized in terms of variations from the normal state: '(a) pathology is not different in any kind from the normal; nature ... passes from the normal to the pathological continuously. (b) the normal is the center from which deviation departs' (Hacking 1990: 164).

The notion spread into different spheres, among them psychology and sociology, its migration to sociology being essential for the argument made in this chapter. By his adherence to Broussais' principle, Comte carried on a certain construction of the continuity between the pathological and the normal, in fact from the pathological to the normal, for the purpose of bringing about the laws of normalcy. The continuity between the normal and the pathological is reaffirmed so that the knowledge of the normal can benefit from it. At the opposite extreme, the thinking of C. Bernard, whose hostility to Quételet's mean and average we already know about, goes the other way around, from the normal to the pathological for the purpose of a rational action upon the pathological. Here the continuity between the normal and the pathological is reaffirmed in favour of an empirical correction of it. These two conceptions were very influential in the nineteenth century.[13]

Comte transferred the notion of normality to the social domain from the medical one; he is considered responsible for the displacement from physiology to sociology of this conception of the normal and the pathological which he found in Broussais' work. The latter's understanding becomes in Comte's mind a general axiom. This conception can be summarized as follow: illnesses are nothing else than effects of simple changes of intensity in the action of stimulus essential to the support of health (Canguilhem 1966: 19). Such a proposition

---

[13] For a complete overview of these two conceptions of the normal and the pathological, see Canguilhem's key work, Le normal et la pathologique (Canguilhem 1966). He gives a very stimulating account of Darwin's decisive role in introducing into biology a criteria of normality based on the relationships of the living form to life and death (Canguilhem 1977: 132).

comes as the main argument in support of Comte's fundamental sociological principle: 'progress is nothing but the development of order; it is an analysis of the normal state'. Consequently, every modification in the social reality's order is a matter of intensity, not a change in the nature of the phenomenon itself.

The important point to note for our purpose concerns the identification of structures of order both reliable and fallible within the living. This is why the concept of normality was proposed.[14] On the other hand, Comte's position is the illustration of what he called the political road to the true normal state. Moving normality to the political sphere, Comte twisted the idea of normal from the healthy to the purified state that one should aspire to. Hacking however argues that Comte 'expressed and to some extent invented a fundamental tension in the idea of the normal – the normal as existing average, and the normal as figure of perfection to which we may progress' (Hacking 1990: 168).

The connection between the principles of Broussais and Comte will give a better idea of the effect that such a theory of the normal can have upon the child in the work of Durkheim, whose idea of normality is deeply embedded in the medical construction as well as being indebted to Comte.[15] Durkheim proposes that the average gravitate around the central dense mass represented by a single number: the normal in a society is indicated by an average. In *Suicide*, he uses statistics to document his argument about the normality of suicide: year after year in the different European countries surveyed, he found that the rate of suicide was amazingly regular and that the number of candidates for suicide was constant. Inasmuch as suicide rates are averages, they then ought to betoken what is normal (Hacking 1990: 172). Thus, from Durkheim's perspective, suicide was a normal and functional phenomenon.

The relevant question, then, is how the social scientist can tell when a social phenomenon is normal or pathological? Durkheim answers like the biologist who seeks to set apart in the human organism the spheres of normal and pathological physiology. The functional

[14] Canguilhem gives a very stimulating account of Darwin's decisive role in introducing into biology a criterion of normality based on the relationships of the living form to life and death (Canguilhem 1977).

[15] Durkheim's conception of normality/pathology is synthesized in the introduction to *The Division of Labour in Society* (Durkheim 1933).

explanation of suicide trusts that such a social practice is a response to a need expressed in one way or another. This helps to keep society together. It is the increase in suicide that is considered abnormal or pathological. Dysfunctional practice has a dismantling effect on society and is seen as pathological.[16] No form of probability thinking influenced Durkheim's reasoning: that is why he did not consider the abnormal as a simple deviation from the normal, but as pathology. This reflects his preoccupation with morality; the normal was moral.[17] This conception of abnormal as pathology raises the question: what kinds of childhood behaviour would be classified as such? One can think of delinquency, truancy and teenage prostitution, but what else?

Finally, the third form of normality, normal as acceptable, appeared later. Hacking states that these two conceptions, average/probability and healthy/pathology are deeply embedded in western culture as part of a crucial transformation that goes, to put it bluntly, from determinism to probability theory and from the notion of human nature to the idea of normality (Hacking 1990: 179). But some researchers, including the author, doubt that these two above-mentioned forms deplete the practice and the regime of normality that impinged upon children at the turn of the twentieth century. Consequently, the hypothesis of a third form of normality as acceptable, removed from the work of Hacking, pertains to Foucault's work, at least from a theoretical perspective.[18] Hacking's main concern revolves around the question of the rise of indeterminacy. Our task is to some extent

---

[16] Generally speaking, a social phenomenon is considered functional when it is a response to a need. The link between dysfunctionality and pathology is provided by a moral construction of normality. Giddens formulates a relevant point about Durkheim's conception of normality: 'No aspect of Durkheim's writings has been more universally rejected than his notion of normality and pathology, and rightly so' (Giddens 1986). This conception of normality pervades all aspects of Durkheim's work.

[17] Durkheim's first published paper on suicide and birth rate was subtitled: '*Étude statistique morale*' ('A Study of Moral Statistics'). Statistics could be moral then, and Durkheim stated that he wanted to practice a science of morality. See *Revue Philosophique*, 26, 1886.

[18] Foucault's lectures at the Collège de France in 1974–1975 were about the abnormals: a series of eleven lessons which studied the formation of the concept of abnormality in the western world. They are part of a more elaborate cycle of research into psychiatric practices: '*Les anormaux*', published in 1999.

different in that this analysis is trying to track down the notion of the normal child in its various materializations, the way it was translated, circulated and so on.

Instead of going directly to Foucault's figures, it seems more interesting to introduce it progressively through other works and authors, two of whom were already encountered: Beekman and Wong. In his book, *The Mechanical Baby*, Beekman devotes a whole chapter to the question of the normal child. He had formerly framed the gap between Victorian ideals and technology – the application of technology to childcare and, hence, the commodification of childcare – which was already carrying parents and children into the nascent culture of that period: 'If science could prevent disease as Koch and Pasteur had shown, why couldn't it also prevent psychological disorder? And social disorder? Personal failure and poverty? If technology could guarantee consistency in manufactured goods, why couldn't it also guarantee the production of consistently wonderful children?' (Beekman 1977: 112).

This was the culture of middle-class American parents raised during the Great War. Facing such considerable demands from parents, is it surprising that scientific research took a very specific turn which ought to be referred to as the technology of child-raising? This proposition – child-raising as a technology of standardization – is rather close to a Foucaldian perspective concerning the relationship between power and knowledge, albeit far from the most important point. This statement raised the question of the outcome of this standardized system which pertains to the normal child: a particular form of the normal as good based upon the weight of science. Normal as good comprises a huge range of behaviours drawn from group studies by both physicians and experts, although the relationship of good to normal was a problem Gesell, for one, found troubling because to a certain extent it constraints parents in assuming this precise range of behaviours. According to Beekman, this was a 'mathematical abstraction' (Beekman 1977: 158).

Beekman introduces the perspective of normal as good which he does not elaborate conceptually; it is as if he had just suggested the idea without being bothered to unravel and frame it. Wong's conception, the normal as an ideal, is considered as a prolongation as well as a clarification of the latter. Wong is interested in the progressive transformation of the concept of normal from its early meaning acquired in the 1830s up to the 1870s with the British anthropometric studies – a child of a certain age weighing that much and standing just so tall[19] – to its more intricate meaning at the end of the century: its extension to a child's behaviour, psychological attributes, cognitive abilities and social capacities. The transformation of the concept bore important effects for children (Wong 1993: 96).

Wong's argument revolves around the discovery of children's minds, labelled as mental development. If the early studies focused primarily upon children's physical features – one can refer to the authority of the height and weight chart – the new century saw a decisive turn towards the child's mind: emotional and intellectual development became the centre of enthusiasm of those involved in childhood research.[20] Wong shows how ambivalent the concept of normalcy has historically been. Balancing between average and healthy, it can be either descriptive or evaluative. The situation becomes further complicated by a non-statistical use of the concept, as when the normal heralds the typical. 'The implication is plain: the "normal child" may not be the average child; rather it may well be an ideal...and hence the norm by which others are gauged. Rather than being merely average or mediocre, the normal child may well be elitist' (Wong 1993: 102).

Wong's form of normalcy, the normal as ideal, is the main outcome of the trend which consists of huge studies in the child's mental development yielding standards along which parents, teachers and the like would gauge children's development. Not only had children to grow up properly, but they were 'moulded to conform to the scientific picture of how they ought to develop' (Wong 1993: 107). The normal child is an abstraction, an ideal, which parents, children and experts must all strive for.

The appropriateness of Foucault's conception of normalcy to the logic of this case is relevant when discussing a third form of it. In his lectures to the Collège de France, Foucault identifies, around the

---

[19] Studies, such as those by Henry Bowditch, Charles Roberts and William Porter, provided a great amount of knowledge about children's physical features. Paediatrics was also instrumental in adding to the knowledge of children's bodies (Tanner 1981).

[20] This enthusiasm is expressed by the *Revue Philosophique* and *Mind* in which both Taine and Darwin set up a cycle of debate around these questions at the end of the 1870s. Sully and the *Cornhill Magazine* are also considered as part of this ongoing debate.

questions of discipline and normalization, what he thinks are the three
main figures of abnormality: the monster that refers to the laws of
nature and society's norms; the undisciplined taken hold of by the new
dispositifs of body training; and the onanist that sustains a vast
campaign aiming at disciplining the modern family. The problem is
that Foucault admits that he developed the first and the last figures
while leaving the second one in the shade.

It is, however, undeniably the second figure that turns out to be
appealing for this discussion. As Foucault's argument is composite,
complex and polymerous, I shall sort out its most relevant propositions to work out the third form of normalcy already briefly outlined.

- as psychiatry becomes a science and technique of abnormality, so
  I shall consider psychology as a science and technique of normality,
  both of these being technologies of social intervention;
- anomaly as deviant and aberrant behaviour is the main object of
  psychiatry's intervention giving birth to the aforementioned figures
  of the monster and the onanist;
- the medicalization of the abnormal finds its structural corollary in
  the psychologization of the normal; psychology's cognizance relates
  to a non-pathological object;
- childhood is the historical condition of the generalization of
  psychological as well as psychiatric knowledge;
- the undisciplined child relates to the normal child and its small
  deficiencies, related to a lateness in development, different from the
  monster and the onanist.

Thus the form of normal as acceptable pertains foremost to the
normal child with small or mild deficiencies, a deviant or dysfunctional child[21] which sound monitoring can put back on track in
accordance with the prevailing norms. Foucault's ideas about the
training of the body bear on the undisciplined child: the setting up of
new techniques and procedures of body-training is related to the

[21] Small or mild deficiencies, such as feeble-mindedness or mental retardation are
considered outside the scope of the third form of normalcy, thus of this study.
For an overview of this problem, see Cravens 1988, Richards and Singer 1998
and Zenderland 1999. This distinction between subnormal (mental defect or
low normal intelligence) and abnormal, which refers to psychopathology, will
become crucial in drawing the demarcation line around the third form of
normalcy (Cravens 1987).

technico-institutional emergence of this specific form of child. Although Foucault's undisciplined child includes the retarded, imbeciles and the like (Foucault 1999: 309), it is unlikely that these two categories belong to the third form, normal as acceptable, and conform to the criteria already put forward, most notably the criteria of a non-pathological object. They should then be excluded from this particular form, being accordingly relevant as its opposite: the abnormal.

Normalcy, 'one of the most powerful metaconcepts in human affairs... displaced the Enlightenment notion of Human Nature' (Hacking 1991: 286). The three forms of normality being clearly identified and their boundaries established, they are introduced on a logical basis rather than a chronological order of emergence or implementation, for there is no such order, the forms being intertwined in reality. The next section will look at the first form: normal as average.

4.2 Normal as average

Some key constitutive elements of the normal/average child are already known. Following Quételet in his pursuit of the average man, we became aware of the results of research deriving from large-scale regularities; the height and weight chart was examined as a result of these investigations. The purpose of this section is somehow different and one should not consider it a duplication of the arguments already asserted. Furthermore, criteria and elaboration of new standards of normality are to a certain extent devised by experts on the basis of their claims to a scientific knowledge of childhood (Boli and Meyer 1987; Cohen 1985; Cravens 1985b). Focusing on the narratives concerned with the average child, the aim will be to track down the emergence of this form of normalcy's criteria and standards.

The average child, whose features were outlined previously, is part of a much larger trend, a general groundswell which characterized nineteenth-century thought: the passage from a deterministic to a non-deterministic perspective typified by statistical thinking and probability theory which chiefly meant reasoning with numbers.[22]

---

[22] To be more in line with the core of the argument developed here, it meant the application of numerical reasoning to public-health problems, thus to the area of children.

Although abstract, the notion of *l'homme moyen* (the average man) set the pace for statistical thinking: the average values of large-scale regularities in social phenomena and human characteristics, physical, social and mental, were normally distributed. The question at stake in regard to children is formulated accordingly: what are the common features of the average child? In what respect is he different?

Arising in the second half of the nineteenth century, the intensifying shift of child scientists from the backward to the normal child became also part of a larger transformation of the notion of the national population and of the taxonomy applied to speaking and thinking about it. It is within a global movement of reconstruction of the citizenship and the introduction of a new category of social actor, the child, that this redeployment of normality – and abnormality – is carried out (Ramirez 1989). This shift revolves around the increasing defection from the child at risk – juvenile delinquency being the encapsulated form of the child at risk – to the extensive study of the normal/average child as the main concern of the experts.

The large public-health investigations and anthropometric studies were initiated in both Britain and France and extended later on in most of the western world (Coleman 1982: 10).[23] Looking at these studies, Beekman indicates that the Victorians were 'enraptured' with numbers: through these statistics, a new image of society gradually emerged. Galton is unquestionably the most well-known figure associated with anthropometric studies although he is far from alone in this particular area; we have already encountered, albeit briefly, Roberts, Bowditch and the British Medical Association's anthropometric committee, which 'was appointed to conduct a scientific enquiry as to the "average development and condition of brain power among schoolchildren"' (Caws 1949: 104). The journey into this specific domain was rather hasty. The time has arrived to take a more

---

[23] Coleman insists on the coherent body of method and discovery which constituted the public-health domain through public health of the sanitary condition of discrete populations. 'The hygienists were armed with conceptual and methodological tools... Both British and French physicians had given early stimulus to this movement... it was there, principally in Paris, that *hygiène publique*, or public health, won formal constitution as a science' (Coleman 1982).

systematic look at this to establish the criteria and standards pertaining to the average child.[24]

Children's appalling conditions, 'dreadful in the extreme', it should be borne in mind, are the starting and undisputable point.

- In eighteenth-century Europe, the condition of the poor, and especially of their children...London...was a shanty-town of persons living in broken-down sheds.
- Abandoned and vagrant children were everywhere, and their mortality was such that, from 1756 to 1760 the Foundling Hospital in Coram's Fields opened its doors to all homeless infants and children in London; out of 14,934 admitted just 4,400 survived to be apprenticed.
- In the Foundling Hospital in Paris the survival rate was about the same.

(Tanner 1981: 143)

Hygienic inquiries and public health investigations brought to light crude facts which were first perceived as a malaise, but soon became a predicament; they encapsulated the social problems of industrial societies, especially those primarily affecting children, thus contributing to the quandary of childhood's realm: 'a disheartening record of poverty, sickness, and early death' (Coleman 1982: xviii).

The nub of the question regarding the conditions of the poor is found in the labour of children: factory children. The undeniably hard facts provided a sufficient basis for the reformers to launch the first large-scale inquiries. Children began work in factories and mines as early as the age of five; the usual entry into the work force was at the age of eight. The case of the textile industry is exemplary in this respect. For a long period of time children worked at home at cotton processing; when in the nineteenth century the manufacturing moved from home to factory, the children followed and went with it. 'Small children of only three or four years of age were employed to pick up cotton waste, creeping under unguarded machines where bigger people could not go. The older children worked for fifteen hours a day, and on night work too, under conditions which were often enforced by fear and brutality' (Pinchbeck and Hewitt 1973: 354).

---

[24] The following development will draw on Tanner's scholarly work, *History of the Study of Human Growth*. It is worthy of note that some of these earlier studies took the child as their object of investigation (Tanner 1981).

The children's workhouses were in an awful situation: children were left untrained, in idleness and in general hopelessness. The conditions of agricultural labour for children were hardly better on any account.

As alarming as this situation was, yet it led to an acknowledgement that childhood was a disturbed and chaotic state. Children were threatened by appalling infant mortality rates. Child labour was a highly controversial question; the long process which led over a period of many decades from child work to compulsory education was however divisive; problems such as delinquency, truancy and cruelty to children still needed to be addressed. In short the field of childhood was in a state of disorder and confusion: it needed to be stabilized.[25] Large-scale studies were a first step in the direction of mitigating these conditions (Tanner 1981: 147).

Factory children were the first to be investigated in Great Britain: the Report of the Commissioners on the Employment of Children in Factories (1833) was an inquiry into child labour whose commissioner, Edwin Chadwick, the mastermind of public health reform in England, was presumably well aware of both Quételet's survey of children's heights in Belgium and Villermé's work in France, particularly his 1829 *Mémoire* on adult height.[26] The inquiry was thoroughly carried out and data were mustered on morbidity, mortality, stillbirth, illegitimacy rates, accidents and so forth. In each area of investigation, an appointed Medical Commissioner was requested to ascertain the size of the children. For some unknown reasons, all commissioners, except one, ignored the instructions concerning children's stature; the exception proved too narrow a sample to provide a sufficient basis for any generalization. One interesting remark, however: factory children tended to be smaller than other children. As a consequence

[25] The hypothesis proposed here is drawn from ANT and asserts that, once a specific domain of activities – childhood for instance – is recognized as unstable and in transition at a particular period of time, the relevant question is how and according to which processes it can be stabilized again (Law 1999).

[26] Chadwick's 1842 report, *Report on the Sanitary Condition of the Labouring Population of Great Britain*, produced for the Poor Law Commissioners, contributed to launch public works for cleaning up filthy cities. Quételet had investigated the height of children in Belgium two years earlier. Quételet's concerns were here chiefly methodological. His studies were, however, part of a larger trend which is being described here. Chadwick was probably in contact with Quételet through the British Association for the Advancement of Science, as well as with Villermé in France (Tanner 1981).

of the report, the Factory Regulation Act of 1833 prohibited children under nine years of age from working in certain types of factories.

Chadwick's report was inconclusive with respect to children's height. It would soon have a continuation in another report of the 1830s, Horner's large survey of children's height and weight under-taken in collaboration with Cowell. Honer had twenty-seven physicians appointed to factories to measure 8,469 boys and 7,933 girls aged eight to fourteen. The results were published as an appendix to the translation of Quételet's *Sur l'homme*.[27] This survey was 'the first properly documented cross-sectional survey of children's heights' (Tanner 1981: 156). The inquiry corroborated the hypothesis of the smallness of factory children if gauged by present-day standards, although smallness was not confined to working children. Whatever reasons might be involved – such as severe malnutrition of the pregnant mother, chronic undernutrition of the infant, low birth-weight, unsuitable food and reckless use of narcotics – Horner's survey throws light on the harsh fact of children's shortness and low weight alike.

In France the same type of inquiry took place with Villermé, a reformist physician, academician, statistician and hygienist more or less in the position of Chadwick. His 1828 paper, published by the Academy of Medicine, concerned the connection between mortality and economic status, namely between average income and crude mortality rate: poverty was the most important factor in influencing mortality and growth, infant mortality being one third greater among the poor than among the wealthy (Coleman 1982: 168). His 1832 study of the cholera epidemic confirmed the relations of poverty and increased mortality as he associated death rates among various vicinities housing different social classes. Villermé's ability to link infant mortality to social conditions is considered a noteworthy breakthrough. From this inception,[28] his 1829 *Mémoire* published in the influential *Annales d'hygiène publique*, scrutinized adult stature in relation to the same economic factors. He

[27] Translated as *A Treatise on Man and the Development of his Faculties* (London, 1842).
[28] Villermé knew quite well the préfecture of the Seine's publication of 1821: *Recherches statistiques sur la ville de Paris et le département de la Seine*. Coleman states that 'these data (formed) the foundation of Villermé's first systematic consideration of the presumed connection between mortality and economic status' (Coleman 1982).

was looking for the general causes, which promote or delay growth, thus determining the size of children's stature. Villermé dealt with such specific questions as the conjunction of conception and season, the average duration of diseases at different ages and the age-specific influence of temperature on infant mortality (Villermé 1840). Villermé's concern for the welfare of children found its way into his various studies, which were instrumental in the implementation of the first French law regulating child labour (Garnier 1995). He was highly worried about child labour for he spoke of the incredible suffering of young workers (Chassagne 1998: 246).

Progressively, a new picture of the child, hitherto unknown, emerged from these investigations. The turning point appears to be the measurement of American black slaves, which started after the Bill for the Abolition of Slave Trade was passed in 1807. These measurements, no more intended than the previous as an investigation of children labour in factories, had rather a controlling aim. They reveal much about the conditions of slaves' lives and their nutritional status. Compared to the Hormer inquiry, the slave children are taller for both boys and girls. 'These manifests bear out entirely the comments of English observers of the 1830s and 1840s that the physical conditions of the English factory children were worse than the physical conditions of American slaves' (Tanner 1981: 168). A statistical basis emerged that rendered possible the comparison of children, thus the elaboration of norms of growth.

This emerging trend – large surveys of children, systematic measurements, statistical technology and so on – was reinforced to a large extent in the second half of the nineteenth century, thus allowing the very idea of the normal/average child to take form and consolidate itself. An 1872 British Parliamentary Commission made comprehensive investigations into every aspect of both children's and women's work: systematic examination on an extensive scale, registration of height, weight and dimensions of the chest, recording of malformation or diseases and systematic comparison of factory children with other children. The data of the report showed that urban factory children were, at ages eight to eleven, shorter than non-factory rural or suburban children.[29] This confirmed the tendencies outlined in the previous reports.

---

[29] For details of the differences between the two groups and differences among boys and girls in regard to the question of growth, see Tanner (Tanner 1981).

Roberts, a physician committed to the examination and measurements of children of the 1872 report was keen on anthropometry within the larger upsurge of growth studies of the 1860s and 1870s; he pursued his activity afterwards with his American collaborator, Bowditch, which raised the problem of an international framework for further comparison (Steedman 1995: 76).[30] In two well-known papers, he dealt with the question of children's growth.[31] Carefully examining the 1872 report's series of measurements, he proposed using weight and height as a primary criterion for aptness – how large and strong a child should be before employment – excluding accordingly the children at the lower ends of the frequency distribution. Roberts concluded that almost all the disadvantages of factory children except one (flat feet) must be attributed to social causes such as poverty and sickness rather than factory work in itself. He also produced tables of height and weight, which, along with those of Bowditch, were the first bivariate tabulation of measurements to appear. Contrary to Quételet, he laid great insistence on variation around the mean, which is one of the finest methodological ways of letting the normal/average child emerge.

Roberts' assertion of the significance of variation found a noteworthy echo in Bowditch's work in Boston.[32] A Harvard Medical School professor, he manifested a constant interest in child observation

The Parliamentary Commission of 1872 reported in 1876 on the working of the Factory and Workshop Act (Szreter 1986).

[30] Roberts launched an appeal to *Lancet* readers for help in the completion of a series of observations on the height, weight and chest circumference. 'As my observations vary considerably with the social position, occupation, etc, of the persons on whom the measurements were made, I have divided them into two series: one for the wealthier classes, whose physique has not been influenced by the manual labour either of the children or the parents, and who have been well fed and nurtured; the other consists of the labouring classes and their children' (Steedman 1995: 76).

[31] 'Roberts stated that the permanent and constant elements which modify the development of the human body are age, sex and race, and some of the secondary and temporary ones are diseases, occupation, social habits, nurture, food, exercise, rest, etc.' (Szreter 1986).

[32] Bowditch went to Paris, drawn there as the acknowledged centre of scientific medicine in the 1830s and 1840s. He trained with Pierre-Charles-Alexandre Louis at his Société Médicale d'Observation in a systematic method of investigation. Medical students were attracted by brilliant surgeons and sought training in gynaecology, children's diseases, and supervision of the insane (Cassedy 1984).

and growth studies. Well aware of both the British and French researches in this field, he launched a survey of children's measurements with the collaboration of the Boston School Committee: 24,500 children were measured, twice the number in the British 1872 survey of factory children (Cassedy 1984). He edited growth data considered a classic of international literature: he displayed charts of mean height at successive ages as well as introducing a table of the consecutive differences between the yearly means (Tanner 1981: 191). The availability of such technologies as charts, graphs and tables, the statistical thinking underlying it, were soon to have far-reaching consequences.

Being interested in the growth of the individual child in itself, British physician Percy Boulton became a pioneer in longitudinal studies of a group of children; these data served to yield tables of normal height and weight. He was looking for a reliable and accurate method of assessing the normal waxing and waning of the individual child's growth (Young 1979).

In 1880 Percy Boulton, Physician to the Samaritan Hospital for Women and Children (in London), recalled that ten years before, when he 'commenced weighing and measuring', correct averages were completely unavailable and that he had 'no idea how much a child should grow in a year, so that the scales and measures were practically useless'. He searched for some guide, came across Quételet's work ...

1. That there is a perfect form or type of man and that the tendency of the race is to attain that type.
2. That the order of growth should be regular towards the type.
3. The variation from the type follows a definite law, the law of accidental causes.

     (Boulton's letter to *The Lancet*, quoted in Steedman 1995: 75)

Boulton's letter to *The Lancet* introduces the no-man's land between two different temporalities: before and after the tables. Before, physicians did not have any straightforward guidelines to frame, map out and, to a certain extent, to mould the child's growth: there were no universal referents against which a child's growth could be assessed, the physician's experience being arguably the main term of reference. In between there were more and more accurate ideas, such as Quételet's, produced by statistical thinking (Porter 1986) in regard to children's bodily transformation: regularity, average, variation etc.

Tables and graphs were new and unfamiliar objects in the second half of the nineteenth century. The extent of their circulation was amazing and its consequences have to be reckoned with. Two elements are emphasized at this stage of the argumentation: first, tables meant the standardization of growth measurements as well as normalization of the notion of human maturation, thus the rise of an explicit idea of the normal child as expressed in Table 4. Standardization and normalization are core elements of the process of children's translation into a formal schema, which accelerates their circulation in a given field. What new connections between the entities of the network are now made through the tables?

Second, a material object like a table or a chart is today taken for granted and is not deemed problematic, such was not the case in the nineteenth century: it was then a novelty and an intriguing unusual technique. Physicians like Boulton were looking to tables as a primary source of instructions for the child's growth, while lay persons, although sometimes enthusiastic at the prospect of participating in the upsurge of growth measurements, did not know how to cope with the tables (Gurjeva 1999). They could not envisage how the circulation of such an unfamiliar object would eventually transform their relationships. The restructuring of psychology via the rise and circulation of tables will be indicative in this respect.

It is, unsurprisingly, in the wake of Quételet's pioneering work that statistical psychology emerged as an alternative to experimental Wundtian psychology. It took some time, however, to register the relevance of statistical thinking to psychological questions[33] for psychologists did not want to restrict it 'to the study of individual minds, but rather to extend it to the distribution of psychological characteristics in populations' (Danziger 1990: 75). Statistical regularities in human groups raised some very crucial issues with respect to the relationship between the individual subject and the collectivities into which he is integrated: the continuity assumption not only meant that individual attributes were combinable into aggregates, but group characteristics were considered as the aggregation of individual differences. Galton and Pearson clearly grasped the possibilities offered

---

[33] For an account of the resistance and the transformation of psychology with the introduction of statistical thinking – in regard to German resistance and English enthusiasm alike – see Danziger 1990, Porter 1986.

Table 4. *Height–weight–age table*

TABLE 2.—*Weight-Height-Age Table, for School Children of California—Boys*

Height, In.	Normal Range of Weight, Lb.*										
	5 Yr.	6 Yr.	7 Yr.	8 Yr.	9 Yr.	10 Yr.	11 Yr.	12 Yr.	13 Yr.	14 Yr.	15 Yr.
39	34-40	34-40	.....	.....	.....	.....	.....	.....	.....	.....	.....
40	35-41	35-41	.....	.....	.....	.....	.....	.....	.....	.....	.....
41	36-42	36-43	37-44	.....	.....	.....	.....	.....	.....	.....	.....
42	37-44	38-45	38-45	39-46	.....	.....	.....	.....	.....	.....	.....
43	38-45	39-46	39-46	40-47	.....	.....	.....	.....	.....	.....	.....
44	40-47	41-48	41-48	41-49	42-51	.....	.....	.....	.....	.....	.....
45	42-49	43-50	43-50	43-52	44-53	.....	.....	.....	.....	.....	.....
46	44-51	45-52	45-52	45-54	46-55	.....	.....	.....	.....	.....	.....
47	46-53	47-54	47-55	47-56	48-57	48-58	.....	.....	.....	.....	.....
48	.....	49-58	49-58	49-58	50-59	50-60	50-62	.....	.....	.....	.....
49	.....	51-60	51-60	52-62	52-62	52-63	52-64	.....	.....	.....	.....
50	.....	54-63	54-63	54-65	54-65	55-66	55-67	55-68	.....	.....	.....
51	.....	.....	57-66	57-68	57-68	57-69	57-69	57-71	.....	.....	.....
52	.....	.....	60-70	60-71	60-71	60-72	60-74	60-74	60-75	.....	.....
53	.....	.....	62-73	62-74	63-75	63-75	63-76	63-77	63-78	.....	.....
54	.....	.....	.....	63-76	64-77	64-78	65-80	66-81	66-81	66-82	.....
55	.....	.....	.....	65-78	67-80	67-81	67-83	68-84	68-85	69-86	.....
56	.....	.....	.....	.....	70-84	71-85	71-87	71-87	71-88	73-90	74-92
57	.....	.....	.....	.....	73-87	74-89	74-91	74-91	75-93	76-95	77-96
58	.....	.....	.....	.....	76-91	77-96	77-95	77-95	78-97	80-99	81-101
59	.....	.....	.....	.....	.....	80-98	80-99	81-101	82-102	83-103	84-104
60	.....	.....	.....	.....	.....	84-101	84-103	85-104	86-106	86-107	87-108
61	.....	.....	.....	.....	.....	.....	87-107	88-109	89-111	90-112	91-113
62	.....	.....	.....	.....	.....	.....	91-112	92-113	94-116	95-118	96-119
63	.....	.....	.....	.....	.....	.....	95-117	96-118	97-121	99-123	101-125
64	.....	.....	.....	.....	.....	.....	.....	99-122	101-125	104-129	106-131
65	.....	.....	.....	.....	.....	.....	.....	104-128	106-131	107-133	110-137
66	.....	.....	.....	.....	.....	.....	.....	.....	110-137	112-139	115-142
67	.....	.....	.....	.....	.....	.....	.....	.....	115-142	117-146	119-148

* The weights given represent the approximate permissible range for normal children. Underweight is calculated as pounds under the lower figure; overweight, as pounds over the higher figure. Percentages of under and overweight are not to be computed from these tables. Children whose weights are not within the given range should receive special study and attention. Children whose weights are within the given range are not necessarily free from physical defects, nor are the others necessarily physically defective.

TABLE 3.—*Weight-Height-Age Table for School Children of California—Girls*

Height, In.	Normal Range of Weight, Lb.*										
	5 Yr.	6 Yr.	7 Yr.	8 Yr.	9 Yr.	10 Yr.	11 Yr.	12 Yr.	13 Yr.	14 Yr.	15 Yr.
39	33-38	33-39	.....	.....	.....	.....	.....	.....	.....	.....	.....
40	34-41	34-41	.....	.....	.....	.....	.....	.....	.....	.....	.....
41	35-41	35-42	36-43	.....	.....	.....	.....	.....	.....	.....	.....
42	37-44	37-44	37-44	.....	.....	.....	.....	.....	.....	.....	.....
43	38-45	38-45	38-46	38-46	.....	.....	.....	.....	.....	.....	.....
44	40-47	40-47	40-48	40-48	.....	.....	.....	.....	.....	.....	.....
45	42-49	42-49	42-50	43-50	43-52	.....	.....	.....	.....	.....	.....
46	44-51	45-53	45-53	45-54	45-54	45-56	.....	.....	.....	.....	.....
47	46-53	46-55	46-55	46-56	46-57	46-58	.....	.....	.....	.....	.....
48	.....	47-57	48-58	48-58	48-59	48-60	49-62	.....	.....	.....	.....
49	.....	50-59	51-61	51-62	51-62	51-64	51-66	.....	.....	.....	.....
50	.....	53-63	53-63	53-64	53-66	54-67	54-69	56-72	.....	.....	.....
51	.....	.....	55-67	55-67	55-69	56-70	57-72	58-74	.....	.....	.....
52	.....	.....	59-71	58-72	58-72	58-73	59-75	59-76	.....	.....	.....
53	.....	.....	61-73	61-74	62-76	62-78	62-78	62-80	62-82	.....	.....
54	.....	.....	.....	63-77	64-79	64-81	64-82	65-83	66-85	.....	.....
55	.....	.....	.....	66-81	67-82	67-84	67-86	68-88	69-90	70-91	.....
56	.....	.....	.....	.....	70-86	70-88	70-90	71-92	73-95	74-96	.....
57	.....	.....	.....	.....	73-89	73-91	74-94	75-96	77-99	78-102	82-106
58	.....	.....	.....	.....	.....	76-95	77-98	78-100	80-103	83-108	86-111
59	.....	.....	.....	.....	.....	80-100	81-104	82-106	84-109	86-112	90-117
60	.....	.....	.....	.....	.....	84-105	85-108	86-110	87-113	90-117	95-123
61	.....	.....	.....	.....	.....	.....	89-114	90-116	91-118	94-122	98-128
62	.....	.....	.....	.....	.....	.....	94-120	95-122	95-124	97-126	102-132
63	.....	.....	.....	.....	.....	.....	.....	99-128	100-130	101-131	105-137
64	.....	.....	.....	.....	.....	.....	.....	103-132	104-135	105-137	108-140
65	.....	.....	.....	.....	.....	.....	.....	106-137	108-140	110-143	111-144
66	.....	.....	.....	.....	.....	.....	.....	.....	113-145	113-147	114-149
67	.....	.....	.....	.....	.....	.....	.....	.....	116-151	117-152	118-153

* Measurements are to be taken in indoors clothing, without shoes, coat or sweater. Heights are best taken with heels and head against a wall on which an accurate scale with half or quarter inch divisions has been marked or fastened. The head must be level and the body as erect as possible. The age is taken as that of the nearest birthday.

Source: AJDC 1929

by statistical technologies. Group regularities could therefore be read from a psychological perspective: the individual was classified and assigned a place within the likelihoods offered by group performances.

Danziger proposes a distinction between three models of psychological research: the Leipzig model which is experimental psychology's model set up by Wundt in Germany; the French clinical experimentalists' model with Binet at its core; and Galton's anthropometric model – the science of measuring the human body, including some mental measurements (Danziger 1990: 56). I shall concentrate on the last two. The Galton who sheds light on the normalcy/average form is less the statistician or the innovator of measurement – in the restrictive sense of probabilistic model, inference, contingency, regression etc.[34] – or indeed the theoretician of hereditary than the one who, through his deeds at the Anthropometric Committee, pursued Quételet's pioneering work, thus yielding innovative knowledge of individual performance comparisons.[35] If the latter is known for the average man and the notion of aggregated individuals, Galton on the other hand is acknowledged for his sensitivity to individual differences and their variations, to the variability of human attributes and to the measure of human aptitudes. At the opposite pole from Quételet, he was fascinated by the deviation from the mean, which is estimated by the relative distribution of non-average actors (Desrosières 1993: 140).[36]

---

[34] 'But there can be no better illustration of the bond between diversity of interest and statistical creativity than the career of Francis Galton, who began his scientific work as an African explorer and geographer, became interested in meteorology, ethnology, and anthropology, and was then inspired by his conversion to a creed of eugenic reform to take up biology, psychology, anthropometry, hereditary, personal identification, and the new science of sociology' (Porter 1986).

[35] For a detailed account of Galton's contribution to the advancement of statistics, see among others Desrosières and Porter (Desrosières 1993; Porter 1986). For a more complete overview of Galton's contribution to anthropometric investigation, see Desrosières 1993: 140–150; Hacking 1990: 180–188; Kelves 1985; Mackenzie 1981; Porter 1986: 270–286.

[36] Galton's work – his statistical findings as well as some of his heredity/eugenics propositions – found an echo in Durkheim's own research, particularly in *The Division of Labor in Society*, where explicit references to Galton are made (Durkheim 1933). See also (Hacking 1990; Porter 1986).

One can understand the differences between the yardstick of physical features such as height and weight – which he refers to in his notorious *Hereditary Genius* of 1869 – and the measuring of a human aptitude such as intelligence. Height and weight being a natural standard to order a given population, the question arose of whether the appraisal of human features can be put into the same gauge. It would take some time to orchestrate by techniques such as the IQ specific measures built as indicators of individual aptitudes. With normal distribution and regression analysis, Galton uncovers new spaces for measurement: the relationships between individuals and their relative distribution.

Galton's type of anthropometric investigation and measurement is well known. Gurjeva has insisted on a particular aspect of Galton's inquiry: beyond the fact that tabulation became a vehicle for anthropometric measurements, she emphasized that his laboratories were popular, several thousand subjects (9,000) being measured at the International Health Exhibition in London in 1884. Mass measurements, willingness to be measured, familiarity with the practice of measurement and record-keeping alike 'through a number of everyday practices, including child care' (Gurjeva 1999: 6); these and his investigations of mental inheritance and of sex differences in mental traits were Galton's main contributions to psychology's realignment in this period: 'his greatest contribution to mental testing ... is ... the methods which he used to solve his problems' (Goodenough 1949: 24). This is to say that Galton did not by himself undertake any psychological research, although he decisively contributed to the settling and clarification of statistical techniques that would eventually lead to psychology's crucial contribution to the normal/average form of childhood by paving the way to the measurement of intelligence.

The study of the child's mental development has a convoluted history. Concerns about the child's mind were routinely expressed. The leading figure in medical psychology in England in the 1870s, Henry Maudsley, wrote: 'A psychology which is truly inductive must follow the order of nature, and begin where the mind begins in the animal and infant, gradually rising thence to those higher and more mental phenomena' (Maudsley 1876: 19). Thus in the last twenty years of the nineteenth century, the very idea of the normal/average child was drastically changing: the average child was already no longer either a boy or a girl with specific physical features, but bore intellectual

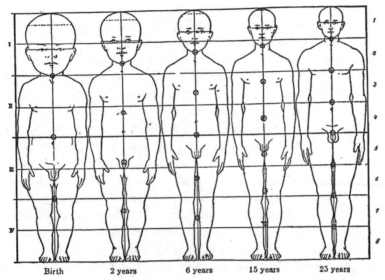

Fig. 3.—Growth: Proportions at Different Age Periods (Stratz).

The figures drawn to scale illustrate the proportions which exist between the head, trunk, and extremities at different ages.

Figure 7: Growth: proportions
Source: Veeder 1926

attributes as well (Figure 7). He or she was also a psychological being whose intellectual peculiarities, appearing on the horizon for the first time, were progressively unveiled. Henceforth, a child's intellectual fulfilment had to be considered as much as its physical growth (Wong 1993: 103). The problem raised, however, serious questions with respect to the link between the child's physical features and its mental traits: 'there is no necessary connection between physical development and mental development' (Adams 1934: 25).[37]

[37] The link between physical and mental development was on its way to becoming a central and crucial question in the collective. In this respect, the whole of Adams' quotation is indicative: 'it is true … that a strong, healthy, well-developed child, who is free of physical defects may have a slightly better chance of succeeding in this world just because he is strong and healthy and well-developed; still there is no necessary connection between physical development and mental development, or between biological growth and intellectual achievement, or emotional stability, or social adaptability, or any of the other factors that make up a successful human life' (Adams 1934).

The context, which saw the rise of children's psychological development, as illustrated in the intelligence-testing movement is well-known. Up until the 1880s, the Germans – Tiedemann, Sigismund, Wundt and others – were active in turning attention to the child's intellectual development. In Britain, journals such as *Mind* and the *Cornhill Magazine* and author such as Darwin and Sully carried on this task. Galton's work was followed by Burt's at the London County Council for the assessment and classification of children as the problem of backwardness was pressing (Sutherland 1984), while, in the USA, European intelligence testing was either translated or adapted by Cattell, Thorndike, Hall, Goddard, Terman and Gesell (Brown 1992). The introduction of compulsory education provided an ideal context to classify children by sorting out those with behavioural problems who might be considered delinquents from the so-called normal children (Hornstein 1988). Schools were looking for a technique that could accurately distribute the children according to their adaptation to the individual school's requirements.[38] An objective evaluation of the child's intellectual ability, thus its classification in relation to others and its placing in the appropriate school setting, arises as the relevant solution (Danziger 1990; Samuelson 1979).

In France, however, a long tradition in psychology, which goes back to Pinel, Esquirol, Séguin, Charcot, Richet and Ribot, was mainly concerned with subjects deviating from the normal pattern, that is the feeble-minded and the insane (Avanzini 1969). Trying to draw a clear distinction between mental deficiency and mental disease, Esquirol for one stated that mental deficiency is not clearly separated from the normal state, and is far from being a discrete category. He sought to find objective criteria by means of which the feeble-minded individual is markedly distinguished from the normal. Meanwhile Richet and Charcot, through their work on hypnosis, did much to bring together normal and abnormal behaviour, for the latter's understanding can inform the normal subject's conduct. Furthermore, Ribot, who was familiar with German experimental psychology and with Galton's

---

[38] Porter gives a stunning indication of the type of problems facing American education. 'The public schools experienced a demographic explosion: from 1880 to 1910, when the number of high schools increased from about 500 to 10,000 and the number of students at that level from 80,000 to 900,000' (Porter 1995).

work, was studying mild deviations in behaviour still considered normal as compared to the pathological (Goodenough 1949).

These earlier studies had already set the ground for an important breakthrough in intelligence testing:

- they depicted manifestly the existence of behavioural sequences, fairly constant from child to child in pattern and order of development; thus tests of development and intelligence could be devised;
- the recognition of extensive individual differences among children in regard to the age where the diverse sequential stages are reached despite the accordance in the recurrent order in which they occur;
- this last point called attention to the requirement for tests establishing the relative position of a child among his peers.

(Goodenough 1949: 32)

This led directly to the pivotal figure of Binet, who introduced an intelligence test device which made correlations between chronological and mental age. His first books, *Psychology of Reasoning* (1899) and *Changes in Personality* (1896), were rooted in the same scientific standpoint: to sketch out individual psychological differences to establish experimentally a classification of characters (Avanzini 1999: 7). His concept of intelligence was a question of patterning and re-patterning images. He happened to be less preoccupied with the universality of mental processes and large-scale investigations, but more involved with the discovery of the individual mind's singularity through a personal and individual approach to each child.[39] He maintained that individual differences were stronger in the higher than in the lower processes of the mind (Binet and Henri 1896: 465). The four main domains of individual psychology were races, mentally ill persons, criminals and children. The last are, to Binet's eyes, favoured collaborators, for they are more spontaneous and confident than adults with respect to psychological investigation. The study of children's intellectual and moral character appeared accordingly as a necessity (Binet and Simon 1908: 2).

Binet was deeply involved in the culture of his time, starting with a major concern with the education of retarded children and the

---

[39] Binet's individual approach to mental measurements differed fundamentally from that of his American colleagues for he never embraced the large-scale quantitative enquiries characterizing the Americans. Binet supported a more personal approach (Brown 1992).

feeble-minded.[40] But his chief interest gradually evolved from that of diagnosing subnormality to securing a better appreciation and discernment of the normal child. Binet's undertaking was successful because he avoided two major setbacks: he refused to conceive of intelligence on the basis of the mind's faculties: 'to measure the richness of intelligence, the sureness of judgment, the subtlety of mind... the immense variety of expression of intelligence' (Binet 1898: 113); he departed from Galton and American psychologists who were trying to infer complex abilities from simple ones. He imagined instead a test that would measure specific mental characteristics previously defined by sorting out particular testing devices, designed to measure eleven mental processes:

1. Memory;
2. Mental imagery;
3. Imagination;
4. Attention;
5. Comprehension;
6. Suggestibility;
7. Aesthetic appreciation;
8. Force of will as expressed by sustained effort in muscular tasks;
9. Moral sentiments;
10. Motor skill;
11. Judgement of visual space.

(Binet and Henri 1896)

Other tests followed where Binet experimented with schoolchildren to establish if the scores improved with age – and to what extent – and if consistent differences were observed in the performances of children whom teachers regarded as bright.

The measure of intelligence is not determined in terms of a quantitatively graded measure, but in terms of an increase with age or school grade (Goodenough 1949: 44).[41] That is, instead of measuring the

[40] His work at both the Société libre pour l'étude psychologique de l'enfant and at the commission appointed by the French Minister of Public Instruction to decide what measures could be taken for the education of maladapted and backward children is indicative in this respect of Binet's orientation (Avanzini 1969).

[41] Age and age grading were always a keystone in developmental theory. 'If the age of a child according to the grade attained is roughly a measure of ability, and memory is also related to this age-ability, then perhaps measures of

amount of time taken to complete the task, the observer would focus on the ratio of children of a specific age who attained a given solution (Hornstein 1988). Observing that very young children found themselves unable to define familiar nouns in one way or another whilst children of five to six years of age gave definitions in operational terms or, some years later, in terms of ordered category, Binet found the relevance of age to be a keystone in mental development. Children's performance was always the key point for evidence. Having gathered an enormous amount of data in regard to children's responses to various sets of tasks, Binet became increasingly aware of the broad range of differences in patterns of ability existing from one child to another at a specific age. The need for a more adapted form of test, measuring mental level, became manifest (Wolf 1973).

The 1905 Binet–Simon test met those objectives: a formal scale for assessing the intelligence of the child.[42] That is to say that they had a relatively clear idea of the nature of intelligence: 'To judge well, to comprehend well, to reason well, these are the essentials of intelligence' (Goodenough 1949: 48).

- They tried to seize directly on what they regarded as the key factor of intelligence: the ability to make sound judgements.
- The test was arranged so the tasks appeared in a gradual order of difficulty instead of their apparent similarity.
- It aimed to fathom a comprehensive idea of the child's mental development across as many different features as possible.
- The test was likely to be a device for classification of children; it relinquished the idea of an accurate protocol for measurement of a specific faculty treated as entity.

---

intelligence could be set up according to age units, a crucial concept for the final development of the scale' (Wolf 1973). Binet was among the first to work in this direction. 'Methodologically, this approach is the direct ancestor of Piaget's work. For Piaget was influenced by Claparède, himself one of Binet's personal friends' (Reeves 1965).

[42] The Binet–Simon scale consisted of a test of thirty items organized in order of difficulty to examine children of three, five, seven, nine, eleven and twelve years of age. It aimed at distinguishing the subnormal from the normal child (Wolf 1973). Binet's experience of children led him replace the long and time-consuming tests – fatigue being a primary factor in a child's performance – by a short test of thirty items ordered in increasing difficulty from those appropriate for the classification of idiots or imbeciles to those suitable for bright children.

- It did not try to measure all the sensory, motor, perceptual and other elements generally understood to be part of what is usually known as intelligence.

The real breakthrough came with the clarification and the settling of the notion of (the child's) mental level in relation to its chronological age (Charts 3 and 4): so as to reckon meaningful comparisons among subjects, that is to classify normal and subnormal children, indicators, norms and benchmarks ought to be ascertained on data relevant to the performances of the normal child at different ages (Wolf 1973). The context which saw the rise of intelligence testing should be borne in mind: public authorities were concerned with the retarded and the feeble-minded and were looking for an objective means to classify children in the school setting. The scale was an instrument of primary usefulness to differentiate the morons (the imbeciles and the idiots), needing special education, from the normal child population. Chronological age became the yardstick for normalcy in childhood; a normal/average form primarily constructed against backwardness.

The rules which Binet and Simon apply are two: (i) *A child has the intelligence of that age all the tests for which he succeeds in passing.* If a child succeeds in the tests of his age he is normal. If he can succeed only in those given for a child a year younger than himself he is in Goddard's view *backward* to the extent of one year, and similarly for two or three years. If he is more than three years he is *mentally defective.* (Anonymous 1912: 313)

In 1909, Binet and Simon revised their test and introduced a salient change in it. The 1905 scale was entitled 'New methods for the diagnosis of the intellectual level of the abnormal'; the 1908 test 'The development of intelligence among children'. From the former to the latter, the displacement was noticeable if not significant.[43] Therefore a method of appraising the scarcity of intelligence was transformed into a method of classifying the intelligence of a large range of children: backward, slow, normal and even gifted. The gain in the latter scale lay in the fact that 'it takes express account of age, and it assesses the

---

[43] While the 1905 test consisted of thirty items, the 1909 test retained only fourteen of these without change, dropped nine, modified seven and added thirty-three new items. The test was standardized on about 300 children from three to thirteen years of age (Wolf 1973).

Tests of Binet and Simon, grouped according to Age

Three years.

1. Points to nose, eyes and mouth.
2. Repeats two numbers (7, 2).
3. Enumerates objects in a picture.
4. Knows name.
5. Repeats a sentence of six syllables.

Four Years.

1. Knows sex (boy or girl).
2. Recognises and names key, knife, penny.
3. Repeats three numbers (7, 4, 8).
4. Compares two straight lines [as to length].

Five Years.

1. Compares two weights [3 and 12 grams or 6 and 15 grams].
2. Copies a square (in pen and ink).
3. Repeats sentence of 10 syllables [*e.g.*, "His name is John. He is a very good boy"].
4. Counts four pennies.
5. Putting together pieces of a card [a visiting card is cut diagonally, and the child has to make a figure like the uncut card].

Six Years.

1. Distinguishes between morning and afternoon.
2. Defines in terms of use [*e.g.*, fork, table, chair, horse].
3. Copies outline of diamond shape.
4. Counts 13 pennies.
5. Makes aesthetic comparison of faces [from drawings and pictures].

Seven Years.

1. Shows right hand, left ear.
2. Describes a picture.
3. Executes three commissions correctly [*e.g.*, place key on chair; shut door; bring box].
4. Counts nine sous (3 single, 3 double, *e.g.*, 1 1 1 2 2 2).*
5. Names four colours (red, blue, green, yellow).

Chart 3: Binet–Simon three to seven years of age
Source: Anonymous 1912

responses by comparing them to a norm that is a real and living average' (Binet and Simon 1908: 60). They realized the core importance of the three levels of response to a picture – enumeration, description and interpretation – which they located at three, seven and twelve years respectively.

We possess at the present an instrument that allows us to measure the intellectual development of young children whose ages are between three

Eight Years.
1. Compares two objects from memory.
2. Counts backwards, 20–0.
3. Sees picture lacks eyes, nose, mouth, and arms.
4. Gives day and date.
5. Repeats five figures.

Nine Years.
1. Gives change for sixpence or shilling.
2. Defines in terms superior to use [description of articles apart from use].
3. Names nine pieces of money.
4. Enumerates months of the year.
5. Understands simple questions ["What would you do if you missed a train? "].

Ten Years.
1. Arranges five weights in order.
2. Copies design from memory.
3. Criticises absurd statements [*e.g.*, "Is the snow red or black"].
4. Understands a difficult question [*e.g.*, "What would you do if you were delayed in going to school?"].
5. Uses three selected words in one sentence [London, money, river].

Twelve Years.
1. Resists suggestion [length of lines].
2. Uses three words in a simple sentence.
3. Gives 60 words in three minutes.
4. Defines three abstract words [charity, justice, goodness].
5. Puts dissected sentence together.

Fifteen Years.
1. Repeats seven figures.
2. Gives three rhymes.
3. Repeats a sentence of 26 syllables.
4. Interprets a picture.
5. Solves a problem from several facts.

Chart 4: Binet–Simon eight to fifteen years of age
Source: Anonymous 1912

and twelve years ... to know summarily whether a child has the intelligence of his age, or is advanced or retarded ... The general formula is that an individual is normal when he can conduct himself without having need of the tutelage of others, when his intelligence does not take him onto work of a lower classification than that of his parents (like the son of a lawyer reduced to being a petty clerk) (Binet and Simon 1908: 82 and 88).

The normal/average form of the child emerges as part of a larger trend that characterizes nineteenth-century culture and scientific thought: statistical thinking, probability theory and reasoning with numbers. The notion of average man as a typical outcome of statistical thinking was based on large-scale regularities of human characteristics, both physical and mental, which were normally distributed. The physical features of the average child took the form, for instance, of the height and weight tables, thus giving a figure or a visual form to human maturation, growth and developmental normalization as a translation of the normal child. On the other hand, mental attributes were crystallized in intelligence testing even though this could not be as accurate as the aforementioned tables; it nonetheless allowed a classification as well as a formal difference between the normal child and the subnormal, whether moron, imbecile or idiot. The scale also contributed to the translation and circulation of a particular actor. The next section will look at the normal/healthy child as another form of translation.

4.3 Normal as healthy

The normal/average form of childhood, deriving from anthropometric studies, was predicated on the investigation of specific features of children's growth ensuing in large-scale regularities. The worthiness of serial weighing and measuring, the charts issued thereafter in the wake of this movement, were figured in normal standards of development implemented and enforced by public authorities, especially the school apparatus. The use of growth charts and developmental standards did not directly reduce infant mortality, which rather pertained to hygienic reform, limitation of infectious diseases and promotion of nutrition. But at the same period of time, physicians, paediatricians and hygienists recognized that disease affects a child's development: a hindrance of growth or development from normal standards could likely reveal a complex disease process.

Often recognized as a disorder – or an interruption – in the process of child's development, disease and illness betoken the obverse of the normal/average form, namely, the normal/healthy form of childhood. Growth and developmental charts highlighted a construction of normalcy revolving around the average child whilst other scientists (Durkheim, for instance) put forward a conception of the average type identified with the normal, but as opposed to the pathological – not to the gifted or mediocre child of the normal distribution.[44] Disease, pathology and normalcy: aside from developmental standards, although to a certain extent acted upon by it, another form of childhood was already in place, and yet not restricted to medicine: the clarification of the basic elements of the normal/healthy form, their translation and circulation; starting with physicians and paediatricians, I shall investigate its inception in the medical collective,[45] keeping abreast of its gradual widening to other types of practice.

Although social concern over the problem of infant mortality was culminating, it still needed to be addressed on an entirely new basis, both social and technical alike. Children's medicine progressively developed a form of intervention informed by the motto 'scrutinize and regulate as much as possible' known as *puériculture* (infant welfare), following French influences and paediatrics in the Anglo-Saxon tradition (Rodriguez Ocana 1998). The technical sophistication which made possible a decisive breakthrough in the struggle against infant mortality was circulating and redefining the usual categories of child, mother and parent; moreover the network also encompassed important institutional changes and social interventions in infancy and childhood by the spread of medical care for problems such as pregnancy, childbirth and child-raising (Becchi and Julia 1998; Bernardi 1985; Graff 1995).[46]

As the scientific culture was rapidly turning to statistical thinking and to numerical regularities as seen above, the appraisal of the state of health of an individual patient moved away from an individuated standard – instituted as a natural state – towards a population standard known as the normal (Brown 1992: 43). What does the

---

[44] In the normal/healthy form of childhood, the normal is opposed to the pathological whilst in the normal/average form, at least in the Galtonian construction, the normal is opposed to both the gifted and the mediocre at both ends of the normal distribution.

[45] Goodhart published the first edition of his *The Diseases of Children*, in 1885, Hutchison, his *Lectures on Diseases of Children*, in 1904; Garrod, his *Diseases of Children*, in 1913. A Society for the Study of Diseases in Children was established in 1900 and in 1908 it became a Section launching the Royal Society of Medicine (Armstrong 1983). Was the child, accordingly, an invention as a specific object of the medical gaze?

[46] The spread of medical care – in Foucault's terms, medicalization – for events like pregnancy and childbirth could only happen with the displacement of previous beliefs and practices in regard to other forms of care based on traditional knowledge carried out by oral tradition (Turmel and Hamelin 1995).

healthy/pathological form translate to with respect to the status and the form of the normal population standard? My hypothesis relates to the medical collective's population standard of normalcy pertaining to the opposition of healthy/pathological, albeit not totally unfamiliar to the previous form, normal/average, continually circulated in manifold ways in the hybrid socio-medical network.

As one goes back through the paediatric textbooks of the past, one will realize that they have constantly paid much attention to the physical needs of infants and children, much more than to other needs – at first labelled 'spiritual', then later on 'psychological' towards the last quarter of the nineteenth century – which were considered negligible for a very long period of time. Though these physical needs are seen as relatively precise, even measurable – at the opposite of the latter, deemed fuzzy and elusive – the standards established in regard to the former were believed applicable to all normal children. In the context of infant mortality, the child's physical welfare became almost instantly an important focus of attention for both paediatricians and parents: feeding, nutrition, hygiene, sleep and exercise began to be better understood.

Healthy physical welfare for children proved too large a category to be helpful for physicians and paediatricians. It needed to be translated into more circumscribed attributes: additional tangible corporeal features needed to become increasingly accurate so that their circulation in an extended network might accelerate.

The extension of paediatric activities was echoed in Jacobi's 1880 inaugural address to the AMA, its section on diseases of children: recognizing that there are anomalies and diseases which are encountered in the infant and child only, thus not reduced doses of the same diseases in smaller bodies, he confirmed paediatrics' physical orientation towards children's pathological conditions, but translated it beyond its limited physiological boundaries to a more extended network of activities including infant feeding, hygiene and the prevention of disease. In his presidential address to the American Pediatrics Society (1889), Jacobi restated the place of paediatrics in a larger network: individual and public hygiene, diet and nutrition, constitutional and infectious diseases, school and so on. Coit outlines them as follows:

- system and order in routine care;
- regularity in hours of feeding etc.;

- proper judgement and thoughtfulness in the adjustment of the child's food, proper clothing and bed covering;
- selection of suitable rooms for its waking and sleeping hours as regards ventilation, sunshine and quiet.

(Coit 1910: 728)

The daily scientific observation and recording of children took a specific form: regular and systematic: in the most decisive sites of the collective for children: 'in their homes and in the school, through registration of births, infant welfare centres, health visitors, school medical officers...to provide a platform for the deployment of medico-hygienic norms and expertise' (N. Rose 1991: 129).

One cannot be but struck by the emergence in paediatric discourse of categories such as routine, regularity and firmness,[47] which were to become the core of a specific type of practice characterizing the normal/healthy form; hence the hypothesis proposed in this argument. Nothing is more enlightening than these categories for the prospect they open up: they inscribe the difference – one of the more decisive differences – from the normal/average form. The latter is crystallized around the mean and the normal distribution, whilst the former is chiefly concerned with the implementation of a framework intended to assess and improve children's health.

Regularity is best illustrated by the place of the clock in paediatric advice surrounding breastfeeding: scheduled feedings, duration of feedings, feeding intervals, require the timing of feeding. The need of discipline for both the infant and the mother through an imposed scheduled from outside their tight relationship was a common view in the paediatric network to regulate what was seen as an innately confused process; it thus became a keystone in a normal infant behaviour. 'The absence of a regular schedule is thus taken as a sign of abnormality on the part of the infant, the mother, or both ... adherence to the timetable becomes a standard for judging competence, adequacy and normality' (Millard 1990: 219). Infant feeding is, moreover, a cogent illustration of the boundary's displacement and inter-connectedness; scientific literature was prolific about infant and child feeding (Douglas

---

[47] The category of firmness will surface later in paediatric discourse, around the 1920s and 1930s (Camic 1986; Daston 1982). Although important in the normal/healthy form, the category of firmness is much more relevant to the normal/acceptable form.

1905; Richardson 1925; Wilcox 1910); organizations devoted to its betterment, especially milk depots and *gouttes de lait*, emerged in most Western countries whilst their success was mitigated in some of them before being replaced by welfare clinics or societies such as the American Child Health Association (Apple 1987; Dwork 1987; Meckel 1990; Norvez 1990).

One can review the same categories – routine, schedule and regularity – with respect to the question of sleep. From the moment sleep was converted into an issue,[48] sleep problems were enunciated as a health question: adequacy of sleep, requirements of amount, sleep deprivation, sleeplessness and so on (Anonymous 1929). The category of regularity and its correlatives, schedule and routine, were translated in the network as the best habit towards a healthier way of life: regular sleep framed by a schedule is an advantage for a child, helping it in its circulation as stipulated in Chart 5. The AMA expressed it concisely: 'Whatever bedtime the mother sets, it should be regular at all costs. Nothing should interfere with the bedtime habits – neither evening shows nor guests' (Stearns *et al.* 1996: 353).

Carried on mostly by field practitioners in a wide hybrid socio-technical network of professional associations, child welfare activists and parents' organizations, the normal/healthy form of childhood is faced with empirical problems such as infectious diseases, child-rearing questions and various behavioural problems (Comacchio 1993; Cravens 1985b; Turmel and Hamelin 1995a).[49] How these categories came to represent the exact way – in terms of habits, cares, character and so on (Camic 1986; Daston 1982) – of fighting usual misconceptions or disseminated malpractice and of ensuring that children stayed healthy, while improving their general condition, remained to be clarified. The translation of the 'problems' of infant feeding and sleep into categories such as regularity and their circulation accelerated the transformation of the paediatrician/family network.

---

[48] Paediatric manuals of the nineteenth century were unconcerned by the question of sleep, which appeared around the First World War, at least in America. Sleep was seen as a natural matter, later translated into a health issue (Stearns *et al.* 1996).

[49] The gradual widening of paediatric practice from the classic infant and children diseases to child-rearing and to behavioural concerns is one of the most convincing examples of the establishment and implementation of an extensive network, which allows an accelerated circulation (Latour 1994b).

SLEEP REQUIRED BY THE AVERAGE YOUNG CHILD
(Including daytime sleep)

At birth	At 6 months	At 1 year	2–5 years
21–22 hours	18 hours	16 hours	14 hours

SLEEP REQUIRED BY THE AVERAGE OLDER CHILD

6–7 years	8–10 years	11–12 years
12 hours	11 hours	10–11 hours

SLEEP REQUIRED BY THE AVERAGE YOUTH

13–15 years	16–18 years
10–12 hours	9–10 hours

HOW MUCH DOES YOUR CHILD SLEEP?

Chart 5: Sleep – average young child
Source: Children's Bureau, Folder no 11, 1929

The normal/healthy form, however, was much more complex a form than the previous considerations could lead one to think. The categories of regularity and routine were designed as a general mediator circulating between paediatricians' offices and families so as to calibrate family life and children's behaviour. But what is this regulation all about? The classic answer, health, is too restrictive a response for the circulation of the foregoing categories enables a translation of children's health beyond its usual restrained scope. Through its own circulating movement, paediatrics progressively expanded its activities into a wider network reaching outward from its traditional domain (Dwork 1987; Halpern 1988). Thus new bounds were created inasmuch as it associates, combines and redeploys numerous actors in this specific network.

The case of child hygiene is especially appealing in this respect (Veeder 1924: 313).[50] Veeder talks about the rise of a structure, many

---

[50] Child hygiene did not unexpectedly become a critical feature of child health in the 1920s. As hygienists were already at work in the nineteenth century, Veeder

planners having contributed to it, each according to his own design without paying much attention to the whole plan or to whether the foundations could bear the complete arrangement. Child hygiene set the task of educating both mothers and children in the rules and methods of sound health, a task taken up by medical practitioners, thus widening considerably the hybrid socio-technical network of actors in the collective chiefly concerned with children's health: welfare clinics, health education boards, municipal divisions of hygiene and their visiting nurses, science laboratories, Child Hygiene (or Welfare) Associations and so on.[51] 'The activities of the nurse in the direction of "following up" and in particular her frequent visit to the houses and the schools in connection with ailing children have demonstrated her close association with the question of school attendance' (Anonymous 1912: 100).

The effect of this integration of hygiene in paediatrics was to enlarge the vision of children's health from conception through adolescence; the collective progressed from infant feeding to the importance of mental hygiene of the child and the teaching of positive individual health (Veeder 1924: 314). On the other hand, Gesell introduced the concept of complete growth, therefore including mental growth, as the new directing ideal of child hygiene.

The fundamental advantage in this concept lies in the fact that it goes far beyond the traditional ideas of health and disease...it places a new premium upon normality, and gives us the impulse for constructive as well as preventive measures for this normal child. The concept of maximum growth also reveals both the scientific and the practical value of standards of development (Gesell 1926: 46).

Although school in regard to child's health illustrates better than any other aspects the extension of paediatric activities and its pivotal role in a widening community, it has yet to be ascertained as a relevant object related to child's health. Nevertheless, in its incessant effort to connect with a broader network, paediatrics encountered schooling on its way to enhancing child health.

---

is rather referring to the fact that paediatrics became aware of child hygiene (Halpern 1988; Hendrick 1997; Rose 1985).

[51] In this sense, infant feeding can be considered a part of child hygiene, which is more global an approach than the former: it precedes and incorporates it.

it still appears as if our schools were establishments organized to produce near-sightedness, scoliosis, and anaemia, both physical and intellectual exhaustion...The question of school-house building and school room furniture, the structure of bench and table, the paper and type in the books, the number of school hours...the number and length of recesses, the hours and duration of intervening meals, the alternation of mental and physical training, the age at which the individual child should be first sent...have been too long decided by school-boards consisting of...not, however, of physicians (Jacobi 1889: 767).

All of a sudden,[52] new links were established between education and paediatrics whose almost immediate effect was to transcribe school matters – some of them somewhat technical: room furniture, bench, table etc. – into an entirely novel set of interrogations and to translate them into an issue of health: the defective child and its treatment, uncleanliness or verminous conditions among children etc. 'The London County Council have continued their extensive arrangements for the cleansing of dirty and verminous children' (Anonymous 1912: 33). The question at stake pertains to the topic of school hygiene, under the aegis of the medical inspection of school-children. Around the time of the First World War, there were more than 1,500 school physicians employed for medical inspection in American cities and for the medical treatment of the defective child. The system of school hygiene in New York was reputed to represent the highest standard in this case designed to cover the following areas:

1. systematic inspection of all school children for the purpose of early recognition of infectious disease;
2. exclusion from schools of all children so affected;
3. subsequent control of the case with isolation of the patient, and disinfection of the living apartment;
4. control and enforced treatment with the purpose of diminishing the number of children excluded from school attendance;
5. knowledge of unreported cases;
6. complete examination of each school child;

---

[52] 'All of a sudden' can be considered a figure of speech referring not to a specific phenomenon but rather to a general nineteenth-century process that saw the child progressively leave the factory and the mine, child labour in other words, to be directed towards the school system. This transition, one of the most decisive, impinged on and redistributed the whole network of children's relationships.

7. education of the parents;
8. provision of facilities for treatment.

(Anonymous 1912: 18)

Paediatricians demanded their say in school matters, with their re-wording of usual school topics in the language of health, establishing accordingly a new set of relations among families, children, schools, physicians and so on, and widening the notion of health to a whole novel collection of issues. In the context of the implementation of compulsory education, a child's health was at risk not only with issues such as school hours, length of recesses, alternation of mental and physical training, but with uncontrolled predicaments at the periphery of traditional health questions. 'The prevailing tendency of the times is to over stimulation of children. This tendency pervades our whole educational system…Such over-straining and stimulation of the mental and nervous organism cannot fail to cause harmful effects during childhood' (Anonymous 1895: 359).

This transformation came progressively in the wake of paediatrics' growing interest in the topics aforementioned: hygiene, nutrition, feeding etc. Although it appeared at the periphery of the physical health problems – paediatrics' main concern for a long period of time – it is of crucial importance to the reconfiguration of the normal child and the enlargement of negotiations it generates. It is my hypothesis that the transition towards a new form of normal child and a larger hybrid socio-technical network passed in transit through the formulation of problems and the negotiation of solutions raised by these uncontrolled predicaments labelled, after Latour, 'quasi-problems': nail-biting, fear, anger, enuresis, acting-out, temperamental difficulties – in short, ner-vous problems.[53] The nervous child confronted the actors with uncertainty and thus required an entirely new set of answers and relations: 'revived by unexpected events and problems which, for the actors, are trials forcing them collectively to devise new arrangements' (Callon and Rabeharisoa 2000: 4).

The nervous child can, accordingly, be considered a transitional phase in the collective's form: the instalment of a new sequence in an

---

[53] Parents would often seek advice from paediatricians for those specific problems not in the realm of traditional physical questions and which British physician Cameron characterized as 'the influences which mould the mentality of the child and shape his conduct' (Cameron 1919).

already extensive network and the reconfiguration of the collective's boundaries and composition. This movement prompts paediatrics' opening and general reorientation towards what was then designated as children's mental health.

At first the nervous child was a rather loose and hazy class, for it was convenient enough a category to classify miscellaneous problems confronting paediatricians for which their classical knowledge proved less cogent. Nevertheless these difficulties were overcome as paediatricians became gradually aware of the crucial importance of the 'hygiene of the mind'.

The increasing tendency to nervous disease observed in recent years is becoming a subject of interest … in pediatrics … Children and even infants are effected directly and indirectly by the same influences, which generate nervous disorders … The prevailing tendency of the times is to over stimulation of children. This tendency pervades our whole educational system … Such over-straining and stimulation of the mental and nervous organism cannot fail to cause harmful effects during childhood and frequently produce a neurasthenic and nervous temperament in later life (Anonymous 1895: 358).

The standard reorientation towards mental health is based on the classical opposition of the body (physical health as the primary concern of paediatrics) and the mind as something elusive, yet unavoidable (Cameron 1919: 2).[54]

The body of the child is moulded and shaped by the environment in which it grows. Pure air, a rational diet, free movement, gives strength and symmetry to every part. Faults of hygiene debase the quality, although the type is determined by heredity … it seemed as if some mothers whose care for their children's physical health is most painstaking … have had their attention so wholly occupied with the care of the body that they do not appreciate the simultaneous growth of the mind, or inquire after its welfare (Cameron 1919: 5).

The body/mind opposition appears a corner-stone in the emerging discourse on the nervous child whilst contributing to the extension and redeployment of its boundaries. The hygiene of the mind, which is

---

[54] Although I consulted the fifth edition (1946) of the Cameron book, it must be remembered that the book was first published in 1919. I have left aside the two additional chapters added in the subsequent editions.

the main target of intervention with respect to child health, revolves around two key notions: environment and management.[55] The recognition of the worth of the child's environment is in itself a significant advance in a largely Darwinian framework. Provided that the child's mental environment 'is created by the mother or the nurse' (Cameron 1919: 8), the management of the child requires an enlightened involvement as well as constant solicitude. Its faulty management by mothers or nurses is undoubtedly the main source of nervousness for the child. A large variety of signs/disorders are conveyed in the category:

- broken, disturbed or rejected sleep;
- persistent refusal of food or absence of appetite; gastric pain or discomfort after meals;
- irritability, crying, excessive emotional display or ungovernable temper;
- undue timidity, anxiety or fearfulness;
- nervous vomiting, morbid flushing and blushing.

A steady argument, the parents' conduct enhances the main feature of this logic; their management of the child's environment bears the responsibility for its development in regard to the hygiene of the mind. 'Nervous and apprehensive parents who are distressed when the child refuse to eat or to sleep, and who worry all day long over possible sources of danger to him, are forced to watch their child acquire a reputation for nervousness, which, as always, is passively accepted and consistently acted up to' (Cameron 1919: 31). The basic reasoning of such a position, now regarded as a classic in its own right, was then rather unconventional: the child's conduct is dependent upon the mother's state of mind; it is the mother who imparts to her child her own uneasiness, anxieties or distress.

A cognate argument of this kind consists of a translation of the child's situation in the family network and of a redeployment of its boundaries. Although, in the wake of the discovery of the hygiene of the mind, a repositioning of the mother/child bond is under way, one

---

[55] The question of heredity is central to this discourse. The diversity of temperament in children is solely produced by hereditary factors, according to Cameron. 'When a peculiarly nervous temperament is inherited, wisdom in the management of the child is essential...Heredity is so powerful a factor in the development of the nervous organisation of the child' (Cameron 1919).

cannot but take note of the mother's new momentous and pivotal role. The collective normal child is being redefined through appraisal of the nervous child.[56] The network and the boundaries alike are displaced. Paediatricians' willingness to intervene is channelled towards the mother, for their power to model the child is at stake. The network must be both reasserted and redeployed. 'It is through the mother, and by means of her alone, that the doctor can influence the conduct of the child. Without her co-operation . . . we are powerless to help . . . Only so can the doctor intervene to mould its [the child's] nature and shape its conduct' (Cameron 1919: 13).

Paediatrics moved gradually towards mental hygiene under the general umbrella of the child development movement under the aegis of psychology; more precisely that part of psychology concerned with the child's mental development.[57] By the end of the First World War, a change in paediatrics was well on its way with respect to the core value of children's mental life.[58] Even though hygiene of the mind was not something as accurate as physical health – 'Mental hygiene . . . remains a rather nebulous aspiration' (Gesell 1926: 43) – fieldwork experience led to paediatricians' admission of the undeniable prominence of the child's mental development.

As one of the first tangible manifestations of psychology in this respect pertained to the child's individual intellectual ability, the mental testing movement came of age at the beginning of the century by yielding a method of classifying and sort out children according to their ability. Even at the outset of the IQ-testing movement, some paediatricians expressed reservations about this outcome of psychology's orientation. 'Forgetful of the importance of character formation, and more forgetful of physical development in childhood, the attention of the State and of educators has been concentrated upon

[56] The nervous child was always portrayed in a family setting, whilst not being specifically either taught about or acted upon, and yet it is its particular translation and the negotiation of new boundaries for the collective which appear decisive in this respect.

[57] The question at stake here is not whether paediatrics discovered the worth of the child's mental life by itself or whether psychology's advances in this matter were dissemniated in one way or another in paediatrics.

[58] This particular question is an immensely complex problem and the purpose of this development is not to clarify it. The statement amounts solely to a general reminder of psychology's leading role in drawing attention to this aspect of the child's life (Danziger 1990; Halpern 1988; Hearnshaw 1964).

the small part of child education, the development of intellectual capacity' (Jennings 1905: 482). Although useful in the hands of teachers and school administrators, intelligence testing was deemed too unsatisfactory a method – 'The first, and least satisfactory of the methods' (Adams 1934: 27) – to give a careful and proper account of the child's mental development.

It is in such an ambiguous context – both the irresistible rise of intelligence testing and an equivocal doubt about its outputs – and, accordingly, an open situation that the endowment of the child's mental life came into more complete recognition. In a text published in 1910 in *Archives of Pediatrics*, which we have already referred to in defining the classical master concern regarding physical health, the turn towards children's mental health is clearly stated by the author, Dr Henry Coit, thus putting slightly aside paediatrics' traditional orientation. The opening towards children's mental life is clearly asserted.

The mental and moral correspondence of the child and its caretaker will involve in their intercourse the training of the little unfolding mind to recognize and not to fear its surroundings; to regulate and to conserve the lavish waste of nerve force which the sensitive nervous organization is apt to suffer; to isolate it from much of the mental excitement too common in the surroundings of a baby and child; to keep the child quiet (Coit 1910: 728).

Was mental health doomed from the outset to be a string of considerations about the nervous child? The similarity between this text and Cameron's remarks concerning the nervous child is striking. It ought to be more than a pure coincidence as it happens that nervousness appeared at first as cognate to mental life, but dwelled at the very core of it.[59] Though nervous problems were, at least for paediatricians, questions whose translation introduced them to the domain of mental health, it remains to be seen how the boundaries of the collective were neither limited nor reduced to nervousness, but extended far beyond. Though not broadly elaborate, yet Strecker's proposition on the requirements of the normal child in regard to mental hygiene opens new possibilities: 'The greatest tribute I can pay the child is to view him in the light of his adjustment-accomplishment record' (Strecker 1926: 61).

---

[59] These remarks are in line with the hypothesis put forward above: that nervousness is the transitional phase to a genuine account of the child's mental development; in fact, it is its principal entry to children's mental life.

	MENTAL DEVELOPMENT (Use Check Mark √)			
1 Year	2 Years	3 Years	4 Years	5 Years
1 Stands and may attempt to walk with support	1 Walks (18 mos.)	1. Draws circle from copy.	1. Draws cross from copy.	1. Draws triangle from copy.
2 Understands simple commands	2. Uses simple phrases.	2. Combines two parts of cut picture.	2. Repeats sentences of 10 to 12 syllables.	2. Compares two weights.
3 Inhibits simple acts on command	3. Asks for things by name	3. Names three objects in a picture	3. Buttons clothes.	3. Laces shoes.
4. Will hold cup to drink from	4. Folds paper imitatively	4. Points to eyes, nose, and mouth.	4. Washes self.	4. Puts on coat and hat alone.
5. Uses one or two words besides dada and mama	5 Bladder control established	5. Repeats two digits	5. Knows his sex.	5 Counts four pennies

FORM II (Page 1).—DEVELOPMENT RECORD, 1 TO 6 YEARS.

Space for recording the important history for the first year; the common contagious diseases of childhood; immunization data; and a brief outline of mental development.

Form 6: Mental development
Source: Veeder 1926

The preservation of mental hygiene in normal children was always the highest priority of the mental-health movement so that research concentrated on the identification of particular behavioural benchmarks considered normal for children in specified age categories. The Developmental Record Form – including a mental developmental chart – stated specific standards for mental development so that physicians and parents alike could observe stage by stage the progression of the child from infancy to toddlerhood to childhood.[60] A broad examination of the Developmental Form is indicative of what was, during the 1920s, considered standard for mental development and, therefore, developmental schedules. Aside from the classic oral and dental examination – eye, ear, nose and throat; physical examination; measurements (height, weight, circumference of head, chest and abdomen) – the mental development section states the following benchmarks (Form 6):

1 year:
1. Stands and may attempt to walk with support;
2. Understands simple commands;

[60] In this sense, one of the main outcomes of the mental hygiene paradigm lies in the medicalization of normality and legitimation of clinical abnormality (Richardson 1989). Social categories were created and implemented in settings such as schools, nurseries, courts and child guidance clinics, thus classifying and segregating children on the basis of categories.

3. Inhabits simple actions on command;
4. Will hold cup to drink from;
5. Uses one or two words;

3 years:
1. Draws circle from copy;
2. Combines two parts of cut picture;
3. Names three objects in a picture;
4. Points to eyes, ears and mouth;
5. Repeats two digits;

5 years:
1. Draws triangle from copy;
2. Compares two weights;
3. Laces shoes;
4. Puts on coat and hat alone;
5. Counts four pennies.

(Veeder 1926: 193)

According to today's canon in the child's psychological develop-ment, few of these would be considered relevant as a sound criterion of mental hygiene.[61] One cannot but be struck by how the various elements introduced in the form revolve around motor – or what Piaget will call shortly afterwards sensory–motor – development rather than emotional life. This translation of mental health into these standards, which in itself broadens the collective's boundaries can be considered as a transitional phase towards the discovery of the child's emotional life: a second transitional phase, after the nervous child, towards the enlargement of the collective normal-child.

Gesell appears to be instrumental in this respect.[62] His work and research are a yardstick for he was amongst the first to identify stand-ards of mental and emotional development as a necessary condition

---

[61] Gesell and Veeder's standards upheld the official seal of the American Medical Association as they figure in one of its record forms. It is possible to derive from this plain but pivotal fact an awareness that these criteria were, in the 1920s, acknowledged as state-of-the-art in this particular collective.

[62] Gesell's plea for the child was passionate and unconditional: the child was the gateway to everything else. 'Some day society will realise that the well-developed child is the most valuable possession of the race... "The conservation of the child life" is more than a phrase. It fully represents the deepest and most central of all problems and duties' (Gesell and Gesell 1912).

of good health for normal children.[63] One of the basic touchstones of his work lies in the postulate of the parallel and at the same time intertwining of both mental and physical development (Gesell 1926: 48). The child, he had already propounded, is a unity and must be dealt with as such: unity of the body and mind, unity of mind in its various manifestations.

The mind is a living unit, but a unit with three expressions: thinking, feeling, and doing... Hygiene recognizes the natural unity of the mind, and insists that mental health depends on a proper coordination of all three expressions... Intellect, feeling, and will should function together, reinforcing one another. In this trinity, feeling is both central and fundamental (Gesell and Gesell 1912: 291).

The introduction to emotional life, although as acute a part of mental health, must be read as a component of the mind understood as a whole and a unity.

Acknowledging that mental development in infancy and childhood is rapid, Gesell goes on to concede that most of the time it rivals or exceeds that of stature. The noteworthy consequence of such a statement – the scaling of standards of mental health – occurs in the formulation of monthly increments of behaviour. 'The growth of the mind scientifically conceived, therefore, is essentially the development of a sequence of behaviour values which are correlated with the maturation of the nervous system' (Gesell 1926: 47). Gesell answers in a quite different vein from Veeder and the motor perspective in most respects; his response denotes a translation that displaces and expands the boundaries of the collective normal-child.[64] Normality of mind, he adds, can be formulated in terms of:

1. Wholesome habits of eating, of sleeping, of relaxation, and of elimination: These are often regarded as 'purely physical' matters. Actually they are of basic psychological importance. They are ways of

---

[63] The context in which Gesell's research took place is specific. He speaks of the vast latent pre-scientific prejudice, a return to imperfect folklore, to erroneous superstition, ignorance and quackery. Gesell will always talk from a scientific standpoint inasmuch as medicine appears the only safeguard against such possibilities (Gesell 1926).

[64] The fact that Gesell's answer differs from Veeder's and the motor development perspective ought not to be interpreted as a disavowal of the latter. He fully recognizes its importance.

living; they require proper organization of the nervous system. The child who is not well trained in these everyday habits has not learned even the first letters of the alphabet of nervous or mental health.

2. Wholesome habits of feeling: Here again we deal with the organisation of the nervous system [and] of emotional life. Happily, the feelings respond to training. It is all-wrong to think that temper tantrums, morbid fears, timidity, jealousy, sensitiveness, suspiciousness, and other unhealthy mental states are beyond control. The thoroughly normal child has positive emotional habituations...Consistent training and favourable home atmosphere will bring him under the spell of socialised good will ...

3. Healthy attitudes of action: Self-reliance is a cardinal virtue in the code of mental health. Growing up...means attaining sufficient stamina to meet the demands of life squarely on one's own resources. It is a steady process of detachment, first from the apron strings. Later from the home itself.

(Gesell 1926: 49)

Gesell thus proposes that normality in the field of mental growth is as valid a notion as normality in regard to physical growth, each of them requiring a distinctive hygiene. Moreover he stresses the core importance of personal–social behaviour, through which the child's emotional life and his capacity for socially adaptive behaviours are expressed. The wellbeing of the developing mind bear heavily upon the quality of the parent–child relation.[65] Although the regulation of nutrition can be broadened to include psychological factors affecting mental health, the influential parent–child relation has yet to come to terms with the flaws of childcare: beating, slapping, rough handling, excessive shouting, scolding, threats and so on. 'A calm, kind, consistent parent–child relation is the most important essential in improving the mental health of these young children' (Gesell 1926: 50).

Later, in the 1930s, Gesell was to introduce the first timetables of normative chronological schedules of child development,[66] thus

---

[65] If the parent–child relationship was so essential, Gesell was furthermore aware of the cardinal value of the teacher–child relation. 'It means that pedagogical methods should not be tested by their success in imparting prescribed subject matter, but by their effect on the health of the mind' (Gesell and Gesell 1912).

[66] The notion of normative chronological schedules was met with scepticism and, sometimes, with direct criticism: 'children do not follow standard chronologic patterns of advance in their mental and behaviour development any more than

Sequence of Stages

	Stage 1 Equilibrium	Stage 2 Disequilib.	Stage 3 Equilibrium	Stage 4 Disequilib.	Stage 5 Equilibrium	Stage 6 Disequilib.	Stage 1 Equilibrium	
	Smooth, Consolidated	Breaking Up	Rounded, Well-balanced	Inwardized	Vigorous, Expansive	Neurotic, Inwardized, Troubled	Smooth, Consolidated	
Cycles						Birth	4 weeks	**Duration**
1st	4 weeks	6–12 weeks	16 weeks	20 weeks	24–28 weeks	32 weeks	40 weeks	0.7 years
2nd	40 weeks	44–48 weeks	52–56 weeks	15 months	18 months	21 months	24 months	1.2 years
3rd	2 years	2½ years	3 years	3½ years	4 years	4½ years	5 years	3 years
4th	5 years	5½–6 years	6½ years	7 years	8 years	9 years	10 years	5 years
5th	10 years	11 years	12 years	13 years	14 years	15 years	16 years	6 years

Chart 6: Sequence of stages
Source: Gesell 1946a

giving concrete expression to the idea of sequential phases of development (Chart 6). The normal course of development for children would then amount to achieving specific physical and psychological prescriptive attainments (Varga 1998). Accordingly, the normal child was not the average child, but the one who could develop to the utmost of its capacities/abilities whether physical, mental or intellectual in a sequence of consecutives stages (Cravens 1985b). The translation of the child's development would then take the form of sequential phases, thus becoming a cognitive form.

The normal/healthy form of the child emerges as part of a huge trend in public hygiene, medicine and psychology. The notion of health was first understood as the physical growth of the child, which referred to a particular translation of the normal child while sorting out its boundaries in a no less specific way: from the regulation of infant mortality rate to the control of the complex disease process characteristic of childhood, it is possible to follow the complexities of child development. Through the passage of the nervous child and motor development as transitional phases the reconfiguration of the

they do in their physical development. In both instances there are spurts and retardation, both in general and in particular phases of developmental advance...that have little bearing on the final outcome' (Brennemann 1933: 21). Nonetheless, these schedules of development would become as real as children's height and weight and the very way in which every child should conform. 'The features by which we in Western culture think and talk about children...In sum, such knowledge transformed the way in which we understand and see children' (Wong 1993: 129).

collective normal-child was progressively resettled. The normal/ healthy form was not completed until the standards and protocols framing mental development were introduced. Gesell fitted those into chronological schedules and into sequential phases of development. The next section will look at the normal/acceptable form of childhood.

4.4 Normal as acceptable

The normal/healthy form of childhood, deriving from paediatrics as well as psychological studies, was first predicated on the opposition between health and pathology: the normal child was, accordingly, a healthy child, whilst forms of disease, illness and sickness all pertained to the pathological/abnormal child because they affected its development. In the realm of mental hygiene, developmental standards emphasized the dichotomy after intelligence testing gave it both a new translation and a new impetus. Much as disease was recognized as a disorder in child development, pathology was not yet restricted to illness: it could allude to behaviour. The experts were already taking aim at the delinquent child.

Though chronological schedules and sequential development highlighted a form of normalcy – revolving around the healthy child – it did not utterly deplete the translation and circulation of its opposite, the pathological child, in the collective. Here is outlined the figure of the child at risk and its surrogates: delinquents, runaways, truants, vagrants and prostitutes. In the second half of the nineteenth century, the delinquent child is endowed with the epitomized form of society's worst problems by public authorities or public opinion.[67] Thereupon arose a construction of normalcy related to acceptable behaviour, but as opposed to pathological demeanour leading to social disorder – not to the healthy child of paediatrics or psychology.[68] Conduct,

---

[67] This section will concentrate on the case of the delinquent child rather than having an overall view of all the other figures (vagrants, prostitutes and so on). The umbrella figure of the delinquent child adequately translates the other forms of the pathological child in the collective.

[68] Beeckman talks of the normal as good. 'The weight of science stood behind the statistical concept of normal as good. Yet, while a child . . . may be good simply by virtue of his not being bad, to be normal implies conformity to a fixed list of behaviour that science has drawn from group studies. Good can encompass a whole range and variety of types and behaviours' (Beeckman 1977). As long as it

pathology and normalcy: above developmental standards, although connected to them to a certain extent, another form of childhood was already carried out in the collective.

The basic elements of the normal/acceptable form of childhood and their translation and circulation in the collective will be clarified. The emergence of the delinquent child goes far back in the history of society, as this figure is constant in the western world since the early Middle Ages. This section will ascertain the translations of the delinquent child during the period under consideration and will, accordingly, register the transformations of the collective. From the guilty child sent to prison, to the victim child handled by the philanthropists, to the maladjusted child taken charge of by psychiatry, one can find the various translations bestowed upon the delinquent child, the first of which provides 'the initial recognition in legislative terms of juvenile delinquency as a separate category' (Hendrick 1994: 27).

From the 1850s in England, the delinquents mostly belonged to what was termed the 'dangerous classes', this urban proletariat racked by social agitation. The delinquent child is then frightening on several accounts. Not only is he threatening the social order for which public authorities and fractions of the population – the bourgeoisie and the middle classes – are seeking regulations and controls aimed at containing the delinquent within the boundaries of civil society, but he raises above all very acute and pressing questions: can he be a child? How to restrain such threatening youth? How is such conduct acceptable?

It raised the question of the extent of the concept of childhood: were the delinquents still children? What constituted childhood with respect to the process leading to delinquency? Reformers such as M. D. Hill, the Recorder of Birmingham, were at the forefront of the reasoning surrounding these interrogations. Their reflections sums up to general considerations concerning the self-reliance of the delinquent, the mis-directions of his own behaviours, the scarcity of trust in those in charge of him; hence the lack of control and protection. The answer: he has to be turned into a child again (Hendrick 1994: 27).

The Youthful Offenders Act of 1854 – with further acts in 1857, 1861 and 1866 – started to provide answers to these queries. The first

refers to behaviour, it seems more appropriate to speak of normal as acceptable to avoid any moral connotations.

response revolved around the implementation of juvenile courts, thus establishing a clear distinction between delinquents and adult criminals; if children were to be brought to court for grave misdemeanours, it would be under specialized youth offence courts rather than general courts, in which children were amalgamated with adult criminals. An equivalent principle of separation of children and youth from adults, while incarcerated, prevailed. The second outcome of the acts introduced the idea of reformation with the intention of handling and retrieving delinquents – through reformatory schools – rather than solely punishing them. Reformation and punishment came into sight, by the mid-nineteenth century, as the two opposite categories regarding delinquency; the same phenomena were translated into entirely different terms in the collective, thus launching a renewed context for relationships setting up distinct networks among actors. Once the juvenile courts were set up, a new gaze of scrutiny bore upon the families of troublesome children: procedures such as the case conference or diagnostic forum, new supervising staff such as social workers and probation officers, and a cutting-edge framing protocol led to the normative assessment of children and their families (L. Rose 1991: 129).

Punishment has been for a very long period of time the usual, common and conventional translation in the collective in regard to delinquent behaviour. By mid-century, however, in the wake of increasing criticism concerning the unintended consequences of punishment upon delinquent children, a novel translation, the reformatory, came to light as the instalment of a new sequence and the reconfiguration of the collective's boundaries. The Society for the Prevention of Cruelty to Children (NSPCC) is deemed a transitional phase in both broadening the collective's boundaries and resettling the form of a new collective normal-child.[69]

Cruelty to children is reckoned to be the structural inversion of delinquency from an analytical point of view; it bears on a translation of childhood into an enlargement of the normal child's form. The former alludes to violence towards children mostly by parents and adults, whilst the latter pertains to brutality enacted by children and

---

[69] It is intriguing to realize that both British and American Societies for the Prevention of Cruelty to Children were set up in the aftermath of their counterpart, the Societies for the Prevention of Cruelty to Animals (Ferguson Clement 1985). See also Hendrick for the British version (Hendrick 1994).

adolescents. Although both of these violences were at the forefront of public concern, yet innovative ways were found to come to terms with this ferocity. Child abuse and child neglect alike were regarded as a major social problem and it seemed that time had come for a decisive intervention (Quincy-Lefevre 1997).

Reformation was proposed by the Poor Law in Great Britain, by the 1850 law concerning the education of young offenders in France, and by institution-building – refuges, asylums, orphanages, reformatories, schools – in the USA. Thus reformation was steadily becoming an imperative requirement for reformers and child-savers of the same mould. In England, philanthropists such as Lord Shaftesbury, Baroness Angela Burdett-Coutts, Florence Davenport-Hill and Mary Carpenter initiated a campaign for better protection of children.[70] The NSPCC as a movement proceeded cautiously giving priority to education – educating parents and reforming the home – rather than prosecuting criminals. 'Saving children' as a watchword – especially those children categorized as at risk – paved the way for a double differentiation: first, a keen social demarcation among families, with the bourgeois family 'self-contained, private, patriarchal, loving, religious, hierarchical and civilised' (Hendrick 1994: 51) being contrasted with the poor family, characterized by irresponsibility, brutality, moral bankruptcy, thriftiness, callousness and the like. The second distinction, between punishment and reformation, remained remarkably relevant for the question of delinquency, as well indeed as the first distinction.

Incarceration of young offenders was no longer, by mid-nineteenth century, an adequate translation of the delinquency quandary – that is, connecting poverty, urbanization and immigration, in the USA, at least – with juvenile crime.[71] The pace moved steadily towards reformation. The basic idea consisted of setting up a mediation

---

[70] The battle for a better legal protection of children would receive a first political acknowledgment with the passing of the Prevention of the Cruelty Act in 1889 (Hendrick 1994).

[71] The American experience is a striking example of a translation of the delinquency predicament that has varied according to the parameters of sex and race. Reformatories for instance admitted only white boys, as black children were most of the time locked up with adult criminals or rigidly segregated from whites in the few establishments that admitted them. On the other hand girls were incarcerated not for any petty larcenies usually characterizing boys, but for precocious sexual behaviour, a misdemeanour for which boys were virtually never indicted (Ferguson Clement 1985: 257).

between the child and the external world: circles of protection so to speak, home and school, for these two sites of the collective appeared crucial as templates of experience (Finkenstein 1985). Deserted or rebellious children or those of decisively mischievous propensities had previously crossed the circles of protection and were herded together in a network, not of punishment any more, but of reformation, education and discipline.[72] Widespread suspicions of various reformers, philanthropists and the like, as well as the failure of the penitentiary authorities, were instrumental in a novel translation of the delinquency question.

The passage from punishment to reformation in the picking up of the delinquents generally meant a displacement towards the family – bolstering and reforming the family – and towards an extensive use of probation. The family was bestowed a pivotal position in the collective, a key mediation, as the young delinquent is translated as a victim of the poor family's moral bankruptcy rather than a sole individual accountable for its own behaviour. Moral concern appeared central in this translation; Binet and Simon's collaborator, Miss Bonnis, was the head of a service intended for children in moral danger (Quincy-Lefevre 1997). The cardinal difference between the guilty child and the victim child was the slippage from the individual to the familial stratum: namely, from the child's misconduct to the family's deviance.

Four innovations characterized this passage:

• The child's general condition in the family and at school rather than specific acts or behaviour, was the most important feature to take account of in assessing it; the responsibility was not individual, but clearly familial.
• Separate detention facilities were set up provided the number of delinquents was sufficient; girls and blacks constituted in that respect a specific issue, were dealt with later, thus raising the question: what and who is a child.

---

[72] Though the pace was progressively moving from punishment to reformation, professionals working with delinquents assumed that there was a clear line delineating the normal from the subnormal. Here the explanations contrasted sharply. In America for instance, Henry Goddard, a biological determinist, insisted that the cycle of the Mendelian dice established the child's conduct, whilst William Healy, a psychiatric determinist, argued that mental and emotional disorders induced delinquency (Cravens 1985b: 428).

- Adults could be convicted for contributing to youth delinquency in one way or another, thus emphasising the networking aspect of the question.
- Probation, regulation and adjustment were stressed rather than punishment with the launching of reform and industrial schools; home, family, school constituted the collective's enlargement aimed at the rehabilitation of the delinquent.

(Cohen 1985)

It is widely recognized in France that compulsory schooling, by bringing and fixing all children to such a specific network site as the school, greatly furthered the observation of families and its pedagogical penetration with its moralizing aim (Donzelot 1977).[73] The child who resisted school rules and regulations was, therefore, considered as a victim of family disorders, its moral bankruptcy, its hereditary defects and the like. Even Binet and Simon, whose *Société Libre pour l'Étude Psychologique de l'Enfant* published its first survey in 1899, investigated, for instance, schoolchildren's lies, which they attributed to family brutality, morality or alcoholism (Renouard 1990: 65). Kergomard, a key figure of France's kindergartens (*salles d'asiles*) once stated: 'I dream ... of having the family invaded by the school' (Renouard 1990: 69).

The broadening of the alliance, previously foreseen, between the physician legitimized by scientific progress, the teacher whose authority rested on the transmission of basic knowledge, and the psychologist promoting a unique vision of the child's needs paved the way for a programme of recommendations, advice and notifications intended for both the child's and the family's education. Its coherence was secured by the vision of the child as a victim of his family and an education harmful to his development (Boltanski 1969). The medical and the school apparatus, with psychology's active collaboration, translated the child's situation into a new wording and new places: to protect the child from the aggressions of the adult world by creating, for instance, a specific site where the child will be protected and able to maximize its chance of development. In this rational organization of foresight, the delinquent also has places of protection: the reform and industrial schools; a particular instance in the court system as well as separate detention facilities.

---

[73] It is possible to outline the influence of Foucault in this immense process of family observation.

The great laws of childhood protection emerged within this temporality in most western societies. One might plausibly think of the laws regarding compulsory schooling and child work. It is, however, rather the laws pertaining to the abandoned child and the ill-treated child, which translated primarily the moralizing vision of delinquency and the new responsibility borne by families. These laws legitimized the medico-administrative intervention of experts in families based on a new principle, the interests of the child. Both the school and the court started to understand delinquency in terms of family deviance: psychological knowledge asserted the weight of education upon the evolution of the child.

The role of psychological knowledge points henceforth to a novel orientation, that is an unconventional translation of delinquency in the collective and the rise of unusual relationships in the hybrid network. Psychology and psychiatry were to play a decisive role in this reconfiguration and the translation of delinquency into the figure of the maladjusted child.[74] This double process – translation and mediation – of child psychiatry's implementation in the collective will be the focus of the analysis hereafter.

By the 1920s and the 1930s, it was widely agreed that the delinquent was no longer a 'victim', but rather a maladjusted child, a translation put forward in various settings, under the large umbrella of mental hygiene notably and the sponsorship of the Rockefeller Foundation in the USA, Rollet and Heuyer in France, Newman and Miller in Britain. The mental hygiene movement conveyed an extraordinarily broad notion of what constituted an at-risk child, finding signs of deviance in everyday behaviour of the normal child and thus emphasizing its psychiatric orientation. Moreover, it coined the term 'pre-delinquent', acknowledging a preventive approach to the problem which had an abiding effectiveness in the network.

Hence psychiatry will extend remarkably across juvenile delinquency in the collective; namely, its translation of the problem prevailed and its mediation in the network became gradually unavoidable. The gradual development of child psychiatry is related to

[74] The establishment of psychiatry in the collective goes back to the turn of the twentieth century, mainly around the question of the schooling of the abnormal, with Binet and Simon, Goddard and the Vineland Training School for the Feebleminded in the USA, and Burt and London County Council in London. See also Seguin 1895 for the education of the abnormal.

its implementation in the increased management of all forms of deviance. The connection between delinquency and maladjustment emerged in the 1920s in Britain when Newman, the Chief Medical Officer, acknowledged that emotionally disturbed children could develop into delinquents; the Tavistock Clinic, in close relationship to the Home Office and the probation service, evolved from the growing influence of psychiatry (Hendrick 1994: 164). It is indicative in this respect to note that, in 1925, the Sorbonne school of medicine created a clinic of child psychiatry whose main goal was to track down the mental anomalies – either irregular psychological or emotional development – of delinquents. The core of this sub-discipline is delinquency, which, in a certain sense, gave birth to it (Heuyer 1952).

The juvenile justice system set the stage for translating juvenile crime as a medical problem which is linked to public confidence in medical solutions to social problems: translating the child offender not as a criminal nor a victim, but as a maladjusted child which, as a general category, also included the neglected child, the child in the street (truant), not to mention the delinquent (Richardson 1989). Medicalization[75] of juvenile crime, that is psychiatrization of the maladjusted child, is appraised in the growing focus on individual differences, as opposed to the family deviance of the 'victim' child, although child guidance kept the parent–child relationship at the heart of its concerns.

Can the medicalization of juvenile crime be translated as a transitional phase towards the medicalization of normality and, therefore, as the legitimation of clinical abnormality through the psychiatrization of delinquency? Child psychiatry introduced two disruptions into the particular trend of the medicalization of childhood. The first related to asylum considered as a network site of exclusion rather than adaptation (its new motto) while the second pertained to the overpowerful medicalization of adult psychiatry. The question, however, remains open, although a precautionary stance leads to scepticism with regard to a strong Foucaldian wording of the issue. Unlike Donzelot and others, I am less concerned by the extension and professionalization of specific problems such as delinquency, and more

---

[75] Medicalization must be understood within the framework of actor–network: the central and key position in the network that allows physicians and psychiatrists to mediate – translate and interfere – in children's lives.

interested in the patterning of the childhood collective, as well as the design of the network arising from it.

It should be borne in mind that delinquency was deemed, especially in reformers' eyes, to depend on environmental causes such as poverty or family moral bankruptcy. By the mid-1920s, this translation of delinquency is already pushed aside; a more thoroughly psychiatric restatement asserted that the mind of the adolescent is being enforced as an unavoidable analytical momentum in the network. The question at stake revolved around the role of mental conditions in regard to the prevalence of delinquency. Healy's work in America as well as Heuyer's in France and Burt's in Britain were heading in the same direction: the core importance of the delinquent's psyche in finding a relevant course to adapt the maladjusted child to its environment.[76] This, however, did not betoken a similar treatment, i.e. readjustment, for all delinquents (Hendrick 1994).

The most specific site of the maladjusted child is the child-guidance clinic, where child psychiatry settled. In the aftermath of punishment and reformation, a third phase, maladjustment, redefines the normal-child collective around psychiatry, an emerging force that offered a credible alternative to philanthropists' reformation. It puts the psychiatrist in a key network position; the reconfiguration of the hybrid network is punctuated by the insertion and the increasing domination of psychiatry in parent–child relations with respect to delinquents along with the activities of other figures such as physicians, psychologists, probation officers and social workers (N. Rose 1991: 129).[77]

---

[76] Burt's study, *The Young Delinquent* (1925), is considered a benchmark in the normal-child collective.

[77] It should be borne in mind that when I refer to psychiatry or psychiatrists, I always have in mind child psychiatry. The various editions of Henderson and Gillespie's leading *Textbook of Psychiatry* are indicative in this respect of this translation and, accordingly, of psychiatry's involvement in childhood.

In the first edition, published in 1927, no mention was made of either children or childhood in the index, though children's problems were described in terms of 'emotional defect'...The second edition, 1930, had one reference to child-guidance clinics, which noted that it was now widely accepted that the seeds of many mental disorders are 'sown in childhood'...By the third edition, published in 1932, there was a separate chapter on the psychiatry of childhood, which could no longer be ignored since the CGC had shown it to be 'an important part of the psychiatric domain' (Hendrick 1994).

The relevant question to be addressed, therefore, pertains less to the medicalization of delinquency than to the sociological conditions upon which psychiatry built its key network position.[78] Two basic elements should be underlined: first, a new translation of delinquency in terms of maladjustment, rather than victimhood, which paved the way for the implementation of psychiatrists' knowledge and the competence of those who mastered it. Second, by disqualifying the philanthropists' management of delinquency, psychiatrists proposed, as a counterpart, original methods of investigation and treatment designed according to their distinctive translation. Psychiatry's intervention was directed at the counterproductive inefficiency of philanthropists' ways of taking charge of delinquents as victims. Psychiatrists came in the collective to rationalize it, so they interposed themselves, not primarily as researchers, but rather as managers or counsellors who implemented a process of orientation and selection based on a diversified nosography, for instance the distinction between morons, idiots and imbeciles.

Psychiatrists provided a more accurate classification and categorization whose common denominator was mental anomaly; delinquents were, accordingly, presumed to be mentally defective. 'Mental anomaly is found in various degrees in almost all of school abnormal and juvenile delinquents' (Heuyer 1914: 316). A more sophisticated and discriminating classification is a crucial element in a rationalization of the collective as it calls for a specialization of the management of delinquency – observation, selection, professional rehabilitation and adaptation[79] – while bringing out the amateurish nature of philanthropy, its confusion and disorder. Philanthropy's indifference towards classification is noted in its indistinct admission of all delinquents without any preliminary selection.

Thus, whilst reformatory aimed at moralizing the family and the victim child, psychiatry sought to link the adaptation of the

---

[78] Even though a few philanthropists, chiefly Rockefeller, directed their intervention in the collective so as to make a social problem such as delinquency a public health question.

[79] The treatment of delinquency, which was reduced to a uniform minimum in the reformatory period, became more elaborate with the maladjusted child. For each particular anomaly there was identified a specific treatment generally oriented towards the professional insertion of delinquents and their adaptation into the labour market (Renouard 1990).

maladjusted child to the external world: professional, domestic and academic achievement. Following Healy's view, delinquents' problems were generally split up into three components: inner problems, i.e. medical; those associated with the school, i.e. educational; finally, those in the family, i.e. domestic or social (Cravens 1985b). With regard to the family, nothing provides a sharper contrast than philanthropy and psychiatry's practices in the collective. The former tried to shield the child from its family inasmuch as the latter has always considered the family as the basis of the child's mental hygiene. Adaptation–readaptation prevailed over most other forms of supervision in psychiatrists' management of delinquency, as young offenders were in need of effective training to take them out of the streets and integrate them, notably, into the labour market. A condition for an effective adaptation was to set up institutional devices to meet this goal: welfare services, professional and scientific psychiatry, and centres for professional orientation. Reformatory and industrial schools were among those institutional devices.

The normal/acceptable form of childhood emerged from the nineteenth century onward as part of society's bewilderment – predominantly that of public authorities, the bourgeoisie and the middle classes – at some children's awkward behaviour. The image of children's innocence, which prevailed for so long in western culture as an ideal childhood, was already suffering through threatening behaviour in the streets of the great industrial cities, with the delinquent, the truant, the neglected or the abandoned child. The normal/acceptable form refers to a specific translation of childhood, while clarifying its boundaries in a no less particular way: from the regulation of undesirable child-adolescent behaviour to the mastery of the complex process of child development, it is possible, first, to follow the transformations of both the normal-child collective's configuration and the network's set of relationships, such as the integration of the home with the school and the juvenile court to produce properly attuned citizens (Hendrick 1994: 162). Second, the singular translation of delinquency by child psychiatry emphasized adolescence as a distinct developmental stage of life with its own peculiarities, thus highlighting developmental process in a more global way while making it more complex characterized by specific and discrete stages.

The previous chapter looked at the languages and devices of children's textual inscription – the technologies of regulation – as a way of embodying them. In this respect, children are not only textually inscribed, but also codified through technical devices, which are patterned in normative ways, the most important of these being the normal child. The single idea of the normal child was a complex cultural and technical concept. This chapter followed the emergence of the normal child and the various forms it took in the collective as an outcome both of an abstract idea and of technical devices. The sociological status of the technical objects being to activate the capacity for action of various social groups in the collective constituting childhood, new forces, symbolic and technical alike, introduced into the network were enabled to translate and circulate, i.e. to mould, the child according to an entirely new scheme: the developmental process in ordained sequences.

Statistical thinking, both as a political–administrative and a cognitive device, emphasized the great quest for measuring children as a social object worthy of concern for public authorities. This huge activity of measurement presupposed a system of registration (collecting numerical data), coding, tabulation (performing statistical operations), and publication, which induced a peculiar way of thinking – numerically, statistically and probabilistically – about social actors. Numerical regularities paved the way for a process of normalization which bore three different set of meanings that have been investigated above: normal as average, as healthy and as acceptable.

The average child shares common features and characteristics with all children, physical, mental and social alike, that are normally distributed by large-scale regularities. The elaboration of norms of growth came as a result of extensive enquires concerning infant mortality, factory children – smaller than other children – tables of normal height and weight, mental tests contributing to the advent of a universal referent to assess children's growth, thus designing the average child.

Furthermore, these developmental standards did not prevent infant mortality or smaller children per se. Child experts recognized that disease affects child development: a deviation from normal standards manifested a complex disease process. The normal child was healthy, as the core opposition of this form was health/pathology. The main focus of attention revolved thereupon around the child's physical welfare; other needs, such as psychological, were considered negligible at the outset. In the aftermath, they came to be a crucial feature of the child's health.

Although disease is recognized as a disorder in child growth, and developmental standards provided a new translation to mental hygiene, pathology is not restricted to illness: it could also allude to behaviour. Accordingly, the pathological child extends nonetheless to the figure of the child at risk: the delinquent. The normal/acceptable form of childhood was granted three different sets of translation in the collective: punishment, reformation and maladjustment. Child psychiatry emphasized adolescence as a distinct developmental stage of life. The next chapter will look at the sequential development process as a cognitive form whose main achievement is to stabilize the childhood collective.

5 | *Developmental thinking as a cognitive form*

By the 1920s and 1930s, development was not only an outlandish idea emerging from researchers in isolated laboratories. It was, more broadly, becoming both a way of thinking and acting legitimized in the scientific community and in the larger childhood collective; thus, slowly percolating several activities pertaining to childhood. Growth, which chiefly means children's physical progression, was not any longer the central concern in the collective for the questions of hygiene, nutrition and so on were already on the agenda of experts and families, and mental hygiene was likewise becoming a crucial aspect of children's lives, therefore extending widely the emerging concept of development.

It is understood that developmental thinking paved the way to the idea of the normal child, to which it is tied by numerous connections, as much mental and physical normality with respect to the child's maturation. Based on statistical technologies in extensive focused enquiries, large-scale regularities contributed decisively to outline what a normal child would look like, both physically and mentally. Although normality was far from being unequivocal as a notion,[1] different actors from the childhood collective – parents, teachers, paediatricians, nurses and welfare activists, social workers – started to be on the look-out for new criteria that would be suitable for adults in their daily relations with children. Developmental standards were implemented in the collective; thus, children's progression was measured in accordance with these standards. Moreover, parents, teachers and the like gradually fell in line with this particular way of

---

[1] What is said here about the idea of normality is essentially relevant to the notion of development. The latter also has a convoluted history, embroiled in interminable debates among experts (Kellogg 1926; Porter *et al.* 1915; Veeder 1924).

thinking.[2] From statistical technologies to developmental standards, an emerging cognitive device is becoming a way of thinking/acting towards children.

The idea as well as the symbolism of normality – its intricate set of lexicons, measurements, categories, visual depictions and so on – shaped the way in which the child is conceived of and acted upon.[3] The situation of children was being translated into novel standards and criteria of behaviour. The introduction of new practices in the collective such as mental hygiene, intelligence testing, various measurements, different school operations and so on induced a translation of children's predicaments into a broad question of normality/development. A primary consequence of this translation consisted in a major redistribution of the socio-technical network of relationships surrounding the child, whose focus was displaced towards normal and abnormal children. The network is, thus, both reasserted and redeployed along this keen and straightforward difference. Development brings stabilization to the collective, but nonetheless its boundaries must be re-negotiated.

This chapter will further investigate specific aspects of the associations between development and normality. The analysis takes place within the larger context of developmental thinking: how such an idea emerged and was implemented, what it meant, how it became a cognitive form. This progressive mutation emphasizes, and here lies the crucial point to note, the double pattern of developmental thinking as both a cognitive form and a hybrid object. The investigation of the links between normality and development will raise fundamental questions for social theory revolving around the question of the child's

---

[2] A double movement is outlined here: on the one hand, experts are identifying developmental standards which public authorities are trying to implement; on the other hand, various people in the collective are not only acted upon by these criteria, but actively participate on their own terms in their enforcement. Therefore, this double movement relates to regulation of control and autonomous regulation. The hypothesis focuses on the idea that developmental thinking emerges at the intersection of these two forms of regulation.

[3] Both normality and development bear two different aspects that need to be distinguished. They are a practice of extensive investigation, thus control of children. They are also, at the same time, a practice of category building. Therefore it is not only a professional practice, but also a cognitive form (Molino 1984).

ontological status and contingency. I shall address these, first, by following the rise of the double form of developmental thinking; second, by mapping the configuration of developmentalism in its essential patterns; third, by making a basic critique of developmental theory; and fourth, by establishing how developmental thinking moved steadily towards a cognitive form, by retracing the different steps of its translation into this specific type of form.

5.1 The rise of developmental thinking

Both as a seminal idea and as an inventive practice, normalcy is linked to the rise of statistical technologies as well as the fading away of determinism. On the other hand, normalcy appears a much wider and complex lineament than its single representation as an outcome of statistics, especially in its late extension as developmentalism. Whilst normalcy undeniably originates from statistics (Hacking 1990), the three forms in which it materialized, afterwards, percolated in the collective, were surprisingly diversified.[4]

The perspective, therefore, is slightly different, for the main line of argument was displaced and is taken up from a singular angle, the other way around as it were, that is, transversely. Across the three forms already acknowledged, I shall focus on the general configuration emerging from normalcy and recognized as developmental thinking in its two salient patterns: a cognitive form and a hybrid object. Besides looking closely at the transformation of the category – from physical growth to mental development and beyond, I shall investigate the startling direction the conceptualization of development took: the stage theory in its different forms. Later, I shall consider developmental thinking today as well as its links with socialization theory.

From the nineteenth century onwards, in almost all western societies, especially in England, France and the USA, the primary concern, and the most disrupting in its effects, was bestowed by the appalling rates of infant mortality, the noticeably critical threat to the collective, as well as its most worrying. Childhood happened to be in a

---

[4] I shall rather focus on the consequences of the delimitation of criteria, standards, for this appears to be the core of the hybrid circulating in a given collective.

chaotic and disturbed state in need of stabilization. The already known – the relationship between infant mortality and poverty – however important, became an increasingly insufficient assertion. Not only was infant mortality connected to poverty in myriad ways, but also the various enquiries were pointing to a novel association/ translation between poverty, growth and child mortality: children suffering from growth deficiencies were statistically in a more vulnerable position regarding mortality. From then on, researchers went on investigating the general causes promoting or delaying growth in childhood.

A new picture of the child, hitherto unknown, emerged from these investigations based on statistical technologies: large surveys of children, systematic measurements, methodical examination on an extensive scale and so on. The regular registration of height and weight, the recording of malformation and diseases, the formal comparison of children among themselves – and, of groups of children, one next to the other – constituted an adequate basis to render possible the contrast of children, therefore, the elaboration of norms of growth. The comparison of children in large-scale inquiries opened up possibilities for original knowledge: the norms of growth are directly related to these possibilities as both the examples of British factory children and American slave children have compellingly indicated.

The alarming situation surrounding infant mortality had the acute effect of focusing the collective's attention upon the child's physical growth, which, in return, became the central concern for adults. Two main outcomes of this effect revolved around, on the one hand, the various growth charts which gave a visual depiction of human maturation concentrated on the child's physical features. On the other hand, public authorities implemented substantial measures to fight effectively infant mortality: hygienic reform, improvement of nutrition, regulation of infectious diseases etc. The introduction of these new forces in the collective were, according to some experts, the main reason for the relative decline of infant mortality, although everyone agrees that growth charts did not directly reduce infant mortality.

The question at stake in this line of argument concerns the steady mutation in the ways such problems were thought about. There lay the real innovation happening in the collective. Large-scale inquiries opened up an imaginative prospect: the comparison of groups of children among themselves set up the pace for norms of growth relevant for all children; they constitute the core basis from which developmental thinking came forth.[5]

The same form of social process briefly outlined above happened with the question of children's mental hygiene. Under the broad aegis of psychology,[6] and in the wake of Binet's breakthrough, the IQ testing movement yielded a method to classify and sort out children according to their ability, within the school system and for its benefit. In the context of compulsory schooling, school administrators looked for a device that could help them to categorize children on a 'scientific' basis. Much as this problem did not pertain exclusively to backwardness and feeble-mindedness, yet a solution was imagined that proved efficient and manageable for all children, and not only for the retarded.

The novelty of Binet's approach consisted of introducing an intelligence test device correlating chronological with mental age. Departing from Galton and American psychologists trying to induce complex abilities from elementary ones,[7] he worked on a test measuring specific mental characteristics – memory, attention, comprehension etc. The test became a scheme for classification of children: backward, slow, normal and gifted. It focused on the measurement of specific tasks appearing in gradual order of difficulty revolving around judgement, comprehension and reasoning. The measure of intelligence was not settled on a quantitative graded scale, but in terms of an increase with age. Binet investigated if scores improved with age and to what extent. The genuine breakthrough came with the ordainment of the child's mental age in relation to its chronological age. Although age was already a relevant parameter in physical growth, Binet found it to be a keystone in mental development.

---

[5] For the moment, no distinctions are introduced between the notions of criteria, standards, norms of growth and development, although the progression from criteria to standards of growth can be considered as consolidation of developmental thinking.

[6] Intelligence testing was the most visible outcome of psychological research, at the beginning of the century. 'The general mental test stands today as the most important single contribution of psychology to the practical guidance of human affairs' (Lee Crombach, quoted in Sokal 1987b: 113).

[7] As already noted above with Durkheim and his analysis of religion, it was a nineteenth century general trend to try to analyse complex forms of social life and to explain them as if they derived from elementary forms, conceived therefore as their inception.

Paediatrics was not anymore considered as a practice restricted to the sole cure of children's diseases. The enlargement of paediatric intervention towards hygienic conditions, infant feeding, nutrition and the like, that is, beyond its traditional restricted scope, enabled an original translation of children's health: in this respect, child hygiene – the task of educating both mothers and children in the methods of sound physical health – is indicative of an ingenious translation. Under the large umbrella of the child development movement, paediatrics gradually veered towards mental hygiene, even though as Gesell stated, mental hygiene was rather a nebulous idea at that period of time. A global image of the child was gradually emerging that included mental hygiene as a major constituent of child development, from conception through adolescence.

Gesell is especially meaningful in this debate for he was amongst the first researchers to identify particular behavioural benchmarks, which were considered as standards for mental development for children in specified age categories.[8] The Developmental Record Form included a mental development chart: specific standards of mental development were contrasted so that physicians and other actors could observe the child step by step from infancy to adolescence. This breach in mental behavioural benchmarks was a specific translation of mental health, which took the form of developmental schedules drawn up in line and standards provided by Gesell and Veeder (Veeder 1926).

These various graphs, tabulations, schedules etc, along with standards introduced by experts, are especially indicative for they visualize in a compelling, yet convincing way the mapping and charting of children's growth, and ultimately its extensive development. These devices

---

[8] Morss is highly critical of Gesell and bluntly dismisses his contribution to developmental thinking. 'Gesell's own stage theory has been of too little scientific influence to merit detailed discussion here, consisting of summary descriptions of "the" three-year-old, "the" four-year-old, and so on' (Morss 1990). He nevertheless recognized Gesell's practical influence (Morss 1990: 51). Is it necessary to state that I strongly disagree with Morss' appreciation? Gesell might not be a sophisticated theoretician, but he was certainly an experimenter who cannot be bypassed or ignored, and a truly innovative researcher with brilliantly conceived plans, forms and technologies with respect to developmentalism. Experimentation, observation and the technology sustaining them (such as instruments) do not play a secondary role in developmental thinking. They were, on the contrary, central and decisive (Hacking 1983).

amount to the technical translation of a social problem and its under-lying human relations. Graphs or tabulations circulate and add new resources to the network, as they forge new ties in it (White 1992: 66ff.). I now turn to the visualization of bodily elements through the various devices. What is precisely visualized in the latter? How is it done?

Cognitively speaking, a chart or an intelligence test crystallizes, in a particular visual form, specifically identified elements of the child's body – for instance, height and weight on one hand and IQ on the other; these elements ordered along discrete parameters bear extensive characteristics such as universality, comparability, flexibility and malleability. Relating directly to the descriptive organization of see-ing,[9] the devising of a technical device, however clear and simple the device might be, set in motion a complex transaction (Latour 1994a). The question here at stake is how the network is mobilized and, afterwards, stabilized via the circulation of devices such as graphs. The elaborate activity of translating children's bodily elements is a process of ordering through patterning explicit areas of the child's body – those parts of its body that are either dubious, puzzling or unsure – into an entity which, by way of visualization, furthers and accelerates the circulation in the socio-technical network, thus becoming co-extensive with actors (Callon 1986).[10]

Beyond the extended characteristics of the technical device already imparted, readability and discussability appear to be the two indis-putable lineaments of the patterning entity that is, for example a, graph. To be prevailing in the collective, namely to further the circu-lation among differentiated actors, and to stabilize it, an operative cognitive device must bear appropriate attributes: readability and discussability are likely to encounter such features, as they provide accessibility to abstract characteristics for lay persons as well as intro-ducing new forces into the social fabric. A quick reminder to that effect: so as to answer the question – what does a cognitive device bring up and

---

[9] As Law and Lynch have cogently worded it in their text concerning observational activity: 'Lists, field guides, and the descriptive organization of seeing: Birdwatching as an exemplary observational activity' (Law and Lynch 1990).

[10] Besides stabilizing the network, a cognitive device circulates in it at certain precise conditions to be elucidated (Breslau 2000; Latour 1990; Star and Griesemer 1989).

gather into the social fabric? – a prerequisite is required. If charts and graphs were to make new connections between the various entities in the collective while accelerating the circulation among them, a few basic operations have to be met. The modification of the fabric made through technical mediation focuses on three operations: new forms of child observation, of inscription, and of visualization of the previous two. It is a formal basic condition that data of the child's body tabulated into an abstract figure must be accessible – in the form of traces, numbers or diagrams – by being legible and discussable among all of the collective's components, not solely experts or professionals. Accessibility to the cognitive device entails the indispensable condition for securing the whole connection between families, peers, schools, clinics, hospitals, the state etc.

In this respect, the impetus towards the establishment of orderly categories in developmental thinking became an integral part of the quest for rationality, measurement or regularity (Hacking 1990). What was in consequence the most performing design for these orderly categories? Visually accessible categories in child development's devices based on readability and discussability features took the form of age-grading structuration – and eventually age norms – in the broader process of classifying children in the collective (Bernardi 1985; Graff 1995; Hockey and James 1993; Kertzer 1989; Quentel 1997).[11] Paediatricians spoke of age as an etiological factor and developmental psychologists recognized age from the outset as a crucial feature.[12] Although this cognitive pattern came along with the cultural rediscovery of childhood as a peculiar category of bounded life course, it must be understood that institutions were not yet structured according to either age-determined rank or age-related

---

[11] My line of argument differs significantly from Chudacoff's. That 'age norms were being fashioned by physicians' and that 'we attached scientifically defined biological and psychological characteristics to specific ages' (Chudacoff 1989), are propositions which were extensively supported in the previous chapters. The point in need of clarification focuses on the particular features of age as being the most effective criteria for a cognitive device's operativeness in the collective.

[12] French physician, Charles Billard, whose book, *Traité des maladies des enfants nouveau-nés et à la mamelle* (1828) became a landmark in child medicine on the pathology of childhood diseases. The book 'was one of the first texts to list what Billard and other doctors believed to be the norms for the weight, size, and shape of growing children and their organs' (Chudacoff 1989).

behaviour. On the contrary, child development's framework is, therefore, considered a decisive impulsion towards the generalization of age-grading structuration in western societies.

Age norms as well as age structuration embody a specific translation which enables social actors to go into different relationships by bringing up new forces and, above all, by stabilizing the hybrid network.[13] The translation of children's general behaviour – physical and psychological maturation alike – into age standards entails a genuine breakthrough for it initiated a whole mutation of the collective around age structuration: it pragmatically meant age-related diseases or age-related psychological behaviour: 'in an ordered form, managing their variability conceptually, and governing it practically' (N. Rose 1991: 132). This form of translation offered the possibility of stabilizing the collective, which was confused by threats such as infant mortality and puzzled by uncontrolled childhood diseases or behaviour. Age framework,[14] therefore, domesticated the threats – children's frailty, precariousness or unpredictability – while offering the possibility to master their proliferation by putting forward a cognitive device to understand the predicament, visualize its translation into an image and, subsequently, intervene efficiently in the collective.

For straightforward as they are nowadays, and indisputable as they seem in everyday life, age standards were a totally novel form of wording by visualizing the issue of children's disruptive situation; and above all, stabilizing a precarious plight. 'Children are ephemeral, shifting, elusive ... the images make the child stable' (N. Rose 1991: 146). At the beginning of the twentieth century, hygiene, paediatrics, child psychology and so on did not proceed from unmitigated ideas such as criteria, regularity, schedules or firmness, pertaining to their object, but within laboratories, their dispositifs and their instruments – measurement, technical apparatus, schema, clinical and experimental

[13] Age norms, for instance, are the findings of the gathering of comparable data on a huge number of children along a temporal axis, emphasizing a developmental scope (N. Rose 1991: 142).

[14] Both as a framework and as the central feature of a cognitive device, age was not restricted to health. School was completely reshuffled around age structuration and age-grading at the same period of time depending on the country considered (Graff 1995; Hockey and James 1993; Kett 1976; Luc 1998; Luc 1997; Tyack 1974).

research protocols – which are techniques of inscribing individual differences. Laboratories' dispositifs provide the technologies of inscription with the status of a cognitive device and the legitimation of science. Scientists and experts, on the other hand, do not operate empty-handed in the collective; they act with hybrid entities such as graphs and charts which are circulated in the collective since their readability and discussability allows the network's lengthening as well as its stabilization and consolidation.

Age is the structural attribute of the cognitive device in regard to children. Binet found in the category of age the key abstract lineament for ranking individuals according to their abilities, thereby creating a hierarchy of the normal. Age sustains the possibility of differentiated behaviour among social actors with respect to formal age-related standards enabling the entities to be co-extensive with the network. The several social technologies encountered in this investigation are all, in one way or another, ordered by age as their central lineament.

- Isolation and hospitalization of sick children;
- compulsory vaccination;
- child hygiene booklets and manuals;
- systematic measurements of height, weight, chest, girth etc;
- medical supervision of children and regular medical visit for healthy children;
- atlas of infant growth;
- nutrition and diet standards;
- posture charts;
- compulsory schooling and medical monitoring of school children;
- IQ-testing;
- developmental benchmarks and record forms;
- normative summaries of expected mental behaviour;
- mental development guidelines.

The various devices indicate a decisive change in scaling within a collective on its way to a new orientation. After the threats of infant mortality and infectious diseases were overcome, the beginning of a peculiar phase came in, as the category of childhood appeared openly in its uniqueness, perhaps for the first time in modern times. It put forward a translation focused on children's particular features – their individuality – that carried out the notion of graduality applied to children's growth. The cardinal breakthrough lies in the capacity to show, namely to visualize, unsettled aspects of children's situation. It inaugurated 'a regime of visibility' (N. Rose 1991: 132).[15] Graphs, charts and tabulations set up age structuration as the best fulfilment of graduality; it operates as a new entity, network and actor being co-extensive as a hybrid entity, which did not have much of an existence for mankind prior to this period. These entities rearranged the collective by sustaining the socio-technical network, codifying it around age standards, therefore stabilizing it by securing social actors and behaving in accordance with these hybrid entities.

Age as the central feature of developmental thinking's cognitive device took the form of age standards or age norms; the fulfilment of developmentalism in various settings was organized from the notion of age structuration. In 1842, British physicians Evanson and Maunsell, in their *Practical Treatise on the Management and Diseases of Children*, introduced a division of childhood into two age-enacted categories: birth to age one and age one to age eight, dentition being the boundary and the onset of the second phase. From cases such as the latter, which expanded over the century, and under a generalization of discrete yet articulated categories of childhood, a new lexicon emerged in experts' circles to be relayed to the larger collective: behind time, ahead of time or on time progressively became part of developmental discourse as a direct effect inferred by standardized measurements (Chudacoff 1989). Therefore there ensued a reordering of the categories pertaining to childhood.

The reordering of age-based categories of childhood into a continuum of phases – later to become stages – turned out to be a fundamental protocol in developmental thinking. Inasmuch as age structuration mustered children into a coherent classification which set the pace for the collective's stabilization, the delineation and fulfilment of phases in the course of childhood paved the way to a more explicit, yet formal, conception of childhood through reliable stages of development. The transition from age structuration to phases of

---

[15] Rose's regime of visibility could well be understood within the framework of actor–network theory: collective, network, stabilization and so on. Rose sees that the observation activity in its linguistic form is rapidly transformed into a different material form, such as graphs and diagrams, and thus into means of visualization and techniques of inscription. 'Inscriptions must render ephemeral phenomena into stable forms that can be repeatedly examined and accumulated over time' (N. Rose 1991: 133 et seq.).

development, although important, is considered as a proper translation of children's general condition (health, predicament, behaviour and so on) which will be documented further on. The translation of age categories into phases/stages of development goes back as far as the nineteenth century's advisedness with natural growth in its physical and intellectual materializations. Paediatrics' key role enabled physicians, through observation, experimental or clinical research, to clarify their knowledge and refine their findings. They articulate progressive age standards with growth phases as well as the specific circumstances surrounding children's diseases, thus distributing more systematically childhood into age-graded stages. In France, in the aftermath of the Bichat era, the medical discovery of a 'second childhood' between three and six years of age comes shortly after the fundamental steps of walking and speaking, which are major characteristics of infancy (Luc 1998). On the other hand, Bowditch was one of the most explicit advocates of such a translation, that is of new connections between disparate elements previously isolated. 'The statistics of growth taken in connection with those of disease might very possibly reveal unexpected relations between periods of slow and rapid growth and the age at which certain diseases most frequently occur' (Bowditch 1881: 469).

Stage became a key constituent of childhood in developmental thinking. This translation gives an idea of the immense step forward carried out by the concept of stage. When British physician Boulton[16] started weighing and measuring children in the 1870s, correct averages being unavailable, he had not a clear idea at what rate a child should grow in a year. Conversely, in 1894, Starr put forward the statement that 'under normal circumstances children grow in height and weight according to a regular rate' (Chudacoff 1989: 52). Starr assessed that the data collected indicated what should be the normal proportions (height and weight) of a child at each age; such an indication was clearly prescriptive, legitimized by the authority of science. Starr abundantly documented age-graded stages of growth in his well-known textbook.[17] Holt's book, *The Care and Feeding of Children*, links growth to nutrition and diet while it delineated varying

---

[16] Percy Boulton was a physician to the Samaritan Hospital for Women and Children in London at the end of the nineteenth century.

[17] Louis Starr edited a widely influential paediatric text of the 1890s: *An American Textbook on the Diseases of Children*, Philadelphia, PA, W.B. Saunders, 1894.

nutritional needs of children in relation to their age, thus setting the pace not only for age standards but also for stages of growth. Finally, Binet's major breakthrough pertains to the elucidation of firm relationships between mental capability and chronological age which provided him with the core device for ranking individuals according to their abilities; stages of mental development were soon to follow well above the IQ-testing movement.[18]

From age-based categories to stages of growth, a continuum of phases appears as a watermark. In this translation, stages of growth are not disorderly identified by researchers. Either primary and secondary childhood or accurate stages of growth in height and weight emerge from the logically articulated idea of a morphological organization of the child's development. A continuum of phases was very likely the first form through which this concept found its way publicly into the collective. Although rather elementary, the first acknowledged stages already pertained to a more formal conception of childhood as they inserted notions such as measurement, steps, regularity, benchmark, requirement and so on. Progressively, children's situation was widely understood through these notions in the network, and not only in the experts' circles.

The passage from phases/stages to sequences of development, as a third level of developmental thinking, came later in the 1920s for their developmental chart enabled standardization and normalization to go further in the regulation via the construction of norms. Piaget's genetic psychology is usually considered as the epitomized pattern of this cognitive form. Along this passage, researchers went from an extensive description of the child's physical condition to an understanding of its mental capability – mainly intelligence – and, later with Piaget, a whole depiction of the structuring of thought through the acquisition of cognitive competencies in compliance with a universal sequence: from sensory-motor intelligence after birth, through pre-conceptual thought, intuitive thought, and concrete operation up to the level of formal operations (Archard 1993: 65). 'These stages are chronologically ordered but also hierarchically arranged along a continuum from low status, infantile, "figurative" thought to high status, adult, "operative" intelligence' (Jenks 1996: 23).

[18] This issue relates to the historical origins of psychological research (Danziger 1990).

Piaget personifies in the 1930s, the finest of developmental thinking in its sequential form. In this cognitive form, each stage of the structuring of thought consisting of specific schemata or pattern is articulated to both the preceding and the following stage in a coherent sequence in which no child can bypass a step. 'The move from each stage ... to the succeeding one represents a passage from the simpler to the more complex whereby the later stage included ... the earlier one as a component reintegrated at a higher level' (Archard 1993: 33). The necessary connectedness of one stage to the other presumes that each stage is completely gone through, as an unavoidable requirement of the passage to the next. These stipulated stages, which all children must go through, do not pertain to specific contents of thought or behaviour, at least in the Piagetian theory, but relate to structures or predispositions whose mastery empowers the child to make progress.[19] The general design outlines a progress towards a higher order which is a more definite state for children at the end of the journey.

Although Piaget's genetic psychology is widely criticized for over-emphasising abstraction, logico-deductive reasoning and mathematical operations (Lee 1998; Lee 1999; Morss 1990), the sequencing of developmental processes in a teleological model presupposes the state of adulthood to be the ultimate goal, the terminus. As the capacity for formal operations, abstract thinking, adulthood is the core reason why maturity as the concluding state of adulthood is deemed a higher order. Whether Piaget's developmental model is biologically rooted or genetically secured is peripheral to our argument, the main point is the sequencing of the model into a set of more and more complex stages, quite unlike however and somehow further formally elaborated than the sequencing of Veeder, Gesell and others.[20]

Age structuration, stage and sequence as the three major phases leading through stage theory to developmental thinking, were the

[19] These structures can also be understood in the Foulcaldian sense of 'dispositif', or in the Bourdieusian sense of habitus. Bourdieu's psychological reference is Piaget, yet he is first and foremost a sociologist of socialization.

[20] Developmental psychologists have acknowledged their theory took the form of a sequence of stages articulated in a specific way. 'Child development can best be understood in terms of a sequence of stages. Stages have been tested as configurations of mental structures governing the child's interactions with its environment. Development consists, in this view, of a sequence of reorganizations of adaptive systems with later stages representing more differentiated and better integrated versions' (Cole 1983).

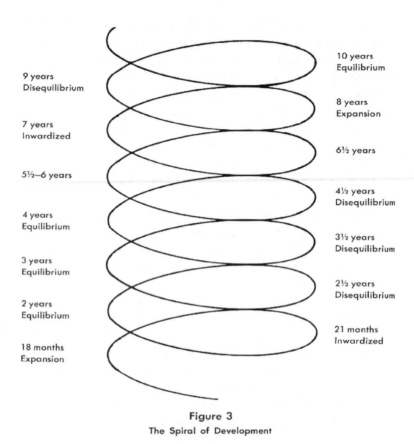

9 years
Disequilibrium

7 years
Inwardized

5½–6 years

4 years
Equilibrium

3 years
Equilibrium

2 years
Equilibrium

18 months
Expansion

10 years
Equilibrium

8 years
Expansion

6½ years

4½ years
Disequilibrium

3½ years
Disequilibrium

2½ years
Disequilibrium

21 months
Inwardized

Figure 3
The Spiral of Development

Figure 8: Spiral of development
Source: Gesell 1946a

intricate pattern of bringing up the child in regard to physical growth
and mental hygiene (Figure 8). Gradually the collective is re-ordered
around a hybrid object offering such a firm anchorage on children's
transformations: the collective's participants are acted upon by this
device as well as cooperating in their own terms in its requirements.
The network is rearranged accordingly along the main features of this
hybrid object: children's behaviour is slowly being monitored with
remarkable thoroughness via these devices.

The knowledge and artefacts systematized in developmental thinking mould into a cognitive form that inform the ideas and practices

concerning childhood; such a form is therefore understood as the culturally legitimated way of thinking and acting towards children.[21] Developmental thinking, as a cognitive form that I am trying to single out in its historical specificity, is an integral part of a broader movement: rationalization of the social in a Weberian meaning. Weberian rationality finds its most expressive figure in bureaucracy although not be limited to it. The foremen of the Taylorian factory, army officers, nineteenth-century schoolteachers and Prussian civil servants do proceed from this model. So do the hygienists, paediatricians, psychologists and nurses of the child collective.

The cognitive form is a formalization of a particular knowledge constructed by researchers through a systematic observational model, which conveys a methodical knowledge for local traditions. Hence it slowly percolates in the collective remodelling its network of relationship; thus joining the general movement of rationalization supported by an age-based hierarchy and a sequence of stages ushering into adulthood. It carries on a translation of child-rearing into scientific wording revolving around developmental psychology, yet not confined to it.

As a cognitive form, developmental thinking set aside lay traditions of child-rearing to the advantage of a scientific perspective for this intuitive familiarity or understanding always appears a partial and local knowledge of childhood. The tradition in upbringing refers to both the oral discourse transmitted from one generation of mothers to the next as well as its general ineffectiveness towards children's predicaments. A developmental perspective offers a proper counterbalance to heretofore prevailing theories of human maturation: Locke's empiricism and tabula rasa metaphor; Rousseau's natural, unpolluted and virtuous child developing himself far away from the evils of a corrupted urban society; finally, the innocent child – the ideal childhood of western culture – both in its Christian and timelessly natural form.[22] So by the 1930s, developmental thinking was

[21] A cognitive form is less an object to think with than a form in which to think about an object, that is the child. This culturally legitimated way of thinking and acting with children bears a universalistic underpinning which states that children are, ontologically speaking, trans-historically and trans-culturally constant social actors (Lesnik-Oberstein 1998).

[22] 'Precisely because the modern concept of childhood was an invented cultural ideal, it required representations ... To a great extent, childhood innocence was

the primary form of knowledge and the master framework in which to think and act upon the child. How does this cognitive form link with socialization theory by then?

The socialization paradigm is still pervasive in social sciences although decidedly criticized more recently. Its basic assumption consists succinctly of a rather simple postulate presupposing that the child's nature is in becoming an adult headed towards the ultimate goal, namely adulthood as embodiment of maturity and reason. This complex process of 'becoming' is observed in children's growing up – their maturation – and conceptualized as development. Although the focus is on developmental thinking as a cognitive form, it is understood that this device is not solely a discursive phenomenon, but is moreover institutionalized as a powerful mean of establishing children's everyday lives.

The core of socialization theory, seen as the best way to integrate the child in a society, is crystallized in the Parsonian paradigm understood in its two pivotal forms: transmission of culture and becoming human. It converges towards the uninterrupted bonds constructed, between socialization/becoming human/child development. The Parsonian paradigm, recognized as the highest form of conceptualization of socialization in a general theory, was unable to conceptualize it and yielded to child development the difficult trust of theorizing this specific field on its own terms. Whether in the sites of the family, the school or the peer group, whether through the procedures of constraint, inculcation or patterning, a homogeneous process is ongoing under the umbrella of developmental thinking: to transform a child in becoming into a competent, rational, mature adult being.

The question now at stake is the following: how relevant – or appropriate or suitable – is the concept of development with respect to children in sociology? If social sciences gave up to child development in its attempt to conceptualize socialization in the Parsons era and after, does it have to restate the same scenario again and again? Is there a possibility nowadays of theorizing children's 'growing up' above developmental thinking? The next section will examine these

considered an attribute of the child's body, both because the child's body was supposed to be naturally innocent of adult sexuality, and because the child's mind was supposed to begin blank. Innocence therefore lent itself to visual representation' (Higonnet 1998: 8).

disturbing questions while setting out the pattern of developmental thinking – the bonding of physical and mental growth – focusing on the conditions that made it so prevalent.

5.2 The pattern of sequential developmental

Thus ... we are on the highway towards the doctrine long ago enunciated by Pestalozzi, that alike in its borders and its methods, education must conform to the natural process of mental evolution – that there is a natural sequence in which the faculties spontaneously develop ... that spontaneous unfolding which all minds go through in their progress to maturity.[23] (Herbert Spencer)

Developmental theory is so pervasive, so overwhelmingly accepted from the outset that the socio-technical network of relationships between parents, children and others is thoroughly reshuffled in an amazingly complex institutional setting as actors act towards the child with respect to the main synopsis of sequential theory. It is almost hopeless to imagine any alternative. With the rise of developmental theory, are we allowed to raise the appropriate question: how did children come to be historically consigned to developmental thinking? This enquiry will announce the dawn of a new direction in the analysis, that is, tracking down the seizure of the child in the net of developmental framework. This section will first examine the emergence of a globally coherent developmental theory from its earliest days; second, it will probe the nub of developmental thinking, namely the bonding of physical and mental growth.

Developmental enquiry goes back to the early period of investigation in psychology, to researchers such as Preyer, Sully and Hall if not Freud himself;[24] and to Tiedemann, Pestalozzi and Darwin to go further back in history (Cavanaugh 1981). From the outset, psychologists studying the phenomenon of growing-up mustered data and translated them into rising developmental assessments globally

---

[23] (Morss 1990: 48).

[24] Freud's psychosexual theory of children's development is crystallized in an age-based schema of development whose stages are: oral stage, anal stage, phallic stage, latency stage, genital stage. Freud's theory being the best known of all, I shall insist on its prominence although I do recognize its weight in the processes described here.

understood as a stage theory.[25] Darwin's work was instrumental in the emergence of developmental theories. He posited that a singular actor was an abbreviated replica of the development of the race, therefore postulating that phylogenetic – the stages through which the human specie has passed during its evolution – is recapitulated in ontogenesis, that is the development of the individual. Objections to recapitulation theory point that it could not account for the particular sequence of ontogenesis. On the other hand, utility theory, more relevant in this respect in that only those characteristics already selected on the basis of their utility will deepen into tendencies coming into sight in ontogenesis; thus a specific individual's attributes condense only a small and suitable specimen of the earlier tendencies of the species.

A preliminary form of stage theory had already been set forth by Darwin, Spencer and Hall. Relying on these theories, some experts activated the concept of stage as a more commonsensical data-based approach than recapitulation theory. As already examined, the paediatrician often acts as an expert on developmental benchmarks of childhood in terms of increasingly differentiated stages, which were set up as behavioural expectations or age appropriate behaviour, soon becoming a normative expectation.[26]

The first stage theories concentrated on the physical determinants of development, therefore leaving psychological and cognitive traits. Holt was especially concerned with the influence of nutrition on physical development, outlining the mutable nutritional exigencies of children according to their age. Although Holt was rather a popularizer of scholarly research, he nevertheless was a specialist in nutrition, feeding and diet. He was among the first to put out height and weight tables, as his books were supplemented with numerous charts and tables specifying age-defined standards, behavioural

---

[25] I am indebted for this clarification to Cavanaugh's indispensable paper: 'Early Developmental Theories: A Brief Review of Attempts to Organise Developmental Data prior to 1925' (Cavanaugh 1981). Although Cavanaugh's text is limited in its scope and purpose, he gave the essential inspiration for my own analysis.

[26] The translation of behavioural expectations – age-based appropriate behaviour – into normative benchmarks is a crucial question that needs to be addressed. Are behavioural expectations doomed to become norms once they circulate in the collective and transform accordingly the relationships in the network?

criteria and scheduled norms. In its table, the Middle Months period, comprised between the third or fourth month and the tenth or eleventh month, is also divided in sub-categories, indicating therefore the accuracy of the stage framework in the early period of infancy with respect to physical development. This framework was not restricted to infancy, but was furthermore appropriate to toddlerhood and childhood as well. 'Holt's book was certainly the most detailed diateray curriculum ever concocted. Each of the early stages of life was divided into a "period" with an entire series of formulas prescribed for the child' (Beekman 1977: 114).

The trend in paediatrics was already progressing towards stage theory as Holt's reasoning figures. From that period onward, it became widespread as the extensive diffusion of the height and weight tables compellingly attest. Afterwards, the regular publication of textbooks is a cogent indication of the consistent pervasiveness of this cognitive schema in paediatric practice. From a developmental perspective, growth, maturation and related questions were all thought via stage theory, thus progressively raising it to a way of thinking. Beyond Holt, stage schema was not restricted to paediatrics. Foremost, examples of early stage theories (Table 5), although quite elementary, give a remarkable overview of it, mostly in psychology in fact (Cavanaugh 1981: 41).

The psychosocial paediatricians showed broad concerns for children, much larger than the usual restricted scope of paediatrics (Halpern 1988). Veeder, one of the most distinguished among them, was carrying mental hygiene through paediatrics with respect to normalcy. The path leading from children's diseases, paediatrics' primary concern from the beginning, to growth, normalcy and deviations from normal development is indicative less of a novel translation of children's situation while going deeper into stage theory as an attempt to figure out diverse issues related to development. Hence diverse constituents of development – notably mental hygiene and personality traits[27] – were promptly integrated into an invariant theory in its sequences, but nonetheless setting the pace for a more

---

[27] For some researchers, the passage from character to personality is given the status of a fundamental change in the culture of American society (Camic 1986; Meyer 1988; Youniss 1990). I would rather consider this 'cultural' change as a new translation of the data gathered about children in the collective, yielding fresh associations and connections.

Table 5. *Stage theories*

TABLE 1

Six Examples of "Stage" Theories Examining Children from Birth Through Adolescence

Edward L. Thorndike (1903)	Edwin Kirkpatrick (1911)	Irving King (1903)
1. Infancy (0-1)	1. Presocial (0-1)	1. 0-3
2. Babyhood (1-5)	2. Imitative and Socializing (1-3)	2. Play Period (3-6)
3. Childhood (5-12)	3. Individualizing (3-6)	3. Early teens
4. Transition (12-14)	4. Competitive Socialization (6-12)	4. Latter half of teens
5. Early Adolescence (14-18)	5. Pubertal or Transitional Period (12-18)	
6. Later Adolescence	6. Later Adolescence (18-24)	

Joseph Lee (1915)	John M. Tyler (1907)	Ella L. Cabot (1921)
1. 0-3	1. 0-3	1. Infancy (0-3)
2. 3-6	2. Early Childhood	2. Dramatic Age (3-7)
3. 7-11	3. Development of motor instincts (6-9)	3. Angular Age (7-11)
4. 11-14	4. Pubertal years (9-15)	4. Early Adolescence— Paradoxical Age (12-14)
5. Apprentice Age (14-21)	5. Adolescence (15-18)	5. Age of the Gangs or Team Play (11-16)
6. Romantic Age (16-21)		6. Age of Romance (15-18)
		7. Age of Problems (16-21)

Source: Cavanaugh 1981

differentiated rate of progress for individuals through the successive stages.

To basic stage theories, it seems appropriate to add more complex and sophisticated cases. Although the cognitive perspective is not pre-eminent in their thought, Binet, Veeder and Gesell's scholarly work appears relevant in this particular context for they were amongst the first to articulate explicitly children's characteristics within a stage/sequence theory. As a paediatrician, Holt was a leading figure in this respect. In psychology, this role belongs to Binet who, for the first time, started to interpose a clear-cut difference between intelligence and thought. It should be borne in mind that his main innovation, in regard to child development, consists of establishing stable correlations between mental capabilities and chronological age; he thus provided an empirical device for the classification of children consistent with their abilities (Form 7 and 8). Binet was empirically as ingenious as was needed to overcome the various obstacles over

GENERAL INFORMATION—FORM I

ame ....Age............... Grade............ High or low. ....

ame of School...City ....

ate: Month and day.................................Year............... Are you a boy or girl?.................

Test	Score	Age Equivalent	Grade Equivalent
1			
2			
3			
4			
Total			

TEST 1. GEOGRAPHY, HYGIENE AND ELEMENTARY SCIENCE

Draw a line under the word that makes the sentence true as shown in the two samples.
Samples: 1. The number of cents in a dollar is   100   200   300
             2. New York is in   England   France   United States

egin here.
Christmas comes in   December   January   July 1
A food that grows under the ground is the   cabbage   potato   tomato 2
A sweet-smelling flower is the   daisy   poppy   rose 3
Alfalfa is a kind of   corn   fruit   hay 4
Soap is made from   fats   lemons   sugars 5

Bacon comes from the   cow   hog   sheep 6
A bird that makes its nest on the ground is the   quail   robin   swallow 7
Raisins are dried   currants   gooseberries   grapes 8
A baboon is a kind of   bird   fish   monkey 9
Ivory is obtained from   elephants   shell-fish   reefs 10

The number of inches in a yard is   36   24   12 11
Tarts are a kind of   drink   pastry   vegetable 12
The tractor is used in   farming   mining   racing 13
Planes are used chiefly by   barbers   blacksmiths   carpenters 14
Rubber is obtained from   animals   oil   trees 15

Anchors are used on   autos   ships   wagons 16
The number of quarts in a gallon is   2   4   6 17
Muslin is a kind of   cloth   color   drink 18
The burro resembles most the   cow   donkey   horse 19
A flower that grows from a bulb is the   lily   marigold   poppy 20

Turn over the page to number 21

e Stanford Achievement Test. 192?. Terman prepared the Stanford

Form 7: Terman's General Information Form
Source: Chapman 1988

Scale A. Form 1

Test 2

Write on each dotted line one word to make the sentence sound sensible and right.

SAMPLES
{ Sugar.... *is* ....sweet.
{ ... *Birds* ...sing.

Begin here

1   The dog.................black.
2   An airplane is able to.................a great distance in a short time.
3   Mother is.................doughnuts.
4   There are seven.................in the rainbow.
5   Rain.................snow fall from the clouds.

6   We love liberty.................the United States.
7   Twenty-five cents make one.................of a dollar.
8   Bananas grow in.................climates.
9   He tried to.................his ball among the bushes.
10 Jack came to.................me mow the lawn.

11 Trees are.................than bushes.
12 Winter is.................in the North and short in the.................
13 The man.................aids his fellows will.................his reward.
14 A.................is made up.................an engine and coaches.
15 You should never go.................a crowd when.................have a cold.

16 Several.................have gone by since the end of the greatest.................
    in history.
17 Labor unions.................the right to.................for higher wages.
18 The visitor.................the child.................name.
19 Poverty cannot.................down a man.................is intelligent and
    ....hard.
20 ....should prevail in churches and libraries.

National Intelligence Tests, Test 2. Using materials developed in the First
World War, Terman and other psychologists created the National Intelligence
Tests and by 1920 nearly half a million exams had been published and sold to
the public schools. (Reprinted by permission of the Special Collections Department and University Archives, Stanford University Libraries.)

Form 8: Terman Test 2
Source: Chapman 1988

which Galton failed, and invent a test designed to sort out children according to their mental abilities in relation to their age (Avanzini 1969).

Before Binet's accomplishments, mental capacity was a fuzzy notion, a form of 'terra incognita' where lay persons and experts did not have the slightest idea of its manifestations and its progress. From Binet onwards, mental capacities are understood as the development of intellectual capacity, which is a specific translation generating renewed associations with families and schools: a careful reallotment of responsibilities between families, schools, clinics and others, which materialized in a vast reform of primary school curriculum around the main outcomes of sequential development theory. Binet started mapping children's mental capacities in as accurate a way as was empirically conceivable:[28] he assigned an age level to those intellectual operations ranking from the simplest to the more complex (Wooldridge 1995: 89). The measurement of mental capacities gives an interesting translation of children's condition:

a. Some logical ordering close to the rationale of mathematics: counts backwards from twenty to zero; gives change for sixpence or a shilling; arranges five weights in order; counting etc.
b. The practice of memory, quite elementary at the beginning: repeats two numbers; more elaborate later on: repeats seven numbers; memory for words, objects, designs, verses etc.
c. Language skills, such as enumerating objects in a picture; repeating sentences; writing words, sentences, completing sentences; understands simple questions etc.
d. Judgement skills, such as: defines in terms superior to use; criticizes absurd statements; resists suggestion etc.
e. Common-sense knowledge: gives day and date; enumerates months of the year etc.
f. The beginning of abstract thinking: defines three abstract words; puts dissected sentence together; interprets a picture; solves a problem from several facts etc.

---

[28] Binet's approach was personal and individualistic, less interested in the massive investigation of large-scale population or the universality of mental processes. He was fascinated with the discovery of the individual mind's singularity.

The core of Binet's test rests on the apprehension of children's capacities: logic, memory, language, judgement, abstract thinking and their measurement. His concept of intelligence was explained in terms of patterning and re-patterning of sensory experience (Reeves 1965: 242). Binet put forward the notion of intellectual level designed to measure the child's mental ability to perform certain tasks in relation to its chronological age; it served to rank children among their peers and in relation to the curve of normal development (Wooldridge 1995).

Veeder and Gesell wrote in the 1920s; they represent the archetypal schema articulating physical and mental traits, largely centred around motor development. Commenting on his Developmental Record Form, Veeder asserted that it elucidated 'the character of the norms at different levels' (Veeder 1926: 79).[29] I shall first examine Veeder's Developmental Record Form, to investigate more closely what was translated by the label mental development in the 1920s.

Although both Holt and Veeder work within a stage framework, the distance between them is indeed quite astonishing as the former was a paediatrician in the conventional sense focusing on physical traits, whilst the latter was a psychosocial paediatrician concerned by a global approach of child development integrating both normalcy and mental hygiene in the 1920s. I shall probe more rigorously what mental development meant to a paediatrician in the 1920s, and what was translated into this new category. This last point is especially cogent as it figures the translation of mental development:

- at one year old, stands and may attempt to walk with support, will hold cup to drink from etc.;
- at two years old, walks, folds paper imitatively etc.;
- at three years old, points to eyes, nose and mouth, repeats two digits etc.;
- at four years old, buttons clothes, knows his sex etc.;
- at five years old, laces shoes, counts four pennies etc.;

---

[29] The ascent of scientific norms proved to be a decisive question in the rise of modernity and, therefore, the brushing aside of traditional society. In the scientific area and the health domain, the childhood collective occupies a particular place for it was a new space for social intervention and rationalization. Regarding the mutation of the norms, see: (De Munck 1999; De Munck and Verhoeven 1997).

In Veeder's Developmental Record Form, the distinction between mental and motor development looks, at first sight, quite thin.[30] Nevertheless the aforementioned distinction revolves around the content of development – for example a little more motor here or a slight emphasis on emotions there – whilst I am concerned with the topic of the form of development: the cognitive form in which actors think about childhood. The nub of the question is not crystallized in the fact that there are meaningful differences between physical, motor and emotional development, which everyone recognized, even then. It is vested in the common morphological framework of stage/sequence theory impinging upon the conceptualization of development either in the laboratory or in its implementation in the collective. Above the differences in the pace of development, an identical framework – figuring a common translation of children's situation – redirects social action towards the hybrid socio-technical network while bestowing on it a new impulsion: to help stabilize the collective.

Gesell's researches are probably, in themselves, the most mesmerizing pieces of literature in the area His work was acknowledged as being instrumental in widening paediatrics' task to the investigation of mental hygiene: 'there have been no carefully worked out studies of mental norms until last year, when Arnold Gesell published the results of his observations at the Yale Clinic' (Veeder 1926: 79). In Gesell's instance, it is insufficient to take note of the constant presence of the stage framework which appears in every aspects, both physical and mental, of his developmental theory. The observer must go further.

Gesell devoted his entire academic life to child study, working to sort out a consistent, logical and shrewd developmental perspective. He wrote more than twenty books, clarifying in book after book his position on child-rearing while also refining his ideas. Much as Gesell is considered one of the main figures in devising developmental thinking, yet it remains to see how it operated from the outset as a cardinal framework in his own research. In order to clarify these questions, two key issues should be examined to give as accurate an insight as possible as to how far Gesell's thinking was framed by developmental thinking. The first key topic relates to the specific mode

---

[30] The difference between mental and motor development raises the question: was mental development or the development of the mind broader than motor development for Veeder and the other psychosocial paediatricians?

along which Gesell's books were sequentially systematized around the aforementioned framework:

- *The Mental Growth of the Pre-School Child*;
- *Infant and Child in the Culture of Today*;
- *The First Five Years*;
- *The Child from Five to Ten*;
- *Youth: The Years from Ten to Sixteen*.

So as to complete this global picture, a book such as *The Child from Five to Ten*, is, in itself, organized sequentially, in the same way as the age-based categories. The second part of the book goes through child development at each age: five, six etc. Each one of these successive years of age is also treated in accordance with a common schema of maturity traits[31] as indicated in Table 6. 'The maturity traits are set forth in brief, informal statements which reflect the everyday happenings of home and school life. We do not set up these traits as norms, but rather as indicators of the child's behavior equipment at a given level of maturity' (Gesell *et al.* 1977 (1946): 57).[32] The schema suggests a remarkable continuity from one age to another while also yielding the possibility of comparisons (Table 6).

The second key topic regards his standpoint about developmental thinking. Gesell being a crucial element in the rise of the culture of developmentalism, it concerns its progressive mutation into a cognitive form. He puts forward the proposition of a science of child development as a cultural force:

The culture of tomorrow will begin and always rebegin with the development of individual infants and children; for, as Malinowski aptly said, culture is nothing but the organized behavior of man ... the limiting factors in this conditioning mechanism. They are growth factors. They are the laws of child development. Indeed, it might be well to reserve the term matrix for the maturational mechanisms which literally establish the basic patterns of behavior and of growth career. A matrix is that which gives form and foundation to something which is incorporated, in this instance, through

---

[31] The notion of maturity traits put forward by Gesell might be considered as a possible answer to the previous question: what is mental development all about?

[32] It is very instructive to realize that Gesell do not give maturity traits the status of norms but rather of gradient – growth gradients, although in his 1925 book, *The Mental Growth of the Pre-School Child*, Gesell includes a chapter (32) entitled: 'Normative Summaries'.

Table 6. *Maturity traits*

Classification of
Maturity traits and Gradients of Growth

1. **Motor Characteristics**
   Bodily Activity
   Eyes and Hands

2. **Personal Hygiene**
   Eating
   Sleep
   Elimination
   Bath and Dressing
   Health and Somatic
     Complaints
   Tensional Outlets

3. **Emotional Expression**
   Affective Attitudes
   Crying and Related
     Behaviors
   Assertion and Anger

4. **Fears and Dreams**
   Fears
   Dreams

5. **Self and Sex**
   Self
   Sex

6. **Interpersonal Relations**
   Mother–Child
   Father–Child
   Siblings
   Family and Grandparents
   Manners
   Teacher–Child
   Child–Child
   Groupings in Play

7. **Play and Pastimes**
   General Interests
   Reading
   Music, Radio, Television,
     and Movies

8. **School Life**
   Adjustment to School
   Classroom Demeanor
   Reading
   Writing
   Arithmetic

9. **Ethical Sense**
   Blaming and Alibiing
   Response to Direction, Pun-
     ishment, and Praise
   Responsiveness to Reason
   Sense of Good and Bad
   Truth and Property

10. **Philosophic Outlook**
    Time
    Space
    Language and Thought
    Death
    Deity

The foregoing areas of behavior in ten major sectors of child development are treated by ages in chapters 5–10 and by gradients in chapters 11–20.

Source: Gesell 1946b

growth. By growth we do not mean a mystical essence, but a physiological process of organization which is registered in the structural and functional unity of the individual. In this sense the maturational matrix is the primary determinant of child behavior (Gesell and Ilg 1949: 357).

Growth factors, laws of child development, basic patterns of behaviour and the maturational matrix (Table 6): a science of child development aimed at a global understanding of the child that requires further clarification within a framework binding mental and physical hygiene with growth as well. Gesell's questioning is worded as follow:

- How are the natural growth characteristics of infant and child brought into harmony with these cultural pressures?
- What are the relationships between the pressures of natural growth (maturation) and the pressures of the social order (acculturation)?
- The answers to these questions will determine our attitudes and our practices in the psychological care of infant and child.

(Gesell and Ilg 1949: 1)

In Gesell's eyes, culture helps the child achieve his developmental potentialities, the process of acculturation being limited by the child's own natural growth process. The author goes on to affirm: chronological age and maturity level are indispensable concepts (Gesell and Ilg 1949: 2). Binet demonstrated the usefulness of chronological age for child development. Growth, maturation, accretion, heightening, enlargement of every child ought to be strictly 'codified in terms of age to clarify the generic, innate sequences of development, and to define some of the more usual deviations which determine the individuality of the child' (Gesell and Ilg 1949: 2).

Age, thereby, is given the status of a sine qua non condition in the form of an unequivocal codification to establish clearly – that is, graphically and visually – the stages/sequences of child's development. So deviations from normal development can be fixed quite accurately and attested on age-based categories.[33] Age is granted the status of the most convenient or manageable category for classifying and monitoring children. The idea that a child of seven or ten years of age is normally expected to perform such and such a task widely acknowledged by experts, filtered down gradually through the collective.

Child development closely links mental and physical growth within a global and comprehensive perspective. It conceals the possibility of patterning child's behaviour[34] in as accurate a way as was possibly

[33] The crucial point revolves around both age-based categories and stage/ sequences as the central piece of Gesell's developmental theory, the question of deviation from the normal being relegated to the periphery.

[34] Gesell's definition of the patterning of behaviour is the usual mark of a definition which tends to be formal. 'A behaviour pattern is simply a movement

conceivable at that period of time. The latter relates to age/stage/ sequences as it allows a clear-cut figure of what is expected from a child at every step of its maturation. Gesell's ideas denote some of the most thoughtful pieces of material concerning child development. Developmentalism is, here, at its peak.

a. Mental growth, like physical growth, is a modelling process which produces changes in form. Or we might say that mental growth is a patterning process, because the mind is essentially the sum of a growing multitude of behavior patterns.

b. All child development proceeds with reference to the future. When the time comes the child is normally ready for what we may expect at that time ... Environmental factors support, inflect and modify; they do not generate the progressions of development. The sequences, the progressions come from within.

c. The nervous system with its prodigious capacities of growth and learning is the medium through which the mental life of the child is organized in terms of the past, and projected forward in terms of the future. This mental life embraces three levels of reality: (1) the vegetative functions of respiration, alimentation, elimination; (2) the world of things, in time and space; (3) the world of persons in home and community.

d. The child develops as an integrated unit, and he must simultaneously combine his adjustments at all three levels of reality. His mind does not grow on the installment plan. It grows as a unit ... As the mind grows it must be socialised ... he must become a person among persons in a WORLD OF PERSONS. This constitutes the most bewildering task for the infant and child reared in the complicated culture of today. The organization of his personality depends on the manner in which he adjusts to human relationships.

(Gesell and Ilg 1949: 16 et seq.)

This long quotation shows quintessential developmentalism. The age/stage/sequence framework is scarcely mentioned, yet it must be supplied with propositions, observations, connections and graphics,

or action which has a more or less definite form ... Behaviour has form or shape in virtually the same sense that physical things have shape ... These movements will have a certain degree of pattern. We shall call them behavior patterns as soon as they take on a characteristic form. The growing mind consists of countless such patterns of behavior, made possible by the progressive organization of the nervous system' (Gesell and Ilg 1949). Patterning consists of a movement having a form or a shape: or a movement along which an object – a child for instance – takes a specific form or shape.

every element of which contributes to a novel translation of the child's situation and its circulation among clinics, offices, laboratories, diverse institutions, but also among paediatricians, nurses, teachers, experts, school administrators, neighbours and parents. These propositions relate to the activities of patterning, ordering and organizing into a hierarchy, which is exactly what Gesell put forward above. To the question raised: what is being upheld, aggregated, taken away by such objects as charts and tabulations in the process of circulation and stabilization?, Gesell's theory is the beginning of an answer demarcated by its completeness.

As a modelling process, patterning of behaviour produces a change in form, the changing form being the child itself[35] either in a physical or mental outlook. Although the idea of the plasticity of the form goes back to Locke and the metaphor of the blackboard, the idea of the child as a modelling process – the process of modelling a form as an integrated unit indisputably physical and mental – is thought-provoking while opening up new possibilities for conceptualizing childhood: the modelling of a changing form – the child – outstretched towards its own development through the processes of growth and maturation. This departs from theorization such as childhood as a biological category, as immaturity and so on.

The child is considered a living form, yet mental life is believed to be the crucial piece of this changing form, the one that gives the decisive impulse for change; a hierarchy is thereby outlined in the modelling process of the integrated unit. Development is forward/future oriented, the child being constructed in a state of becoming; and it implies a particular organization, an articulated structure both internal or from within and external with environmental factors. Socialization is hovering around, as a child lives in a world of persons with whom it is associated in multiple ways, and with whom it has to learn to dwell in the long run. The characteristics of development as forward oriented opening onto socialization are cardinal elements of the theory which will be closely examined later.

From the outset – that is from Tiedemann, Pestalozzi, Darwin, Sully and others – both paediatricians and psychologists, fascinated with the matrix of mental life, mustered data leading to the knowledge of

---

[35] The child as a living form, a form that grows, maturates, expands, ripens from a physical, psychological and social point of view.

its main vectors. I examined how mental life was configured in Holt's, Binet's, Veeder's and Gesell's work: which translations of children's situation were specifically carried on to bond physical and mental growth. The next section will investigate what interrogations this pattern of developmental thinking raises while setting out an extensive critique of the vectors that made it so predominant.

5.3 The critique of developmental thinking

As ubiquitous as it was from the 1920s onwards, developmental theory was hardly accepted without opposition. It presumes a translation of the situation of children which resulted in a significant reshuffling of the collective and a circulation of a children as well: it initiated a renewal of relationships among actors. Though the transformation of the collective was major, it remains to be seen how its critique came of age and how it was formulated. Nevertheless, although recent years have seen the emergence of a basic critique from within, by psychologists themselves, the critique of developmental thinking is not recent despite being constant for a long time.

One can identify a polymorphous critique, external and internal, the former not necessarily overlapping with the latter. These critiques attracted a lot of attention so that some psychologists have now integrated parts of them (Elder *et al.* 1993; Modell 2000; Rogoff and Chavajay 1995; Woodhead 1990).[36] This section will first peruse the critique of developmental thinking mainly through the work of Burman, Stainton Rogers and Morss; secondly, how it was partially integrated into the core of developmental thinking, which disturbed the patterning of the continuum of development.

What we are talking about here is mainly definition and categorization: 'Thus developmentalism – the set of ideas about child and childhood systematised and promulgated by child psychology – is what dominates and weaves through our current orthodox western understandings of the young' (Stainton Rogers and Stainton Rogers 1992: 37). Developmental thinking's ascendancy, warranted by science, lies in its reverberance with common-sense knowledge,

---

[36] Particularly instructive is the postscript – 'Beyond Children's Needs' – of the 1997 new edition of Woodhead's text in the same book by James and Prout (James and Prout 1990a: 77–81).

'deeply and enduringly sedimented in western thought' (Stainton Rogers and Stainton Rogers 1992: 38), which is another way to take note of its transformation into a cognitive form. Although they overlap, differences ought to be established between developmental psychology, thinking and theory as much as these discrete categories are articulated one to the other. The classic critique, historically speaking, revolves around four cardinal assumptions about which developmental thinking was criticized for a long time:

a. Ahistorical and acultural: it sets the focus without any regard to the historical or cultural conditions in which the child was raised; no variations to location are expected.
b. Individualistic: the development of a child is constructed as an internal process and for whom social interactions or external encounters such as economic constraints play no part or are simply subject to individualistic interpretations.
c. Universalistic: by extension, rational and prescriptive; the device applies to all children in all circumstances whatever their historical context, cultural, social or economic conditions are.
d. A natural, biological process, based on evolutionary assumptions and centred around both psychological and physical features of child's maturation, 'a process that is "wired in" to the human organism, and which inexorably unfolds just as, say, green leaves turn to red and gold in the autumn, or tadpoles turn into frogs in the spring'.

(Stainton Rogers 1998: 179)

Burman's *Deconstructing Developmental Psychology* is set forth as a critical introduction to developmental psychology:[37] 'I use the term "deconstruction" in the sense of laying bare, of bringing under scrutiny, the coherent moral – political themes that developmental psychology elaborates' (Burman 1994: 1). The tone is set, although Burman admits that she writes from within developmental psychology, and that her critique is an integral part of it.

I shall put aside Burman's critiques deemed external, such as the link she detects between developmental psychology and bourgeois democracy through the production of the appropriate moral citizens

---

[37] Child development is the core of developmental psychology. I shall focus almost exclusively on child development as the consolidated form of developmental thinking whilst stating at the same time that other domains of practice, paediatrics for instance, played an important role in its emergence.

(Burman 1994: 177).[38] Acknowledging the powerful impact of developmental psychology in our everyday lives, she ask why, how and in what ways the complex set of depictions – measurements and technological artefacts[39] – of developmental psychology operated within its domain, but outside it also: in welfare policies of childcare, the incorporation of Piaget's work in the school curriculum etc. (Walkerdine 1984).

Despite developmental thinking being so widely diffused, Burman notices that the training of a nurse, social worker, counsellor or teacher give much space to Piaget whose stage model of cognitive development is a keystone of their learning. Developmental thinking informs professional practices, particularly those involved in the child collective such as visiting nurses, social workers, teachers, school administrators, welfare director and child association activists. The circulation of knowledge thereby becomes a key element as it is put to use on a daily basis in the transactions and negotiations surrounding children's situation in the collective. Hence it plays a key part in stabilizing children's condition by putting forward a translation of the latter which is decisive in many ways as it introduces new forces in the collective. It is indicative of developmental psychology's pervasive sway in the larger culture; much more ubiquitous than within psychological theory itself. For instance:

- The premise of the law courts' definition of a child's best interest?
- The rationale of a social worker's conception regarding a child's 'social and emotional needs' in mainstream schools?
- The criteria of adoption agencies in evaluating parents' skills in an adoption situation?

'These are some of the ways in which developmental psychology reverberates far beyond the theory' (Burman 1994: 5).

A second cogent critique concerns developmental psychology's shifting primary focus from children to mothers reflecting wider references to social regulation considered as psychology's main Achilles' heel. Developmental investigations are largely directed to mothers through

---

[38] One of Burman's aims, as stated in her Introduction, is to bring under scrutiny the moral–political topics specified by developmental psychology.

[39] Or hybrid objects as identified earlier in this work; as hybrid objects, these artefacts have a relative agentic capacity in the collective, notably in the circulation of children.

an active intervention in their lives. It happens to have an impact upon them as mothers actively subscribe to developmentalism's accounts of how children develop: the best way to raise them, to handle specific problems such as tantrums, enuresis and jealousy. 'It is the adequacy of mothering that developmental psychology is called upon to regulate' (Burman 1994: 3). These remarks catch up with Brennemann's own analysis concerning mothers trying to live up to developmental standards. Although children were the targets of investigations, mothers and families were regulated – that is, submitted to the developmental gaze – for children to behave appropriately. As the social context of the collective is never taken into account and theorized, it reinforces individualistic dispositions already operating in developmental thinking.

Two other critiques of Burman's cannot be overlooked, the first one generally agreed upon for a long time as Brennemann's paper attests: the transfer of children's empirical descriptions, somewhat normative in its tone, to naturalized prescriptions.[40] This passage is closely connected to the call to classify children into a hierarchy in diverse settings, notably the school. The other critique pertains to Piaget and his particular brand of developmental psychology: a general account of the emergence of knowledge – with an emphasis on abstract knowledge and its particular operations – rather than an accurate analysis of how a child achieves this acquisition. Is this orientation consequential on developmental psychology's mainstream?[41] As committed as Piaget was to science and to developmental psychology as a modern project,[42] yet he put his faith in a qualitative model of

---

[40] Brennemann noticed the problem with the question of standardization, whilst Gesell, well aware of its effects, fought this trend with vigour. He taught that developmental standards were benchmarks for mothers, parents, teachers and the like, not prescriptions (Gesell and Ilg 1949).

[41] This question is raised in a general sense with respect to developmental psychology's mainstream orientations. Methodologically speaking, it is well known that Piaget clashed with the Anglo-American empiricist tradition and the broad differences of view around methodological issues. 'Piaget's investigations with children took place as the social sciences were moving from informal observation and experimentation to developing standardised forms of assessment, a tendency that Piaget, in general, vigorously opposed. His «clinical method» ... is a flexible semi-structured interviewing technique ... designed to provide a profile of each child's thinking' (Burman 1994).

[42] As opposed to social Darwinism's competition ethos, Piaget's faith in science as the promotion of well-being and peaceful coexistence among humans is

development acutely based upon stages/sequences theory. Children's developmental trajectory, being a continuous adaptation to social environment's complexity, abides by a hierarchical model of cognitive structures. 'As such it is thoroughly normative' (Burman 1994: 158).

With Stainton Rogers' *Stories of Childhood*, I shall concentrate on the 'troubled' origins of developmental thinking. Their stimulating proposition, after the linguistic turn, proposes the idea that the circulating discourse around childhood – what is said to account for childhood – is a story, a narrative: developmental psychology is the dominant story at the moment and has been for a while. This story is an endeavour to intertwine two different sets of knowledge: the outcomes of nature (biological sciences) and of nurture (the sciences of culture).[43] Developmental psychology is the narrative of an encounter of nature with nurture and an agenda of reconciling two sets of conflicting practices; socialization was therefore designed as a developmental process. This story is crystallized around the alembic myth.

The alembic myth is the most relevant and convincing way to metaphorically figure the alchemical transformation of two processes: 'a semi programmed, vital material frame (nature) and an impinging and pro-active cultural medium (nurture)' (Stainton Rogers and Stainton Rogers 1992: 40), each of which furnishes capacities to bring about personhood. The nature/nurture composite of the myth is wrought by three constituents: a biological material frame, a cultural repertoire and environment and their translation into a child. Problems arise when one raises questions about what these terms means, and how they were channelled to answer queries about becoming mature humans. The material frame invokes the intermingling of biology, body and genetics. These three notions do not admit strict commonality: there are strict and stringent differences between body, biology and genetics, that is between being a body and having a body.

A human being always hovers in a balance between being and having a body, the child's body being not totally granted either by

deeply rooted in the modern celebration of reason, rationality and morality alike.

[43] It is the Stainton Rogers' hypothesis that psychology achieved an independent academic status as a bio-social science designed to study how we become socialized, enculturated and so on, childhood being the prime location to investigate in this respect, in short, how nurture infringes on nature (Stainton Rogers and Stainton Rogers 1992).

biology or genetics. This distinction is crucial for a child from a 'growing up' perspective because it recasts the balance between these two aspects of the body. As for the translation of the previous two (biology and genetics) into a child through the cake-making metaphor, developmentalism's weak concept of culture is confine to a loose interaction as a transducer of nurture into nature in a softer version of a hard form of determinism (Galton). Without a satisfying articulation of the biological and the cultural which has not yet been reached, such a solution is always worrisome. This knowledge of developmental psychology congeals the child in invariable truths and essentialism about their nature.[44]

John Morss' project, *The Biologising of Childhood: Developmental Psychology and the Darwinian Myth*, is somehow different both in its scope and purpose. His ambition is first and foremost epistemological,[45] that is aiming to track down developmental psychology's foundations, especially its core biological assumptions, its pre-Darwinian endowments – Lamarckian evolutionary change, recapitulation theory, ontogeny and phylogeny etc. Globally, Morss' focus is centred

---

[44] Developmentalism is a story, sustained by the power of rhetoric and narrative. 'The variety of narrative forms used by developmentalists ... would best be put across by recasting them as a set of Chaucerian Tales' (Stainton Rogers and Stainton Rogers 1992).

   Development as steady increase of growth of assets;
   Development as topological changes: a transformation of proportion;
   Development as a series of crucial events: dentition, sitting up, acquiring breast-buds, menarche, etc.
   Development as branching out: the child's faculties unfold from the simple to the complex;
   Development as transformation: series of metamorphoses;
   Development as planning: the passing along of a decisional tree (choosing piano over football etc.);
   Development as chain reaction: one thing leading inevitably to the other (precocious sexuality, drug use etc.);
   Development as a sequence of challenge: the child meets and resolves a series of problems.

[45] Epistemology in a broad sense goes beyond biological assumptions in developmental thinking. For instance, Morss referring to James Mark Baldwin whose book, *Mental Development in the Child and the Race* (1895), we hinted at previously, asserts that Baldwin considered philosophy indispensable for a sound understanding of individual development. In regard to empiricism, he deemed that 'empirical research and observation played a secondary role to theory' (Morss 1990).

around the predominance of biological ideas in developmental thinking (Morss 1990). Beyond biological determinism and Darwinian epistemology, some of Morss' critiques are nevertheless relevant for an assessment of developmental thinking's general framework.

Morss notes that children's maturation is nowadays universally constructed as development, which implies a uniform schedule of developmental stages connected into a unitary sequence from infancy to adulthood. A sequence of developmental stages is progressive, evolutionary in its framework, a systematically ordered series of hierarchical states. Translating childhood into sequential development was then seen as a decisive scientific step forward away from a conventional definition in moral terms or in terms of rights.[46] The author points up a fundamental postulate to most developmentalists, namely 'cognitive or intellectual primacy, an understanding of the physical world being treated as a prerequisite for social interaction' (Morss 1990: 83). Hence developmental thinking's standard hierarchy of children's features assumes that infancy is less affected by the cultural environment than childhood; such an assumption is the basis from which is posited a crucial distinction of the self from the world.[47]

The idea of progress linked to evolutionary theory is at the core of the concept of development, thus to the stage/sequence framework, the latter being the most influential model proposed by developmentalists: 'the notion that the individual gets better and better as times passes has been central to most developmental thinking ... Stage theories of individual development generally constitute concrete realisations of the doctrine of progress' (Morss 1990: 174). Pivotal to the stage/sequence framework is the notion of periodicity: the idea of phases, stamped by regularity and repetition, the progress from one phase to the other coming about through a series of thrusts. Periodicity in behaviour emerges as an overruling characteristic in the linear

---

[46] Definitions of childhood, either in moral or rights terms, were predominant from the outset up to the nineteenth century. Archard's book explores this question both in its religious and legal forms (Archard 1993).

[47] This distinction of the self from the world must be situated within the precise context of an infancy cut off from its cultural environment. It is then possible to draw some similarities between the thought of infants and that of 'primitives', 'primitive thought' being more or less the analogue of Levy Bruhl's 'primitive mentality'. In this form of understanding, the child is basically an animal before entering human society (Morss 1990).

progression towards adulthood: best illustrated by the staircase metaphor (Case 1991), linear progression pertains to the fact that each step/stage must be completely gone through before reaching the next one. Individual development being sized up against a background of universal change, hence emerges the centrality of the whole sequence of developmental stages (Morss 1990).

Morss acknowledges that Gesell's Developmental Record Form for children gradually gained precedence in the collective. Confirming that developmental expectations intrinsic to mental testing should not be overlooked, he recognizes that development is deemed as the regular accretion of age-based acquired abilities. Gesell's project embodies the quest for behavioural norms related to chronological age by the observation of the normal child's behaviour: stability and regularity of developmental course, centrality of physical and mental growth in a maturational model of development, an articulated sequence of stages culminating in adulthood as shown in Figure 9. On the other hand, Piaget's developmental sequence is more complex for it is entirely constructed around language acquisition, reasoning, logic and formal thought. Although more keenly refined than Gesell's, Piaget's sequential development pertains to the same pattern of children's assessment, if not the same architecture.

Although Morss tracks down the influence of biological ideas, I shall now focus on the basic schema of developmental thinking as a cognitive form. What is developmental thinking's structural framework? By the 1920s and 1930s, its predominant design embodies:

- an accurate process framed into a series of stages chronologically ordered, hierarchically arranged and rationally organized in a sequence;
- a shift or gap from one stage to the next in the transitional process – the higher stage including and extending the lower at a proper rate;
- a causal connection – connectedness and directionality – binding each level to the next in a methodical and universal sequence;
- the latter concealed in an endogenous teleological form, which presupposes a self-propelled progress towards an ideal end, maturity and adulthood;
- a mapping of child's development hinging on homeorhesis, namely the tendency for developmental processes to maintain a steady trajectory beyond various perturbations.

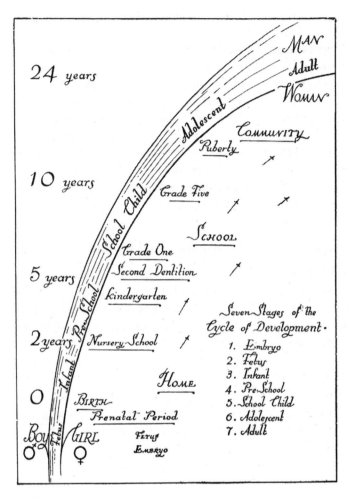

Figure 9: Stages of development
Source: Gesell 1946b

This common schema raises crucial questions that need to be addressed. Is the child's development theorized as a spatial form, as a topology – with knots, intersections, and the like – of children's life-course? From the psychometric tradition of Galton and Binet linking mental development to chronological age through Gesell's maturational pattern of growth to Piaget's final stage of formal operations, what models conform to developmental thinking's transformation into a cognitive form?

The concept of stage and of sequential development was established as the genuine nucleus of developmental thinking. We recalled the withering critique directed at developmental psychology: its universalistic, individualistic, naturalistic stance, as well as its ahistorical and acultural bias. The general character of these severe criticisms must not overshadow the fact that they paved the way to pointing the features, which constitute the hard core of developmental thinking while raising the most earnest questions about the topology of linear developmentalism. The next section will address these questions within the context of developmentalism's mutation into a cognitive form.

5.4 Development as a cognitive form and beyond

From the 1920s and 1930s onward, developmental thinking was established as the predominant frame of reference, prevailing over all other schemas in this respect. The arcaneness of developmentalism exposed its complex yet coherent framework, namely layers of age-structuration, series of hierarchically ordered stages, arranged into a sequence. The status of this intricate set of ideas, measurements, categories, visual depictions, patterns of behaviour etc. is recognized as a cognitive form.

Relevant questions still need to be addressed. What is a cognitive form and how does it operate? The general hypothesis of developmental thinking as a cognitive form must not be understood as a closed compilation of formal knowledge; it is both formal knowledge and hybrid objects, as I shall clarify in the first place by focusing on the pivotal part of hybrid objects in a cognition not restricted to isolated individuals, thus distributed and shared among them. Clearly stated, this hypothesis opens up to an additional one pertaining to the operative character of a distributed cognition: developmental thinking operates an essential stabilization of the collective through artefacts.

As a cognitive form, developmental thinking cannot be reduced solely to a primary form of codified knowledge in regard to the child: it is already the master framework in which to think about and act upon the child. I shall propose that sequential development is considered a cognitive form if, and only if, the latter sustains unambiguously and cohesively the two aspects of thinking about and acting upon the child.

Acknowledging Pickering's framed distinction between science as practice and science as knowledge (Pickering 1992), I see developmental thinking as a process embedded in both practice and knowledge; moreover, 'it is through dissolving the distinction between knowledge and practice that we can better see the processes in action' (Clarke 1992: 8). Furthermore, the question of skills, abilities, capacities and knowledge – secured empirically via social practices – is the very condition of developmental theory's effectiveness and pervasiveness by means of the network connecting together the actors of the childhood collective on an entirely novel basis.

With this specific clarification in mind, a more tightly formulated definition of the concept of cognitive form is needed.[48] Veron's concept of a socialized cognitive framework is put forward in a book emphasizing a theory of discursivity, which is far from being the thrust of my argument. Despite a strong emphasis on classic cognition–discursivity argument, Veron's socialized cognitive framework remains a decisive contribution. The operative capacity of a text – it fulfils a pivotal disposition in social activity – can be extended to artefacts and hybrid objects. This concept pertains to the socialized character of cognition, which is another way of highlighting its distributed property in a given factual situation.

Cognition does not lie in the mind of an isolated individual acting solely within the restricted scope of its own competence. It comes under the aegis of dynamic systems in motion linked to a specific social situation – namely, here, children's situation in the collective. It triggers a process which requires a shared, distributed cognition among both actors and artefacts involved. The dynamic systems in motion entail hybrid objects, social actors in interaction and a process of temporal spreading (Hutchins 1995). A hybrid object such as an instrument, a diagram, a chart, a text or an image circulates in the collective and its simple circulation rests on a proficiency presuming a socialized cognition: in Veron's terms a common grammar of production and of recognition. An individual's slightest act-in-society requires the bringing into play of a socialized cognitive framework (Veron 1987: 123).

---

[48] So as to do so, I shall draw upon Veron's concept of socialized cognitive framework (Veron 1987) as well as Ramognino's critique of it (Ramognino 1988) and De Munck's concept of collective cognitive dispositif (De Munck and Verhoeven 1997), for all of them present a convincing argument in regard to a distributed cognition.

How does one operate a distributed cognition? To bring to light the heuristic character of socialized cognition, De Munck adduces the norm.[49] It comes out as a pattern of behaviour providing paradoxically both large and specific indications, and some understanding, to the actors with respect to a given situation. This pattern bears simultaneously on cognitive and practical aspects. Hence the norm supplies a knowledge in the form of a 'map of the world' allowing one to qualify a particular situation (De Munck 1999; De Munck and Verhoeven 1997). The norm is enforced within an institution, which I prefer to call a collective, that not only says what must be done, but above all how to decide in various situations how to adjust or orient oneself.

Beyond a hierarchy of knowledge, the differences between norm, common-sense and socialized cognition do not intrinsically come into view. Heuristically speaking, socialized cognition consists of a double operation – there and back – of institutional legitimation of the partners and the hybrid object circulating among them. It seeks a minimal understanding, such as the sharing of categorization, classification, grading or taxonomy, which informs[50] the reality of social actors on the one hand and, on the other, strengthens the relationships among them. In other words, it is a matter of consolidating social bonds by stabilization, which exact a distributed cognition; the latter allows both an objectivity of the outside world by reducing its complexity through categorization, classification, norms etc. and the possibility of a relationship among actors (Ramognino 1988: 33).

In brief, a cognitive form pertains to:

a. the operative capacity of the reflexive actor as well as a relative operative capacity of the hybrid object circulating among actors;
b. the distributed property of cognition in dynamic systems in motion which rests on a complex network of heterogeneous social relations and shared categories;

[49] Following Favereau, De Munck defines the norm as a heuristic in a process of training. The norm is a heuristic insofar as it never applies mechanically to a given situation which it is supposed to govern as it presumes reflexivity from the actor (De Munck and Verhoeven 1997).
[50] A minimal knowledge such as categorization and classification informs, that is pre-forms or pre-determines, the reality of social actors with respect to childhood. Hacking gives a convincing example of the operativeness of a category with the case of child abuse (Hacking 1991; Hacking 1992).

c. the providing of visual knowledge to qualify and translate specific situations such as children's illnesses;

d. shared practice and knowledge-strengthening relationships among actors to stabilize the network in regard to children's problematic situation.

Additional attributes of the hybrid object's status as a cognitive form must be provided. Developmental thinking is intertwined in both a set of ideas and a practice, and yet recognizing that it remains to observe how social actors act and interact with artefacts in a given situation: how objects translate the situation into a visual depiction whilst furthering the whole process previously hindered, children's predicaments seemingly assessed as insuperable. What does an artefact introduce into a collective? How are charts and diagrams practically grounded? How, afterwards, do they redistribute the stakes in the collective on the basis of technical skills partly made of tacit and incorporated knowledge?

The practice of child development whose tools/objects constitute a central dimension is made up of a contingent work. In order to carry out these tasks, one must establish the objects, fulfil the tasks and discipline the objects so that they stay appropriate, and, finally, modify them in the temporal process of developmentalism (Acker 1997; Clarke 1992). At this stage of the line of argument, I shall give special attention to the inscriptive and operative character of the hybrid object.

Inscriptions are operations which allow us to produce basic and developmental straightforward facts (Callon and Law 1997).[51] The concept of inscription in regard to children's embodiment is adumbrated with explicit connections to corporeal dispositions: in brief, how child-rearing is not only a matter for culture through learning, narratives and memory, but pertains to the incorporation/inscription of the social structure upon the child's body. I mentioned an inscription scheme alluding to science's innovative instrumentation, namely measurement and statistics with their specific protocols. This scheme is illustrated by the cognitive conditions, the technical

---

[51] With regard to scientific facts in laboratory life, is it appropriate here to go into a hazardous discussion of the status of developmental facts: whether developmental facts are scientific facts or not. I shall consider that the notion of inscription is relevant and valuable for this analysis: facts about the child's body, the growth of its body, and so on.

instrumentation and the various requirements of physicians' intervention in the field of childhood. It is now time to qualify the frame of
their intervention and their technical instrumentation, not to mention
the hybrid objects, which play such a pivotal role through inscription
in developmental thinking.

To do so, I shall concentrate on two standardized forms,[52] the
standard scorecard and the developmental record, for they clarify
compellingly the inscriptive and the operative character of the hybrid
object, well above its conception as a repository of information. The
standard scorecard[53] displayed a chart of the infant's development: a
duplicated form, for both parents and paediatricians, gave a record of
the child's growth and development. It requested data, along with
demographic features and general information (health history etc.)
under five different headings: mental development; oral and dental
examination; eye, ear, nose and throat; physical examination; measurements. Included for the first time in a record form, a heading is
dedicated to mental development, beside other headings pertaining
to physical growth. It gave a thoroughly new picture of a child's
maturation in the perspective of its development. The committee
responsible for the standardization of the form attested its range: it
sought to promote 'intelligent' motherhood, to prevent sickness, to
place the child under supervision and therefore to restructure the
hybrid socio-technical network of relationships in children's collective.

The Developmental Record Form departed from the standard
scorecard in many ways, the most salient of these being as complete an
assessment as possible of the child's whole progress, notably by listing
an index of behavioural benchmarks considered normal for children

---

[52] How can such a mundane artefact as a record form be defined? Berg and
Bowker on this subject: 'we will be using a broad definition of the "medical
record" as all written, typed, or electronically stored traces of any aspect of the
patient treatment that has official status within the hospital system and is in
principle stored for a period of time' (Berg 1997: 515). They also include in
the definition that the record is not a single object as it combines the record the
expert keeps in a folder at hand with the (physically separate) record of the
nurses and physicians 'in house'.

[53] Especially appealing is the Standard Score Card, issued by the American
Medical Association in 1914, in an effort to standardize the numerous types of
record forms used in American hospitals, paediatricians' clinics, state agencies
etc. This standardization indicates what I mean by constructing the object,
fulfilling the tasks and their appropriateness.

in specified age categories. A developmental examination was considered as an assessment of the child's progress in physical growth, in mental maturation, in emotional stability and in other aspects of normal healthy childhood including personal social reactions, reasoning and the handling of factual material, mechanical intelligence and ability, and self-reliance. Gesell was instrumental in the introduction of a mental developmental chart: it contains a space for the history of the first year, the common contagious diseases of childhood, immunization data and a brief outline of mental development. In discrete age categories, normal behavioural benchmarks could be ticked off: 'draws circle from copy'; 'combines two parts of cut picture'; 'names three objects in a picture'; 'repeats two digits' etc.

The developmental form became a vital object in forming as complete a picture as required of the individual child whilst measuring it against other children of the same age category on a comparative scale. Great emphasis is laid on the construction of behavioural benchmarks for children, the specification of age categories, tasks involving mental maturation, reliance and emotional stability. The task of producing the record form was a large, intricate one, including some key features:[54]

a. developmental record as a force in itself translates and transforms the relations that act through it, while playing a constitutive of ordering the processes of shaping and furthering a child's trajectory;
b. developmental record achieves these tasks through practices of observing, recording and visualizing which are decisive in the practices of reading, leafing through, jotting down notes, communicating or dispatching frame a decisive site in developmental work;
c. developmental record is a key part of the process transforming of the child's problem into a manageable situation for the paediatrician's or the psychologist's working routines;
d. every note entails the operative production of historical information[55] and of visual overview – data, sources, relevancies – in a

---

[54] I am indebted to Marc Berg's acute analysis of the medical record as a sociological artefact for some of the following propositions (Berg 1996, 1997, 1998).

[55] 'The record produces a patient with a medical history; the accumulation of sets of traces configures a medical past for a specific patient ... This produces a linear, stable history; this activity performs the temporality that Foucault sees as a crucial innovation of the modern, clinical gaze' (Berg 1997: 516).

temporal process so as to furnish a clear-cut frame in which to gaze upon the child, to ponder and elaborate further;

e. the record predetermines, due to its categories, design and format, a problem-definition which is developmentally relevant while mediating the expert–child–parents interactions; it is a device where all tasks relating to a child's trajectory must begin and end;

f. this durable set of multiple inscriptions not only yields explicit tasks, but also affords action at a distance: via writing recommendations to perform thereafter and via enabling past and distant work to be brought into the present; thus, triggering a continual reconstruction of the present.

As hybrid objects, the record forms constitute a key site of the socio-technical network – or dispositif – within which the child acquires its particular mode of existence as a social actor: the site where inscriptions accumulate, where developmental experts' tasks begin, are coordinated and end, where the temporal process unfolds progressively. The record mediates the relations that it coordinates as well as children's bodies configured through it. The record produces the child's map of maturation and development by demanding in an ordered fashion that the same measurements be made at fixed intervals and by sequentially designing behavioural yardsticks for particular age categories. Inscriptions made in the record lead to interventions in the child's development as inscribed in the individual case record. The latter does not simply describe a situation: it structures the way the child's development is rewritten (Berg 1997).

The question – is developmental thinking a cognitive form? – can now be approached in a more informed way. Bearing on the two aspects of thinking about and acting upon the child, this general question must be clarified and reworded as follows: how does sequential development as a social form pertaining to thinking about and acting upon the child stabilize a disturbed collective?[56] In this sense, cognition does not lie in one's head, but rather in the dynamic processes of the childhood collective.

[56] A chaotic childhood collective is understood as a collective seriously disturbed and disrupted by an uncontrolled level of children's predicaments. At first linked to children's physical growth: various infectious diseases, height and weight problems, they became later on manifold behavioural problems, which accelerated the coming of age of developmental thinking.

The answer ought to be qualified as it involves at once the hybrid object circulating in the collective, those among whom the hybrid object is circulating and the reshuffling of the relationships already established in the collective through the first two. The connections among elements are complex, multiple, transformative, occasionally contradictory, ever more conflicted. Let it be restated that sequential development alludes primarily to the implementation of technical devices – the objects – to perform specific tasks. Those devices have something to do with agency, with strengthening and furthering the agentic capacity of actors. Accordingly, they are also an integral part of social action. Such an assumption is underpinned by the proposition that actors are regulating their activities through these devices: design and connection of objects are parts of actors' conduct for they participate in their interactions (Heath 1997). It remains to be seen what type of action is involved in this collective and how objects proceed into action.

Children's disturbed condition is already established and well documented. The question at stake is the stabilization of the collective: how it operates and how it does so correctly. It consequently comes back to breaking down the argument into three different entities: how to conceive and construct feasible technical devices with respect to children's disordered condition; how these perform the task of stabilization; how the translation of a chaotic situation into a specific technical device to stabilize it is stamped as appropriate or not. Although crucial, the question of translation[57] appears to be subsidiary nature with respect to its own effect: the stabilization of the childhood collective.

Much as the childhood collective was faced with several uncertainties with respect to its own future, yet uncertainties were pertaining to an unstable situation described by physician Percy Boulton, for instance. As reliable averages were unavailable in the 1870s, he had no clear idea at what rate a child should grow during a specific period. What could he tell parents seeking advice? By the end of the century, both physicians L. Starr and E. Holt had height and weight tables at hand; they could, accordingly, indicate the normal growth of a child

---

[57] Callon's analysis, *Some Elements of a Sociology of Translation*, with its identification of four moments in the translation process, is usually considered as the most elaborate and convincing example of a sociology of translation (Callon 1986).

at each age, whilst connecting growth to nutrition and diet in regard
to age categories, hence establishing the first steps leading later to age
standards, norms and stages of growth.

What happened between those two moments, 1870 with Boulton in
London and 1894–1895 with Starr and Holt in the United States, is a
noteworthy process of translation and, therefore, of stabilization.
Although the focus will not review the activity of translation in itself, a
few critical indications concerning what is being translated are
worthwhile. Translation consists of associating entities forming alliances – among actors and between actors and hybrid objects as well –
that will eventually bring stabilization to a collective. The fabrication
of the collective entails the enrolment of non-human entities. A translation reverts to a displacement where what actors do is expressed in a
particular visual language, which, if successful, see people of the
collective speaking/acting in unison accordingly; namely, using a
common language to speak of the same questions while using a common framework to operate upon the problems disturbing the collective.

A presupposition supports such an assumption: at the starting point,
disordered clusters of actors can not interact effectively for they do not
have a mutual problematization of the situation: that is, among other
things, a cultural repertoire and language to word it. The childhood
collective was unable to track down the problems it encountered, let
alone to name them.[58] Translation provides, and stabilization operates
from, a common ground by means of negotiations and reciprocal
adjustments. Stabilization conveys a shared framework which raise
actors and hybrid objects to common-ness with regard to children's
chaotic situation: shared schemas and understanding as a prerequisite
for action and focused intervention to provide a stabilized collective.

Stabilization is brought forth through the elaboration of the
appropriate tools for specific assignments – the devices and their
operative dispositions. The objects/devices are a cardinal constituent
of social activity: images and information sustained by the technical
devices acquire their operational effectiveness by the way they
perform within the interactions among participants. Actors become

---

[58] Despite the fact that large-scale inquiries were already implemented and
ongoing, their findings and their conceptualization – the statistical concept of
population for instance – was not yet circulating in a broader network of lay
persons. Accordingly, the childhood collective was not aware of these findings.

involved in the collective with and via objects so that the very possibility of action is partly inserted in the objects themselves (Norman 1993). This last assumption raises the question of feasible devices: how are feasible technical devices fabricated with respect to children's disordered situation?

The construction of feasible technical devices requires a complex space–time process, the identification of the problem at stake – that is, to outline, delimit, establish the frame and the figures of children's development – will entail a set of specific investigations related to particular problems. These combine two main areas, both internal and external. The first area pertains to skills, strategies, tasks to perform, including obtainable materials and data, to set out a feasible and cogent device. The second area refers to diversified supports in both the wider scientific community – the extant laboratories for example – and the extrascientific world for funding, but also for access to diffusion channels with socio-technical networks of professional associations, hospitals, clinics and so on.[59]

Stabilization designates the handling of divergent standpoints given the heterogeneity of the multiple actors in the collective, which indicate furthermore the necessity to craft reliable connections among these entities considering the wide array of circumstances within which they interact. The most decisive connection, from a developmental perspective, to establish and implement, is that between paediatrics and psychology: how paediatrics gradually veered towards mental hygiene to include it as a major constituent of child development. 'The physician must not only be concerned with the body health of his patients, but with their mental health. In pediatrics we are more and more recognizing the necessity of a knowledge of the psychology of children' (Veeder 1926: 65). For developmental thinking could not

---

[59] Relations between the scientific community and the extrascientific world are always delicate, not to say conflictual. This can be read as connections building rather than strictly corporatist interests. 'This needs particular emphasis, for the field of child health has attracted and developed many non medical health workers, and many experimental methods and phases have been accepted by them as of fixed and permanent value. The physician, upon whom the knowledge and development of child hygiene fundamentally depends, as all knowledge of nurses, nutrition workers and the like is purely secondary and derived from medical knowledge, should keep this broad aspect clearly in the background of his mind and should maintain a scientific attitude toward the work' (Veeder 1926).

thrive without such a crucial link, which would yield cooperation and bring about the collective beyond children's disturbed situation.

Designing a persuasive developmental device raises at once a question of integration – integrate previous devices and further them into a new developmental scheme: the design of an effective framework for developmental tasks. At first, the measurement of height and weight was considered as 'the most obvious and striking characteristics of growth in children', which amounts to 'the simplest method of following the development' of the child (Veeder 1926). However, height and weight convey physical measurements related to the child's nutritional condition, which on the other hand involves other factors such as tissue tonus, muscular development, anaemia and posture. In brief, that is to say:

- measurements of height and weight provide the best method of recording the development of the child;
- the weight curve supplies the most accurate index of the progress of the child;
- keeping a record of the child's development, in form of graphic chart is appropriate.

(Veeder 1926: 29)

This was the starting point of Veeder's argument; overlapping with the argument around regularity, the debate concerning firmness with children was also circulating in the collective. Links with psychology were established in the aftermath raising the feasibility of a developmental form that encompasses mental hygiene and mental growth, habit formation and psychometric tests. Veeder's assertions concerning the connection between paediatrics and psychology are indicative in this respect:

So far we have been concerned with the growth and development of the body of the child. Of equal importance to this is the subject of the growth and development of the mind ... The close interrelation between physical growth and mental growth and the interdependence of the two has been slow in gaining recognition, but the importance of this relationship is at last being recognised ... Mental hygiene is only a phase of the general hygiene of the child, but a phase whose importance is steadily gaining recognition. (Veeder 1926: 65)

Connecting with psychology as a body of formal knowledge, and designing a feasible developmental form, meant that experts and researchers coordinated their experimental capacities to put out an appropriate form and their empirical possibilities of implementing such a device. Feasibility pertains to the complex task of pulling disparate elements together in the right sequence to achieve the goal of a developmental form. Articulating diverse elements in a coherent sequence requires appreciation of the hindrances, possibilities and resources of each element engaged in the construction of the form. From this standpoint, Veeder draws up a parallel between mental and physical growth.

A striking parallelism exists between the mental growth and development of the child and the physical growth. Both are continuous processes and the conditions existing at any time are influenced to a large extent by what has gone before. Moreover, there is a distinct periodicity of the curve of mental growth somewhat similar to the periodicity pointed in discussing physical development (Veeder 1926: 65).

Untangling a developmental form purported to the translation of the vague notion of mental growth into a workable object for practitioners. If psychology alludes to knowledge of the mind – 'how it develops, how it works, how it reacts, and the conditions influencing its working' (Veeder 1926: 68) – then taking hold of the mind's operations is of primary importance: how these are measured in as accurate a way as statistical technologies allows. This operation entails overcoming such speculative notions as instincts, consciousness and ideas.[60] and to concentrate on aspects of the child's body indicative of its mental development: the IQ tests either in the Binet–Simon or the Stanford–Binet forms. What was so cogent about mental measurements lies in 'the establishment of norms or levels of intelligence for age periods'

---

[60] The reaction of the paediatrician to some of these psychological notions, instinct for instance, and their contribution to developmental thinking is suggestive of the negotiations going on in the collective:

We are interested rather in what we may gather from them in relation to the mental growth and development of the child which is of practical importance to the pediatrician. Thus a discussion of the exact meaning of the term 'instinct', whether it is a concrete or an abstract idea, and differences between an instinct and the emotional state accompanying the instinct is of little interest or importance to the physician; but the conception of instinct and emotion has definite practical value in explaining some of the phenomena of a child's reactions and behavior which is of real importance to the physician (Veeder 1926).

(Veeder 1926: 78). The question of norms – norms for children at different stages of their lives – appears decisive in the 1920s in regard to the processes of stabilization, for they are the core elements with which stabilization proceeds.

Although a form of stabilization of the collective is brought about by mental measurements' norms, yet a question arises with infants and pre-school children for they do not have complete access to language required by the tests; the Binet tests are characterized as tests of the language function. How, then, can the pre-school child be taken notice of in a developmental perspective? 'The use of language (in order and in response) cannot be utilized and hence tests are largely motor in character' (Veeder 1926: 79). The feasibility of the Developmental Record Form lies in this operational articulation between motor and language tests. Stabilization of the child's disordered situation is achieved by a normative process, which tends to fixing appropriate physical and mental behaviour for assorted age categories. Norms not only say what must be done, but above all how to decide in various situations, how to adjust or orient oneself.

It is with a device such as a developmental record form that stabilization is introduced in the childhood collective as a critical moment of coherence in a space–time process, most notably by bringing the manifold actors of the collective to commonness with and vis-à-vis children. Furthermore a distributed cognition yields an objectivity of the outside world by reducing its complexity via categorization, classification, norms and so on.

The developmental form appears as a standardized package – metaphorically, an interface – which favours social bonds and furthers integration in the collective among actors coming from different social worlds: it operates in several intersecting social worlds (Clarke 1992). A stabilizing device is both legible and discussable by the collective's components for the mapping of the child is carried out in an optically consistent way, thus allowing one to qualify a peculiar situation (De Munck 1999; De Munck and Verhoeven 1997). It circulates in the collective without being altered or depleted, is combinable with other objects to further circulation and enhancement of the capacities for action. In brief, it is a compelling illustration that non-humans can be active in the co-production processes of childhood.

The novel idea of development, and its extension in developmental thinking, was a complex scientific scheme. This chapter focused on the general configuration which emerged from the notion of normalcy and its continuation in the figure of the normal child, where it was recognized as development. Hence, the mapping of developmental thinking in its two most salient patterns: a cognitive form and a hybrid object. The line of argument followed the emergence of developmental thinking and the various forms it took since its inception in the childhood collective as an outcome both of an abstract concept and of various technical devices. Far from being a homogenous and coherent concept, developmental thinking swung back and forth between physical growth and mental development and beyond whilst migrating progressively in the startling direction of a stage theory: that is, ordained sequences.

Developmental theory in its age/stage/sequential form became entirely pervasive, as soon as the device circulated in the collective, everyone acting towards the child with respect to the main outline of sequential theory. The emergence of a globally coherent developmental theory took place mainly in the overlap between paediatrics and psychology. From the outset, scientists studying maturation translated data into developmental assessments globally understood as a stage theory. The first stage theories converged on the physical determinants of development, the paediatrician set up developmental benchmarks in terms of increasingly differentiated stages of physical maturation unravelled as normative expectations or age appropriate behaviour. But the nub of developmental thinking rests in the bonding of physical with mental growth and hygiene. From a developmental perspective, growth, maturation and intelligence were all thought of via stage theory, therefore raised to a way of thinking, and a cognitive form. The patterning of children's behaviour appears to be the modelling of a child in a sequential process.

Developmental theory was hardly agreed upon unanimously for it presumes a translation of children's situation and a stabilization of the collective which initiated a renewal of relationships among actors; the training of nurses, social workers and so on places greater emphasis on developmental thinking, whose stage model of development is a keystone of their learning. Nevertheless, the critique of developmental thinking was constant for a long time; Morss, for one, criticizes acutely the predominance of biological ideas upon developmental thinking, the idea of progress and of linear progression as the core of developmental thinking (Morss 1990).

Developmental thinking is progressively established as the predominant frame of reference, prevailing over all other existing schemas, for it provided a noteworthy stabilization to the childhood collective, which operates by way of the inscriptive and operative character of artefacts. The sociological status of hybrid objects is to enhance the capacity for action of different actors. New forces introduced into the hybrid socio-technical network stabilized by moulding the child according to the schema of developmental thinking. Stabilization is assured by normative expectations, for it specifies how to decide in distinct situations, how to adjust oneself and so on.

Conclusion

This book is a tribute to the relevance of the sociology of childhood, and an acknowledgement of the fruitfulness of a historical sociology of developmental thinking. It argues forcefully that the latter became the predominant way of thinking and acting with relation to the child in western societies and, certainly, beyond. The analysis arises from a critical stance with regard to the positions provided by both psychology's perspectives and socialization enquiries. Arriving at the end of our journey in the historical sociology of developmental thinking, the main line of argument of this volume must be reasserted. The final remarks, however, will assume that the outcomes derived from developmental thinking's leading position can arguably be an overture to a purposeful shift in the childhood collective.

The argument

In the course of the analysis, I maintained that childhood is a crucial condition for sociological theory to be as general – a totality – and constructive as possible. The point of departure relates to the scientific investigation of children which started to observe, measure, weigh and describe them: their social inscription was hence provided largely by recording devices such as graphs, charts and tabulations. Along the way it is suggested that a novel child figure is carried forward by the activity of measurement, classification and codification via diverse social technologies working to put into operation standardized variables and developmental benchmarks for monitoring children. As a consequence, statistical reasoning introduced a new way of thinking and acting with relation to the child, whilst standards and criteria translated children's situation into the complex cultural framework of normality/development; the normal child came of age, in varied forms. In accordance with several assessments, the childhood collective is described as disturbed, chaotic and in need of stabilization;

developmental thinking is set forth as a cognitive form, now extended to mental hygiene, as the most credible effort ever implemented to stabilize the collective by bringing common-ness, i.e. shared schemas and understanding, to it.

Although much is said about the sociohistorical context of contemporary childhood, what about the child himself, one might legitimately ask? This question raises the status of the social context in a study aimed at shedding light onto the historical roots and foundations of western childhood. The gradual autonomization of the category of children within the national population occurred partly in the wake of the scientific investigation of children. The case of developmentalism provides a telling example in this respect. Clearly, sociologists ought to question developmentalists, not only regarding their universalist assertions, but primarily in relation to their surprising abilities and their startling effectiveness in stabilizing the childhood collective in the first half of the twentieth century; namely, the historical context that allocates them a predominant position in the collective. Together with socialization theory, developmentalism is deemed the dominant framework of the collective (Lee 2001).

This book provides a cautious yet resolute answer to the questioning of the predominant position of developmentalism and socialization within the collective; it proposes substantial answers about how it reached that position and how, in the aftermath, it upheld it throughout the twentieth century. One of the arduous tests in designing such a research device lies in establishing a legitimate stance for sociology, for this field is already occupied by both developmentalists themselves and historians. A critical examination of their research agenda will be worthwhile as it will allow sociology to outline its specificity in this respect. In their influential book, *Children in Time and Place*, Elder *et al.* set up an interdisciplinary research agenda to explore the ways in which the construction of childhood changed across time. The agenda identifies five sets of issues all of which are especially relevant to this study:

- The first set of issues concerns the boundary conditions of the stage of childhood itself;
- A second issue concerns the norms or expectations of development;
- A third set of issues concerns the presumed determinants of or relevant influences on development;

- A fourth set of concerns focuses on the end goals of development;
- A fifth issue focuses on beliefs and ideas concerning the role played by individuals in fulfilling the developmental agenda.

(Elder *et al.* 1993: 247)

Accordingly, the authors put forward a three-step research process that is particularly appropriate for this work:

1. The nature of the construction of adults and children needs to be retrieved from historical record.
2. The contexts provided for children that flow from these constructions require descriptive work.
3. Research should focus on the implications of these environments for children's developmental agenda.

(Elder *et al.* 1993: 249)

A historical sociology of childhood is settled on to go beyond the evident drawbacks of the pragmatic descriptions of past events, and yet the latter are still an unavoidable starting point. Its basic assumptions rest upon the thesis that childhood is primarily a sociohistorical phenomenon; consequently, that no legitimate conception of the contemporary child can be sustained without a thorough historical standpoint. But this is far from sufficient for an effective sociology of childhood, as most historians provide, to some extent, such an outlook. Thereupon, they usually afford the historical viewpoint in the dominant framework's terms, which is problematic. A credible and quite different alternative based on an undeniable sociological proposal is offered here.

This may be why historians have not, thus far, put forward an alternative view of developmental thinking as a cognitive form to rival that offered by the dominant framework. In consequence, a historical sociology of childhood is basically preoccupied with putting this reliable standpoint back into a more general scheme; thus the concept of totality, which opens up the possibility of drawing parallels between children's situation and some broader movements in the larger society (Thornton 2005). Children were not an isolated unit in society, growing up in a closed world. Furthermore, it seeks to establish from these acknowledged findings a sound conceptual appraisal of the child as well as of the society within which the child is recognized as such. The last proposition needs additional explanations in particular with regard to developmental thinking.

Lee has proposed the argument that one of the most crucial differences between the dominant framework and the sociology of
childhood lies in terms of their approaches to time. In the former case,
time is restricted to chronological age – and hence to sequential
development – as the key parameter distinguishing children and
adults. Chronological age, hence, becomes the crux of developmental
thinking's leading line of argument, which all other forms of variations between children and adults – maturity–immaturity, rationality–
irrationality, nature–culture and so on – are measured against,
therefore operating as the yardstick to organize the collective and,
above all, to stabilize it. For the latter, on the other hand, the parameter of chronological age is not as determinant a constant as it is for
the dominant framework. For, obvious though time seems to be for a
common-sense public, I shall speak rather of the settling of a specific
time–space for children, where time, far from being chronological or
an arrowed line along which children travel unidirectionally, is
noticeably multifaceted: many lines loosely interlaced all running and
shifting at different speeds in different situations.

Review

This conception of a particular space–time for children emerges as the
core of a historical sociology of childhood. The review of the key
arguments presented so far began by addressing the question: what is
childhood from a sociological standpoint if it is no longer either a
residue of social theory or a peripheral phenomenon of adult society?
A second question followed at once: intersecting both the question of
the child's status and the interrogation of children's circulation in the
collective, what is a child from a sociohistorical perspective? Finally,
what are the crucial parameters upon which our contemporary
understanding of children is built?

Chapter 1 accounted for children's situation in the collective.
Building upon the inherent limitations of sociology's sole concept of
childhood, socialization, which some social scientists find unilateral,
homogenizing and, frankly, boring, the seeds of a legitimate historical
sociology of childhood, disentangled from the basic shortcomings
of sociology's children, are now sown around the implementation of
the category of childhood and the rise of the normal child. This
comprehensive operation goes together with a deep reoutlining of a

national population in accordance with its rationalization, the beginning of population studies yielded by statistical thinking, which ushered in the systematic investigation of childhood. Therefore, the awakening of specific scientific domains – public hygiene, paediatrics, psychology, education and so on – opens up an exact space–time for social intervention, thus for childhood regulation.

The research issue at stake in this chapter pertains to the particular translation of children's situation brought in by the nascent sciences of childhood: that is, how developmental theory, backed up by its cognitive lineaments and its hybrid objects, mutated into a cognitive form which turned out to be the usual way of thinking about and acting with regard to children that has endured ever since. An account is made that encompasses the performative interactions of both social actors and technical devices whereby actors interact with each other. An ongoing debate is sustained around such issues:

1. As the status of the child and the social construction of childhood, by resetting it within a broader sociohistorical phenomenon opening up a specified space–time of social intervention.
2. As structure and agency, by setting out an unconventional conceptualization of the social as a complex set of interrelated heterogeneous entities that could take into account the child as a social actor of its own.
3. As the circulation of children in the collective and the puzzle of hierarchy/symmetry, by considering how actor–network theory's relational materialism gives a convincing account of the performative interactions of social actors and technical devices.
4. As the translation of children's predicaments, by presenting several analytical propositions pertaining to the translation of children's predicaments into a knowledge-driven activity paving the way to the stabilization of the collective.

The second chapter points out that the figure of the child and the very idea of childhood alike were sustained in science and in literature above all. Besides the enormous advice literature afforded by various welfare groups, a growing body of scientific texts became available, initially in specialized circles and, afterwards, to the wider public. This specific discourse involved an inscription of children whose form is different from the previous ones. As a background to twentieth-century scientific

practices, a detailed account of the first forms, as well as the more
elaborate forms of child observation and recording, was documented.
In the latter case, hopeful fields of investigation with their effective
technologies, as the main outcomes of population studies, come into
sight throughout the century: some scientists saw opportunities in these
outcomes and pervaded the emergent childhood collective, which was
then under the authority of welfare activists. Thus, they restructured it
by introducing new forces – it supported a standardized classification
and categorization of children – and by rearranging its network of
relationships on the edge of a stabilization schedule.

The new resources introduced by scientists were emphasized as they
outlined how the scientific observation of children yielded technical
devices furthering original knowledge. From the outset, the constant
appearance of graphs, charts and tabulations in scientific journals and
books related to the empirical study of children is striking: it departed
ceaselessly from a more mundane form of children's inscription, the
diary. The radical novelty introduced by this specified inscription of
children was scrutinized in the form of technical devices conveying
a complex set of descriptions, vocabularies, reasonings and visual
depictions. These original ways of observing the child are connected
with the increase of knowledge about childhood, notably technical–
empirical knowledge, in such fields as anthropometry, hygiene,
paediatrics and psychology that took the child as a subject of study.
As it transformed the collective, it also ushered in a new conception of
the child.

This argument lead to an examination of the main graphs as well as
their specific constituents and effects: Chapter 3 investigated the
processes of social change initiated by technologies' contribution to
repositioning children in the collective with respect to a particular
society. A child becomes an object of knowledge when it is identified
as such, different from other social actors, and as methods of observation, subsequently of recording, are put into place. These methods
rest on two fundamentals: measurement and classification. Recording,
especially in its scientific rather than its diary form, requires the
practice of measurement according to fixed predefined parameters:
height–weight–age tables personify the carrying out of children's
measurement put into place on that occasion. Measurement of children
in conformity with discrete parameters entails a system of categories:
the activity of classifying children is essential in this respect.

Taxonomy, enumeration, classification and data collection concerning children have certain consequences. Classifications directly affect the children classified: this is regulation – bringing forth standardization. On the other hand, resistance is offered by social actors to both regulation and standardization. In between stands an apparatus in charge of monitoring children's behaviour by way of social technologies, considered as a by-product of the scientific investigation of childhood, both of the observation/recording methods and of the activity of classification. The perspective is twofold – regulation/resistance – and, furthermore, it takes into account the point that these forms vary in time and space accordingly. It concerns some of the most cogent social technologies set up to supervise and regulate children's behaviour; their reactions, as well as their those of parents, to this supervision. The attention is focused upon the technologies that paediatrics and child psychology established, those which public authorities and reformers implemented in the aftermath: the charts, the record forms, the well–child conference, intelligence testing and the child-guidance clinic.

Chapter 4 probed the social forms of normalcy in the larger context of statistical thinking and children's measurement. We argued that a normal child is recognized as such when it is classified in the relevant categories as it put up with the standards of development, implemented and generalized in the collective. Standards of development came to symbolize normalcy, even though the analysis tried to track down when, if and how the two are equivalent, or substitutable one for the other. The turn of the twentieth century's enthusiasm for normalcy and standardization could not bypass the child collective for it was in the process of becoming a distinct entity of its own, well above public authorities' concerns about the chaotic condition of children. Developmental standards, which are yielded at one and the same time by technical devices and politics of regulation, bring about three different forms of normalcy: the normal child as average, as healthy, and as acceptable. We first looked to the form of the normal child as average, for it is an outcome of large-scale inquiries and regularities. We investigated the form of the normal child as healthy, for disease and illness are recognized as a disorder – or an interruption – in the process of a child's development. We finally queried the form of the normal child as acceptable, for pathology is not restricted to illness as it can also allude to behaviour.

Measurement, collection of data and classification gather numerical facts concerning children whose unintended consequences achieve a new framework of thinking about and acting upon children in the collective. Statistical reason, both in its cognitive and administrative lineaments, introduces consistency and regularity in the knowledge of the child. This way of reading reality pertained to childhood as well: the institutional knowledge of children read its object in terms of statistical laws and probability, therefore bringing in a whole awareness of the child. In this context the normal soon met probability, mean and so on and overlapped with these notions. The normal child emerged both as a cognitive form whom parents, teachers and physicians taught about and as an administrative device to rationalize. This analysis takes place within the larger context of the rise of statistical thinking and the processes of its contribution to children's position. It pertains to some of the most cogent meanings of the figure of the child, whilst resituating it in larger social trends in which it was embedded and shaped. The analytical perspective focused on the emergence of a singular entity in the collective, the normal child and its three social forms of normalcy.

Chapter 5 documented the mapping of developmental thinking in its essential double configuration – namely, to think about and act upon the child; so, developmental thinking heralded the idea of the normal child, which it is secured to by numerous connections, as much mental as physical normality with respect to the child's maturation. Based on statistical technologies in extensive focused inquiries, large-scale inquiries contributed decisively to outline what the regularities of a normal child would look like. Although normality was, in the first part of the twentieth century, a notion far from being unequivocal, different actors in the childhood collective – parents, teachers, paediatricians, nurses and welfare activists – started to be accordingly on the look-out for new standards that would be appropriate for adults to frame their customary relationships with children. Much as developmental standards were implemented in the collective, children's progression was nevertheless measured in accordance with these standards. Furthermore, parents, physicians and the like began to conduct themselves according to this particular way of thinking/acting, hence the very condition of developmentalism's effectiveness and pervasiveness.

From statistical technologies to developmental standards, a cognitive device is becoming a way of thinking about and acting towards children. The extensive mutation of sequential development into a cognitive form conveys a socialized or distributed property as a vital requirement of its operative capacity supplying knowledge in the form of a 'map of the world' and allowing it to qualify a peculiar situation. The idea as well as the symbolism of normality completely shaped the way in which the child is apprehended, moreover acted upon. Children's situation is translated into novel standards and criteria of behaviour; the translation of children's predicaments into a broad question of normality/development displaced the focus of the crucial distinction towards normal and abnormal children. We noticed in addition that the introduction of new forces and practices in the collective such as mental hygiene, intelligence testing, assorted measurements, different school operations, have something to do with agency, with strengthening and furthering the agentic capacity of actors in the collective.

Development brings stabilization to the collective, but nonetheless its boundaries have to be renegotiated. One of the primary consequences of this translation/stabilization consisted in a major redistribution of the network of relationships surrounding the child, the connections among the various elements of the collective being complex, multiple, transformative, occasionally contradictory, ever more conflicted. This chapter investigated the specific aspects of the various associations between development and normality, actors regulating and stabilizing their activities with developmental devices. The analysis takes place within the larger context of the institutionalization of childhood: how such an idea emerged and was implemented, what it meant, how developmental thinking moved steadily towards the stabilization of the collective. Stabilization brings about actors' behaviour in a particular visual language which, if successful, will accordingly see people in the collective speaking/acting in unison; that is, using a common language to speak of the same questions while using a common framework to operate upon the problems disturbing the collective. Common-ness with regard to children's chaotic situation conveys shared schemas and understanding as a requirement for purposeful intervention to endow a stabilized collective.

This progressive mutation emphasizes, and here lies the crucial point, the double pattern of developmental thinking as both a cognitive form and a hybrid object. The investigation of the links between normality and development raised fundamental questions for social theory revolving around the question of the child's ontological status and contingency.

Overture

The gist of the question, as our analysis decisively indicated, lies in the capacity to stabilize the childhood collective. Public authorities and welfare activists, among others, were highly concerned about the chaotic and disturbed condition of children: their understanding of children's situation was irresolute and, consequently, they hesitated over the most efficient approaches or methods to monitor their behaviour. They were looking, however, for resourceful devices that could fulfil their managerial needs; height and weight chart, intelligence testing embodied such a device, especially for teachers and school administrators. Piaget's form of developmentalism went even further.

From a broader stance, developmental thinking performed in startling ways. It stabilized the collective through standardized packages bringing a mutual understanding of the situation: namely, common-ness or a common framework carrying on shared schemas as a prerequisite to operating a focused intervention upon the problems disturbing the collective. It provided actors with the likelihood of tracking down and overcoming the predicaments it encountered.

There remains developmental thinking's unsurpassed strength and brightness, which enabled the dominant framework to operate its unrivalled capacity to stabilize the childhood collective. It does so, however, by streamlining a very complex question, by ordering, after Binet, children's long path towards growing up along chronological age, age categories and sequential stages leading steadily to maturity. Although we acknowledged much was gained with the implementation of a cognitive form like developmentalism, yet there remain crucial problems to be addressed. The relevance of a sociology of childhood here comes into view, as one of its main tasks consists in reintroducing some complexity in this field – beside Bourdieu's claim to the right to intricacy in explaining the social – and questions the basic tenets of developmentalism as well as the powerful and passionate rhetoric of children's needs, rights and interests.

The question of time, invoked by Lee, appears to be central with regard to the stabilization of the collective. A more complex conception of time indicates primarily a differentiated, yet variably tightly or loosely interrelated set of children's times: the time of play, of study, of interactions, the latter being divided between family and peer interactions and so on. In brief, there is a profusion of different forms of time which children move between very rapidly. These have to be strictly identified, their characteristics and parameters brought to light as well as their articulation – the way they are interlaced one with the other. This raises the fundamental question: can we think of the child without first assigning age as the central parameter? If not age – and in its wake sequential stages – what then? What is the child's specific time–space and how could we give an account of it?

A stimulating answer, although partial, is given by Lee when he suggested that 'growing up is a slowing down, a decrease in the rate at which a person can pass from one social order to another ... It sets limits to the pace of personal and social change' (Lee 2001: 137). Looking at this proposition through the lens of social relationships, and trying to take it further, I shall rephrase it this way: growing up is a time in accelerating the pace of building a network of heterogeneous social relationships in need of stabilization, whilst adulthood is a time of slowing down and consolidating that network. Childhood is then considered as a space–time of initiating, building and diversifying relationships, first in the family, then at school, afterwards with peers – establishing that these several stages are not sequential.

Appendix

Table 7. *History of child development*

OUTLINE: HISTORY OF CHILD DEVELOPMENT

	Before 1920	1920-29	1930-39	1940-On
University Units	**Individuals** Darwin 1809 — Wallin 1876 Galton 1822 — Koffka 1886 Preyer 1841 — Bühler, C. 1893 G. S. Hall 1846 — Werner 1890 Binet 1857 — Piaget 1896 J. M. Baldwin 1861 — Freud 1856 Thorndike 1874 — Watson 1878 Stern 1871	10 Gesture Fund became ICW; U Washington [Smith 83] 17 Iowa C W Research Station [Baldwin 75, Sears 08] 24-34 CWI, Teachers College, Columbia [Woolley 74, Jersild 02] 25 ICW, Minnesota [Anderson 93, Scammon 83, Goodenough 86] 25 ICW, Toronto [Blatz 95] 25 CO3-U, Cornell [Waring] 26 Yale Psycho-Clinic [Gesell 80] 27 ICW, California [Jones 94] 27 Child Research Council, Colorado [Washburn 95] 28 Brush Foundation, W.R.U. [Todd 85] 30 Research in Child Dev., Michigan [Olson 99] Committee Human Dev., Chicago		48 Child Study Dept., Yale
College Units			29 Fels Institute, Antioch [Sontag 01] 35 Char. Research Proj., Union [Ligon 97]	
Clinics	96 Psychological Clinic, University of Pennsylvania [Witmer 67]			
Independent Units	08 Vineland Research Laboratory [Goddard 66, Porteus 83, Doll 89] 08 Elizabeth McCormick Memorial Fund	20 Merrill-Palmer School [White 80, McGinnis 93]	30 Moosehart Laboratory for Child Research [Raymart 83]	
Longitudinal Projects		22 Stanford Gifted Children [Terman 77]	Harvard Growth Study [Dearborn 78] Chicago Growth Study [Freeman 80] 30 Neuromuscular Dev. of Infants and Johnny and Jimmy [McGraw 98]	
Handbook or Manual			31 [Murchison 87]	46 [Carmichael 98]
Foundations		18-38 Laura Spelman Rockefeller Memorial [Ruml 94, Frank 90] 18 Commonwealth Fund 24 Child Guidance Clinics [Stevenson 92]		
U. S. Government	White House Conferences .1909	12 United States Children's Bureau 1919	1929 1940	
Voluntary Lay Organizations	88 Child Study Association of New York [Gruenberg 81] 97 National Congress of Parents and Teachers 98 Child Study Program, American Association of University Women	25 Association for Family Living, Chicago [Lawton]		
Professional Organizations	1909 Hall's abortive attempt	20 Committee on Child Development, National Research Council [Woodworth 69] 26 National Association Nursery Education 26-41 National Council of Parent Education	33 Society for Research in Child Development	46 Division of Childhood and Adolescence, A.P.A.

Source: Anderson 1956

Bibliography

AASPIM (1910). *Transactions of the First Annual Meeting.* Johns Hopkins University, Baltimore, MD.

ACHA (1918). Report on Procedure and Record Form. In American Association for Study and Prevention of Infant Mortality (ed.), *Transactions of the Ninth Annual Meeting.* Baltimore, MD: Franklin Printing Co.

(1920). A Plan for Maternity Care. *Transactions of the Tenth Annual Meeting.* Headquarters of the Association, Baltimore, MD.

Acker, F. (1997). Sortir de l'invisibilité: Le cas du travail infirmier. *Raisons Pratiques* 8, 65–93.

Adams, G. (1934). *Your Child is Normal.* New York: Covivi, Friede.

Alanen, L. (1992). *Modern Childhood? Exploring the 'Child Question' in Sociology,* Vol. 50, Jyväskylä: Institute for Educational Research.

Alanen (1997a). Sociological Perspective on Childhood: The Quest for a Structural Perspective. *Zeitschrift fur Sozialisationsforchung und Erziechungssoziologie* 17 (2), 162–177.

(1997b). Review. *Childhood* 4 (2), 251–256.

(1997c). *Sociologies of Childhood and the Politics of Growing Up.* University of Jyväskylä.

Alpers, S. (1983). *The Art of Describing.* University of Chicago Press.

Ambert, A.-M. (1986). Sociology of Sociology: The Place of Children in North American Sociology. In P. Adler and P. Adler (eds.), *Sociological Studies of Child Development* (pp. 11–31). Greenwich, CT: JAI Press.

Ames, L. B. (1989). *Arnold Gesell: Themes of his Work.* New York: Human Sciences Press.

Anderson, J. E. (1956). Child Development: An Historical Perspective. *Child Development* 27 (2), 181–196.

Anonymous (1890). A New Apparatus for Infant-feeding Based on the Infant's Weight Instead of its Age. *Archives of Pediatrics* VII (6), 470–472.

(1895). Editorial. *Archives of Pediatrics* XII (5), 357–360.

(1912). Annual Report for 1911 of the Chief Medical Officer of the Board of Education. London: HMSO.

Anonymous (1914). Infant Mortality: Two Resistant Groups. *Archives of Pediatrics* 31, 643.

(1926). Health Show and Conference held by the Children's Bureau. *Child Health Bulletin* 2 (5), 130–134.

(1929). *Why Sleep? Sleep Helps Children Grow.* Washington, DC: Children's Bureau.

Apple, R. (1987). *Mothers and Medicine: A Social History of Infant Feeding, 1890–1950,* Madison, WI: University of Wisconsin Press.

(1995). Constructing Mothers: Scientific Motherhood in the Nineteenth and Twentieth Centuries. *Social History of Medicine* 8 (2), 161–178.

Archard, D. (1993). *Children. Rights and Childhood.* New York: Routledge.

Armstrong, D. (1983). *The Political Anatomy of the Body: Medical Knowledge in Britain in the Twentieth Century.* Cambridge University Press.

(1986). The Invention of Infant Mortality. *Sociology of Health and Illness* 8 (3).

Ashmore, M., Wooffitt, R. and Harding, S. (1994). Humans and Others: The Concept of 'Agency' and its Attribution. *American Behavioral Scientist* 37 (6), 733–740.

Atlan, H. (1979). Créativité et réversibilité du temps: Une réflexion sur la science à la lumière de la tradition hébraïque. *Prospective et santé* 8, 17–32.

Avanzini, G. (1969). *Alfred Binet et la pédagogie scientifique.* Paris: Vrin.

(1999). *Alfred Binet.* Paris: Presses Universitaires de France.

Baldwin, B. T. (1924). The Use and Abuse of Weight–Height Tables as Indexes of Health and Nutrition. *Journal of the American Medical Association* 82 (1), 1–4.

Barad, K. (1998). Getting Real: Techno-scientific Practices and the Materialization of Reality. *Differences: A Journal of Feminist Cultural Studies* 10 (2), 88–128.

Becchi, E. (1998). Le XIXe siècle. In E. Becchi and D. Julia (eds.), *Histoire de l'enfance en occident* (pp. 147–223). Paris: Seuil.

Becchi, E. and Julia, D. (eds.) (1998). *Histoire de l'enfance en occident.* Paris: Seuil.

Beck, U. and Beck-Gersheim, E. (1995). *The Normal Chaos of Love.* London: Polity.

Beck, U., Giddens, A. and Lash, S. (1994). *Reflexive Modernization.* London: Polity.

Beekman, D. (1977). *The Mechanical Baby: A Popular History of the Theory and Practice of Child Raising.* Westport, CT: Lawrence Hill and Co.

Bellah, R. (1991). *The Good Society.* New York: A. A. Knopf.

Berg, M. (1996). Practices of Reading and Writing: the Constitutive Role of the Patient Record in Medical Work. *Sociology of Health and Illness* 18 (4), 499–524.

(1997). The Multiple Body of the Medical Record: Toward a Sociology of an Artefact. *The Sociological Quarterly* 38 (3), 513–537.

(ed.) (1998). *Differences in Medicine*. Durham, NC: Duke University Press.

Bernard-Bécharies, J.-F. (1994). Quels paradigmes pour une théorie de l'enfant acteur? *Revue de L'Institut de Sociologie* 1–2, 21–37.

Bernardi, B. (1985). *Age Class Systems: Social Institutions and Polities Based on Age*. Cambridge University Press.

Bijker, W. E., Hughes, T. P. and Pinch, T. (eds.) (1987). *The Social Construction of Technological Systems: New Directions in the History and Sociology of Technology*. Cambridge, MA: MIT Press.

Binet, A. (1898). La mesure en psychologie individuelle. *Revue philosophique* 46, 113–123.

(1903). *L'étude Expérimentale de l'Intelligence*. Paris: Schleicher Frères.

Binet, A. and Henri, V. (1896). La psychologie individuelle. *Année Psychologique* t.2, 411–465.

Binet, A. and Simon, T. (1907). *Les enfants anormaux. Guide pour l'admission des enfants anormaux dans les classes de perfectionnement*. Paris: Armand Colin.

(1908). Le développement de l'intelligence chez les enfants. *Année psychologique* t.14, 1–94.

Blanton, S. (1925). Helping the Child Adapt Himself. The Work of the Child Guidance Clinic. *Hygeia*, 639–640, 689–691.

Bliss, M. (1991). *Plague: A Story of Smallpox in Montréal*. Toronto: HarperCollins.

Block, N. J. and Dworkin, G. (eds.) (1976). *The IQ Controversy: Critical Readings*. New York: Pantheon Books.

Bloor, D. (1991). *Knowledge and Social Imagery*, 2nd edn. London: Routledge and Kegan Paul.

Boli, J. and Meyer, J. (1987). The Ideology of Childhood and the State: Rules Distinguishing Children in National Constitutions, 1870–1970. In J. W. M. George, M. Thomas, Francisco O. Ramirez and John Boli (eds.), *Institutional Structure Constituting State, Society and the Individual* (pp. 217–241). Newbury Park, CA: Sage Publications.

Boltanski, L. (1969). *Prime éducation et morale de classe*. Paris: La Haye, Mouton.

Boring, Edwin G. (1923). 'Intelligence as the Tests Test it'. *The New Republic*, 35, 6 June 1923.

Bourdieu, P. (1980). La 'jeunesse' n'est qu'un mot. In P. Bourdieu (ed.), *Questions de sociologie* (pp. 143–154). Paris: Éditions de minuit.

(1986). L'illusion biographique. *Actes de la recherche en sciences sociales*, 62–63, 69–72.

Bourdieu, P. (1990). *In Other Words*. Cambridge: Polity Press.

Bourne-Taylor, J. (1998). Between Atavism and Altruism: The Child on the Threshold in Victorian Psychology and Edwardian Children's Fiction. In K. Lesnik-Oberstein (ed.), *Children in Culture: Approaches to Childhood* (pp. 89–121). London: Macmillan.

Bowditch, H. (1881). Relation Between Growth and Disease. *Boston Medical and Surgical Journal* 104, 469.

Bradley, B. S. (1989). *Visions of Infancy: A Critical Introduction to Child Psychology*. Oxford: Polity.

Bradley, F. S. and Sherbon, F. B. (1917). *How to Conduct a Children's Health Conference*. US Children's Bureau.

Brennemann, J. (1933). Pediatric Psychology and the Child Guidance Movement. *Journal of Pediatrics* 11 (1), 16–21.

Bresci, M. and Livi-Basci, M. (1994). Le mois de naissance comme facteur de survie des enfants. *Annales de démographie historique* (pp. 169–186). Paris: Edition de l'Ecole des Hautes Etudes en Sciences Sociales.

Breslau, D. (2000). Sociology after Humanism: A Lesson from Contemporary Sciences Studies. *Sociological Theory* 18 (2), 289–307.

Brown, J. (1992). *The Definition of a Profession: Authority of Metaphor in the History of Intelligence Testing, 1890–1930*. Princeton University Press.

Brown, S. D. and Capdevilla, R. (1999). Perpetuum Mobile; Substance, Force and the Sociology of Translation. In J. Law and J. Hassard (eds.), *Actor–Network Theory and After* (pp. 26–50). Oxford: Blackwell.

Burkitt, I. (1998). Relations, Communication and Power. In I. Velody and R. Williams (eds.), *The Politics of Constructionism* (pp. 121–131). London: Sage.

Burman, E. (1994). *Deconstructing Developmental Psychology*. London: Routledge.

Callon, M. (1980). Struggles and Negotiations to Define what is Problematic and what is not; the Socio-logic of Translation. In K. D. Knorr and A. Cicourel (eds.), *The Social Process of Scientific Investigation. Sociology of the Sciences Yearbook*. Boston, MA: D. Reidel Publishing Company.

(1986). Some Elements of a Sociology of Translation: Domestication of the Scallops and the Fishermen of St-Brieux Bay. In J. Law (ed.), *Power, Action and Belief: A New Sociology of Knowledge?* (pp. 196–229). London: Routledge and Kegan Paul.

(1991). Techno-economic Networks and Irreversibility. In J. Law (ed.), *A Sociology of Monsters: Essays on Power, Technology and Domination.* London: Routledge and Kegan Paul.

(1992). The Dynamics of Techno-economic Networks. In R. Coombs, P. Savitotti and V. Walsh (eds.), *Technological Change and Company Strategies: Economic and Sociological Perspectives.* London: Academic Press.

(1999). Actor–network Theory – the Market Test. In J. Law (ed.), *Actor Network Theory and After* (pp. 181–195). Oxford: Blackwell.

Callon, M. and Law, J. (1997). After the Individual in Society: Lessons on Collectivity from Science, Technology and Society. *Canadian Journal of Sociology* 22 (2), 165–182.

Callon, M. and Rabeharisoa, V. (2000). Articulating Bodies: The Case of Muscular Dystrophies. In M. Akrich and M. Berg (eds.), *Bodies on Trial: Performance and Politics in Medicine and Biology.* Durham, NC: Duke University Press.

Cameron, H. C. (1919). *The Nervous Child.* London: Oxford University Press.

Camic, C. (1986). The Matter of Habit. *American Journal of Sociology* 91 (5), 1039–1087.

Canguilhem, G. (1966). *Le normal et le pathologique.* Paris: Presses Universitaires de France.

(1977). *Idéologie et rationalité dans l'histoire des sciences de la vie.* Paris: J. Vrin.

Canto-Klein, M. and Ramognino, N. (1974). Les faits sociaux sont pourvus de sens. *Connexions* 11.

Case, R. (1991). *The Mind's Stair-Case.* Hillsdale, NJ: Erlbaum.

Cassedy, J. H. (1984). *American Medicine and Statistical Thinking, 1800–1860.* Cambridge, MA: Harvard University Press.

Cavanaugh, J. C. (1981). Early Developmental Theories: A Brief Review of Attempts to Organise Developmental Data prior to 1925. *Journal of the History of Behavioural Sciences* 17, 38–47.

(1985). Cognitive Development Psychology before Preyer: Biographical and Educational Records. In W. Eckardt, W. Bringmann and L. Sprung (eds.), *Contributions to a History of Developmental Psychology* (pp. 187–207). Berlin: Mouton Press.

Caws, A. G. (1949). Child Study Fifty Years Ago. *Bulletin of the British Psychological Society* 1 (3), 104–109.

Chapman, P. D. (1988). *Schools as Sorters. Lewis Terman, Applied Psychology and the Intelligence Testing Movement, 1890–1930.* New York University Press.

Chassagne, S. (1998). Le travail des enfants aux XVIIIe et XIXe siècles. In E. Becchi and D. Julia (eds.), *Histoire de l'enfance en occident* (pp. 224–272). Paris: Seuil.

Chauvenet, A. (1988). Les professions de santé publique de l'enfance: entre police administrative et éthique communicationnelle. *Sociologie et Sociétés* XX (2), 41–54.

Chenery, W. (1919). Standards of Child Welfare: A Report of the Children's Bureau Conferences. Washington, DC: US Children's Bureau Publication.

Chudacoff, H. P. (1989). *How Old are You? Age Consciousness in American Culture*. Princeton University Press.

Clarke, A. and Fujimura, J. H. (ed.) (1992). *The Right Tools for the Job: At Work in the Twentieth-Century Life Science*. Princeton University Press.

Clarke-Steward, A., Friedman, S. and Koch, J. (1985). *Child Development: A Topical Approach*. New York: Wiley.

Cohen, R. (1985). Child-saving and Progressivism, 1885–1915. In J. Hawes and R. Hiner (eds.), *American Childhood: A Research Guide and Historical Handbook* (pp. 273–311). Westport, CT: Greenwood Press.

Cohen, Y. and Pestre, D. (1998). Presentation. *Annales HSS* 4–5, 721–744.

Coit, H. (1910). Factors in the Conservation of Child Life. *Archives of Pediatrics* XXVII (10), 721–731.

Cole, M. (1983). Society, Mind, and Development. In F. Kessel and A. Siegel (eds.), *The Child and Other Cultural Inventions*. New York: Praeger.

Coleman, W. (1982). *Death Is a Social Disease*. Madison, WI: University of Wisconsin Press.

Collins, R. (1999). *Macro History. Essays in Sociology of the Long Run*. Palo Alto, CA: Stanford University Press.

Comacchio, C. (1993). *Nations are Built of Babies: Saving Ontario's Mothers and Children*. Montreal: McGill-Queen's University Press.

Connerton, P. (1989). *How Societies Remember*. Cambridge University Press.

Corsaro, W. (1998). *Sociology of Childhood*. Thousand Oaks, CA: Pine Forge Press.

Coutard, O. (1999). *The Governance of Large Technical Systems*. London: Routledge.

Cravens, H. (1985a). The Wandering IQ: American Culture and Mental Testing. *Human Development* 28, 113–130.

  (1985b). Child-Saving in the Age of Professionalism, 1915–1930. In J. Hawes and R. Hiner (eds.), *American Childhood: a Research Guide and Historical Handbook* (pp. 415–488). Westport, CT: Greenwood Press.

  (1987). Applied Science and Public Policy: the Ohio Bureau of Juvenile Research and the Problem of Juvenile Delinquency, 1913–1930. In

M. Sokal (ed.), *Psychological Testing and American Society, 1890–1930* (pp. 158–194). New Brunswick, NJ: Rutgers University Press.

(1988). *The Triumph of Evolution*, 2nd edn. Baltimore, MD: Johns Hopkins University Press.

Crisler, J. E. (1984). 'Saving the Seed': The Scientific Preservation of Children in France during the Third Republic. Unpublished thesis, University of Wisconsin.

Cunningham, H. (1991). *The Children of the Poor: Representations of Childhood since the Seventeenth Century.* Oxford: Blackwell.

Curtis, B. (2002). Surveying the Social: Techniques, Practices, Power. *Histoire Sociale/Social History* XXXV (69), 83–108.

Danziger, K. (1990). *Constructing the Subject. Historical Origins of Psychological Research.* Cambridge University Press.

Darwin, C. (1877). A Biographical Sketch of an Infant. *Mind* 2, 285–294.

Daston, L. (1982). The Theory of Will versus the Science of Mind. In M. G. Ash and W. R. Woodward (eds.), *The Problematic Science: Psychology in Nineteenth Century Thought* (pp. 88–115). New York: Praeger.

Delanty, G. and Isin, E. F. (eds.) (2003). *Handbook of Historical Sociology.* London: Sage Publications.

De Munck, J. (1999). *L'institution sociale de l'esprit.* Paris: Presses Universitaires de France.

De Munck, J. and Verhoeven, M. (1997). *Les mutations du rapport à la norme: Un changement dans la modernité?* Brussels: De Boeck.

De Staël, A. (1896). *Lettres.* Paris: Calman-Levy.

Desrosières, A. (1992). Discuter l'indiscutable. *Raisons pratiques* 3, 131–154.

(1993). *La politique des grands nombres.* Paris: Editions La Découverte.

DeVilbiss, L. A. (1915). Opportunity for the Co-operation in the Medical Profession in the Baby Health Conference Movement, with a Report. *Archives of Pediatrics* 32 (4).

DiMaggio, P. J. and Powell, W. W. (1991). Introduction. In W. W. Powell and P. J. DiMaggio (eds.), *The New Institutionalism in Organizational Analysis* (pp. 1–41). University of Chicago Press.

Dolto, F., Rapoport, D. and This, B. (eds.) (1981). *Enfants en souffrance.* Paris: Stock/Laurence Pernoud.

Donnelly, M. (2005). William Farr and Quantification on Nineteenth-Century English Public Health. In G. Jorland, A. Opinel and G. Weisz (eds.), *Body Counts: Medical Quantification in Historical and Sociological Perspectives* (pp. 252–265). Montreal: McGill-Queen's University Press.

Donzelot, J. (1977). *La police des familles.* Paris: Minuit.

Douglas (1905). A Feeding Chart for Infants. *Archives of Pediatrics* XXII (10), 745–753.

322   Bibliography

Douglas, M. (1986). *How Institutions Think*. Syracuse University Press.

Dumont, L. (1986). *Essays on Individualism*. University of Chicago Press.

Durkheim, E. (1933). *The Division of Labor in Society*. New York: Macmillan.

Dwork, D. (1987). *War is Good for Babies and Other Young Children: A History of the Infant and Child Welfare Movement in England, 1818–1918*. London: Tavistock Publications.

Edgarton, S. (1975). *The Renaissance Rediscovery of Linear Perspective*. New York: Basic Books.

Ehrenreich, B. and English, D. (1978). *For Her own Good: 150 years of the Expert's Advice to Women*. Garden City, NY: Anchor Press.

Elder, G. H. J., Modell, J. and Parke, R. D. (eds.) (1993). *Children in Time and Space: Developmental and Historical Insights*. Cambridge University Press.

Elias, N. (1978). *The History of Manners*. New York: Pantheon Books.

  (1987). The Retreat of Sociologists into the Present. *Theory, Culture and Society* 4, 223–247.

Eyler, J. (1979). *Victorian Social Medicine: The Ideas and Methods of William Farr*. Baltimore, MD: Johns Hopkins University Press.

Faber (1920). Study of Growth of Infants by New Weight Chart. *Archives of Pediatrics* 37 (4).

Fabian, J. (1983). *Time and the Other: How Anthropology Makes Its Object*. Cambridge University Press.

  (1984). The Other and the Eye: Time and the Rhetoric of Vision. *Communication et Information* VI (2–3), 290–322.

Farr, W. (1875). Letter to the Registrar-General on the Mortality in the Registration Districts of England During the 10 Years 1861–70. Supplement to the Thirty-fifth Annual Report of the Registrar-General.

Ferguson Clement, P. (1985). The City and the Child, 1860–1885. In J. Hawes and R. Hiner (eds.), *American Childhood: a Research Guide and Historical Handbook* (pp. 235–272). Westport, CT: Greenwood Press.

Finkenstein, B. (1985). Casting Networks of Good Influence: The Reconstruction of Childhood in the United States, 1790–1870. In J. Hawes and R. Hiner (eds.), *American Childhood: a Research Guide and Historical Handbook* (pp. 111– 152). Westport, CT: Greenwood Press.

Fonssagrives, J.-B. (1869). *Livret maternel pour prendre des notes sur la santé des enfants*. Paris: Hachette.

  (1882). *Leçons d'hygiène infantile*. Paris: Lahaye.

Foucault, M. (1999). *Les anormaux: Cours au Collège de France, 1974–75*. Paris: Hautes études/Gallimard/Seuil.

Freeman, F. N. (1917). A Critique of the Yerkes–Bridges–Hardwick Comparison of the Binet–Simon and Point Scales. *The Psychological Review* XXIV (5), 484–490.

Freeman, R. (1914). Weights and Measurements of Infants and Children in Private Practice Compared with Institution Children and Schoolchildren. *Archives of Pediatrics/Transactions of the American Pediatric Society* 31, 203–208.

Fries, M., Brokaw, K. and Murray, V. F. (1935). The Formation of Character as Observed in the Well Baby Clinic. *American Journal of Diseases of Children* 49 (1), 28.

Fujimura, J. (1992). Crafting Science: Standardized Packages, Boundary Objects, and 'Translations'. In A. Pickering (ed.), *Science as Practice and Culture* (pp. 168–211). University of Chicago Press.

Gagan, R. (1988). Mortality Patterns and Public Health in Hamilton, Canada 1900–1914. *Revue d'Histoire Urbaine*, XVII (3), 161–176.

Gardin, J.-C. (1974). *Les analyses du discours*. Neuchatel: Delachaux et Niestlé.

Garnier, P. (1995). *Ce dont les enfants sont capables. Marcher, travailler, nager. XVIIIe–XIXe–XXe siècle*. Paris: Editions Métaillé.

Gergen, K. J. (1994). The Limit of Pure Critique. In H. Simons and M. Bilig (eds.), *After Postmodernism: Reconstructing Ideology Critique*. London: Sage.

(1995). Social Construction and the Formation of Identity Politics. Online. www.swarthmore.edu/SocSci/kgergen1/text8.html.

Gesell, A. (1926). Normal Growth as a Public Health Concept. *Transactions of the Third Annual Meeting of the American Child Health Association* II (Part 1), pp. 43–51.

(1929). *Infancy and Human Growth*. New York: Macmillan.

(1952). *Infant Development: the Embryology of Early Behavior*. New York: Harper.

Gesell, A. and Gesell, B. C. (1912). *The Normal Child and Primary Education*. London: Ginn.

Gesell, A. and Ilg, F. (1949a). *Child Development. An Introduction to the Study of Human Growth: Infant and Child in the Culture of Today*, Vol. 1. New York: Harper and Row.

(1949b) *Child Development. An Introduction to the Study of Human Growth: The Child from Five to Ten*, Vol. 2. New York: Harper and Row.

Gesell, A., Ilg, F. and Bates Ames, L. (1977 [1946]). *The Child from Five to Ten*. New York: Harper and Row.

Giddens, A. (ed.) (1986). *Durkheim on Politics and the State*. Palo Alto, CA: Stanford University Press.

Gomart, E. and Hennion, A. (1999). A Sociology of Attachment: Music Amateurs, Drug Users. In J. Law and J. Hassard (eds.), *Actor Network Theory and After* (pp. 220–247). Oxford: Blackwell.

Goodenough, F. (1949). *Mental Testing, its History, Principles and Applications.* New York: Rinehart.

Gould, S. J. (1981). *The Mismeasure of Man.* New York: W. W. Norton.

Graff, H. J. (1995). *Conflicting Paths: Growing Up in America.* Cambridge, MA: Harvard University Press.

Gurjeva, L. (1998). Everyday Bourgeois Science: The Management of Children in Britain, 1880–1914. Unpublished thesis, King's College, Cambridge.

   (1999). Tabulation Of Child Development Around 1900. London, Institute of Education: unpublished.

Habermas, J. (1979). *L'espace public.* Paris: Payot.

   (1984). *The Theory of Communicative Action.* London: Heinemann.

Hacking, I. (1983). *Representing and Intervening: Introductory Topics in the Philosophy of Science.* Cambridge University Press.

   (1990). *The Taming of Chance.* New York: Cambridge University Press.

   (1991). The Making and Molding of Child Abuse. *Critical Inquiry* 17, 253–288.

   (1992). World-making by Kind-making: Child Abuse for Example. In M. Douglas and D. Hull (eds.), *How Classification Works: Nelson Goodman among the Social Sciences* (pp. 180–238). Edinburgh University Press.

   (1995). *Rewriting the Soul. Multiple Personality and the Science of Memory.* Princeton University Press.

   (1998). On Being More Literal about Construction. In I. Velody and R. Williams (eds.), *The Politics of Constructionism* (pp. 49–68). London: Sage.

Halpern, S. (1988). *American Pediatrics. The Social Dynamics of Professionalism, 1880–1980.* Berkeley, CA: University of California Press.

Halsan Hølskar, A. (2001). Underage and Under Fire: An Enquiry into the Use of Child Soldiers 1994–1998. *Childhood* 8 (3), 340–360.

Hardman, C. (1973). Can There Be an Anthropology of Children? *Journal of the Anthropology Society of Oxford* 4 (1), 85–99.

Hardyment, C. (1983). *Dream Babies: Child Care from Locke to Spock.* London: Cape.

Harkness, S. and Super, C. M. (1983). The Cultural Construction of Child Development: A Framework for the Socialization of Affect. *Ethos* 11 (4), 221–231.

Hearnshaw, L. S. (1964). *A Brief History of British Psychology.* London: Methuen.

Heath, C. and Hindmarsh, J. (1997). Les objets et leur environnement local: La production interactionnelle de réalités matérielles. *Raisons pratiques* 8, 149–175.

Hendrick, H. (1990). Construction and Reconstruction of British Childhood: An Interpretive Survey, 1800 to the Present. In A. Prout and A. James (eds.), *Constructing and Reconstructing Childhood: Contemporary Issues in the Sociological Study of Childhood* (pp. 35–59). London: Falmer Press.

(1994). *Child Welfare England, 1872–1989.* London: Routledge.

(1997). *Children, Childhood and English Society, 1880–1990.* Cambridge University Press.

Herrnstein, R. J. and Murray, C. (1996). *The Bell Curve: Intelligence and the Class Structure in the United States.* New York: Free Press.

Heuyer, G. (1914). *Enfants anormaux et délinquents juvéniles: Nécessité de l'examen psychiatrique des écoliers.* Paris: G. Steinheil.

(1952). *Introduction à la psychiatrie infantile.* Paris: Presses Universitaires de France.

Higonnet, A. (1998). *Pictures of Innocence: The History and Crisis of Ideal Childhood.* London: Thames and Hudson.

Hockey, J. and James, A. (1993). *Growing up and Growing Old: Aging and Dependency in the Life Course.* London: Sage.

Holt, L. E. (1914). *The Diseases of Infancy and Childhood: For Use of Students and Practitioners of Medicine,* 6th edn. Appleton.

Hopkins, E. (1994). *Childhood Transformed. Working-class Children in Nineteenth Century England.* Manchester University Press.

Horn, M. (1989). *Before it's Too Late: The Child Guidance Movement in the United States, 1922–1945.* Philadelphia, PA: Temple University Press.

Hornstein, G. A. (1988). Quantifying Psychological Phenomena: Debates, Dilemmas and Implications. In J. G. Moraski (ed.), *The Rise of Experimentation in American Psychology* (pp. 1–34). New Haven, CT: Yale University Press.

Hutchins, E. (1995). *Cognition in the Wild.* Cambridge, MA: MIT Press.

Ivy, M. (1995). Have You Seen Me? Recovering the Inner Child in Late Twentieth-Century America. In S. Stephens (ed.), *Children and the Politics of Culture* (pp. 79–104). Princeton University Press.

Jacobi, A. (1889). Presidential Address to the APS, 1889. *Archives of Pediatrics* VI (11), 760–769.

James, A. and Prout, A. (eds.) (1990a). *Constructing and Reconstructing Childhood: Contemporary Issues in the Sociological Study of Childhood.* London: Falmer Press.

James, A. and Prout, A. (eds). (1990b). Re-Presenting Childhood: Time and Transition in the Study of Childhood. In A. Prout and A. James (eds.), *Constructing and Reconstructing Childhood: Contemporary Issues in the Sociological Study of Childhood* (pp. 216–237). London: Falmer Press.

(1995). Hierarchy, Boundary, and Agency: Toward a Theoretical Perspective on Childhood. In A.-M. Ambert (ed.), *Sociological Studies of Children* (pp. 77–100). Greenwich, CT: JAI Press.

James, A., Jenks, C. and Prout, A. (1998). *Theorizing Childhood*. London: Polity Press.

Javeau, C. (1994). Dix propositions sur l'enfance, objet des sciences sociales. *Revue de l'Institut de Sociologie*, 15–19.

Jenks, C. (1996). *Childhood*. London: Routledge.

Jennings, C. (1905). The Medical Supervision of Schools and the Progress of School Hygiene. *Archives of Pediatrics* XXII (7), 482.

Jones, J. A. and Hand, J. G. (1935). The Child Health Clinic. *Archives of Pediatrics* 52 (4), 259–274.

Jones, K. (1983). Sentiment and Science: the Late Nineteenth Century Pediatrician as Mother's Adviser. *Journal of Social History* 17, 79–96.

Kamin, L. J. (1974). *The Science and Politics of IQ*. Potomac, MD: Erlbaum Associates.

Karsenti, B. (1997). *L'homme total: Sociologie, anthropologie et philosophie chez Marcel Mauss*. Paris: Presses Universitaires de France.

Kellogg, V. (1926). Determining the Normal. *Transactions of the Third Annual Meeting of the American Child Health Association* II (Part I), 77–82.

Kelves, D. J. (1985). *In the Name of Eugenics: Genetics and the Uses of Human Heredity*. Berkeley, CA: University of California Press.

Kertzer, D. (ed.) (1989). *Comparative Perspective on Age Structuring*. Hillsdale, NJ: Laurence Erlbaum Associates Inc.

Kett, J. (1976). The History of Age Grouping in America. In A. Skolnick (ed.), *Rethinking Childhood: Perspectives on Development and Society*. Boston: Little, Brown and Company.

Kincaid, J. (1992). *Child Loving. The Erotic Child and Victorian Culture*. London: Routledge.

Klaus, A. (1993). *Every Child a Lion: The Origins of Material and Infant Health Policy in the U. S. and France, 1890–1920*. Ithaca, NY: Cornell University Press.

Kohs, S. C. (1917). The Stanford (1915) and the Vineland (1911) Revisions of the Binet Scale. *The Psychological Review* XXIV (2), 174–179.

Kugelmass, I. N. (1935). *Growing Superior Children*. New York: Appleton-Century.

Lahire, B. (1998). *L'homme pluriel: Les ressorts de l'action*. Paris: Nathan.

Lallemand, S. (1993). *La circulation des enfants en société traditionnelle: Prêt, don, échange*. Paris: Editions l'Harmattan.

Latour, B. (1986). *Laboratory Life. The Construction of Scientific Facts*. Princeton University Press.

(1987). *Science in Action: How to Follow Scientists and Engineers Through Society*. Cambridge, MA: Harvard University Press.

(1990). Drawing Things Together. In M. Lynch and S. Woolgar (eds.), *Representation in Scientific Practice* (pp. 19–68). Cambridge, MA: MIT Press.

(1994a). Pragmatonies: A Mythical Account of How Humans and Nonhumans Swap Properties. *American Behavioral Scientist* 37 (6), 791–808.

(1994b). *We Have Never Been Modern*. Cambridge, MA: Harvard University Press.

(1999a). On recalling ANT. In J. Law and J. Hassard (eds.), *Actor–Network Theory and After* (pp. 15–25). Oxford: Blackwell.

(1999b). *Pandora's Hope*. Cambridge, MA: Harvard University Press.

Law, J. (1999). After ANT: Complexity, Naming and Topology. In J. Law and J. Hassard (eds.), *Actor–Network Theory and After* (pp. 1–14). Oxford: Blackwell.

Law, J. and Lynch, M. (1990). Lists, Field Guides, and the Descriptive Organization of Seeing: Birdwatching as an Exemplary Observational Activity. In M. Lynch and S. Woolgar (eds.), *Representation in Scientific Practice* (pp. 267–300). Cambridge, MA: MIT Press.

Lee, N. (1998). Toward an Immature Sociology. *The Sociological Review* 46 (3), 458–482.

(1999). Faith in the Body? Childhood, Subjecthood and Sociological Enquiry. In A. Prout (ed.), *The Body, Childhood and Society* (p.). London: Macmillan.

(2001). *Childhood and Society. Growing Up in an Age of Uncertainty*. Buckingham: Open University Press.

Lee, N. and Stenner, P. (1999). Who Pays? Can We Pay Them Back? In J. Law and J. Hassard (eds.), *Actor–Network Theory and After* (pp. 90–112). Oxford: Blackwell.

Lesnik-Oberstein, K. (1998). Childhood and Textuality: Culture, History, Literature. In K. Lesnik-Oberstein (ed.), *Children in Culture: Approaches to Childhood* (pp. 1–28). London: Macmillan.

Lewis, J. (1980). *The Politics of Motherhood: Child and Maternal Welfare in England, 1900–1939*. London: Croon Helm.

Lomax, E., Kagan, J. and Rosenkrantz, B. (1978). *Science and Pattern of Child Care*. San Francisco, CA: W. H. Freeman.

Low, B. (1998). NFB Kids: Portrayals of Children by the National Film Board of Canada, 1939–1989. Unpublished thesis, University of British Columbia.

Luc, J. N. (1997). *L'invention du jeune enfant au XIXe siècle: De la salle d'asile à l'école maternelle* (p. 16). Paris: Belin.

(1998). Les premières écoles enfantines et l'invention du jeune enfant. In E. Becchi and D. Julia (eds.), *Histoire de l'enfance en occident* (pp. 304–330). Paris: Seuil.

Lynch, M. (1998). Toward a Constructivist Genealogy of Social Constructivism. In I. Velody and R. Williams (eds.), *The Politics of Constructionism* (pp. 13–32). London: Sage.

(2005). The Production of Scientific Images: Vision and Re-Vision in the History, Philosophy, and Sociology of Science. In L. Pauwels (ed.), *Visual Cultures of Science. Rethinking Representational Practices in Knowledge Building and Science Communication* (pp. 26–40). Hanover, NH: University Press of New England.

McCleary, G. F. (1935). *The Maternity and Child Welfare Movement.* London: P.S. King and Son Ltd.

McEwan, I. (1993). *Black Dogs.* London: Picador.

Macintyre, A. (1984). *After Virtue. A Study in Moral Theory.* South Bend: University of Notre Dame Press.

McKeen Cattell, J. (1890). Mental Tests and Measurements. *Mind 15,* 373–381.

Mackenzie, D. A. (1981). *Statistics in Britain 1865–1930: The Social Construction of Scientific Knowledge.* Edinburgh University Press.

(1990). *Inventing Accuracy. A Historical Sociology of Nuclear Guidance Missiles.* Cambridge, MA: MIT Press.

Maudsley, H. (1876). *The Physiology of Mind.* London: Macmillan.

Mayall, B. (ed.) (1994). *Children's Childhood: Observed and Experienced.* London: Falmer Press.

(1996). *Children, Health, and the Social Order.* Buckingham: Open University Press.

Mechling, J. (1975–1976). Advice to Historians on Advice to Mothers. *Journal of Social History* 9 (2), pp. 44–63.

(2001). *On My Honor: Boy Scouts and the Making of American Youth.* University of Chicago Press.

Meckel, R. A. (1990). *Save the Babies. American Public Health Reform and the Prevention of Infant Mortality 1850–1929.* Baltimore, MD: John Hopkins University Press.

Meigs, G. L. (1918). *Children's Year Campaign: Transactions of the Section on Diseases of Children of the AMA.* Chicago, IL: AMA Press.

Ménoret, M. (2002). The Genesis of the Notion of Stages in Oncology: The French Permanent Cancer Survey (1943–1952). *Social History of Medicine* 15 (2), 291–302.

Meyer, J. (1988). The Social Construction of the Psychology of Childhood: Some Contemporary Processes. In E. Mavis Hetherington, R. M. Lerner and M. Perlmutter (eds.), *Child Development in Life Span Perspective* (pp. 47–65). Hillsdale, NJ: Lawrence Erlbaum Associates.

Millard, A. V. (1990). The Place of the Clock in Pediatric Advice: Rationales, Cultural Themes, and Impediments to Breastfeeding. *Social Science and Medicine* 31 (2), 211– 221.

Modell, J. (2000). How May Children's Development be Seen Historically? *Childhood* 7 (1), 81–106.

Modgil, S. C. E. (ed.) (1987). *Arthur Jensen: Consensus and Controversy*. New York: Falmer Press.

Molino, J. (1974). Sur les titres des romans de Jean Bruce. *Langage* 35, 87–116.

(1978). Sur la situation symbolique. *L'Arc* 72, 20–25.

(1984). Vers une nouvelle anthropologie de l'art et de la musique: A propos d'un ouvrage de Steven Feld, 'Sound and Sentiment'. *Revue de musique des universités canadiennes* (5), 269–313.

Moran-Ellis, J. (1998). Documenting Children's Physical Development: A Methodology for Analysing the Textual Recording of Children's Bodies. Paper to ISA 14th World Congress, Montreal, Canada.

Morel, M.-F. (1987). Médecins et enfants malades dans la France du XVIIIe siècle. *Lieux de l'enfance* 9–10, 13–46.

(1989). Les soins prodigués aux enfants: Influence des innovations médicales et des institutions médicalisées (1750–1914): Médecine et déclin de la mortalité infantile. *Annales de démographie historique*, 157–181.

Morrison, B. (1997). *As If: A Crime, a Trial, a Question of Childhood*. London: Picador.

Morrow, V. (1994). Responsible Children? Aspects of Children's Work and Employment outside Schools in Contemporary UK. In B. Mayall (ed.), *Children's Childhood: Observed and Experimented*. London: Falmer.

(1995). Invisible Children? Toward a Reconceptualisation of Childhood Dependency and Responsibility. In A. M. Ambert (ed.), *Sociological Studies of Childhood* (pp. 207–231). Greenwich, CT: JAI Press.

Morss, J. R. (1990). *The Biologising of Childhood; Developmental Psychology and the Darwinian Myth*. London: Lawrence Erlbaum.

(1996). *Growing Critical: Alternatives to Developmental Psychology*. London: Routledge.

Moscovici, S. (1988). *La machine à faire des dieux*. Paris: Fayard.

Näsman, E. (1994). Individualisation and Institutionalisation of Childhood in Today's Europe. In J. Qvortrup, G. Sgritta and H. E. Wintersberger (eds.), *Childhood Matters: Social Theory, Practice and Policy*. Aldershot: Avebury Press.

Naussbaum, F. (1988). Eighteenth Century Women's Autobiographical Commonplaces. In S. Benstock (ed.), *The Private Self*. London: Routledge.

Necker de Saussure, A. (1828). *L'éducation progressive ou étude du cours de la vie*, Vol. 1, 1828; Vol. 2, 1838. Paris: Garnier.

Newman, G. (1906). *Infant Mortality, a Social Problem*. London: Methuen.

Norman, D. (1993). *Les artefacts cognitifs. Raisons Pratiques* 4, 15–34.

Norvez, A. (1990). De la naissance à l' école. Santé, modes de garde et préscolarité dans la France contemporaine: INED.

Nye, R. A. (1984). *Crime, Madness, and Politics in Modern France: The Medical Concept of National Decline*. Princeton University Press.

O'Shea, M. V. (1924). *The Child: His Nature and His Needs*. Valparaiso, In The Children Foundation.

Palmer, G. T. (1925). Weight and Height as an Index of Nutrition in Infants. *Child Health Bulletin* 1, 5.

 (1930). The Measurement of Nutritional Status. *Child Health Bulletin* 6 (2), 45–50.

Parsons, T. (1951). *The Social System*. London: Routledge and Kegan Paul.

Pickering, A. (1992). *Science as Practice and Culture*. University of Chicago Press.

Pinchbeck, I. and Hewitt, M. (1973). *Children in English Society*. London: Routledge and Kegan Paul.

Place, B. (1999). Constructing the Bodies of Ill Children in the Intensive Care Unit. In Prout A. (ed.), *The Body, Childhood and Society*. London: Macmillan.

Pomian, K. (1984). *L'ordre du temps*. Paris: Gallimard.

Popham, W. H. (1847). *Nursery Guide, or, Practical Hints on the Diseases and Management of Children*. London: Simkin, Marshall.

Porter, L., Huffaker, A. and Ritter, A. (1915). Mental and Physical Survey of Supposedly Normal Children. *Transactions of the Section on Diseases of Children of the AMA*. San Francisco, CA: AMA Press.

Porter, T. M. (1986). *The Rise of Statistical Thinking, 1820–1900*. Princeton University Press.

 (1995). *Trust in Numbers. The Pursuit of Objectivity in Science and Public Life*. Princeton University Press.

Prendergast, S. (1992). *This is the Time to Grow Up: Girls' Experience of Menstruation in School*. Cambridge: The Health Promotion Trust.

(1995). The Spaces of Childhood: Psyche, Soma and the Social Existence. Menstruation and Embodiment at Adolescence. In J. Brannen and M. O'Brien (eds.), *Childhood and Parenthood*. London: Institute of Education.

Preston, M. (1935). Child Guidance in Out-Patient Pediatrics. *Journal of Pediatrics* 7 (4), 452–464.

Preston, S. and Haines, M. R. (1991). *Fatal Years: Child Mortality in Late Nineteenth-Century America*. Princeton University Press.

Prout, A. (1996). Actor–network Theory, Technology and Medical Sociology: an Illustrative Analysis of the Metered Dose Inhaler. *Sociology of Health and Illness* 18 (2), 198–219.

(ed.) (1999). *The Body, Childhood And Society*. London: Macmillan.

(2005). *The Future of Childhood*. London: RoutledgeFalmer.

Prout, A. and Christensen, P. (1994). Children and Medicine Use: Theorizing the Cultural Differences. In P. Bush, D. Trakas, A. Prout and E. Sanz (eds.), *Children, Medicine and Culture*. Bingham, NY: Haworth Press.

Prout, A. and James, A. (1990). A New Paradigm for the Sociology of Childhood? Provenance, Promise and Problems. In A. James and A. Prout (eds.), *Constructing and Reconstructing Childhood: Contemporary Issues in the Sociological Study of Childhood* (pp. 7–34). London: Falmer Press.

Punch, S. (1998). Children's Strategies for Controlling their Use of Time and Space: Negotiating Independence in Rural Bolivia. Paper presented at the International Sociological Association Conference, Montreal.

Py, G. (1997). Rousseau et les Educateurs: Etude sur la fortune des idées pédagogiques de J.-J. Rousseau en France et en Europe au XVIIIe siècle. Unpublished thesis, University of Paris: IV.

Quentel, J.-C. (1997). *L'enfant: Problèmes de genèse et d'histoire*, 2nd edn. Brussels: De Boeck.

Quincy-Lefevre, P. (1997). *Une histoire de l'enfance difficile: 1880 – fin des années trente*. Paris: Economica.

Qvortrup, J. (1990). A Voice for Children in Statistical and Social Accounting: A Plea for Children's Right to be Heard. In A. James and A. Prout (eds.), *Constructing and Reconstructing Childhood* (pp. 85–103). London: Falmer Press.

(1993). Nine Theses about 'Childhood as a Social Phenomenon'. Childhood as a Social Phenomenon: Lesson from an International Project European Center for Social Welfare Policy and Research, Vienna: Eurosocial. Report no. 47, pp. 7–18.

(1995). Childhood in Europe: a New Field of Social Research. In L. Chisholm, P. Buchner, H.-H. Kruger and P. Brown (eds.), *Growing*

Up in Europe. Contemporary Horizons in Childhood and Youth Studies (pp. 7–20). New York: Walter de Gruyter.

Qvortrup, J., Sgritta, G. and Wintersberger, H. E. (1994). *Childhood Matters: Social Theory, Practice and Policy.* Aldershot: Avebury Press.

Ramirez, F. (1989). Reconstituting Children: Extension of Personhood and Citizenship. In D. Kertzer (ed.), *Comparative Perspective on Age Structuring.* Hillsdale, NJ: Lawrence Erlbaum Associates Inc.

Ramognino, N. (1987). Renouvellement de paradigme ou traduction-trahison de la tradition sociologique: pour une positivité de l'objet sociologique. *Sociologie et société* 19 (2).

(1988). La recherche d'une pertinence. In N. Ramognino (ed.), *La politique s'affiche: Les affiches de la politique* (pp. 11–43). Didier Erudition/Presses de l'Université d'Aix-en-Provence.

(1998a). Epistémologie, Ontologies et Théories Sociales Pratiques. Unpublished paper.

(1998b). Le travail social a-t-il encore besoin des sciences sociales? *Cahiers de l'ADEUS* 1, 92–122.

(2000). L'enfance handicapée. Unpublished paper.

Reeves, J. W. (1965). *Thinking about Thinking: Studies in the Background of Some Psychological Approaches.* London: Methuen.

Renouard, J.-M. (1990). *De l'enfant coupable à l'enfant inadapté. Le traitement social et politique de la deviance.* Paris: Centurion.

Retan (1920). Measure and Development of Nutrition. *Archives of Pediatrics* 37 (1), 32–38.

Richards, P. and Singer, G. H. S. (1998). 'To Draw out the Effort of His Mind': Educating a Child with Mental Retardation in Early Nineteenth-century America. *Journal of Special Education* 31 (4), 443–466.

Richardson, F. H. (1925). Breast Feeding – Past, Present and Future. *Archives of Pediatrics* 42 (10), 651–657.

Richardson, T. (1989). *The Century of the Child: The Mental Hygiene Movement and Social Policy in United Stated and Canada.* State University of New York Press.

Richardson, T. and Johanningmeir, E. (1998). Intelligence Testing: The Legitimation of a Meritocratic Educational Science. *International Journal of Educational Research* 27 (8), 699–714.

Rodriguez Ocana, E. (1998). *Children's Medicine: From Puericulture (Prevention) to Pediatrics (Medical Care) in Twentieth Century Spain.* Paper presented at the European Social Science History Conference, Amsterdam.

Rogers, A. C. (1913). The Desirability of Early Diagnosis of Mental Defect in Children, and Mental Tests as an Aid. *Transactions of the Section on Diseases of Children (AMA)* (64th annual session), 293–304.

Rogoff, B. and Chavajay, P. (1995). What's Become of Research on the Cultural Basis of Cognitive Development? *American Psychologist* 50 (10), 859–877.

Rollet, C. (1990). *La politique à l'égard de la petite enfance sous la IIIè République*. Paper presented at the European Social Science History Conference, Amsterdam.

(1993). La lutte contre la mortalité infantile dans le passé: essai de comparaison internationale. *Santé publique* 5 (2), 4–20.

(1994). La mortalité des enfants dans le passé: au delà des apparences *Annales de démographie historique* (pp. 7–22). Paris: Edition de l'Ecole des Hautes Etudes en Sciences Sociales.

(1998). Infant Welfare: A Comparison of some Local European Experiences (France, Great Britain). ESSHC.

(2003). History of the Health Notebook in France: A Stake for Mothers, Doctors and State. *Dynamis. Acta Hispanica ad Medicinae Scientiarumque Historiam Illustrandam* (23), 143–166.

(2004). Le carnet de santé pour les enfants en Europe. *Medicina e storia* IV (7), 31–55.

Rose, L. (1991). *The Erosion of Childhood: Child Oppression in Britain, 1860–1918*. London: Routledge and Kegan Paul.

Rose, N. (1985). *The Psychological Complex. Psychology, Politics and Society in England, 1869–1939*. London: Routledge and Kegan Paul.

(1991). *Governing the Soul. The Shaping of the Private Self*. London: Routledge.

Rosenkrantz, B. (1978). Reflection on 19th Century Conception of Childhood. In E. Lomax, J. Kagan and B. Rosenkrantz (eds.), *Science and Patterns of Child Care*. San Francisco, CA: W. H. Freeman.

Ross, D. (1972). *G. Stanley Hall: The Psychologist as Prophet*. University of Chicago Press.

Rotch, T. (1910a). Comparison in Boys and Girls of Height and Weight. *Archives of Pediatrics* 27 (7), 568.

(1910b). Public Work of the Society. In L. E. L. Fetra (ed.), *Transactions of the American Pediatric Society*. New York: E.B. Treat and Co.

Rothstein, W. G. (2003). *Public Health and the Risk Factor: A History of an Uneven Medical Revolution*. University of Rochester Press.

Rusnock, A. (2005). Quantifying Infant Mortality in England and France, 1750–1800. In G. Jorland, A. Opinel and G. Weisz (eds.), *Body Counts. Medical Quantification in Historical and Sociological Perspectives* (pp. 64–86). Montreal: McGill-Queen's University Press.

Samuelson, F. (1979). Putting Psychology on the Map: Ideology and Intelligence Testing. In A. R. Buss (ed.), *Psychology and Social Context* (pp. 103–168). New York: Irvington.

Sayles, M. B. (1932). *Child Guidance Clinic.* New York: The Commonwealth Fund.

Schweber, L. (1996). L'histoire de la statistique, laboratoire pour la théorie sociale. *Revue française de sociologie* 37, 107–128.

Sears, R. (1975). Your Ancient Revisited: a History of Child Development. In E. M. E. Heatherington (ed.), *Review in Child Development Research.* University of Chicago Press.

Seguin, E. (1895). *Rapport et mémoire sur l' éducation des enfants normaux et anormaux.* Paris: Bibliothèque d'Education Speciale II.

Sereny, G. (1999). *Cries Unheard: Why Children Kill: The Story of Mary Bell.*

Sewell, W. H. (1992). A Theory of Structure: Duality, Agency, and Transformation. *American Journal of Sociology* 98 (1), 1–29.

Snyderman, M. and Rothman, S. (1988). *The IQ Controversy, the Media and Public Policy.* New Brunswick, NJ: Transaction Books.

Sokal, M. (1987a). Introduction: Psychological Testing and Historical Scholarship – Questions, Contrasts and Context. In M. Sokal (ed.), *Psychological Testing and American Society, 1890–1930* (pp. 1–20). New Brunswick, NJ: Rutgers University Press.

 (1987b). *Psychological Testing and American Society, 1890–1930.* New Brunswick, NJ: Rutgers University Press.

Stainton Rogers, R. W. (1998). Word Children. In K. Lesnik-Oberstein (ed.), *Children in Culture: Approaches to Childhood* (pp. 178–203). London: Macmillan.

Stainton Rogers, R. and Stainton Rogers, W. (1992). *Stories of Childhood. Shifting Agendas of Child Concern.* Hemel Hempstead: Harvester Wheatsheaf.

Star, S. L. and Griesemer, J. R. (1989). Institutional Ecology, 'Translations', and Boundary Objects: Amateurs and Professionals in Berkeley's Museum of Vertebrate Zoology. *Social Studies of Science* 19, 387–420.

Stearns, P. N., Rowland, P. and Giarnella, L. (1996). Children's Sleep: Sketching Historical Change. *Journal of Social History* 30, 345–366.

Steedman, C. (1992). Bodies, Figures and Physiology. In R. Cooter (ed.), *In the name of the Child, Health and Welfare, 1880–1940.* London: Routledge.

 (1995). *Strange Dislocations. Childhood and the Idea of Human Interiority, 1780–1930.* Cambridge, MA: Harvard University Press.

Stevenson, G. S. (1930). The Child Guidance Clinic – Its Aims, Growth, and Methods. *Proceedings of the First International Congress on Mental Hygiene.*

Strathern, M. (1999). What is Intellectual Property After? In J. Law and J. Hassard (eds), *Actor–Network Theory and After* (pp. 156–180). Oxford: Blackwell.

Strecker, E. A. (1926). What Constitutes Mental Health in Childhood. *Transactions of the Third Annual Meeting of the American Child Health Association* II (Part 1), 55–61.

Stuart, H. C. (1928). Pediatric Service in City Health Depatment Centers Provided by Medical Schools in Boston. *Transactions of the American Child Health Association.*

(1933). Appraisement of the Child. *Child Health Bulletin* 9 (1), 29–32.

Suchman, L., Trigg, R. and Blomberg, J. (2002). Working Artefacts: Ethnomethods of the Prototype. *British Journal of Sociology* 53 (2), 163–179.

Sully, J. (1881). Babies and Science. *Cornhill Magazine* (43), 539–554.

Sussman, G. D. (1982). *Selling Mothers' Milk. The Wet-Nursing Business in France 1715–1914.* Chicago, IL: University of Illinois Press.

Sutherland, G. (1984). *Ability, Merit and Measurement. Mental Testing and English Education, 1880–1940.* Oxford: Clarendon Press.

Sutherland, N. (1976). *Children in English–Canadian Society: Framing the Twentieth-Century Consensus.* Toronto: University of Toronto Press.

Sutton, J. (1983). Social Structures, Institutions and the Legal Status of Children in the United States. *American Journal of Sociology* 88/5, 915–947.

(1988). *Stubborn Children: Controling Delinquency in the United States, 1640–1981.* Berkeley, CA: University of California Press.

Swann, A. D. (1990). *The Management of Normality.* London: Routledge.

Szreter, S. (1986). The First Scientific Social Structure of Modern Britain 1875–1883. In L. Bonfield, R. M. Smith and K. Wrightson (eds.), *The World We Have Gained* (pp. 337–354). Oxford: Blackwell.

(1988). The Importance of Social Intervention in Britain's Mortality Decline c. 1850–1914: A Re-Interpretation of the Role of Public Health. *Social History of Medicine* (1), 1–37.

Tanner, J. (1981). *A History of the Study of Human Growth.* Cambridge University Press.

Thom, D. (1925). Mental Handicaps of Childhood. *Hygeia*, 29–30.

(1992). Wishes, Anxieties, Play, and Gestures. Child Guidance in Interwar England. In R. Cooter (ed.), *In the name of the Child, Health and Welfare, 1880–1940.* London: Routledge.

Thorne, B. (1993). *Gender Play: Girls and Boys in Schools.* New Brunswick, NJ: Rutgers University Press.

Thornton, A. (2005). *Reading History Sideways: the Fallacy and Enduring Impact of the Developmental Paradigm on Family Life.* University of Chicago Press.

Touraine, A. (1992). *Critique de la Modernité.* Paris: Fayard.

Turmel, A. (1986). Le discours savant à rebours. In P. Ouellet and K. Fall (eds.), *Les discours du savoir* (pp. 104–121). Montreal: *Cahiers de l'ACFAS.*

(1993). L'interpellation: Sur les rapports entre sociologie et sémiotique. *Sociologie et Sociétés* 25 (2), 137–156.

(1997). Le retour du concept d'institution. In A. Turmel (ed.), *Culture, Institution et Savoir* (pp. 1–24). Quebec: PUL/CEFAN.

(1997a). Absence d'amour et présence des microbes: sur les modèles culturels de l'enfant. *Recherches Sociographiques* 38 (1), 89–115.

(1997b). The History of Children in Canada. *Paedagogica Historica* 33 (2), 509–520.

(1998). Childhood and Normalcy: Classification, Numerical Regularities, and Tabulations. *International Journal of Educational Research* 27 (8), 661–672.

Turmel, A. and Hamelin, L. (1995). La grande faucheuse d'enfants: La mortalité infantile depuis le tournant du siècle. *Revue canadienne de sociologie et d'anthropologie* 32 (4), pp. 439– 462.

Turmel, A., Hamelin, L. and Irambona, C. (1991). Les représentations de l'enfant: Rapport de recherche soumis au CRSH: 410–88–1383.

Tyack, D. B. (1974). *The One Best System: A History of American Urban Education.* Cambridge University Press.

Urwin, C. and Sharland, E. (1992). From Bodies to Mind in Childcare Literature: Advice to Parents in Inter war Britain. In R. Cooter (ed.), *In the Name of the Child: Health and Welfare, 1880–1940* (pp. 174–199). London: Routledge.

Valentine, E. R. (1999a). The Founding of the Psychological Laboratory, University College of London: 'Dear Galton ... Yours truly, J. Sully': History of Psychology. Unpublished paper.

(1999b). Introduction to James Sully's *Studies of Childhood.* Unpublished paper.

Varga, D. (1991). The Cultural Organisation of the Child Care Curriculum: The University of Toronto Institute of Child Study and Day Nurseries, 1890–1960. Unpublished thesis, University of Toronto.

(1997). *Constructing the Child: A History of Canadian Day Care.* Toronto: James Lorimer and Co.

(1998). Technologies, Methodologies and Discourse in the Production of Twentieth Century Child Development Knowledge. *Canadian Childhood Conference*, Edmonton.

Veeder, B. (1924). The Trend of Pediatrics. *Transactions of the First Annual Meeting of the American Child Health Association*. Detroit, 15–17 October, 1923: J. J. Little and Ives Company.

(1926). *Preventive Pediatrics*. New York: Appleton and Cie.

Veron, E. (1987). *La sémiosis sociale: Fragments d'une théorie de la discursivité*. Paris: Presses Universitaires de Vincennes.

Villermé, L.-R. (1840). *Tableau de l'état physique et moral des ouvriers employés dans les manufactures de coton, de laine et de soie*. Paris: Renouard.

Waksler, F. C. (ed.) (1991). *Studying the Social World of Children. Sociological Readings*. London: Falmer Press.

Walkerdine, V. (1984). Developmental Psychology and Child-centered Pedagogy. In J. E. A. Henriques (ed.), *Changing the Subject: Psychology, Social Regulation and Subjectivity* (pp. 153–202). London: Methuen.

Wallace, J. E. W. (1914). *The Function of the Psychological Clinic*. New York: Wood.

Wasburn and Putnam (1933). Child Care. *The Journal of Pediatrics* II (5).

Weinland, T. P. (1989). Book review of: Michael M. Sokal, *Psychological Testing and American Society, 1890–1930*. New Brunswick, Rutgers University Press, 1987: JHBS.

WHC (1931). Body Mechanics: Education and Practice. White House Conference on Child Health and Protection. Report of the Subcommittee on Orthopedics and Body Mechanics; Robert B. Osgood, Chairman.

White, H. (1992). *Identity and Control: A Structural Theory of Social Action*. Princeton University Press.

White, S. (1990). Child Study at Clark University: 1894–1904. *Journal of the History of Behavioural Sciences* 26 (2), 131–150.

Whitney, A. (1930). The Weighing and Measuring of School Children. *Child Health Bulletin* 6 (2).

Wilcox, H. B. (1910). *Infant and Child Feeding*, Vol. 12. D. Appleton and Co.

Wile, I. (1910). Educational Responsibilities of a Milk Depot: Prevention of Infant Mortality. *American Academy of Medicine*. New Haven, CT.

(1920). Health Classes for Children. *Archives of Pediatrics* 37 (3).

Wolf, T. H. (1973). *Alfred Binet*. University of Chicago Press.

Wong, J. (1993). *On the Very Idea of the Normal Child*. Unpublished thesis, University of Toronto.

Wood, T. D. (ed.) (1924). *How Far May Weight be Relied upon as a Measure or Index of Child Health?* New York: Little and Ives.

Wood, T. D. and Lerrigo, M. O. (1925). Care of the School Child's Health. *Hygeia*, 549–551.

Woodhead, M. (1990). Psychology and the Cultural Construction of Children's Needs. In A. James and A. Prout (eds.), *Constructing and Reconstructing Childhood: Contemporary Issues in the Sociological Study of Childhood*. London: Falmer Press.

Wooldridge, A. (1995). *Measuring the Mind. Education and Psychology in England, 1860–1990*. Cambridge University Press.

Yerington, H. H. (1928). Clinical Supervision of the Well Baby During the First Year. *Transactions of the American Medical Association Section on Diseases of Children*.

Young, J. A. (1979). Height, Weight and Health: Anthropometric Study of Human Growth in Nineteenth Century American Medicine. *Bulletin of the History of Medicine* 53, 214–243.

Youniss, J. (1990). Cultural Forces Leading to Scientific Developmental Psychology. In C. B. Fisher and W. W. Tryon (eds.), *Ethics in Applied Developmental Psychology*. Norwood, NJ: Ablex.

Zenderland, L. (1987). The Debate over Diagnosis: Henry Herbert Goddard and the Medical Acceptance of Intelligence Testing. In M. Sokal (ed.), *Psychological Testing and American Society, 1890–1930*. New Brunswick, NJ: Rutgers University Press.

  (1999). *Measuring Minds: Henry Herbert Goddard and the Origins of American Intelligence Testing*. New York: Cambridge University Press.

Zinnecker, J. (1997). Children as Agents: The Changing Process of (Re)producing Culture and Society between Generations. *Childhood and Children's Culture*. Paper presented at a conference, Esbjerg, Denmark.

Index

child (children) (cont.)
  lack of universal child 25
  material/corporeal entity 32, 33
  as modelling process 278
  monitoring *see* monitoring of
    children
  as "muted group" 19
  as object of investigation,
    evolutionism 93
  phases of development/life 87
  as psychological and physical
    being 41
  similarities to adults 24
  as sociological category 39
  threats to 8
  "under good control" (growth) 130
  universal, in psychology 6
  wild (Victor) 90
  see also childhood; *specific topics*
    relating to
child abuse 56, 238
child at risk 235
child care 63
  flaws in 233
  Holt's book 113–114
  literature 89
  manuals 89
  techniques 38
  technology application 194
  see also infant care
child conduct, dependence on mother's
    state of mind 227
child development 33
  see also development
child guidance 174
  aims and children requiring 176
  classification of children for 173
  clinical protocol 177–178
  collaboration of parents 179–180
  contradictory forces 180
  definition/meaning 177
  lack of uniformity in practice
    178–179
  mobilization 180
  mobilization of social groupings 179
  role 174
  shift from advice to parents to
    suggestions to children 179
  shift from delinquency 173
  as technology 179

child guidance clinic 173–180
  British 176
  for maladjusted children 243
  records 179
    as inscription devices 180
  as technology 177, 179
  USA 174, 176
Child Guidance Council 176
child health
  schools and 223–224
  see also health
child hygiene 222–223
  see also hygiene
child interest 241, 281
child investigation 101
child labour 54–55, 200
  child workers' classification 54
  Villermé's concern 202
  see also factory children
child neglect 238
child offenders 56–57, 242
child prostitution 55
child protection 240, 241
child psychiatry *see* psychiatry, child
child psychology
  development of 94–95, 96
  see also developmental psychology
child-rearing/raising 291
  social technologies in 122
  technology 194
child relation map 119
child-soldiers 55
Child Study movement 98, 101, 102, 103
child welfare 154, 155
  children's year campaign (US)
    132–133
  national variations 154–157
  Villermé's concern 202
child welfare clinics 154
child workers *see* child labour; factory
    children
childbirth
  in hospital 146
  physicians taking charge 146
childhood 313
  Ariesian proposition and shaping
    forces 3, 6–7
  body/representation 32
  as component of personhood, of
    totality 32, 64